YO-CFU-147

Edited by David Brewster

SEATTLE BEST PLACES

A definitive guide to the city's finest restaurants, shops, hotels, nightlife, arts, sports, sights, and short tours

Sasquatch Publishing/Seattle

Copyright © 1983 by Sasquatch Publishing Inc.
All rights reserved
Printed in the United States of America

ISBN 0-912365-00-5

Editorial director: Susan Gough Henly
Editorial assistant: Pamela Hafey
Design: Heckler Associates
Drawings: Fred Hilliard
Maps: Jois Child and Jane Rady
Production: Weekly Typography and Graphic Design
  Margaret Elson, Chad Haight, Roberta Huff, Richard T. Jameson, Renee Marquette, Irene Mitchell, Laura Perry, Rose Pike, Jane Rady, Meg Robson, Vickie Ryan, Wanda Terry, Linda Tipping, Midge Williams
Proofreaders: Miriam Bulmer, Jann Hattrup, Charles Smyth
Contributors and researchers:
  David Alecock, Tim Appelo, Bruce Betz, Rebecca Boren, David Buerge, Miriam Bulmer, Paul de Barros, Ryan de Mares, Roger Downey, Pamela Hafey, Carol Hermer, Linda Hoffman, Ron & Glenda Holden, Richard T. Jameson, Jane Lotter, Susan Mendelsohn, Catherine Mueller, Carla Noble, Warren Payne, Martin Rudow, Eric Scigliano, Wanda Terry, Will Urban, Nona Weglin, Peg World

The Best Places guidebooks have been published continuously since 1975. Readers are advised that places listed in previous editions may have closed or changed management, or are no longer recommended by this series. The editor greatly appreciates information conveyed by users of this book, as long as they have no financial connection with the establishment reported on. A report form is provided at the end of the book. Seattle Best Places is available at bulk discounts for corporate gifts, conventions, fund-raising sales for clubs and organizations, and other purposes.

Also by Sasquatch Publishing Inc.
  The Best Places: Washington, Oregon, and British Columbia

Seattle Best Places
1932 First Avenue, Suite 605
Seattle, Washington 98101

Table of Contents

Introduction	*v*
Lodging	*1*

Restaurants	*11*	
	11	Top 200
	52	Other restaurants

The Arts	*65*

Nightlife	*78*

Shopping	*97*

Touring Seattle	*174*	
	174	Touring with Emmett Watson
	187	Other tours

Sports	*215*

Out of Town Tours	*245*

Services	*260*
Index	*285*
Report Form	*291*
Maps	*244* Puget Sound region
	Inside back cover Downtown Seattle and Greater Seattle

Introduction

Seattle—so the quip goes—is a great place to live, but you wouldn't want to visit there.

Not so long ago, the quip had some truth to it. The city did little to open itself up to visitors, suffered from a shortage of hotel rooms, and had allowed itself to be spooked enough by the rainy winters to think that no investment in year-round tourism was ever wise. The World's Fair in 1962 started to change this mentality; the King Tut exhibition in 1978 nudged things along futher; and the development of full-fledged convention facilities (including a hotel boom downtown) and major-league sports finished the task. The Emerald City—to use the semi-accepted new nickname that signaled full emergence into the competitive world of visitor-luring—is now a great place to live. And to visit.

The paradox remains, however: Seattle is pleasant to visit precisely because it makes relatively little fuss over tourists. It's a city where a traveler can feel part of the city, not stigmatized and quarantined to the tourist quarters. Whenever I'm flying out of Seattle and meet some visitors to the city returning to their homes, I always ask them how they liked Seattle. They almost invariably liked it, a lot. They found it clean and safe-feeling. They found it very convenient and compact, but with a lot to do (though not quite enough). And they found that the natives were friendly, took the strangers right in and made them feel welcome. The conversation finishes up in the same vein: "If I weren't so happy with my job in _____, Seattle is the place I'd like to live. In fact,..." At this point, I change the subject.

We've written this book in the spirit of helping visitors fit right in. Our method was simple: tell the folks who visit us exactly what we try to tell the people who live here. Where are the best things, the places with the most distinctive and individualistic touches, the places the locals come back to time and again, the spots with good value. Our theory was that if we produced a book we would use ourselves, then it would also turn out to be the most helpful guide for visitors. The best tourism in Seattle is the kind that isn't tourism at all in the usual sense: it's just being part of an agreeable, open city that feels almost like home.

Another principle of our guidebooks is to concentrate on the places we consider to be the best in their category, and then to tell you enough about them, in fairly blunt language, so that you can see if you agree with our ratings after going there. Most guidebooks I am familiar with are written in a prose that emits such a cloud of positive adjectives that one soon recoils into doubt. Our ideal is to sound like that slightly jaded, wise uncle in a strange town, who knows that you don't have unlimited funds, time, or patience, and want the straight dope.

All these uncles have their biases and we do, too. We prefer smaller places, just as we prefer living in a smaller city. By the time "formula" places get to this corner of the country, they have usually lost a lot in the translation; so we're not too fond of them. We think you ought to stay downtown—few downtowns in America are as convenient to walk around in or have such splendid views. We advise getting out of town, or to the edges, where the natural wonders abound. Even though the city, the youngest of the great American metropolises, has relatively little historical "depth," we think the places with history, like the Public Market, are uncommonly attractive (possibly because the history is so recent as to be still alive). Maybe because the city errs on the side of staidness, we like places with lively individualists in command. Few cities in the world have a better growing climate, so we commend our horticultural glories. And Seattle may be a smaller American city, but she is a big actor on the stage of global commerce: so we like to direct you to her rich, thoroughly interwoven international aspects.

Yes, Uncle, but what about the rain? The topic does come up. And the rain does

v

indeed fall, taking a long time to drop not very much moisture. From November to May Seattle is mild, but cloudy and rainy more days than not. Springs are long, filled with splendid stretches, warmish from March on—and always raining again when you thought that was done with. Summers are clear and cool, with crisp nights—the latitude here is the same as the northern tip of Maine—and it stays light for a long time. Fall weather, very chancy, lingers on in good fashion just until the Huskies start getting beaten by the California football teams. Winters are dark early, glum, never very cold (January, the coldest month, averages 38 degrees), and relieved by very short, very helpful stretches of cruelly sunny weather. The official garment of the Seattleite is the lined raincoat, followed closely by the down parka. Umbrellas are a good idea, but they tend to get blown inside out by the strong gusts off the harbor, and the natives have never quite got the hang of them. The proper native attitude is to thrust a stoically bare head into the shower, as if the rain is just a temporary inconvenience, about to stop. Sometimes it does.

Twelve top attractions

1. **The Pike Place Market.** The finest remaining farmer's market in the nation, and the true soul of Seattle. It is always alive with shoppers, voluble merchants, people of all classes and costume, and visitors from everywhere. Three blocks and four stories of things to buy, plus excellent restaurants and views of the harbor. Hours are Monday-Saturday, 9-6; see Emmett Watson in Touring Seattle chapter for more information.

2. **Pioneer Square.** One of the most extensive and architecturally consistent "old towns" in the country, Pioneer Square is lovely for strolling in, shopping for gifts, gallery-hopping, dining (it's particularly popular at lunch), and carousing before and after Kingdome events. Developers have rejuvenated most buildings, including the upper floors, rather than putting tourist traps on the street level as in most revived old districts. See Emmett Watson in the Touring Seattle chapter for more information.

3. **Seattle Art Museum.** At its Volunteer Park home, a lovely Art Deco facility, SAM displays a fine collection of oriental art and puts on important touring shows and exhibits from its own collections; a branch museum, The Pavilion, is at Seattle Center. See The Arts chapter for details.

4. **Pacific Science Center.** This lovely facility, built around reflecting pools, is a legacy of the 1962 World's Fair, and includes a planetarium, laser beam-and-music shows, hands-on exhibits of computers, mathematics and physics, natural life in Puget Sound, and volcano displays featuring current seismic readings from Mount St. Helens—even an Indian longhouse. Admission: $2-3. Hours: 10-5; 382-2887. See "Touring Seattle" for more details.

5. **University of Washington.** Few large universities have a more beautiful campus than this one, on a bluff overlooking Lake Washington and the Cascades. A full menu of museums, bookstores, sporting events, and cultural performances is offered. See University District in the Touring Seattle chapter for more information.

6. **The Arboretum.** Seattle is one of the grand horticultural areas of the world, and this magnificently laid out park displays the widest array of plantings in the city. A walk in the spring down Azalea Way ending up at the Japanese Tea Garden will set you up for the year. See Green Seattle in the Touring Seattle chapter for more details.

7. **The Aquarium.** Small, intricately designed, full of intelligent signage, and very wide-ranging in the aquatic environments displayed, this facility is one of the best in the land. It includes a salmon fish ladder, a touch tank for children, and a domed underwater room that lets you look up at fish "flying" overhead. A great view of the Sound climaxes your visit. Hours: winter, 10-5; summer, 10-9. Admission: $.75-$3.25. Phone: 625-4358.

8. **The Zoo.** Amid the relics of old zoo buildings are some outstanding, internationally admired displays. Particularly fine are the African Savannah, with lions, giraffes, and hippos roaming seemingly free, and an extensive children's zoo with lots of young animals to cuddle. The grounds are extensive and well landscaped. See Green Seattle in Touring Seattle chapter for more information.

9. **The Ferries.** The nation's biggest fleet of ferries presents an easy opportunity for a short cruise from the downtown waterfront, across Elliott Bay, and back: fine for admiring the skyline, soaking up sun on the top deck, and (if you bring your own lunch rather than using the cafeteria), a great lunch break. See Transportation in the Services chapter for more details.

10. **International District.** Small, not especially touristy, full of excellent stores and foodstuffs, and rich with restaurants of Chinese, Japanese, Filipino, and Vietnamese cuisines, the district makes a dandy spot for lunch or for a meal before a game at the nearby Kingdome. See the Touring Seattle chapter for more information.

11. **The Ship Canal.** The Hiram M. Chittenden Locks, opened in 1917, connect Lake Washington with Puget Sound, and here you can watch the local armada of pleasurecraft being gently levitated, observe salmon leaping through the fish ladder, and picnic in the park gardens. To round out the visit, visit nearby **Fishermen's Terminal**, the working home of 650 gillnetters, trollers, seiners, draggers, and crab-boats; and stroll down Market Street in Ballard, the heart of the city's Scandinavian enclave.

12. **Mount Rainier.** Pick a clear day, and drive (or take a bus) down to one of the most awesomely bulky mountains in the world, clad with glaciers and girt about with wildflower meadows, fine trails, and virgin forests. It is the best symbol of the brooding presence of the Northwest's mighty and magnificent natural forces. See the Out of Town Tours chapter for more information.

How to use this book

Star-rating system. We rate lodging and the top 200 restaurants according to the following scale:

★ ★ ★ ★   *The very best in town.*
★ ★ ★   *A distinguished place.*
★ ★   *Several outstanding qualities.*
★   *A good place.*
(no stars)   *Worth knowing about.*

Cost. When we indicate a restaurant's price range, we use the following rough scale:

Expensive: *A dinner for two (exclusive of drinks) would be more than $30; most entrees are more than $10, a la carte.*
Moderate: *The dinner for two (no drinks) would be $15-$30.*
Inexpensive   *The dinner for two (no drinks) would be less than $15.*

Map indicators. Most of the attractions in the book are keyed to the fold-out maps attached to the inside back cover. The code is found in the margin next to the attraction. For example:

F7: refers to the Downtown Seattle map.
FF7: refers to the Greater Seattle map.

Users of the map should note that the miles and meters scale on the Downtown Seattle map is unfortunately wrong, and this error was discovered too late for us to correct in this printing. The scale is actually 6 inches (roughly) to a mile.

Finding things. A short index on the first page of each chapter serves as a guide for that section. There is also a full index in the back. In the restaurant chapter, the Top 200 restaurants are listed alphabetically. We have also divided them up by various categories, added other restaurants to that listing, and used this section as an additional index which can be found immediately after the Top 200 restaurant reviews.

A final caution. The information in a book like this, with thousands of listings, is bound to erode over time. The listings here are current as of late Spring, 1983. It is always a good idea to call ahead and make sure that the place you want to visit still has the same hours as those we list. Where hours tend to change often, as with shops, we have omitted exact hours.

If you find your experience of a place we have reviewed to be quite different from our account—either better or worse—or if you find good places that we have overlooked, please use the report form at the back of the book and let us know. Scores of sources have contributed to this book, and we'd be delighted to include you.

UPDATES for second printing, October 1983

Restaurants

p. 11. A la Francaise (at 2325 Fourth Ave) no longer operates a restaurant at its bakery, which continues to be a successful supplier of French baked goods.

p. 12. Al-Waaha has closed.

p. 12. The Alexis Restaurant is now offering Northwest nouvelle cuisine under the direction of Bruce Naftaly and Robin Sanders, both formerly of Les Copains.

p. 13. Andy and Jemmy's Wok now has a three-star rating based on recent reports.

p. 17. Cafe Sabika is now open for lunch (11:30-2 Tues-Fri), in addition to dinner.

p. 19. China North has been demoted to a one-star rating based on recent reports.

p. 22. Duke's has opened a cafe around the corner from its original Queen Anne establishment (236 First Ave W, 283-4436). It serves deli snacks, seafood appetizers, wines, cognacs, desserts, and coffees (hours: 11am-1am Mon-Fri, 5:30pm-1am Sat & Sun).

p. 25. The Goose's correct address is 1301 Fifth Ave.

p. 25. All the branches of Gretchen's Of Course have changed their phone numbers. The new numbers are 467-4002 for 1111 Third Ave, 467-4001 for 909 University, 467-4004 for 94 Stewart, 467-4006 for 1513 Sixth Ave. A new Gretchen's Of Course has opened in Bellevue at 411 108th NE (453-2603; hours: 7am-5pm Mon-Fri; closed Sat & Sun).

p. 33. Les Copains has closed.

p. 35. Malia's Northwest has closed.

p. 38. Mukilteo Cafe has closed.

p. 41. Phoenicia has closed; the Meenar restaurant, serving Pakistini and Middle Eastern food, has opened in its place (hours: 11-10 Tues-Fri, 4-10 Sat-Sun; closed Mon).

p. 42. The Rainier Pub has closed.

p. 44. Russets has closed.

p. 51. The Washington Post Cafe, renamed the Washington Post Restaurant and Catering, has a new owner and an adventurous Northwest nouvelle cuisine menu executed by the same chef (Hugh Kohl). New phone number: 623-8100; new hours: 11-11 Mon-Fri, 9am-11pm Sat & Sun.

p. 51. Yangtze Szechwan's correct address is 1320 156th NE.

p. 52. A la Francaise is now a bakery only; Malia's Northwest has closed.

p. 53. Russets has closed.

p. 54. Washington Post Cafe has changed name, menu, ownership, phone number, and hours—see above.

p. 55. Soup, salad, and sandwich restaurants—Soupourri has closed.

p. 59. French restaurants—A la Francaise, Les Copains, Mukilteo Cafe have closed.

p. 60. Mediterranean—Alexis now serves Northwest nouvelle cuisine.

p. 60. Middle Eastern—Al-Waaha, Phoenicia have closed.

p. 62. Dessert and coffee places—A La Francaise is a bakery only.

Nightlife

p. 79. Malia's Northwest has closed.

p. 88. Seattle Concert Theater has been razed.

p. 88. The Blarney Stone has been replaced by The Talk of the Town Restaurant and Bar (621-0900).

p. 89. Ernestine's has closed.

p. 89. Michael J's has closed.

p. 90. Dez's 400 has closed.

p. 92. The Medieval Cellar is now a new-wave club.

p. 92. The Rainy Town Folk Music Club has closed.

p. 93. The Silver Spoon Restaurant has moved to a new location at 26399 NE Cherry Valley Road (788-2734). The old location (now the Good Old Spoon, 788-4107) holds Friday night movies and Saturday night folk music in its upstairs concert hall.

Shopping

p. 106. Rumpelstiltskin has closed its Broadway store; other locations: Northgate Mall 365-0400, Southcenter 246-8750.

p. 112. Maxims has opened a new store on the Eastside at 454 Kirkland Park Place, 828-4393; open every day.

p. 120. A new branch of A la Francaise has opened in The University Village (524-9300).

p. 121 & p. 126 The Quicherie has closed.

p. 125. Les Copains has closed.

p. 139. Royal City Antiques has closed.

p. 142. Tashiro's Japanese Tools has moved to 707 S Jackson; same phone number.

p. 148. The Goldern Horn has moved to 317 First Ave S; same phone number.

p. 154. Computerland has moved its Yesler Way branch to 822 First Avenue, same phone number.

p. 155. Pioneer Square Gardens has closed.

p. 162. Prasad's has closed.

p. 166. Gregg's Greenlake Cycle's correct phone number is 523-1822.

p. 169. Reggae City has closed.

p. 170. Great Winds Kite Shop has moved to 402 Occidental Ave S; same phone number.

Touring Seattle

p. 175. The clock is in the heart (not the north end) of the Pike Place Market.

p. 200. The Suquamish Museum is open 10-5 every day.

Sport

p. 216. Del Crandall has replaced Rene Lachemann as manager of the Seattle Mariners baseball team.

Out of Town Tours

p. 248. The Inn at Wapato Point is now exclusively a time-share and full-ownership condominium complex.

p. 252. The Silver Spoon Restaurant has moved to spiffy new quarters at 26399 NE Cherry Valley Road, same phone number. The old location (now the Good Old Spoon, 788-4107) still holds Saturday night folk music concerts upstairs (also Friday night movies).

p. 253. The Laurel Point Inn is no longer owned by Delta.

Services

p. 263. Correct phone number for Language Bank is 323-2345.

Lodging

Hotels and motels	*1*	Downtown
	4	Denny Regrade/Seattle Center
	5	Airport area
	6	Eastside
	6	University District and North End
Other lodgings	*7*	Bed & Breakfast
	9	Condominiums
	10	Hostels
	10	Camping

Hotels and motels — Downtown

★ **Alexis Hotel**   *624-4844*
★ **First & Madison**   *D $85, Suite $175*
★   *(includes continental breakfast and service fees)*
★
L8   Few cities have as elegant a hotel as the Alexis, newly carved out of a stylish, turn-of-the-century building near the waterfront. It's small (54 rooms), full of tasteful touches (televisions concealed in armoires, a free *New York Times*—even on Sundays—in the room), and decorated with a suave modernity as up-to-date as Michael Graves' post-modernist colors. It's a great place for being pampered, with Jacuzzis in the tubs, fireplaces (real wood) in some of the suites, and concierge at the ready. It's very quiet, too—sipping sherry in the lobby, drinking in the cozy bar, or dining on the Spanish-accented fare in the spacious, sedate dining room. Rooms opening onto the inner courtyard are preferred. The suites make splendid rooms for private meetings, incidentally. No convention facilities: the Alexis favors well-heeled travelers on the Stanford Court/Pierre circuit.

★ **The Baker Apartment Hotel**   *365-8615*
GG7 **1121 Broadway E**   *$25-$35*

While not really downtown, this 1910 apartment hotel is situated on a quiet street near the bustling inner-city district of Capitol Hill. Recently renovated with great care, the hotel offers studio and one-bedroom apartments with full kitchens, china, and linens. Refurbished claw-footed tubs and second-floor veranda reflect the building's turn-of-the-century style. Color TV and phone in each room. Laundry facilities and free parking.

★ **Camlin Hotel and Cabanas**   *682-0100*
14 **1619 Ninth Ave**   *D $49, Suite $150*

Open bright lobby and stylish quarters in this refurbished 1926 hotel. Most accommodations have small sitting areas off the bedrooms. Rooms ending in the number ten have windows on three sides. Huge closets and spotless bathrooms,

1

Lodging

some with original porcelain fixtures. Free parking. Excellent bell-cap services.

| ★ **Four Seasons Olympic** | 621-1700 |
| ★ **Fourth & University** | D $110, Suite $325 |

★
★
L6

The Olympic has been a Seattle landmark since the 1920s, and now it has been refurbished in a style befitting its earlier grandeur. Rooms (451 on 12 floors) are now quite spacious, furnished with period pieces, muted lighting, televisions in the armoires, and such welcome touches as a terrycloth bathrobe for each guest. A team of well-informed concierges also offers a wealth of personal services. The public rooms are grand verging on gaudy: armchairs, potted plants, marble galore, tapestries, wood paneling, etc. You can lounge in the Garden Court, taking high tea if you wish, amid enormous plants and arresting skylights. The showcase dining room is The Georgian Room, a handsome space; downstairs is the livelier Shuckers, an oyster bar with excellent mixed drinks. There are several elegant meeting rooms, and the ornate Spanish ballroom for large affairs. A delightful health club rounds out the amenities. Prices are stiff, especially since there are few views, but it certainly is a venerable hotel with all the trimmings and the best location in town.

| L6 | **Hotel Seattle** | 623-5110 |
| | 315 Seneca | D $50, Suite $77 |

The lobby decor is somewhat tattered, but the remodeled rooms and sprightly service are commendable. Parking is free, and location is excellent.

| ★ | **Kennedy Hotel** | 623-6175 |
| L6 | **Fifth & Spring** | D $31.95, Suite $48 |

A small but elegant lobby with Oriental appointments reflecting the largely Japanese clientele. The rooms are undistinguished though large; a few feature kitchenettes, but they must be booked far in advance. Free parking and complimentary continental breakfast; no room service or air-conditioning.

| ★ | **Madison Hotel** | 583-0300 |
| ★ | **Sixth & Madison** | D $90, Suite $140 |

★
M5

Scheduled to open in mid-1983, this stylish downtown hotel next to I-5 will join Seattle's family of luxury lodgings. The rooms are very tasteful with handmade cabinets and brass fittings and many command some superb views. Facilities include two restaurants, lounges, and a 24-hour espresso bar, as well as a universal gym, sauna, and 40-foot swimming pool. The hotel opened just at press time so service and restaurants could not be considered for rating.

| ★ | **Mayflower Park Hotel** | 623-8700 |
| ★ | **405 Olive Way** | D $50, Suite $80 |

I6

They haven't quite settled on a style for refurbishing this hotel, but they keep working at it. The rooms are plain, but well proportioned, and the double-pane glass keeps out the street noises; you can get a large suite for only $90. The downstairs bar is snazzily done in glass and steel, and it has a dandy view of a busy street corner. The real advantages are two: a location smack in the middle of the department stores, and bargain prices.

| ★ | **Pacific Plaza** | 623-3900 |
| L6 | **Fourth & Spring** | D $52, Suite $92 |

The recent renovation retained the 1929 brass and porcelain fixtures. There's no air-conditioning, but ceiling fans are planned for each room. Services include fresh fruit on each floor, and daily papers for suite occupants. Excellent downtown location.

Lodging

★ **Park Hilton** 464-1980
★ **Sixth & Seneca** D $93, Suite $130
★
L5 The narrow, tall hotel has just about the right combination of bustle and compactness, completeness and coziness. The architecture is handled with dash and assurance; the views are quite panoramic (above the 12th floor); and the level of sophistication and intimacy is positively Manhattanish. There's a tiny French restaurant, a posh piano bar (the pianist once ran for mayor), and a cafe that opens into a sunny little park. Rooms are well appointed and fairly capacious; north-facing rooms overlook the city's celebrated over-the-freeway park. The service is very good, the location is right by the freeway and the downtown hotels and shops, and you won't be bothered by conventioneers.

★ **Seattle Hilton** 624-0500
K5 **Sixth & University** D $83, Suite $110

This hotel has been criticized because the lobby sits above the parking garage, but the bay windows in each room give these digs a homey feel, and the location is central. Northern exposure offers the best views. Popular night club on top floor.

★ **Sheraton Hotel** 621-9000
★ **Sixth & Pike** D $95, Suite $125

K5 Seattle's new Sheraton is an 880-room tower rising as a sleek triangle over a somewhat "transitional" neighborhood. It aims at the convention business, so the rooms are smallish and standard, and the emphasis is on the meeting rooms and the restaurants. The Cafe offers mediocre international fare, plus a 27-foot-long dessert spread. Better to eat lunch in Green's, by night a music lounge but an easy hideaway by day. Fuller's is the fancy restaurant, adorned with outstanding Northwest paintings. The top floor will soon open a seafood grill, called Cirrus. The overall architecture is bland and confusing, but the Sheraton has done a nice job in commissioning Northwest artists to decorate the walls. Convention facilities are very complete, and the kitchen staff can handle the most complex assignments. Snootier business travelers will head for the upper four floors, where a hotel-within-the-hotel offers its own lobby and considerably more amenities in the (same size as economy) rooms.

★ **Sorrento Hotel** 622-6400
★ **900 Madison St** D $90, Suite $120
★
M4 When the Sorrento opened in 1909, in time for the Alaska Yukon Pacific Exposition, it commanded a bluff overlooking the young city and the Sound. For years thereafter, it was the most elegant hotel in the city—Renaissance architecture modeled after a castle in Sorrento, with Honduras mahogany in the lobby and a famous dining room on the top floor. That faded badly, and the view was lost as the city grew around the hotel; then in 1981 it was all fixed up and reopened. It's a real beauty. Downstairs is a clubby restaurant, and the mahogany lobby, now turned into a lounge that is a fine place for talking. The rooms (76 of them) are decorated in muted, tasteful coziness with a slight Oriental accent. We recommend the 08 series of suites, in the corners, or room 615, one of the few with a good view. Suites on the top floor make nice rentals for special meetings or parties. The location, up the hill five blocks from the heart of downtown, can be somewhat inconvenient for some, but it's quieter.

I5 **Vance Hotel** 623-2700
   620 Stewart St D $38

The wood-paneled lobby is reminiscent of Booth Tarkington; upstairs is a nest of corner rooms and cramped hallways. Service is good and the parking is free. Full-service coffee shop and lounge.

Lodging

★ **Warwick Hotel**	625-6700
★ 421 Lenora	D $67, Suite $325

★
H6 This new hotel in the Denny Regrade aims a straight pitch at the corporate traveler. Rooms are unpretentious and comfortable, very well soundproofed, and well stocked with executive services. The restaurant is nothing much, and the pool is only four feet deep; nor is the lobby what you'd call grand. If you want to impress somebody here, you'll have to take a grand suite, complete with a marble bathtub/Jacuzzi that commands a panoramic view of the city. The location, a few blocks north of the department stores, is mid-nowheresville.

★ **Westin Hotel**	624-7400
★ Fifth & Westlake	D $100, Suite $250

★
H5 Westin, a major international chain, is headquartered in Seattle, so this flagship hotel has quite a few extras. The twin cylindrical towers may be called corncobs by the natives, but they afford rooms with superb views, particularly above the 20th floor. The convention facilities are quite complete, spread over several floors of meeting rooms. There is a large pool, along with an exercise room supervised by qualified conditioning experts. On the top floors are some very ritzy suites. The location, near shopping and the Monorail station, is excellent. The recently enlarged hotel has also improved its restaurants: Trader Vic's is still here, one of the better ones in the chain, and there is now a posh restaurant called The Palm Court, with an outstanding adjoining wine bar; a good, though overpriced, Market Cafe; and a handsome seafood bar in the Gatsby-era style.

Hotels and motels — Denny Regrade/Seattle Center

★ **Century House**	624-6820
F4 2224 Eighth Ave	D $46

It's like a motel off a slick side street in a B-movie. Stella does the cleaning. But the 1950s-ish rooms are large, with colorful tilework in the bathrooms. The front-desk staff is taciturn but helpful. Free parking, full restaurant, and continental breakfast.

★ **Edgewater Inn**	624-7000
F9 Pier 67, 2411 Alaskan Way	D $46

You don't need a license to fish from your window here and many guests in the shoreside rooms do just that. Avoid the in-shore rooms, which overlook the parking lot, or the smallish top-floor rooms. A good motel, with restaurant and bar, that makes use of its unique location on the bay. Free parking.

★ **Executive Inn**	628-9444
B4 200 Taylor N	D $56, Suite $71

Large rooms and spacious, cheerful halls. The mini-suites have couches, wet bars, refrigerators, and whirlpool baths. All the rooms have original, colorful batiks by the owner's daughter—a welcome alternative to the standard wall art. Parking, food, and liquor. In the shadow of the Space Needle.

★ **Loyal Inn**	682-0200
F5 2301 Eighth Ave	D $44

Blue rooms with blue doors. Large indoor whirlpool and adjoining sun deck and saunas give this standard motel a boost. No restaurant, coffee shop, or bar. Some rooms have wet bars and refrigerators. Close to Seattle Center.

Lodging

G6	**Regency Motor Inn** **2200 Fifth Ave**	*682-9785* *D $45*

Somewhat sterile, but good-size rooms and excellent location close to the department stores. Restaurant, lounge, and free parking. Family discounts available.

B3	**TraveLodge** **200 Sixth Ave N**	*623-2600* *D $45*

Fully tiled showers in clean rooms decorated in burnt orange and browns. Small swimming pool next to the front door. Across the street from the Seattle Center.

Hotels and motels — Airport area

PP4	★ **Doubletree Inn** **205 Strander Blvd, Tukwila**	*246-8220* *D $77, Suite $85*

The woody interior and lobby fireplace create a relaxing atmosphere for a motel fixed between Interstate 5 and Southcenter shopping mall. First-floor rooms open onto a pool area. Guests can also use the Jacuzzi and sauna located across the street in the Doubletree Plaza Hotel, a luxury inn with suites only. Valet service is also available.

OO5	★ **Hyatt Seattle** **17001 Pacific Hwy S**	*244-6000* *D $64, Suite $150*

Thoughtful management and high staff morale ensure solid service. Rooms are comfortable and the closets large. Pool, sauna, and massage available. Avoid rooms across from the United Airlines hangar. Full restaurant.

PP6	★ **Sea-Tac Holiday Inn** **17338 Pacific Hwy S**	*248-1000* *D $49, Suite $55*

The clay-colored walls and dark-green furnishings make these accommodations unusually tasteful fare for a hotel chain. No charge for children (under 18) bunking in the same room with parents. Babysitting service is also available. Coffee shop and rooftop restaurant.

PP6	★ **Sea-Tac Red Lion Inn** **18740 Pacific Hwy S**	*246-8600* *D $64, Suite $110*

You may pass Willy Loman in the dark, cavernous halls of this 850-room mega-motel. Sleeping rooms are decorated in lime and olive greens; public rooms in purple and red. The inn's east-facing rooms have views of the Cascade Mountains. Full restaurant and bars.

	★ **Seattle Airport Hilton Hotel** ★ **17620 Pacific Hwy S**	*244-4800* *D $75, Suite $205*

PP6 This low-lying building miraculously manages to create a resort atmosphere along an airport strip. Plush rooms (at posh prices) circle a large, landscaped courtyard with pool and indoor/outdoor Jacuzzi. The architecture, recently refurbished, is by the distinguished national firm of SOM. Weather permitting, there's outdoor dining. A versatile menu offers Northwest game and fish.

	★ **Seattle Marriott at Sea-Tac** ★ **3201 176th S**	*241-2000* *D $72, Suite $175*

PP6 Another mega-motel, but on a human scale. Alaskan motif is warm though somewhat cluttered in the lobby. Pool and courtyard area are part of a covered atrium.

5

Lodging

Jacuzzi, sauna, and well-equipped exercise room. Lobby and disco bar. Spacious suites.

NN4	**Sheraton Renton Inn**	*226-7700*
	800 Rainier Ave S, Renton	*D $55, Suite $69*

Twenty-four-hour limousine service to Sea-Tac Airport and free parking privilege while away make this an ideal stopover for vacationers who need a night's rest before taking off. Limousine services are also extended free of charge for guests making local calls. An up-to-date, midrise motel decorated in mauves and neon. Youthful, helpful staff. A convenient place to stay for people doing business at Boeing.

Hotels and motels — Eastside

★	**Bellevue Hilton**	*455-3330*
HH3	100 112th Ave NE, Bellevue	*D $68, Suite $125*

Fresh fruit at the front desk typifies the personal service for which these hotel professionals strive. Rooms sport soft, warm colors and lights that illuminate without glare. Small indoor pool with Jacuzzi and sauna. Regular business travelers receive a special rate ($49) plus complimentary *Wall Street Journal* and other extras. Valet service and all-night cafe round out this full-service inn.

★	**Bellevue Holiday Inn**	*455-5240*
★	11211 Main St, Bellevue	*D $57*

HH3 Standard motel fare that neither stimulates nor overloads the senses. Rooms with comfortable, simple furnishings, surround a well-manicured lawn and heated swimming pool. Full-service gourmet restaurant and good coffee shop. The campus-style architecture is excellent.

HH3	**Bellevue Thunderbird**	*455-1515*
	818 112th NE, Bellevue	*D $53*

Probably the only motel in town that gives you a map to find your room. Spacious accommodations with Spanish-style furniture. Swimming pool and restaurant.

★	**Greenwood Inn**	*455-9444*
HH3	625 116th NE, Bellevue	*D $51, Suite $85*

Brightly colored rooms with ceiling-high windows. Inside quarters surround a lovely courtyard with azaleas and rhododendrons. Two-floor suites have wet bars and fireplaces. Free coffee and local newspaper with your wake-up call. Full bar and popular restaurant.

★	**Red Lion Inn**	*455-1300*
HH3	300 112th Ave SE, Bellevue	*D $75, Suite $150*

Even the most seasoned traveler could become disoriented in this low-tech hall of mirrors and glass. Tastefully decorated rooms make up for the gaudy atrium lobby. The 355-room motel specializes in convention trade.

Hotels and motels — University District and North End

★	**The College Inn**	*633-4441*
★	4000 University Way NE	*D $24, Suite $44*
FF7		

Burgundy carpets, window seats, antique writing tables, and pastel comforters create a cozy atmosphere in this hospitable inn designed along the lines of a European pension. Newly tiled bathrooms are located at the end of each hall. A continental breakfast is included in the room price and served under the sloping roof of this renovated 1909 Tudor structure in the University District. Pub downstairs.

DD7	**Ramada Inn** **2140 N Northgate Way**	*365-0700* *D $53, Suite $80*

This roadside inn barely lifts its head above the tangled I-5 interchange and the vast parking lots of Northgate shopping center. Heated swimming pool, 24-hour restaurant, and airport-shuttle service.

FF7	**Sherwood Town and Country Inn** **400 NE 45th**	*634-0100* *D $48, Suite $120*

The drab outside contrasts oddly with the medieval decor inside. This inn's location next to Interstate 5 and not far from the University makes it a favorite for traveling sports teams. Several rooms open onto the pool, which is motel-modern.

	★ **University Tower Hotel** ★ **4507 Brooklyn Ave NE**	*634-2000* *D $58, Suite $69*

FF7 The preferred hotel in the University District. Close to Interstate 5, but not too close. The architecture is distinguished 1930s design, and the hotel is conveniently located for shopping along The Ave. Each room has a bay window with a good view, and those on the south side are sun-filled, when the sun's out. Sparkling bathrooms. Suites offer little more than standard doubles.

Bed & Breakfast

Bed and Breakfast International (Registry)
151 Ardmore Road   *Jean & Harry Brown*
Kensington, CA 94707   *(415) 527-8836 or 525-4569   D $28-$60*

Founded in 1978. Each of their Seattle member houses has four years of experience. Homes are on or near Capitol Hill, Volunteer Park, University of Washington, and Queen Anne Hill. For local information, call Patricia Reese, 323-2467. The national list includes over 300 homes, mainly in California, Hawaii, and New York City. They range from "city apartments to ocean-beach villas with swimming pools and tennis courts." Rates include a full American breakfast. Send self-addressed stamped envelope for a list of homes. Three-night minimum stay in major cities, two nights in others.

Bed and Breakfast League, Ltd (Registry)
2855 29th St NW   *Diana MacLeish*
Washington DC 20008   *(202) 232-8718*

Membership organization: $25 a year. Toll-free phone number and annual bulletin for members only. Operates in 42 states, 300 cities worldwide (US, Canada, Europe). Forty-five homes in England. Office closed December 21–January 2. Six listings in Washington State; four in Seattle, one in Edmonds, one on Bainbridge Island.

GG8 **Galer Place** (Independent and registry-listed)
318 W Galer St   *Rod Garritson & Dick Fusco*
Seattle, WA 98119   *282-5339   D $35-$45*

Lodging

Built in 1906, this B&B's three double bedrooms (The Oak, The Brass, and The Mahogany) are furnished with antiques, as are the parlor and dining room. Hosts freely advise on out-of-the-way cafes, events, and country outings. Lots of fresh fruit for breakfast. Backyard hot tub. The South Queen Anne location makes it within downhill walking distance of the Seattle Center and near downtown attractions. Bus service at the front door.

Heather House (Independent)	*Harry & Joy Whitcutt*
1011 B Ave	778-7233
Edmonds, WA 98020	D $25, S $20

This one boasts a lovely view of Puget Sound and the Olympic Mountains. Pier, beaches, museum, and restaurants nearby. Breakfast is extra: full English $3, continental $2.

GG6 | **Interlaken Bed and Breakfast (Independent)** | |
|---|---|
| 2149 E Interlaken Blvd | *Genie Hagar* 323-0760 |
| Seattle, WA 98112 | D $35, S $25, $7.50 *per child* |

Old Seattle home in Interlaken Park. Two adjoining guest rooms, separated by a half-bath; shower available. Leaded windows and Oriental rugs. Breakfast served in a formal dining room. On bus line.

Northwest Bed and Breakfast Inc. (Registry)	
7707 SW Locust St	*Gloria Shaich & Laine Friedman*
Portland, OR 97223	(503) 246-8366
	D $18-$40 *(family rates also available)*

Membership organization with fees at $15 single and $20 family. Every home is inspected to meet registry standards. Homes vary from Victorian to modern, with private baths or shared, in the city or suburbs. Guest members receive directory with maps and rates.

Pacific Bed and Breakfast (Registry)	*Irmgard Castleberry*
701 NW 60th St	784-0539
Seattle, WA 98107	D $26-$42

Their $2 directory lists 65 homes throughout Puget Sound located in such serene-sounding places as Whidbey Island, Mount Vernon, and the San Juans.
In-town accommodations include: a private upstairs apartment with a double bed, a full bath, and stocked kitchen in a Queen Anne home; the second-floor rooms (with kitchenette) of an 1890 mansion featuring stained-glass windows, an oak staircase, and afternoon tea and cakes in a gazebo overlooking Green Lake; and a University language professor's Tudor home on Capitol Hill with down comforters and gourmet breakfast.
Off-the-tourist-track locations include: a farmhouse (with airstrip) near Mount Rainier; a Mercer Island home offering wine in the afternoon; and a swank two-story houseboat on Lake Union.
Languages spoken: Scandinavian, German, French, Italian, and Dutch. Babysitting available in some homes.

PT International (Registry)	
1318 SW Troy St	1-800-547-1463
Portland, OR 97219	

Call toll-free for information on 36 homes and eight inns in Washington State. Reservations can be made on the same number or through a travel agent after you determine which PT's Bed and Breakfast is best for you. In total, the Oregon outfit lists 2,500 B&Bs in 11 countries.

Lodging

Travellers' Bed and Breakfast (Registry)
Box 492   *Jean Knight*
Mercer Island, WA 98040   *232-2345   D $28-$50*

English-born Jean Knight brings years of experience to choosing over 50 B&Bs located between Gig Harbor, Washington, and Victoria, BC. Her directory, which includes some inns, costs $3. Knight takes pride in such personal attention as surprise birthday parties, or champagne and flowers for honeymooners and anniversary couples.

The registry includes such gems as an 80-year-old Victorian home (with exquisite furniture, a grand piano, and lace bedspreads) across the street from Volunteer Park and the Seattle Art Museum; a turn-of-the-century Lake Union houseboat (former Bunk House to Alaska) equipped with a kayak and rowboat; a Mercer Island retreat with a pink bedroom, English engravings, an antique tea table, and a four-poster bed complete with canopy; and a delightful Lake Washington waterfront home in a wooded setting—breakfast is served in the atrium overlooking the lake.

MM8 **West Coast Bed & Breakfast (Registry)**
11304 20th Pl SW   *Jean Hartzell*
Seattle, WA 98146   *246-2650   D $25-$50*

A select group of 30 homes mostly in greater Seattle, some with excellent waterfront locations. Almost all are five to ten minutes from downtown. One elegant turn-of-the-century home has a double room with a deck overlooking Portage Bay. Located near the Broadway shopping and movie district, it is owned by a former restaurant manager who cooks up a storm. A West Seattle split-level cedar home shares space with wooded Lincoln Park and a two-mile beach. A double room with deck opens onto the water. A ladder to a refurbished attic offers additional beds and a gangbusters view. A 1915 home near the banks of Green Lake is decorated in American Federal and English Regency antiques; the guest room opens onto a private patio with hot tub. Freshly baked bran muffins are offered for breakfast.

The registry also books reservations for the Swan Inn, patterned after a 14th-century English roadhouse, on rural Vashon Island, a 15-minute ferry ride from Seattle.

Condominiums

Condominium Rentals of Seattle
555 116th Ave NE, Suite 201, Bellevue   *454-2800*
HomeFires Condominium Rentals, Inc.
855 106th Ave NE, Bellevue   *454-7888*

Shot glasses, free phone calls, fireplaces, linens, and kitchens with everything from cutlery to colanders are just a few of the amenities condominium rentals offer travelers staying a three-day minimum. Washers and dryers are standard; boat slips are extra.

Condominium Rentals of Seattle has apartments in the Arlington Building, a classy Cornerstone Company renovation project strategically placed between Pioneer Square and the Pike Place Market. The accommodations offer a clean, modern look with wood and marble appointments.

Both rental outfits provide condominiums throughout Seattle and Bellevue. Some

Lodging

one-bedrooms begin at $49. Two- and three-bedrooms are also available. Prices are pro-rated downward for added days.

Hostels

M6	**YMCA** 909 Fourth Ave	*382-5000* *$19.91–$21.11*

Traditionally small Y rooms with bed, desk, lamp, and chair; phones and TVs in some rooms. Access to all health facilities free of charge.

L6	**YWCA** 1118 Fifth Ave	*447-4888* *$18-$33*

Modest but fairly large rooms, all with sinks, and some with private baths. Large windows give the rooms an airy quality. Singles, doubles, and triples.

Camping

Fay Bainbridge State Park *842-3931*
15446 Sunrise Drive NE, *$5.50 per campsite*
Bainbridge Island

Located on the northeast end of the island, which is only a ferry ride away from downtown Seattle, is a lovely wooded state park right on Puget Sound. It has 36 campsites (but no hookups for RVs), which are available on a first-come, first-served basis. Park hours are 8-5 in the winter and 6:30-till-dark in the summer.

Seattle North RV Park *481-1972*
22910 15th Ave SE, Suite A, Bothell *$11 entry fee for two*

A wooded area north of Seattle (Exit 26, Interstate 405 and the Bothell–Everett Highway) with 153 sites for RVs, campers, and tents. Bathrooms, showers, heated swimming pool, and private bus service to Seattle. Staffers will also provide assistance coordinating excursions into the city.

Restaurants

Top 200	11		
Other restaurants	52	Breakfast	
by category	53	Brunch	
	54	Soup, salad, sandwich	
	55	Pizza	
	56	Hamburgers	
	58	Ethnic	
	62	Dessert and coffee houses	

The Top 200 restaurants

★ **A la Francaise**
F7 **2325 Fourth Ave**
447-1500

B 7-11 Mon-Fri; L 11:30-2:30 Mon-Fri
Sun Brunch 9-2:30
Moderate; Beer & Wine
cc: MC, V

This cafe-bakery is the retail front of one of the city's most successful wholesale suppliers of French baked goods. There's a good and creative Sunday brunch, but otherwise breakfasts are espresso, juice, and exceptional croissants and brioche. Lunch items tend to French-style, including croissant sandwiches and small steaks in several sauces.

★ **Adriatica**
★ **1107 Dexter N**
★ **Res: 285-5000**
A2

D 5:30-9:30 Tues-Thur,
5:30-10:30 Fri & Sat; closed Sun & Mon
Expensive; Full bar
cc: AE, CB, DC, MC, V

Three flights up from a warehouse-lined street, in an old house, is one of the city's most charming and comfortable restaurants. The dining room is cream-colored, with dark wood trim; leafy treetops brush the windows. Co-owner Jim Malevitsis sets the tone in his captain's role. He is relaxed, friendly, knowledgeable, and never pretentious. Another co-owner, John Sarich, runs the kitchen, turning out a short list of Greek, Italian, and Yugoslavian dishes, the most celebrated of which is an appetizer of ideally fried calamari with a perfectly balanced and textured skordalia. Not all the fare reaches that standard. But fish are nicely broiled or sauteed, pastas are well prepared, and occasionally Sarich will display his true worth with a special order of, say, pasta and crunchy shrimp. The wine list is quite good, and Malevitsis often has something new and worthy to recommend. Start with the

Restaurants

calamari and end with a dessert of walnuts and dates in filo served hot with cream, and you will have a memorable meal.

DD7	**Al-Waaha** **543 NE Northgate Way** Res: 364-7300	*11-10 Mon-Sat; noon-8 Sun* *Moderate; No alcohol* *cc: MC, V*

Mohammed Nasser says his is the first Saudi Arabian restaurant in the country. Actually, Al-Waaha (oasis) has a broader range than that. Seating runs from chairs and tables to booths with cushions to the bare floor. Cooking runs from Middle Eastern to East Indian. The Saudi Arabian dishes are worthy: a form of baba ganouj, for instance, where the eggplant skin is charred and the taste of the charring remains; kapsa, spiced rice with chicken or lamb and vegetables; and zurbiyaan, yogurt-marinated lamb mixed with saffron rice and steamed. Nasser also roasts whole lambs for parties.

JJ9	**The Alaska Junction** **4548 California SW** 937-1800	*10-11 Mon-Sat; 9-11 Sun* *Moderate; Full bar* *cc: AE, MC, V*

The informal elegance of this cafe is welcome in downtown West Seattle. The room is nicely decorated in burgundy, roses, and grays. The ceilings are high, and there are fine architectural details; candles and fresh flowers grace the tables. The cooks work in an open kitchen behind a counter, preparing burgers, omelets, steaks, pasta, and seafood, all served in large if not ideally prepared portions. Sunday brunch draws a crowd.

L8	★ **Alexis** ★ **1007 First Ave** Res: 624-3646	*B 7-10:30, L 11:30-2:30, D 5:30-11* *Every day* *Expensive; Full bar; cc: AE, DC, MC, V*

The two-level dining room of the elegant little Alexis Hotel displays European flair: a high ceiling with architectural detail; a color scheme of roses and creams; soft but full light; and spectacular flower arrangements. The menu is mixed European with a Spanish accent, due to the presence in the kitchen of Eugenio Castillano. A thick garlic soup is much admired. Appetizers include pink, tender cold veal with salmon or tuna sauce. Entrees are lightly seasoned and include dishes such as zarzuela, a Spanish seafood stew; prawns sauteed in their shells with paprika, cognac, and herbs; and scallops on a toasted brioche. For lunch, there are salads, osso bucco, and rockfish baked with onions and olives.

J4	★ **The Americana Cafe** **713 Pine** Res: 625-9961	*11-5 Mon, 11-9 Tues-Thur, 11-10 Fri,* *5-10 Sat; closed Sun* *Inexpensive; Beer & Wine; cc: MC, V*

Owner Bill Kraut and two buddies from a decade ago at Seattle Central Community College's cooking school began this small place on the edge of downtown as a showcase for "American" regional cooking, old and new. They're off to an encouraging start with a short seasonal menu that includes hearty fare such as pasties, Texas chili, chicken gumbo, and a sour-cream-based potato salad. At dinner there are monthly specials such as a stuffed pork chop braised in cider, and chicken with wine and cranberries. Prices are low and ambitions high.

FF7	**America's Cup** **1900 N Northlake Way** Res: 633-0161	*L 11-3 Mon-Sat; D 4:30-10:30 Sun-Thur;* *4:30-11:30 Fri & Sat;* *Sun Brunch 9:30-2:30* *Moderate; Full bar; cc: AE, MC, V*

Located in a complex of nautical shops called Mariners Square, this glass-fronted restaurant overlooks Gasworks Park on the north side of Lake Union. The food

—an international mix of seafood, pastas, salads, and sautes—the service, and the sailboat-racing theme are as slick as a fiberglass hull. An inexpensive Sunday brunch-buffet is also served.

CC7	**Andy and Jemmy's Wok** (unrated) **11030 8th Ave NE** **364-6898**	*11:30-9:30 Mon-Thur, 11:30-10:30 Fri,* *4-10:30 Sat; closed Sun* *Moderate; Full bar; cc: MC, V*

Formerly the inspiration at The Wok on First Hill, the brothers Ma, at publication time, were readying their own place near the Northgate shopping center. With Andy in the kitchen and Jemmy in the dining room, there's no reason to believe that this place will be anything less than The Wok was in their hands—which was four-star. Andy plans to recreate his former Szechuan–Hunan–Mandarin menu, which included such marvelous creations as the four-times-cooked Chef's Special Duck; an excellent hot-and-sour soup; dumplings in an extraordinary garlic-chili sauce; Shanghai-style pan-fried noodles; large shrimp in white-wine sauce; and broccoli in an incomparable oyster sauce. He'll also be adding some items, such as orange-peel beef, lobster in white or red sauce, a Hunan dish of sliced chicken and beef in a potato nest, and Shanghai shrimp—huge prawns in a white sauce. Jemmy can be expected to run the dining room with lightning efficiency.

EE3	**Anthony's Home Port** **135 Lake, Kirkland** **Res: 822-0225**	*3-10 Mon-Thur, 3-11 Fri & Sat, 4-10 Sun;* *Sun Brunch 10-2* *Moderate; Full bar; cc: AE, MC, V*
	421 S 227th, Des Moines **Res: 824-1947**	*11:30-10 Mon-Fri; noon-10 Sat; 4-9:30 Sun;* *Sun Brunch 9:30-2:30*
	456 Admiral Way, Edmonds **Res: 771-4400**	*4:30-10 Mon-Thur, 4:30-11 Fri & Sat,* *4-9 Sun; Sun Brunch 10-2*

The original, on Kirkland's waterfront, spawned two clones, in Des Moines and Edmonds. All have nice views, decent seafood, and a good Sunday brunch.

GG8	**Apres Vous Cafe** **1530 Queen Anne Ave N** **Res: 284-9827**	*9-10 Mon-Thur, 9-midnight Fri & Sat* *Sun Brunch 9-2* *Moderate; Beer & Wine; cc: AE, MC, V*

Situated on the second floor of a brick Queen Anne Hill building that is on the Historic Register, this is another of the little cafes sprouting all over town that serve a changing menu of pastas, salads, sautes, and fish specials. Both service and food are earnest but uneven.

	★ **Asuka**	*L 11:30-2 Mon-Fri; D 5:30-10 Mon-Thur,*
L5	**1200 Sixth Ave (Park Place Bldg)** **Res: 682-8050**	*5:30-10:30 Fri & Sat; closed Sun* *Expensive; Full bar* *cc: AE, CB, DC, MC, V*

Setting and decor combine to make this the most serenely beautiful of Seattle's many Japanese restaurants. Glass outer walls give visual access to the greenery and waterfalls of Freeway Park. The decor, particularly of the tatami rooms, is classically restrained. The food is Japanese-modern, too, emphasizing pure taste, texture, and eye appeal. The sushi bar is commendable, and Asuka boasts the only true tempura bar in the city.

J8	**Athenian Inn** **Pike Place Market** **Res: 624-7166**	*B 6:30-noon; L 11-6:30 Mon-Sat; closed Sun* *Inexpensive; Full bar* *cc: MC, V*

The menu is huge but the execution unreliable in this long-established cafe where Pike Place Market regulars bump elbows with visitors. The beer list is remarkable, the view of Elliott Bay splendid, and the heartbeat of the Market all around.

Restaurants

★ **Aurora's of Mexico** *K8* **1414 Alaskan Way** **Res: 343-9370**	*11-10 Mon-Thur; 11-11 Fri & Sat; 4-10 Sun* *Moderate; Full bar* *cc: AE, CB, DC, MC, V*
HH1 **1318 NE 156th, Bellevue** **641-1115**	*11-10 Mon-Thur; 11-11 Fri & Sat;* *4-10 Sun* *Moderate; Full bar; cc: AE, CB, DC, MC, V*

Aurora Ayala-Pena has two restaurants, each offering better-than-average American-Mexican fare in an atmosphere made warm by friendly family members. But what makes Aurora's special are dishes seldom seen in this area: Nopales cactus salad, carne al pastor (marinated pork roasted on a vertical spit), menudo, red snapper with red wine and chiles, and leche quemada (burnt milk with whipped cream and coconut).

★ **The Austrian** ★ **2355 Tenth Ave E** *GG7* **Res: 322-8028**	*L 11:30-2 Tues-Fri; D 5-11 Tues-Sun;* *Brunch 11-2 Sat, 10-3 Sun; closed Mon* *Expensive; Full bar* *cc: AE, CB, DC, MC, V*

One of the better antidotes to nouvelle cuisine can be found in the hearty Viennese cooking here. Begin with, say, herring in wine sauce with pickles and onions. Then savor a potato soup. Then, with an Austrian or German wine, choose from pork loin cutlets in a piquant tomato sauce; Viennese-style smoked ham; roast pork; bratwurst; sauerkraut and heavy, flavorful dumplings; a huge, perfectly breaded and fried wiener schnitzel; pork goulash containing sauerkraut, a large dose of sweet-sharp paprika, and topped with sour cream and dumplings. Homemade strudels provide further relief. And you have a choice of settings: the Schoenbrunner Room with its Viennese-hotel decor of red plush and crystal chandeliers; or the basement Burgkeller with its booths and drinking-inn decor. The menu is shorter in the latter, but there's good German beer on tap.

★ **Avenue 52** ★ **5247 University Way NE** *FF7* **Res: 524-4008**	*L 11:30-2:30 Mon-Fri; D 5-10 Mon-Sat;* *closed Sun* *Moderate; Beer & Wine; cc: MC, V*

Syrian-born Saleh Joudeh studied in Italy, so it follows that his first restaurant in Seattle, this pretty University District place, has a menu combining Arabian and Italian cuisines. The interior is done in shades of violet set off by white lattice and linen. The food and its seasonings are as subtly shaded. Arabian selections from the short list include hummus and the best baba ganouj in the city as appetizers, and a wonderful entree called Upside Down that combines chicken-broth-flavored rice, deep-fried cauliflower, roast chicken morsels, and pine nuts. On the Italian side are dishes such as veal sauteed simply in lemon and wine, and ravioli with butter and garlic.

★ **Bangkok Hut** *O8* **170 S Washington** **Res: 624-7565**	*11:30-8 Mon-Fri; 4-9 Sat; closed Sun* *Inexpensive; Beer* *No credit cards*

Among this area's many new Thai restaurants, this small Pioneer Square cafe stands out for its peanut sauce and its noodle dishes. There's also a splendid spicy shrimp soup and some decent curries.

CC6 **Bella Neapolis** **12501 Lake City Way** **Res: 362-8080**	*L 11:30-3 Mon-Fri; D 4:30-10 Mon-Thur,* *Sun, 4:30-11 Fri & Sat* *Inexpensive; Beer & Wine; cc: MC, V*

Blue carpet, cream walls, dark wood furniture, lots of plants and fabric-shaded lights hanging from the high ceiling—this is a pretty place, in the heart of Lake

City. The menu is long on pasta choices at reasonable prices. Portions are large and saucing is without refinement, sort of Italian-American country-style.

★ G8	**Belltown Cafe** **2309 First Ave** **Res: 622-4392**	*D 5-11 Tues-Thur, 5-midnight Fri & Sat;* *closed Sun & Mon* *Inexpensive; Full bar; No credit cards*

Owner Ben Marks loves artists, frequently trading food for their works, which then hang in his simple cafe. Artists hang out, too, along with assorted wonderful characters who appreciate Marks' low prices. There are daily meat, chicken, fish, and vegetarian specials, all of which are at least hot and filling and served in the friendliest fashion imaginable.

L6	**Benihana of Tokyo** **1200 Fifth Ave (IBM Bldg)** **Res: 682-4686**	*L 11:30-2 Mon-Fri; D 5:30-10 Mon-Thur,* *5:30-10:30 Fri & Sat, 5-9:30 Sun* *Expensive; Full bar* *cc: AE, CB, DC, MC, V*

This national chain's cooking-as-theater gimmick is displayed in a nice setting. Japanese knifemen chop, dice, mince, slice, and then grill before your eyes.

HH3	**Benjamin's** **10655 NE Fourth, Bellevue** **Res: 454-8255**	*L 11-4 Mon-Fri, 11:30-3 Sat;* *D 4-midnight Every day; Sun Brunch 10-2* *Moderate; Full bar* *cc: AE, CB, DC, MC, V*

An exceptional view of the Cascades and Mount Rainier from atop Bellevue's Seattle Trust building, plus omelets, salads, pastas, and fresh seafood prepared in an open kitchen, make this one of the Eastside's most popular restaurants and bars.

GG7	**Boondock's, Sundecker's, and** **Greenthumb's** **611 Broadway E** **Res: 323-7272**	*11-2am Mon-Thur, 11-3am Fri, 9-3am Sat,* *9-2am Sun* *Moderate; Full bar* *cc: AE, MC, V*

One of the city's first "fern" restaurants, Boondock's is the flagship of Gerry Kingen's empire, which includes Lion O'Reilly's, The Lake Union Cafe, and the Red Robin hamburger chain. It's an intimate place, with decor built around wicker, skylights, and, of course, ferns. The enormous menu is offered well into the wee hours, and the food sounds better than it tastes, but comes in large portions. The location, on Broadway, is ideal for the thirtyish crowd Kingen understands so well.

★ ★ N8	**Brasserie Pittsbourg** **602 First Ave** **Res: 623-4167**	*L 11:30-2:30 Mon-Sat; D 5:30-9:15* *Mon-Thur, 5:30-10:15 Fri & Sat; closed Sun* *Moderate; Full bar; cc: AE, MC, V*

Francois Kissel once made this basement cafe the most fashionable and enjoyable place in town, with a clientele of young movers and shakers in the arts, politics, law, and business. But Kissel, an inventive chef capable of the sublime, developed other restaurants, and the Brasserie declined. It's still a wonderful setting: a former soup kitchen of white tiles, pressed-tin ceiling, and ordinary counters transformed by flowers, antiques, and old kitchen utensils. Butcher paper covers the tables, and lunches are served cafeteria-style. There's always an omelet—the eggplant is best—soup, and a couple of entrees such as lamb shanks or chicken breasts. Dinners are classical French fare plus specials such as salmon baked with mushrooms and almonds. It's all good enough, but Kissel is sorely missed.

GG7	**The Broadway** **314 Broadway E** **Res: 323-1990**	*L 11:30-2:30 Mon-Fri; D 5:30-10* *Mon-Thur, 5-10 Fri-Sun; Sun Brunch 11-2:30* *Moderate; Full bar; cc: AE, MC, V*

Restaurants

One of several Broadway District singles places, The Broadway fits the mold: large bar, good drinks, many appetizers, splashy decor, and fare—pasta, steaks, seafood —no better than it has to be and not so good as to distract the patrons.

★ **Browny's Seafood Broiler**	*L 11:30-2:30 Mon-Fri; D 5-9 Sun-Thur,*
BB8 **638 NW Richmond Beach Rd**	*5-10 Fri & Sat*
Res: 542-4766	*Moderate; Beer & Wine; cc: MC, V*

Excellent steamed clams and mussels and an outstanding clam chowder distinguish this cafe as much as its agreeable gimmick: tables covered in butcher paper and cups of crayons to encourage doodling, the best examples of which go on the walls. There are fresh flowers and candles, and white latticework to screen out the surrounding North End shopping center. Fish are fresh and the broiling, over mesquite charcoal, is commendable.

★ **brusseau's**	*7:30-7 Mon-Fri, 8-7 Sat, 8-4 Sun*
117 S Fifth, Edmonds	*Moderate; Beer & Wine*
774-4166	*No credit cards*

In downtown Edmonds, Jerilyn Brusseau has a little cafe in her bakery–cheese shop, where she serves salads, sandwiches on her own bread, and specials such as salmon calzone and a "peasant pie" of sausage, leeks, and cheeses. A flowery patio makes a nice spot for summertime dining, and there's a good list of wines at reasonable prices.

★ **Burk's Cafe**	*11-9 Mon-Sat; closed Sun*
FF8 **5411 Ballard Ave**	*Moderate; Beer & Wine*
782-0091	*cc: MC, V*

The building, constructed in 1891 to house Ballard's first tavern, has been beautifully restored. Terry "Burk" Burkhardt's cooking is the other attraction: limited but authentic Creole and Cajun fare. There's both file and okra gumbo, homemade sausages, local crayfish in season, oyster poor boys, and specials that sometimes include fresh catfish. All the dinners come, classically, with red beans and rice. The rice is Basamati from Texas, an extra-long-grained variety that, combined with grains of wild rice and onion, is exceptionally flavorful.

★ **Cafe Botanica**	*B 7-11 Mon-Fri, all day Sat;*
GG6 **4021 E Madison**	*L 11:30-2:30 Mon-Fri;*
Res: 329-9015	*D 6-9 Mon-Sat; Sun Brunch 10:30-3*
	Moderate; Wine; cc: MC, V

Professional dancers Charles Bennett and Alexis Hoff have created a cheerful, lovely little skylighted garden spot in Madison Park with an interesting and frequently changing menu. Bennett, a talented choreographer, manipulates an espresso machine as adeptly as anyone in town, and his cooking, ranging across the culinary gap, is as inventive as his dance ideas.

K6 **Cafe Casino**	*7-11 Every day; Sun Brunch 7-noon*
Rainier Square	*Inexpensive; Beer & Wine*
622-1188	*cc: MC, V*

This is the first Northwest outpost of a large French cafeteria chain that is rapidly expanding in the American West and eyeing the East. It's located in Rainier Square, overlooking Fifth Avenue on one side and Rainier Square's atrium on the other. An escalator from the street leads to an entrance-area retail outlet for wines, breads, and pastries. The cafeteria, backed by a huge kitchen, spreads out behind the entrance—an attempt, through greenery, neon, and different levels, to replicate a French street cafe. For breakfast there are baked goods, fruit, and egg dishes. Lunch and dinner are identical: baked goods, some salads, and about eight hot

16

entrees, all with a French flavor.

★ **Cafe Juanita**
★ **9702 NE 120th Pl, Kirkland**
EE2 **Res: 823-1505**

D 6-10 Mon-Sat, 5-9 Sun
Expensive; Beer & Wine
No credit cards

You may have to make a reservation a month in advance for weekends, but a visit to Peter Dow's homey Italian restaurant on the Eastside is worth the wait. The menu is limited to six regular selections plus a few specials, usually including rabbit in a red sauce, grilled lamb, and a beautifully prepared fish. First you'll get a wonderful pasta dish and a chance to select from a superb list of Italian wines at reasonable prices. In the summer you can stroll through an attractive garden, visible from the dining room, while you await a table.

★ **Cafe Loc**
D7 **407 Broad Street**
682-7663
(Also in Center House, Seattle Center)

L 11-2:30 Mon-Fri; D 5-8 Mon-Fri,
4-8 Sat; closed Sun
Inexpensive; No alcohol
No credit cards

Minh Chanh Huynh, an American-schooled lawyer in Vietnam before the fall of Saigon, years ago earned a reputation at her little restaurant near Seattle Center for spring rolls served Vietnamese-style—rolled in a romaine leaf with diced carrots, cucumbers, and sprouts. Now her menu, of Vietnamese and Chinese dishes, covers two pages. It's all nicely prepared, but the Vietnamese selections are what make Cafe Loc stand out. There are outside picnic tables, too.

★ **Cafe Optimum**
EE7 **5509 University Way NE**
Res: 527-1033

D 5-10:30 Thur-Sat; closed Sun-Wed
Moderate; Wine
No credit cards

Owner-chef D.J. Zentner's background in nutrition is reflected in her cooking, which emphasizes what is fresh and healthful. Entrees, available a la carte or as full meals, change according to what is available. The accent is on seafood in light sauces, although there are other dishes of mixed ethnic origin, such as couscous and Szechuan chicken. Lace tablecloths and fresh flowers make this house-restaurant a home.

★ **Cafe Sabika**
J2 **315 E Pine**
Res: 622-3272

D 5:30-10 Tues-Sat; closed Sun & Mon
Moderate; Beer & Wine
cc: MC, V

Offbeat in some ways—a room taller than it is wide, jazz played loudly through floor-level speakers, no smoking—this warm, cozy place has a fiercely loyal clientele. Primarily they're drawn by the flair that owner-chef Collins Jones has with home-style French and Italian cooking. The short menu changes only once a month. Usually two pastas, a fish, a chicken, and another meat dish are offered, along with appetizers such as Oysters Rockefeller and Caesar salad. Desserts are homemade and superior.

★ **Cafe Society**
N8 **89 S Washington**
622-9350

L 10:30-3 Mon-Fri; D 5-9 Thur & Fri;
closed Sat & Sun
Moderate; Beer & Wine; No credit cards

The specials when dinners are served can be delicious and unusual, perhaps a spinach pasta in gorgonzola sauce or a classic chicken fricassee. In the daytime, there are soups, salads, sandwiches, and excellent espresso and pastries, the latter a temptation to linger over on a sunny afternoon.

★ **Canlis**
★ **2576 Aurora Ave N**
FF7 **Res: 283-3313**

D 5:30-11:30 Mon-Sat; closed Sun
Expensive; Full bar
cc: AE, CB, DC, MC, V

17

Restaurants

For many older Seattleites, this is still the poshest place in town. It hangs above Lake Union, offering a wonderful view of dark water and twinkling lights. The waitresses are kimono-clad Japanese, quick and quiet. The fare is steak and seafood, with excellent salads and fine accompaniments such as shoestring potatoes. The steaks are the best in town, quality beef properly broiled.

GG8	**Captain's Table**	*11-11 Every day*
	333 Elliott W	*Moderate; Full bar*
HH8	**Res: 284-7040**	*cc: AE, MC, V*

Ivar Haglund serves the masses at his many places. At the moment, this is his most complete seafood house, with a view of Puget Sound (best from the bar) and a long menu. The smoked black cod is particularly good.

GG6	**Cause Celebre**	*10:30-10:30 Mon-Fri; 10-10:30 Sat & Sun*
	524 15th Ave E	*Inexpensive; No alcohol*
	322-1057	*No credit cards or personal checks*

Tofu, burritos, ice cream, and political posters mark this comfortably down-at-the-heels, cooperatively owned Capitol Hill cafe as a counterculture memento. Soups, baked goods, ice cream—everything is homemade, but with more earnestness than excellence. Still, it's a good spot to read or write and there's a large deck for summertime idling over a dish of unadulterated ice cream.

★	**Caveman Kitchen**	*9-9 Mon-Sat; 9-8 Sun*
	807 W Valley Hwy, Kent	*Inexpensive; No alcohol*
	854-1210	*No credit cards*

Dick Donnelly spent years experimenting with methods of smoking ribs, chicken, turkey, sausage, and salmon over apple and cherry. The results are outstanding, especially the chicken, which is moist and pink throughout. His tiny roadside stand has expanded into something like an institution, but trucks still whoosh by a few feet from the al fresco picnic tables and you still have to go across the street for beer. Donnelly has added a teepee, however, to provide some shelter. Most people take out, loading up on the smoked goods and adding accompaniments such as beans, potato salad, coleslaw, smoked potatoes, and a terrific bread pudding with butterscotch-whiskey sauce. The Caveman caters, too.

★	**Chez Claude**	*L 11:30-2 Tues-Fri; D 5:30-11 Tues-Sat;*
★	**417 Main, Edmonds**	*5-10 Sun; closed Mon*
	Res: 778-9888	*Expensive; Full bar; cc: AE, DC, V*

When the excesses of nouvelle cuisine are long forgotten, there will still be classic French cooking. In the Seattle area there is no better spot to be reminded of this than at owner-chef Claude Faure's restaurant in downtown Edmonds. Faure was trained in Lyons, and his room and menu would not be out of place there. Loads of fresh flowers and paintings on the wall give the room color and verve. The menu begins with appetizers such as escargot and quenelles a la Nantua and proceeds through the entire classic repertoire to peach Melba. Along the way there are local favorites such as rack of lamb with artichokes, asparagus, and bearnaise, roast duck au poivre, pheasant choucroute. The wine list is well chosen and the service personal and knowledgeable.

FF7	**China First**	*11-9 Mon-Thur, 11-10 Fri & Sat; 11-9:30 Sun*
	4237 University Way NE	*Moderate; Beer & Wine; cc: AE, MC, V*
	Res: 634-3553	
	6200 196th SW, Lynnwood	

Mandarin-style cooking highlights this popular University District restaurant.

Among the better dishes is eggplant that is briefly deep-fried and then finished in a spicy sauce.

R6 **China Gate**
516 Seventh Ave S
Res: 624-1730

4-2am Every day
Moderate; Full bar
cc: AE, MC, V

The Cantonese cooking is solid but unmemorable in this large International District place, but the dining room is exceptionally handsome in black and red, and the service is friendly.

★ **China North**
★ 12319 Roosevelt Way NE
★ Res: 362-3422

11:30-9:30 Mon-Thur, Sun; 11:30-10:30
Fri & Sat
Moderate; Full bar; cc: MC, V

DD7 Reassuringly plain but clean, this North End spot is the province of master chef Cray Chi-Siung Chen, who was the Uncle Chen of Portland renown and who once cooked in some of New York's fine Chinese restaurants. His menu ranges throughout Northern China: Fukien-style scallops with green vegetables, for example, or Hunan-style smoked duck. Occasionally a dish of, say, prawns in chili sauce can be a disappointment. And the fine Peking duck with ideally crispy skin is unnecessarily tinged with red food coloring. But those are exceptions to the rule of Chen's high standard. The best way of enjoying his art is to arrange a banquet for about eight at a moderate fixed price and allow him to set the menu.

★ **Chiyoko**
Q6 610 S Jackson
623-9347

D 5:30-10 Mon-Sat, 4-8:30 Sun
Moderate; Full bar
cc: MC, V

Tempura enjoys an especially good reputation here, but all of the cooking in this friendly Japanese spot is carefully done. As a bonus, sometimes there are Japanese singalongs and Japanese television shows on a big screen. And Chiyoko is one of the few places in town to offer makunouchi, the delightful Japanese box lunch of hot and cold tidbits.

H6 **Claremont Prime Rib &**
Salmon House
408 Virginia
Res: 622-9411

11-2am Every day
Moderate; Full bar
cc: MC, V

Its name is as straightforward as the food: prime rib, salmon, steak, and, for lunch, soups, salads, and sandwiches. Portions are ample, and quality and prices are both reasonable. The bar is large and sunny. A dance floor in the main room, once the site of a famous Seattle place called the Colony, vibrates to live dance music with a country-and-Western accent.

★ **Clifford's**
P2 1122 Jefferson
Res: 625-0090

L 11:30-2 Mon-Fri; D 5-9:30 Sun &
Mon, 5-10 Tues-Thur, 5-11 Fri & Sat
Expensive; Full bar; cc: AE, DC, MC, V

HH6 6251 Bothell Way NE, Kenmore
Res: 485-7585

D 5-9:30 Sun & Mon, 5-10 Tues-Thur;
5-11 Fri & Sat; Sun Brunch 10-2
Expensive; Full bar; cc: AE, DC, MC, V

Though it seems to occupy somewhat uneasily the former site of one of Seattle's old-line Chinese restaurants, Ruby Chow's, this new fish-house (with steaks on the side) is doing several things right. The style is firmly informal (waiters in tennis shoes), arresting Alaskan-native art hangs on the brick–natural-wood walls, the reasonably priced wine list changes continuously, and the seafood is well prepared. A companion Clifford's in Kenmore shares the same menu.

Restaurants

HH3 **Concord Garden** 30 Bellevue Way NE, Bellevue Res: 451-8787	*L 11:30-2:30 Mon-Fri; D 5-11 Mon-Fri,* *5-10:30 Sat & Sun* *Moderate; Full bar* *cc: AE, DC, MC, V*

Winnie Wang owned Chinese restaurants in Germany's Black Forest before coming to Bellevue, and she acquired a taste for European "romantic" dining there. Thus, her place is beautifully furnished, but not in Chinese style, and her Chinese cooking has a Western tinge, with many dishes being prepared on flambe carts. Better to order ahead and challenge the cook.

★ **Copacabana** ★ **Pike Place Market** *18* Res: 622-6359	*L 11:30-5 Mon-Sat; D 5-9 Mon-Wed,* *5-10 Thur-Sat; closed Sun* *Moderate; Beer & Wine* *cc: AE, CB, DC, MC, V*

Offering Bolivian cooking and a great view, the Copacabana is one of the Pike Place Market's best attractions. The cafe is on the second floor of the Triangle Building. In warm weather, most of the tables are moved to the west balcony, from which Elliott Bay, the throng below, and the flower boxes atop the main Market building across the Place are all clearly visible. Michael Morrow, son-in-law of the late Ramon Palaez, who founded the place, faithfully follows the old Palaez family recipes. Among the best are saltenas, meat-and-vegetable pies; huminta, a spicy corn pie topped with cheeses; a much-admired shrimp soup; paella (Thur-Sat only); fritanga, roast pork cubes in a mild sauce served with white hominy; weekly specials such as cod-and-potatoes in a saffron sauce; and crisp salads. Because the cafe is jammed for lunch on warm days, it's often better to linger over a beer in the late afternoon and then have supper.

FF7 **Costas** 4559 University Way NE 633-2751	*7am-11pm Mon-Thur; 7:30 midnight Fri-Sat;* *7:30-11 Sun* *Moderate; Beer & Wine; cc: MC, V*

The menu has a Greek flavor, but the substantial all-day American breakfast fare and hearty sandwiches, and the opportunity to linger over a book are what make this University District restaurant an institution among the college set.

FF7 **Costas Opa** 3400 Fremont N Res: 633-4141	*L 11-4:30 Mon-Fri; D 4:30-11 Every day* *Moderate; Full bar* *cc: MC, V*

Across from a famed sculpture of ordinary folks "Waiting for the Interurban" in the funky neighborhood of Fremont, this big restaurant serves the gamut of Greek food from avgolemono soup to roast lamb. It's all fine without being refined. Desserts are better because owner Costas Antonopoulos began as a pastry chef in Athens.

★ **Crepe de Paris** ★ 1333 Fifth Ave (Rainier Sq) ★ Res: 623-4111 *K6* 1927 43rd E *GG6* 329-6620	*11-10 Mon-Thur; 11-11 Fri-Sat;* *43rd E only: 11-10 Sun* *Expensive; Full bar; cc: AE, CB, DC, MC, V*

Though the entree and dessert crepes attract the most attention, the real virtue of this elegant restaurant amid the glittering shops of Rainier Square is the skill of co-owner and chef Dominique Place. He mines gems in the region between classic and nouvelle cuisine, working with a short French menu at night and a few specials for lunch. His sauces are exquisite. Steak au poivre here, for instance, is considered the best in town. But Place's forte is fish in light and inventive sauces.

For dinner there are beautifully presented dishes of lamb, game birds, and beef, as well. Lunches are busy and noisy, so try to secure a table on the deck overlooking the atrium. A second Crepe de Paris in Madison Park is fine but does not have Place to give it class.

QQ7 GG7	★ **D'Andrea** **22303 Marine View Dr, Des Moines** **Res: 824-7083** **(Also 109 Broadway E, opening late spring)**	*L 11:30-4 Tues-Fri; D 4-10 Mon-Sat;* *4-9 Sun* *Moderate; Full bar* *cc: AE, MC, V*

The setting is an airy, sparkling Italian cafe and the food—including pizza—is straightforward: good homemade gnocchi, for instance. Still, some dishes are not as good as they could be. Perhaps when the companion D'Andrea opens on Broadway, the cooking will approach the standards recently achieved in Seattle's better Italian restaurants.

OO6	**Dandy's** **14406 Pacific Hwy S** **Res: 246-2626**	*L 11-2 Mon-Fri; D 5-10 Mon-Thur; 5-1am* *Fri & Sat; closed Sun* *Moderate; Full bar; cc: AE, CB, DC, MC, V*

Formerly known as Pepo's, this is an odd place with a Czech chef who turns out quite good Italian, German, and Slavic dishes at night and serves hordes of Boeing workers salads, sandwiches, omelets, and pastas at lunch. The restaurant is large, and there are sometimes dinner shows.

HH6	★ **Daniel's Broiler** **200 Lake Washington Blvd** **Res: 329-4191**	*D 5-10 Sun, 5-11 Mon-Thur,* *5-midnight Fri & Sat; Expensive; Full bar* *cc: AE, CB, DC, MC, V*

The interior is lovely: rusty-brown upholstery, onyx table and counter tops, dark wood trim, and lots of copper, including a spectacular chandelier. The exterior view isn't bad either: Leschi marina, Lake Washington, and the Cascades beyond. The food—steaks, seafood, and pasta—is simple but inconsistently prepared. Plump steamed clams are outstanding. Some regulars swear by huge, puffy deep-fried onion rings, and there are crisply fried potatoes and gloppy desserts.

GG7	**Deluxe Bar & Grill** **625 Broadway** **324-9697**	*11:30am-11:30pm Mon-Wed;* *11:30am-12:30am Thur & Fri;* *10am-12:30am; 10am-11pm Sun* *Moderate; Full bar* *cc: MC, V*

Once the bargain of Broadway for its cheap burgers and steaks, the Deluxe tried to shed its tavern past by opening up a wall to the street in summer and expanding its menu into pastas, salads, nachos, chicken sautes, and so on. It's still a comfortable spot, and the hinged wall was a good idea. But the burgers remain the attraction.

HH3	★ **Domani** **604 Bellevue Way NE, Bellevue** **Res: 454-4405**	*L 11:30-2:30 Mon-Sat; D 5:30-10* *Mon-Fri, 5:30-11 Sat & Sun* *Moderate; Full bar* *cc: AE, CB, DC, MC, V*

For pasta and a smart Eastside lunch setting, nothing beats this spot across from Bellevue Square. Skylights, plants, high-backed wicker chairs, and good service make for a pleasant place. The fare includes veal, chicken, seafood, and beef dishes.

Restaurants

★ **Duke's** GG8 **236 First West** Res: 283-4400	L 11:30-4:30 Mon-Fri; D 5:30-11 Mon-Thur, Sat-Sun; 5:30-12 Fri Moderate; Full bar cc: AE, CB, DC, MC, V
HH3 **10116 NE Eighth, Bellevue** Res: 455-5775	L 11-4 Mon-Fri; D 5-10 Sun-Thur, 5-11 Fri & Sat Moderate; Full bar cc: AE, CB, DC, MC, V

A bar attracting flashy singles and a menu supplying light lunches and suppers for the same keep Duke's, and its Bellevue twin, hopping. The food can be uneven —a splendid spinach salad or a luscious hamburger one night and pale imitations the next—but the steamed mussels and fish specials are reliably good. Duke's is at its best as a late-night cafe.

Eggs Cetera GG7 **220 Broadway E** 325-3447	B 7-9 Mon-Fri, 8-9 Sat & Sun; L & D 11-9 Every day Moderate; Beer & Wine cc: MC, V
GG6 **4220 E Madison** 324-4140	7-3 Mon-Fri; 8-3 Sat & Sun Moderate; Beer & Wine; cc: MC, V

With two locations, Capitol Hill and Madison Park, and a long list of omelets and other egg dishes, Eggs Cetera keeps a lot of hens employed. The food, including sandwiches, burgers, soups, salads, and fresh baked goods, is straightforward and served in ample portions. Don't miss the macadamia nut waffle.

I5 **El Gaucho** **624 Olive Way** Res: 682-3202	11-11:30 Mon-Fri, 5-11:30 Sat (Hunt Breakfast 11pm-3am Fri & Sat); closed Sun Expensive; Full bar; cc: AE, DC, MC, V

There's an El Morocco feel to this dimly lit Seattle institution, heightened by the Runyonesque character of much of its clientele. Pinky rings flash alongside prom dresses, as sporting and business types mingle with high-schoolers on dates. The barbecued ribs and steaks are the main draw. Just before midnight, a huge "hunt breakfast" buffet is rolled out and served until about 3am.

★ **El Puerco Lloron** ★ **1501 Western Ave** J8 **624-0541**	11:30-9 Mon-Sat; closed Sun Inexpensive; Beer & Wine cc: AE, MC, V

For authenticity of decor and cooking, no Mexican place in Seattle beats "The Crying Pig" on the Pike Place Market Hillclimb. The metal card tables and folding chairs, each complete with scars and "Cerveza Superior" logos, were imported from a cafe in Tijuana. The vivid hues of ordinary Mexico—pink, aqua, yellow— were splashed on the ceiling and walls. And the ersatz fare found in American Mexican restaurants was shunned. Instead, everything here is handmade with fresh ingredients. The masa for the tortillas—from American corn, and therefore yellower, is ground daily. The menu is short: taquitos (soft-shelled tacos, as the Mexicans make them) with various fillings, tostadas, homemade pork and chicken tamales, and fresh chili rellenos. It's all delicious.

★ **Elliott Bay Cafe** O8 **101 S Main** **682-6664**	7-11 Mon-Fri; 10:30-11 Sat; noon-6 Sun Moderate; Beer & Wine cc: MC, V

A good idea lies behind this Pioneer Square spot: placing a cafe in the basement of a bookstore. The menu is limited to soups, salads, sandwiches, a quiche, and bread and cheese. The espresso drinks are many and the desserts excellent. And a newspaper reading rack is a boon to breakfast, a reason to linger in the afternoon, and solace at night.

18	**Emmett Watson's Oyster Bar** (unrated) **Pike Place Market** 622-7721	*11:45-5:30 Mon-Thur, 11:45-6 Fri & Sat;* *closed Sun* *Moderate; Beer & Wine* *No credit cards*

Founded by one of the authors of this guide (hence no rating), this is a tiny spot on a back courtyard in the Pike Place Market. There are fresh oysters and other seafood dishes, soups, and a broad beer selection. When the weather's good, diners can eat at tables in the courtyard.

★ J5	**Enoteca** **1522 Fifth Ave (Downstairs)** Res: 624-9108	*11:30-8 Mon-Fri, 11-6 Sat; closed Sun* *Moderate; Beer & Wine* *cc: MC, V*

Billed as "a wine cafe," this quiet spot in a brick cellar across from Nordstrom has tasty food, as well. The menu is limited to a soup, salads, sandwiches, pates, cheeses, desserts, and espresso drinks. One night a week there is a dinner special —chicken curry with many condiments, for instance. Wines are available by the glass, or retail, or they will open a bottle for a $2 corkage charge.

★ OO7	**Filiberto's** **14401 Des Moines Way S, Burien** Res: 248-1944	*L 11-3 Tues-Sat; D 5-10 Tues-Sun;* *closed Mon; Moderate; Full bar* *cc: AE, DC, MC, V*

Few places in the Seattle area elicit such divergent opinions as this family-run Italian roadhouse. Lately, however, an air of neglect has crept in, and it's not enough to say the quality of the food depends on who's in the kitchen. Still, there is a bocce court out back, and some nights the dining rooms can be noisy and fun. And it is possible to pick your way through the large menu and find a good meal.

GG7	**Franco's Hidden Harbor** **1500 Westlake N** Res: 282-0501	*L 11-3:30 Mon-Sat; D 4-11 Mon-Thur,* *4-midnight Fri & Sat; closed Sun* *Moderate; Full bar; cc: AE, DC, MC, V*

John Franco's seafood house has been anchored abeam the yachts on the west shore of Lake Union for nearly 40 years. The menu seemingly never changes, and includes nine ways of serving Dungeness crab. From the orange deck chairs in the waterside dining area to the orange-and-white-clad waitresses, Franco's is reassuringly the same.

J5	**French Invention** **1523 Sixth Ave** Res: 621-9626	*L 11:30-5 Mon-Sat; D 5-9 Mon-Sat;* *closed Sun* *Moderate; Full bar; cc: AE, MC, V*

The quintessential "light meal" house, with modern glass chandeliers, plush booths, and a menu covering pastas, salads, crepes, sautes, quiches, and desserts. All is tasteful, balanced, subdued—a good spot for a dress-up lunch with a friend or a respite from shopping.

★ ★ ★	**Fuller's** **Sixth & Pike (Sheraton)** Res: 621-9000	*D 5:30-10:30 Mon-Sat; closed Sun* *Expensive; Full bar* *cc: AE, CB, DC, MC, V*

K5 Named after the late Dr. Richard Fuller, founder of the Seattle Art Museum, this "fine dining" spot in the Sheraton attains a high standard in spite of itself. Walls and round booths are covered in a tan fabric designed to absorb noise and create a monochromatic backdrop for the works of Northwest painters such as Callahan,

Graves, and Tobey. The effect, though, is akin to eating in a capsule. The captain is theatrical and the waiters oddly hearty; being told, as you are seated, that "you are dining with Tobey tonight" can be disconcerting. The room is saved, however, by the artistry of chef William Mullen, formerly executive sous-chef at the Sheraton–Boston's celebrated restaurant, Apley's. He produces a "Northwest" cuisine with light saucing: salmon with green herb sauce, rainbow trout stuffed with crab, duck sauteed with apples, veal with a pepper-puree sauce. Not everything works, but some dishes—a warm salad of spinach and smoked duck, for example—are outstanding. The wine list is commendable but expensive, and desserts can be superb. For after dinner there are some good specialty coffee drinks and an excellent list of cognacs.

★ **Gene's Place**	*8-2am Every day*
HH6 **2308 E Union**	*Inexpensive; Full bar*
323-6006	*No credit cards*

The best soul food in Seattle used to be served at Helen's Diner. Helen's Diner is now Gene's Place, but the cook, fortunately, is still Robin Caldwell. His menu is short but terrific, including such items as neck bones, short ribs, fried chicken wings, yams (baked or candied), and black-eyed peas. Some days there are specials such as baked grits and gumbo. And there's always cornbread and peach cobbler.

★ **The Georgian Room**	*B 6:30-11 Every day*
★ **(Four Seasons Olympic)**	*L 11:30-2:30 Mon-Fri;*
411 University	*D 6-11 Every day; Sun Brunch 11-3*
L6 **Res: 621-1700**	*Expensive; Full bar; cc: AE, CB, DC, MC, V*

The Four Seasons Olympic did a fine job of restoring this lovely room, still the grandest in the city. The high ceilings, tall palms, chandelier, and huge fresh-flower arrangement combine to make this the favorite special-occasion place for many Seattleites. The fare is sort of post–nouvelle cuisine: sea bass poached in a red-wine sauce, pheasant in a peppercorn sauce, veal medallions in an orange-lemon sauce. It can be excellent, but some dishes—a liquid, so-called "timbale" of scallops, for instance—miss the mark. Service is sometimes slow and awkward, with waiters providing inaccurate information about the day's specials. The wine list is superb but expensive. Enticingly displayed desserts are grandly caloric.

★ **Gerard's Relais de Lyon**	*D 5-11 Tues-Sun; closed Mon*
★ **17121 Bothell Way NE**	*Expensive; Full bar*
BB4 **Res: 485-7600**	*cc: AE, DC, MC, V*

Though the setting, a wonderful old house with a patio garden for summer dining, remains enchanting, this far-suburban French restaurant has undergone a decline. Owner Gerard Parrat, a former student of Paul Bocuse, is capable of preparing a superb meal. But he seems to leave the kitchen in lesser hands at night too often, and the country-style fare can be disappointing when that happens. It's best to ascertain that Parrat will be present, seek his advice, and be demanding. Chances are you will dine truly and well.

F8 **Girvan's**	*L 11-3 Mon-Fri; D 5-10 Mon-Thur,*
2701 First Ave	*5-11 Fri & Sat, 4-9 Sun*
Res: 621-9313	*Moderate; Full bar; cc: AE, MC*

The view of Elliott Bay is the best thing about this popular place atop a First Avenue office building. The fare is tilted to seafood, unevenly prepared.

★ **Golden Palace**	*11:30-1:30am Mon-Fri; 4-1:30am Sat;*
II2 **4056 128th SE, Bellevue**	*4-11:30 Sun*
Res: 746-1132	*Moderate; Full bar; cc: AE, DC, MC, V*

The atmosphere is infectious, with lots of families and large groups to make things jolly, and the hostess, Alice Liu, hugging and fussing over the regulars. The Cantonese cuisine is notable for seafood, clams in black-bean sauce, soft-noodle casseroles in the Hong Kong style, and excellent preparations of fresh Dungeness crab. The restaurant used to be in the heart of the International District, and while the clientele is now suburban at this location across from Factoria Square, the cuisine is still authentic.

K5 **The Goose**
    1326 Fifth Ave
    Res: 682-3066

L 11:30-2:30 Mon-Fri, noon-2:30 Sat;
D 5-11 Tues-Sat;
Expensive; Full bar
cc: AE, CB, DC, MC, V

Underneath the 5th Avenue Theater, this is a nice re-creation of a New York theater-district saloon. The wood is dark, the bar is large, and the front room's booths are cozy. An ambitious new dinner menu is beyond the kitchen's abilities. Stick to simple seafood and steak preparations. Lunch omelets and sandwiches are fine.

★ **Greenlake Grill**
★ **7200 E Green Lake Dr N**
★ **Res: 524-0365**

L 11:30-2:30 Mon-Fri; D 6-10 Sun-Thur,
6-11 Fri & Sat
Expensive; Full bar; cc: MC, V

EE7 Owner-chef Karl Beckley, one of Seattle's most assertive Young Toques, has won a struggle for control of this wonderfully informal cafe. As good as it was, the Grill is getting better. For one thing, Beckley is introducing seasonal fixed menus, with limited daily specials. The fare reflects his convictions about simplicity, quality ingredients, intense sauces, and, take note, undercooking. (Some find his duck with green peppercorn sauce uncuttable, much less edible.) Menus are short but brilliant: appetizers such as rare Olympia oysters on the half shell and perfectly fried Brie; salads such as smoked trout and cucumber, and spinach and prosciutto; pastas such as fettucine with pesto, and linguine with chicken and tarragon; meats such as sirloin marinated in oil and herbs, grilled and served with anchovy butter, and a veal chop with fresh chives. The interior is also classy and simple: black-and-white floor tiles, a high, gray ceiling, and white walls. The wine list has some good and unusual choices, and the best of the desserts are homemade tarts.

★ **Gretchen's Of Course**
L7 **1111 Third Ave**
    621-9225

L3 **909 University**
L4   623-4083

I8 **94 Stewart**
    621-9133

J5 **1513 Sixth Ave**
    (above Mario's Ragazza)
    622-9487

7-5 Mon-Fri; closed Sat & Sun
Moderate; Beer & Wine
cc: MC, V

7:30-2:30 Mon-Fri; closed Sat & Sun
Moderate; No liquor
cc: MC, V

7:30-4 Mon-Sat; closed Sun
Moderate; Beer & Wine
cc: MC, V

8-5 Mon-Sat; closed Sun
Moderate; Beer & Wine
cc: MC, V

Gretchen Mathers is one of the city's busiest caterers, and her cafeteria empire has spread to four places. All have a high-tech look and serve the same food, also with a high-tech look. So beautiful is the food, in fact, that it appears it was designed rather than cooked, and the bland taste sometimes does not match the eye appeal. There are cold salads, such as chicken-with-tarragon and ham-and-cheese in a mustard sauce, soups, a quiche, and two hot daily specials, such as chicken cannelloni and baked salmon. Portions are ample, particularly for desserts, most of which are superior.

R6	★ **Han Il** **409 Maynard S** Res: 587-0464	*11-11 Every day* *Moderate; Full bar* *cc: MC, V*

This Korean restaurant is in the refurbished Bush Hotel in the International District. A glass vault on the south side provides a sunny lunch spot and a view of Hing Hay Park. The menu is extensive, offering a range of spicy Korean food: hot and cold noodles, barbecued beef, homemade kimchee and other vegetable accompaniments, and fancy multi-course dinners. Many items are displayed in plastic replica for the unknowledgeable.

EE3	**Hector's** **112 Lake St S, Kirkland** Res: 827-4811	*B 8-11, L 11-5, D 5-10 Mon-Sat;* *B 8-1, D 4-10 Sun* *Moderate: Full bar* *cc: AE, DC, MC, V*

The bar is Kirkland's liveliest singles scene, attracting Seahawks from their nearby football training site; the food isn't bad, especially the burgers and breakfasts.

GG7	★ **Henry's Off Broadway** ★ **1705 E Olive Way** Res: 329-8063	*L 11:30-2:30 Mon-Fri; D 5:30-10 Every day* *Expensive; Full bar* *cc: AE, CB, DC, MC, V*

The food can be as showy as the mirrored, chandeliered dining room—snails in miniature pastry baskets, for instance, and bon bons over dry ice as a finale. But it's generally well prepared and efficiently served. The menu is in tune with the chic surroundings: veal and lamb, chicken and pasta, steaks and seafood. With his nightly specials, the chef has a chance to be inventive, and he usually shines with such dishes as cream of fennel soup and baked monkfish in a satiny cream sauce rouged with tomato. Even better is the large oyster bar. Here a wide variety of appetizers, including perfect deep-fried zucchini with garlic hollandaise, are cooked to order in front of you—ideal for a light supper.

HH6	★ **The Hi-Spot Cafe** **1410 34th Ave** 325-7905	*B 7:30-2 Mon-Fri, 9-3 Sat-Sun; L 11:30-2* *Mon-Fri; D 5:30-9:30 Thur-Sat* *Inexpensive; Beer & Wine; No credit cards*

A reincarnation of the extremely popular Conscious Exchange, this laidback, cozy little cafe located in a refurbished Madrona house and storefront is famous for its hearty breakfasts and great coffee. Try the fluffy omelets. All the egg dishes are served with a tasty home-fries-and-yams concoction (garlic and shallots too, if you like), fruit, and homemade croissants, cinnamon rolls, or coffee cake. Wholesome soups, salads, and sandwiches are the luncheon fare. Dinners can be uneven; the blackboard menu changes weekly and offers items such as steamed clams, pasta, snapper in filo, and stuffed zucchini.

FF9	**Hiram's at-the-Locks** **5300 34th NW** Res: 784-1733	*L 11:30-2:30 Mon-Fri,* *D 5-9:30 Sun-Thur, 5-11* *Fri & Sat; Sun Brunch 9:30-2:30* *Expensive; Full bar; cc: AE, MC, V*

The ideal place to observe the weekend madness that sometimes ensues at the Locks with boats passing to and from Puget Sound and Lakes Union and Washington. The restaurant's design is interesting, with all its structural elements exposed. The menu is standard seafood, but the chef sometimes ventures forth with a special such as monkfish piccata.

DD7	★ **Hisago** **543 NE Northgate Way** 363-1556	*L 11:30-2 Tues-Fri; D 5-10 Tues-Sun;* *closed Mon* *Moderate; Beer & Wine; cc: MC, V*

Four cooks in a restaurant as small as this one indicates it's serious about food. Indeed, the fare is beautifully prepared, and there are special appetizers, such as beef rolls stuffed with vegetables, that are not normally found in local Japanese places. Omakase dinners are also available. A sushi bar is promised soon.

★ **Hong Kong**　　　　　　　　*L 11-3; D 3:30-11 Mon-Fri, 3:30-1*
R6　**507 Maynard Ave S**　　　　*Sat & Sun*
　　Res: 622-0366　　　　　　*Moderate; Full bar; cc: AE, MC, V*

Widely considered to be the best in town, the dim sum here draws noisy crowds for lunch. Service is rapid, prices low, and the selection broad. The egg tart is peerless. At night, though, the Cantonese selections are ordinary.

★ **Hon's**　　　　　　　　　　*10-3 Mon, 10-8 Tues-Thur & Sun,*
★ **416 Fifth Ave S**　　　　　*10-9 Fri & Sat*
Q7　**Res: 623-4470**　　　　　*Inexpensive; No alcohol; No credit cards*

Don't be put off by the exterior shabbiness of this little cafe in the International District. The Vietnamese-Chinese fare is exceptional. It's all prepared by Lan Do, who, with her husband and children, fled postwar Saigon. She learned to cook before escaping in order to find work in America, and she learned well. Her sauces, such as a non-cloying sweet-sour and a hoisin-peanut-sweet rice, are exceptional. The Vietnamese selections, such as light, refreshing beef or pork noodles and shrimp rolls, are the main attraction. But the Chinese choices, especially Hon's fried rice and wonderfully light deep-fried won ton, are equally rewarding.

★ **Horatio's**　　　　　　　　*L 11:30-2 Mon-Fri; D 5:30-9:30 Mon,*
★ **1200 Westlake**　　　　　　*5:30-10 Tues-Thur, 5-10:30 Fri & Sat,*
A1　**Res: 284-2535**　　　　　*4:30-9:30 Sun*
　　　　　　　　　　　　　　　Moderate; Full bar; cc: AE, MC, V

The decor is undistinguished, but nearly everything else about this Lake Union seafood place is superior. Through ample glass there's a good view of the lake and sleek boats moored nearby. The young waitresses are friendly and efficient. The bar serves good drinks and some of the town's better common appetizers—nachos, for example. Best of all is a wide variety of fresh seafood listed daily on chalkboards. Pacific fish are always well represented, including some from Hawaiian waters. But the real treats to Northwesterners are Atlantic species such as bluefish and scrod. All the seafood is prepared simply. Accompaniments are uninspiring: rice pilaf and a vegetable.

R5　**House of Hong** (unrated)　　*11-midnight Mon-Sat; 4-midnight Sun*
　　409 Eighth Ave S　　　　　*Moderate; Full bar*
　　Res: 622-7997　　　　　　　*cc: MC, V*

Brothers Faye Hong and Hugo Louie once ran the Atlas Cafe, many Seattleites' favorite Cantonese restaurant. Now they have moved a few blocks in the International District to a huge, beautifully decorated, multi-level establishment with a Hong Kong-style barbecue in the front. Early evidence suggests that it will take a while for them to gain control of the kitchen and the dining-room service.

★ **The Hunt Club**　　　　　　　*B 7-11, L 11-2:30 Every day;*
M4　**900 Madison (Sorrento Hotel)**　*D 5:30-10 Sun-Thur, 5:30-11 Fri & Sat*
　　Res: 622-6400　　　　　　　*Expensive; Full bar; cc: AE, MC, V*

Mahogany panelling evokes the Sorrento Hotel's grand past, and the room is laid out nicely so that it is quiet and intimate. Unfortunately, the food has not lived up to the promise of the setting. Some dishes are well thought out and successful; others are a rank disappointment. Daily fish specials are the best choices, and there are good sandwiches and salads at lunch. Homemade ice creams flavored

Restaurants

with liqueur are outstanding.

★ **Il Bistro**	*L 11:30-3 Mon-Sat; D 5:30-11*
★ **Pike Place Market**	*Mon-Thur, 5:30-midnight Fri & Sat,*
★ **Res: 682-3049**	*5:30-10 Sun*
★	*Expensive; Full bar; cc: AE, CB, DC, MC, V*

18 Co-owners Peter Lamb and Frank d'Aquila run this airy cafe in a lower level of the Pike Place Market with unvarying conviction. The result is a cozy, informal dining room and bar (Lamb's province) and limited fare from d'Aquila's kitchen that features seasonal ingredients and is consistently excellent. Nothing is pretentious here. The room has cream-colored walls with a few fabric hangings, fresh flowers, white linen, round tables widely spaced, comfortable "caboose" chairs, and an oak floor. The food largely consists of pastas, sautes, soups, and salads—although there is a roast rack of lamb that might be the best in the city. D'Aquila has a fine eye for ingredients. Here you will find the Northwest's mushrooms—boletus, shiitake, morels, and chanterelles—when they're in season. Fish are carefully selected, and the kitchen has an outstanding veal supplier. Fat mussels come from the East Coast. Herbs and Italian salad staples such as arugula and radicchio are supplied by d'Aquila's father, a winemaker, who is also the source of wonderful cabernet and chardonnay vinegars. From this bounty, d'Aquila fashions dishes such as sliced veal salad, cold braciole salad, prawns with garlic or marinara sauce, cioppino and clam chowder, pheasant breast with a rosemary–green peppercorn sauce, and superb pastas, including house favorite tortellini with white sauce. Pastas are moderately priced, and a single order can be split among an entire party. Lamb's wine list includes unusual and excellent selections, and there are bargains among the more expensive choices. A sublime pecan pie heads the dessert list.

★ **India House**	*L 11:30-3 Every day; D 5-9:45 Sun-Thur,*
★ **4737 Roosevelt Way NE**	*5-10:45 Fri & Sat*
★ **Res: 632-5072**	*Moderate; Full bar; cc: AE, DC, MC, V*

FF7 Genial Chef Kapotra—no first name for such a personage—came to town not long ago to adjust the seasonings at this large University District Indian restaurant. He's also been usefully employed as a publicity foil because he has cooked in New Delhi for the likes of Jackie, Indira, and Princess Meg. (Their photos with him hang on the walls as proof.) The food was good before Chef Kapotra, but it's even better now. And he's instituted a huge weekend buffet at a bargain price and a slightly smaller daily lunch buffet at an even better price. The menu is large and covers all the familiar Indian dishes, including items from the clay oven called a tandoor. Standouts include butter chicken from the tandoor that is finished in a sauce of butter, tomato, cream, and spices; dal maharani, a blend of three types of lentils; and the breads, especially the tandoor-baked naan and the deep-fried puri.

★ **Inn Bin**	*L 11:30-2 Tues-Thur; D 4:30-9 Tues-Thur*
FF8 **5500 Eighth Ave NW**	*& Sun, 4:30-10 Fri & Sat; closed Mon*
784-6388	*Inexpensive; No alcohol; No credit cards*

A friendly, funky neighborhood place, where the Mandarin-style food comes at bargain rates. Some of the favorites are mushi pork, garlic chicken, and imperial shrimp.

KK5 **Italo's Casa Romana**	*11-11 Mon-Fri; 4-midnight Sat & Sun*
6400 Empire Way S	*Moderate; Full bar*
722-0449	*cc: AE, CB, DC, MC, V*
BB6 **14622 15th NE**	*Same as above*
362-8934	

28

There are now two Italo's, but the old basement-of-a-house restaurant down in Rainier Valley is still the preferred version. The food is very uneven, and it helps if you can get Italo himself to assist with the order. The calzone is tasty, as are the veal dishes and the pizza; the pasta is risky. The atmosphere is quite jolly, with many families and regulars on hand, and there is a noisy bar.

★ **Ivar's Indian Salmon House** *L 11:30-2 Mon-Fri; D 5-11 Mon-Fri,*
FF7 **401 NE Northlake Way** *4-11 Sat, 1-10 Sun*
Res: 632-0767 *Moderate; Full bar; cc: AE, MC, V*

Ivar Haglund, Seattle's puckish and ubiquitous restaurateur, gives good value at this replication of an Indian longhouse on the north side of Lake Union. Salmon and black cod are properly broiled Indian-style over a smoky alder fire. For dinner, roast turkey and prime rib are added to the short menu. A takeout window serves deep-fried seafood, and you can eat lakeside on picnic tables amid begging mallards.

O8 **J & M Cafe** *11:30-1:30am Every day*
201 First S *Moderate; Full bar*
Res: 624-1670 *cc: AE, MC, V*

The long, narrow front room has yards and yards of bar space. The back is spacious and full of marble-topped tables. A high ceiling, fans, and old wood recall the earthier days of Seattle's past. The food—chili, a quiche, omelets, sandwiches, etc.—is ordinary. But the noisy lunch scene draws dozens of people who go there daily.

★ **Jake O'Shaughnessey's** *5-11 Tues-Fri; 4:30-11 Sat; 5-10 Sun & Mon*
★ **First & Mercer (Hansen Baking Co.)** *Moderate; Full bar*
GG7 **285-1897** *cc: AE, CB, DC, MC, V*

This Lower Queen Anne spot is where Tim Firnstahl and Mick McHugh first established the formula that has made them among Seattle's most prosperous restaurateurs: saloon-like atmosphere with a noisy bar in front to attract the young and the single; food and drink gimmicks under tight quality control; reasonable prices; young and eager help. The formula and gimmicks are agreeable, although a second exposure to the grinning waiters and waitresses and their by-rote recitation of the fare's virtues makes one want to throttle their masters. In the bar, Jake's boasts the second-largest collection of single-malt Scotches in the world, three dozen cognacs, Guinness Stout from the Dublin brewery on tap, and a singing bartender, Robert Julien. In the dining room are prime rib roasted in rock salt, alder-roasted salmon, huge russet potatoes baked with a spike through them, and good ice creams.

★ **Java Restaurant** *D 5-10 Tues-Sun; closed Mon*
DD7 **8929 Roosevelt Way NE** *Moderate; Full bar*
Res: 522-5282 *cc: MC, V*

A good sampling of Indonesian dishes is available here, in a pretty and spotless house setting. Sates, skewers of grilled meat or fish served with a peanut sauce, are offered, along with such staples as the fried rice dish nasi goreng. There seem to be concessions to perceived Western tastes, however. The peanut sauce for the salad called gado gado is heated. And a delicious thin-sliced pork dish called babi panggang is padded with two scoops of rice. Smoking is not allowed.

HH3 **Jonah and the Whale** *L 11:30-2 Mon-Fri; D 6-10:30 Mon-Fri,*
11211 Main, Bellevue (Holiday Inn) *6-11 Sat; closed Sun*
455-5242 *Expensive; Full bar*
 cc: AE, CB, DC, MC, V

Restaurants

Venison, rack of lamb, lots of carving, cooking, and flambeing at tableside, and a strolling violinist—all in a motel, the Eastside Holiday Inn. Bring your expense account or a special date.

★ **Julia's 14-Carrot Cafe** ★ **2305 Eastlake E** GG7 **324-1442**	*7am-10pm Mon-Sat; 8am-3pm Sun* *Moderate; Beer & Wine* *cc: MC, V*

This is home away from home in the Eastlake neighborhood, crowded morning, noon, and night. It's easy to see why. The place is warm, steamy, noisy, and plain, like eating in your mother's kitchen—provided your mother can turn out dishes inspired by a couple of dozen cuisines. Everything is homemade, including breads, baked goods, and pasta. Little is authentic, as most dishes are given a special—frequently "nutritional"—twist. Breakfasts include all the standards such as omelets and French toast, plus exotica like Tahitian Toast: a grilled, egg-dipped sandwich of sesame butter served with fruit and yogurt. Lunches include hearty salads and inventive sandwiches and burgers, including a meatless nut burger. Dinners also have such vegetarian fare, including many meatless pastas, plus dishes such as Szechuan beef and daily seafood specials.

★ **Kaleenka Russian Cafe** 17 **1933 First Ave** **Res: 624-1278**	*8-8 Mon-Thur; 8-10 Fri & Sat; closed Sun* *Inexpensive; Beer & Wine* *cc: No credit cards*

Capable Russian hands prepare hearty food in this cozy place. The fare, such as eight-vegetable borscht and dumplings called vareniky, has a Ukrainian accent. But there are other regional dishes, too, such as Siberian beef dumplings called pilmeny and a Georgian grilled chicken breast for dinner. The piroshky—cheese, beef, and cabbage—are excellent.

★ **Karawan** FF7 **NE 52nd & University Way NE** **523-7477**	*11-10 Sun-Thur; 11-11 Fri & Sat* *Moderate; No alcohol* *cc: AE, MC, V*

The house specialty, roast leg of lamb, can be a disappointment. Otherwise, the Middle Eastern fare here is fine—including such standards as the eggplant dip baba ganouj, couscous, and a spinach-and-cheese pie called sabanikh. A homemade cheese called jibna is excellent, and happily shows up in many dishes, including an exceptional dessert, kanafa. The long dessert list is also available in an adjacent coffee bar.

★ **Kau Kau** **656 S King** **682-4006**	*10-10 Every day* *Inexpensive; No liquor* *No credit cards*

R6 The front window of this International District place is filled with barbecued meats, Hong Kong–style. There's duck and pork and ribs and all the innards you can imagine. All are available in-house or to go, along with an extensive Cantonese menu and many daily specials.

★ **Kikuya** ★ **8105 161st Ave NE, Redmond** EE1 **881-8771**	*L 11:30-2 Tues-Fri; D 5-10 Tues-Fri,* *4:30-10 Sat & Sun; closed Mon* *Moderate; Beer & Wine; cc: MC, V*

Stuck in the back of a small shopping center in Redmond is this small Japanese place where the fare is prepared uncommonly well. Owner and sushi chef Hiroaki Ito impassively oversees the kitchen, which puts out standard Japanese dishes such as tempura and teriyaki. The room is simply decorated in pale tones; hanging lights are dramatically covered by globular paper shades. Service is excellent.

★ **King Cafe**
R6 **723 S King**
622-6373

11-5 Thur-Tues; closed Wed
Inexpensive; No alcohol
No credit cards

This plain International District place is a lunchtime institution because of its wide variety of dim sum served quickly to a noisy and cheerful clientele.

I14 **Klahowyan**
7811 SE 27th, Mercer Island
Res: 232-8750

D 5-8 Sun, 5-10 Tues-Thur, 5-11 Fri &
Sat; closed Mon
Moderate; Full bar; cc: AE, MC, V

This Mercer Island spot features a round counter with high-backed stools where diners get a closeup view of their meals being prepared. The fare is light, and there are two nightly specials, one fish and one meat, plus a soup of the day. Best of all are the homemade desserts.

★ **Kokeb**
926 12th Ave
HH7 **322-0485**

11-9 Mon-Thur; 11-11 Fri; 3-11 Sat;
closed Sun
Inexpensive; Beer & Wine; cc: MC, V

A rare and charming place: a plain cafe serving authentic Ethiopian fare family-style at remarkably low prices. The way to dine is with a group. Order several dishes (nearly all of them are spicy) such as tibbs, sauteed beef with onions and hot peppers; doro wat, chicken in a red sauce; and messer wat, spiced lentils. Each comes with vegetables such as collard greens and yellow split peas, plus a bland homemade cheese called eyeb, balm for a flaming tongue. The dishes are served on a huge round of enjera, the Ethiopian flat bread that soaks up the sauces and is eaten at the end of the meal.

P7 **Korea House**
212 Fourth Ave S
622-1936

11-9 Mon-Sat; closed Sun
Inexpensive; No alcohol
No credit cards

A little, unassuming place, Korea House is a spot for workingmen's Korean fare such as barbecued beef, Korean chop suey, spareribs, and white radish soup.

★ **Labuznik**
★ **1924 First Ave**
★ **Res: 682-1624**
★
I7

Cafe: D 4:30-10 Tues-Thur, 5:30-midnight
Fri & Sat; closed Sun & Mon
Restaurant: D 5:30-10 Tues-Thur, 5:30-11
Fri & Sat; closed Sun & Mon
Restaurant, Expensive; Cafe, Moderate;
Full bar; cc: AE, MC, V

Owner-chef Peter Cipra's firm convictions about food have served Seattle diners well for more than a decade. He uses choice ingredients, never varies his menu—although he has added nightly specials—and personally approves everything coming out of the kitchen. His cuisine is principally Eastern European (he is Czech, and Labuznik means "lover of good food"), hearty, and deeply flavorful. All Labuznik fans have their favorites, such as the superb roast duck with its crackling skin, or nearly always moist roast pork, or veal Orloff, here done with capers and pickle in the sauce, or the "special" rack of lamb for two. Many dishes come with bread dumplings, sauerkraut, and red cabbage, and these and other accompaniments are as consistently good as the entrees. The quibbles are that service borders on the brusque, and Cipra insists that his kitchen can properly put out only three entree choices per table, meaning a party of four has to double up on one choice. As good as the dining room is, the front cafe, open to the street when weather permits, is even better. Here prices are less, choices are broader, and a light meal is possible: pastas, mustard and green-peppercorn steak sandwiches, beef tartare, fried cheese, fruit, cheese and cold meat trays. Plus desserts and coffees.

GG7 **Lake Union Cafe** L 11-3 Mon-Sat; D 4-midnight Every day
 3119 Eastlake Ave E Sun Brunch 9-3
 Res: 323-8855 Moderate; Full bar; cc: AE, MC, V

Restaurant impresario Gerry Kingen reportedly intended to do penance for his lack of attention to food of distinction by making this a quality Italian restaurant-deli-dessert spot. So far, though it's young, the place seems to be mostly glitter. An old espresso machine, for instance, looks handsome but doesn't work very well.

FF7 **The Lakeside** L 11:30-2:30 Mon-Fri; D 5-10:30
 2501 N Northlake Way Mon-Thur, 5-midnight Fri & Sat; closed Sun
 Res: 634-0823 Expensive; Full bar
  cc: AE, MC, V

This showy Lake Union place owns one of Seattle's great views: across the placid lake to the city lights. The kitchen turns out a seasonal menu based on New California Cuisine: lobster ravioli with anise cream and lobster sauce, for instance, or veal medallions with enoki mushrooms and onion marmalade. The cooks' ambitions, however, exceed their grasp. And if you don't fit the host's idea of what his guests should be, you'll find yourself exiled to the far corner of the bar. When the weather's right, you can dine outside by the water.

 ★ **The Last Exit on Brooklyn** 6am-midnight Mon-Thur; 6-2am Fri;
FF7 **3930 Brooklyn Ave NE** 10-2am Sat; 10am-midnight Sun
 545-9873 Inexpensive; No alcohol; No credit cards

U S chess champion Yasser Seirawan hangs out here when he's home, blending in with the students, chess players, and University District denizens who give this place its special appeal. It's shabby, noisy, smoky, and warm—altogether the ideal off-campus joint. Culinary ambitions are modest—healthful soups, salads, and sandwiches. Baked goods are homemade, and apple pie doused in hot cinnamon sauce is a bestseller.

 ★ **Le Bonaparte** L 11:30-3 Mon-Fri; D 5:30-midnight Mon-Sat;
 ★ **S 216th & Marine View Dr, Des Moines** D 5-11 Sun; Sun Brunch 10-4
PP7 **Res: 878-4412** Expensive; Full bar; cc: AE, CB, DC, MC, V

By mining the territory between traditional French cooking and nouvelle cuisine, this house restaurant draws diners from the entire region to the waterfront community of Des Moines, south of the airport. The dining rooms and upstairs lounge are furnished nicely; lots of white linen and waiters dressed in black complete the setting. The wine list is commendable, desserts are excellent, but service is paradoxical: the waiters are quick and efficient, but the kitchen works slowly, evidently on the understanding that diners are spending the entire evening. Not all of owner-chef Jacques Mason's creations are successful. But he normally has up to four game birds—squab, duck, quail, and pheasant—available in good sauces. And there are surprising touches, such as red snapper with grapefruit. On Sundays, a five-course "champagne" brunch packs the house.

 ★ **Le Pigalle** L 11:30-2:30 Mon-Fri; D 5:30-10 Mon-Thur,
FF7 **1104 NE 47th** 5:30-11 Fri & Sat; closed Sun
 Res: 525-1525 Moderate; Full bar; cc: CB, DC, MC, V

Fresh flowers, little crocks of butter, a creamy garlic house dressing, personal attention from one of the French-accented owners—even the sparse light from the single window—place this small restaurant on a side street in a French provincial town, not the University District. Regulars are happy it's displaced. They also come for the omelets, crepes, and such familiar fare as Boeuf Bourguignon and Coquille St. Jacques.

★ **Le Provencal**
★ **212 Central Way, Kirkland**
EE3 **Res: 827-3300**

D 5:30-11 Mon-Sat; closed Sun
Moderate; Full bar
cc: AE, DC, MC, V

To the relief of those who love it, nothing ever changes at this Kirkland restaurant, where Phillipe Gayte presides with the warmth and charm of a provincial French host. Though augmented by specials, the menu is short and the preparations of favorites such as baked oysters with spinach and bearnaise, and prawns provencale are exact and consistent. Linen, glassware, the fireplace, subdued lighting, and discreet service add up to a soothing setting for a good meal and a quiet conversation.

★ **Le Tastevin**
★ **19 W Harrison**
★ **Res: 283-0991**
★

L 11:30-2:30 Mon-Fri;
D 5-10:30 Mon-Thur; 5-11 Fri & Sat;
closed Sun
Expensive; Full bar; cc: AE, MC, V

A8 Long among the city's better French restaurants, Le Tastevin moved to larger quarters on Lower Queen Anne, expanded its menu, and stepped to the head of the class. West windows offer a view of the Olympics, sunsets, and the Sound, marred only by the intrusion of blocky buildings in the neighborhood. The exterior is of hemlock stained "natural." That theme is repeated in the understated interior, where there are bannered and latticed ceilings, wine racks, and colorful banquettes. Co-owner Jacques Boiroux runs the kitchen along with chef Les Goetz, his longtime student. With admirable consistency, they produce classic cuisine, emphasizing seafood and lighter fare. Scallops, for example, are done a la Nicoise: sauteed in butter, tomato, and garlic; mussels are perfectly steamed in wine, shallots, and herbs. Other favorites on the long menu: kulibiac of salmon, bouillabaise, panfried trout, and a moist broiled chicken breast with tarragon butter. Though dinners rate as expensive, a "curtain-time" menu, featuring items such as sauteed chicken livers and broiled oysters and scallops, is moderately priced. Lunches include smaller portions of some dinner selections plus salads and light items such as poached salmon and chicken crepes. Other delights: the best desserts in town, including a dense truffle torte, souffles, and an incomparable floating island, prepared by Goetz' brother, Darwin; a strong wine list assembled by co-owner and host Emile Ninaud that has excellent Spanish bargains; wide selections of sherries, ports, and iced vodkas; and a free cocktail-hour buffet of hors d'oeuvres such as marinated squid, smoked-trout mousse, prawns, and oysters.

★ **Les Copains**
★ **2202 N 45th**
★ **Res: 633-5753**

D 6-11 Every day
Expensive; Beer & Wine
cc: MC, V

FF7 Bruce Naftaly is perhaps Seattle's most brilliant young chef. He came here to pursue his passion for music and discovered, while working at The Other Place, an equally powerful passion for cooking. The result was this small place in a North End neighborhood that he founded with friends—the "pals" of the restaurant's name. At The Other Place, Naftaly was an expert at sniffing out amateur and professional suppliers of Northwest ingredients. He continues to exploit these sources, turning out a dazzling and daring cuisine based on the finest main ingredients, sauces that often include fruits and nuts, wild salad greens, and edible flowers, and unusual vegetables superbly steamed and flavored with unsalted butter. A typical menu might include these gems: a salad of warm confit d'oie with pickled pears; salmon en papillote with port-and-home-cured-bacon sauce; roast chicken with hazelnut-and-rhubarb sauce; pork medallions with horseradish-rosemary-beet sauce. Desserts, such as a prune-and-cognac tart, are also excellent. The wine list, though short, is well chosen and reasonably priced. The two-level

Restaurants

dining area is beautifully done in dark wood and soft colors. Unfortunately, Les Copains has been unable to shake a "temple of dining" atmosphere compounded of an undue reverence by the staff toward the fare, a rigid no-smoking rule, and live harpsichord music. Closed at press time. Call for possible reopening.

★ **Leschi Lakecafe** ★ **102 Lakeside Ave S** *HH6* **328-2233**	*L 11:30-2 Mon-Fri; D 5-10 Sun-Thur,* *5-11 Fri & Sat* *Moderate; Full bar; cc: AE, MC, V*

The third of Tim Firnstahl and Mick McHugh's formula places. (See listing for Jake O'Shaughnessey's.) This one overlooks the Leschi marina on Lake Washington. A noisy bar attracts singles and/or sailors and features a variety of British and Northwest brews on tap. The menu is short: pasta with fennel sausage, fresh fish, entree salads, huge burgers and omelets, fish and chips, and beef roasted pub-style in butcher paper. For dessert there are baked Alaskas. During the summer, burgers, fish and chips, and fresh-fruit shakes are available from a take-out window.

★ **Lion O'Reilly's &** **B.J. Monkeyshine's** *HH7* **132 Broadway E** **322-1710**	*L 11-4 Mon-Sat; B 9-noon Sat;* *Sun Brunch 9-3; D 4-11 Mon-Sat, 5-11 Sun* *Moderate; Full bar* *cc: AE, CB, MC, V*

This Broadway District hangout for single professionals, another of impresario Gerry Kingen's (Boondock's, Red Robin, etc.) showcases, is done in high-class saloon style: dark wood and dark-green paint, with lots of brass and upholstered booths. Early-evening action is in the bar, over appetizers such as "oyster shooters"—raw bivalves in shot glasses with sauce. Lunch and dinner menus feature fresh seafood, such as "blackened red snapper," pastas, steaks, and chicken dishes. A live lobster tank is a well publicized attraction. On Saturdays there's an elaborate breakfast menu and on Sundays a lavish brunch, with a made-to-order crepe-and-omelet bar.

★ **Linyen** *R6* **424 Seventh Ave S** **Res: 622-8181**	*11:30-1:30am Mon-Fri, 3-1:30am Sat,* *3-11:30 Sun* *Moderate; Full bar; cc: AE, CB, DC, MC, V*

A spicier version of Cantonese cooking is practiced here, making Linyen stand out among the general run of Seattle's many Cantonese restaurants. The printed menu is limited and best avoided, though some regulars swear by the lemon chicken. Better are the daily specials, especially seafood dishes such as crab in black-bean sauce. Snazzy modern decor.

★ **Lofurno's** ★ **2060 15th Ave W** *GG8* **Res: 283-7980**	*D 5-10 Tues-Thur & Sun; 5-11 Fri & Sat;* *closed Mon* *Expensive; Full bar; cc: AE, MC, V*

Chef Bobby Cohen handles a standard Italian-American menu with solid competence and occasional excellence. His marinara sauce and variation of saltimbocca, for instance, are as good as any in town. Try the marinara with mussels. Cohen's cooking, professional waiters, and a third-floor dance hall featuring big-band sounds attract an older crowd that comes for fun. The first floor, part piano-bar and part saloon, is the best place to dine if you don't mind the musical intrusion. There is a wonderful old back bar and eight wood booths set off by a brass-rail-lace-curtain arrangement. The second-floor dining room is quieter and set up for larger groups.

Restaurants

I16 **Louie's Cuisine of China**
5100 15th NW
782-8855

11:30am-12:30am Mon-Thur;
11:30am-1:30am Fri; 4pm-1:30am Sat;
3pm-10:30pm Sun
Moderate; Full bar; cc: AE, CB, DC, MC, V

This is the ultimate Chinese-American restaurant dream: many dining rooms, a large bar, attractive and comfortable furnishings, and a menu that safely stays within the long tradition of Chinese-American cuisine.

HH3 **Mad Anthony's**
1200 112th NE, Bellevue
Res: 455-1776

D 4-9:30 Mon-Thur, 4-10 Fri, 5-10 Sat,
4-9 Sun
Moderate; Full bar; cc: AE, MC, V

Prime rib in many-sized cuts is the centerpiece of this popular Eastside spot. Steak is available, too, of course, and there are broiled and sauteed seafood selections.

★ **Madison Park Cafe**
GG6 1807 42nd Ave E
Res: 324-2626

9-5 Tues-Sat; 9am-10pm Tues-Sat (summer);
9-1pm Sun; closed Mon
Moderate; Beer & Wine; cc: MC, V

This neighborhood spot is best in the summer, when dinners are served on the patio as well as inside the house. Generally there are two pastas, a fish, and a meat dish. In other seasons, only continental breakfasts and light lunches of salads, sandwiches, a quiche, and a special lunch such as chicken breast with paprika in parchment are served. Sunday brunch includes champagne by the glass. No smoking is permitted.

★ **Malia's Northwest**
★ 820 Second Ave
M7 Res: 624-3287

B 7-10:30 Mon-Fri; L 11-3 Mon-Fri;
D 5:30-9 Mon-Thur
Moderate; Full bar
cc: AE, CB, DC, MC, V

Richard Malia doggedly pursues honorable intentions that are gradually improving his restaurant into one of the city's most notable. For instance: breakfast consists of home-baked croissants, rolls, breads, and fresh juices presented self-service beneath a skylight. The bar (fresh juices here, too) includes a large table where singles can be seated. Desserts are home-baked and include delights such as a creamy peanut-butter pie. The wine list is strong on the better Northwest offerings. Rare Olympia oysters are served on the half shell. An excellent bouillabaise is properly accompanied by rouille. Salmon and lingcod are pole-caught and carefully frozen for out-of-season use. And service is exceptionally friendly. Malia specializes in seafood and pasta. Not all preparations are successful, but there are usually several excellent choices among the day's specials.

CC7 **Mama Lontoni's**
14356 Aurora N
Res: 365-4141

L 11-2:30 Mon-Fri; D 5-10 Sun-Thur,
5-11 Fri & Sat
Expensive; Full bar; cc: AE, CB, DC, MC, V

Though its appearance was greeted joyfully by some North Enders eager for relief from fast food and franchises, Mama Lontoni's has not yet found its stride. Improvements are planned, but for now you should approach the pasta dishes gingerly: they are way oversized, and some of the sauces are foolishly excessive. Veal and seafood choices are better, and there are a few gems on the menu, such as sauteed escarole and, occasionally, tripe. The room is lush and dark, with a nice little bar tucked away in back.

★ **Mamounia**
★ 1556 E Olive Way
★ Res: 329-3886
I1

5-10 Tues-Sat; closed Sun & Mon
Moderate; Beer & Wine
cc: MC, V

This small place serves a fair sampling of authentic Moroccan cuisine, one of the world's best. Co-owner Mehdi Ziani has followed the formula that made his two California restaurants successful: a windowless room decorated to resemble a sheik's desert tent; stool or banquette seating around tables of hammered tin; hand-washing ceremonies before and after dinner (this is real finger-food); waiters who can fill a glass with sweet minted tea by pouring from shoulder height; and wonderfully flavorful five-course dinners at an astonishingly low fixed price. First there's a lentil-chickpea soup, then a tomato-eggplant salad, and then a version of Morocco's best-known dish, sweet, flaky pigeon pie (here made of chicken and spelled pastilla). For an entree, each diner chooses from a list of nine, including chicken with preserved lemons, rabbit in paprika sauce, lamb with honey or prunes, couscous and a brochette of moist, tender lamb. For a couple of dollars more, both of two nightly specials are available instead of the single entree from the regular list. All this ends satisfyingly with a fried-dough-and-honey confection called chabbakia and the minted tea.

L8	**The Mark Tobey** (unrated) **1007 First Ave (Alexis Hotel)** Res: 624-4844	*11am-1am Mon-Sat; 11am-4pm Sun* *Moderate; Beer & Wine* *cc: AE, MC, V*

The editor of this guide is a principal in this new establishment, so any judgments here are out of place. The Tobey is an adaptation of an English pub—more like a sociable lounge adjoining a country hotel. Pub lunches are served daily, mixing English items such as ploughman's lunch (cheese, bread, salads, and pickled onions), Scotch eggs, some beef pies and pasties, with smoked meats and fish, soups, and a few continental dishes. Dinners are light, with a daily roast and cold platters, plus trifle for dessert. Fresh local ales, imported beers, Northwest wines, sherries, ciders, and espresso are at the bar. The Tobey, whose name commemorates the great Northwest painter, is located in the Alexis Hotel.

GG6	**Matzoh Momma** **509 15th Ave E** 324-6262	*7am-1am Mon-Thur; 7am-2am Fri;* *8am-2am Sat; 8am-midnight Sun* *Moderate; Full bar; No credit cards*

Arguably, this is the best of a sparse selection of Jewish deli-restaurants in the Seattle area. The menu is standard kosher-style and there is takeout, too. At night, amateur and professional musicians entertain, primarily with jazz, for no extra charge, making Matzoh Momma's a gathering place for North Capitol Hill residents.

★ ★ I8	**Maximilien-in-the-Market** **81A Pike Place Market** 682-7270	*B 7:30-11, L 11:30-4, D 5:30-10 Mon-Sat;* *closed Sun* *Expensive; Full bar; cc: AE, MC, V*

The Brasserie Pittsbourg's Julia and Francois Kissel's French market-cafe oddly suffers a limited reputation, being better known for its view of Elliott Bay than its fare. The food is better than the reputation, although quality can be uneven. In addition to croissants, espresso, and so on, breakfasts include a souffle and homemade sage sausage. At lunch, there are salads such as Napa cabbage with shrimp and crab, vegetable fritters, and herb-flavored hamburgers. Dinners include grilled sweetbreads in mustard-caper sauce, seafood stew, and game hen with apples and veal sausage. Fruit and pastry desserts are beautifully done, and on too-rare occasions Francois's own chocolate sauce over a poached pear is served at night.

★ N6	**McCormick's Fish House & Bar** **722 Fourth Ave** 682-3900	*11-11, Mon-Thur; 11-midnight Fri;* *5-midnight Sat; 5-10 Sun* *Expensive; Full bar* *cc: AE, CB, DC, MC, V*

This downtown fish house has wood booths, a nice bar, a long "fresh sheet," some good touches such as rare Olympia oysters on the half-shell, and excellent desserts. But preparation of the food sometimes is not done with care so that, for instance, a simple grilled salmon arrives charred on the outside and uncooked in the center. An oyster-sandwich bar serves quick lunches and snacks.

★ **F.X. McRory's Steak, Chop &**   *L 11:30-2 Mon-Fri; D 5-10 Sun-Tues,*
★ **Oyster House**   *5-11 Wed-Sat*
P8 **419 Occidental S**   *Moderate; Full bar*
623-4800   *cc: AE, MC, V*

Tim Firnstahl and Mick McHugh's huge food-and-drink emporium across from the Kingdome faithfully follows their formula for success. (See listing for Jake O'Shaughnessey's.) The large and noisy bar's gimmicks are the world's largest collection of bourbons, a list of 80 imported brews, and Anchor Steam beer from San Francisco on tap. In the entrance area there's an oyster bar with standup tables. In the dining room, the principal attractions are roasted lamb and beef finished in bourbon casks, a good variety of fresh fish, oyster and crab stews, an excellent butt pork chop in a spicy sauce, and good ice creams.

★ **Mediterranean Kitchen**   *L 11-3 Mon-Fri; D 5-11 Mon-Sat, 4-11 Sun*
GG7 **4 W Roy**   *Inexpensive; Beer & Wine*
285-6713   *cc: AE, CB, DC, MC, V*
Kamalco   *11-10 Mon-Sat; 4-10 Sun*
HH7 **914 E Pike**   *Inexpensive; Beer & Wine*
Res: 323-7565   *cc: AE, CB, DC, MC, V*

This is the most garlicky kitchen in town. But there are other distinctions, notably the presence of owner-chef Kamal Aboul Hosn, a Lebanese. He serves fare from the entire Mediterranean basin and even has an Afghanistan chicken burger. Quantity plus quality make the place one of the better bargains around. A herby, garlicky salad dressing is outstanding. Entrees include kabobs, steaks done in French and Italian styles, couscous, and a Lebanese farmer's dish of broiled chicken wings and rice in, naturally, garlic sauce. A cousin of the Kitchen, Kamalco, is on the east slope of Capitol Hill. The menu is similar, but prices are a bit higher.

O8 **Merchants Cafe**   *11-10 Mon-Thur; 11-11 Fri & Sat; closed Sun*
109 Yesler Way   *Moderate; Full bar*
Res: 624-1515   *cc: AE, MC, V*

The oldest restaurant in Seattle (1890), Merchants Cafe has a nice, airy bar upstairs and a brick-walled dining room below. Lunch draws a good crowd for sandwiches, barbecued ribs, steaks, seafood stew, and a quiche. Dinners are about the same, with the addition of some light veal and chicken dishes.

★ **Mikado**   *5:30-10 Mon-Sat; closed Sun*
★ **514 S Jackson**   *Expensive; Full bar*
★ **Res: 622-5206**   *cc: AE, DC, MC, V*

Q7 The reputation of this International District culinary landmark as one of the country's finest Japanese restaurants has slipped slightly. Perhaps the owners, Bruce and Irwin Yoshimura, are distracted by their fast-food outlets in the Seattle Center and Bellevue Square and their brand-new restaurant in the Waterfront Center project, Western and Spring. Still, the slippage has been minor, and the perfectionist Yoshimuras likely will restore the formerly flawless food and service. The sushi bar, drawing supplies from Seattle's finest seafood outlet, Mutual Fish, also owned by the Yoshimura family, is superb. The robata bar, where diners select seafood, meat, and vegetables from display cases to be grilled quickly and then passed to them on paddles, is one of the best places in town for a light meal and a long conversation. Tatami rooms are beautiful and the best places to be served omakase, chef Hide Obatake's multi-course dinner in traditional sequence. Pick a price range (preferably in advance) and leave the selections to him.

★ **Mirabeau**
L6 1001 Fourth Ave (Seafirst Bldg)
    Res: 624-4550

*L 11:30-2:30 Mon-Fri; D 5:30-10:30
Mon-Thur, 5:30-11 Fri & Sat; closed Sun
Expensive; Full bar
cc: AE, CB, DC, MC, V*

The view is spectacular, but the French-accented food seldom lives up to the expectations one has of a plush room atop one of the city's tallest bank buildings. Business people and smart shoppers favor the lunches, and it's a nice spot for a late-night drink or dessert.

★ **Miya's**
FF7 5261 University Way NE
     Res: 527-1221

*L 11:30-2 Mon-Fri; D 5-10 Mon-Sat;
closed Sun
Moderate; Full bar; cc: AE, DC, MC, V*

Owner Nagafumi Ninomiya, in traditional style, works the sushi bar and does a fine if humorless job. The tempura is better than average; otherwise, the menu is standard. There are tatami rooms, booths, and a nice country-inn sense about the place.

HH3 **Morgan's Lakeplace**
     2 Lake Bellevue Dr, Bellevue
     455-2244

*11-11 Mon-Sat; 6-11 Sun
Moderate; Full bar
cc: AE, MC, V*

A triumph of marketing, Morgan's sits on a pond grandly called "Lake Bellevue" and offers "foods for all moods" from a huge menu of pastas, salads, seafood, steaks, chicken, sandwiches, and quiche. "Homemade and healthy" is the fare, fashioned from "fresh, first-quality ingredients." The cooks are not as good as the copywriters. The cheesecake, from S&S in The Bronx, is exceptional.

L5 **Morilles (Park Hilton)**
    Sixth & Seneca
    Res: 464-1980

*L 11:30-2 Mon-Fri; D 6-10 Mon-Thur,
6-11 Fri & Sat; closed Sun
Expensive; Full bar; cc: AE, DC, MC, V*

This fancy spot in the Park Hilton is the sort of place that gave hotel restaurants a bad name to all but the expense-account crowd eager to impress clients: condescending service, roses for ladies, matchboxes instantly stamped with a diner's name, flaming tableside preparations providing several downwind parties a heady whiff of steamed vinegar from, say, a warm salad of spinach, squid, and pine nuts (!), and fare that too frequently crosses the line from good to bad taste. The latter category includes a watercress, jicama, and leek salad with a too-sweet blueberry sauce and escargots with sea-urchin roe and hazelnuts. Stick to simpler dishes, such as veal with morels.

★ **Mukilteo Cafe**
★ 621 Front St, Mukilteo
  Res: 347-1400

*D 5:30-10 Tues-Sun; closed Mon
Expensive; Beer & Wine
No credit cards*

This place represents a brave effort to succeed with a French cafe near a ferry dock. The narrow room of unfinished wood paneling is cleverly broken by stepping up two rows of tables. Butcher paper covers the tables, there are candles, and French ballads or Willie Nelson on the tape deck. The kitchen does wonders with a short menu and several specials. Appetizers include steamed mussels, escargot, pate, and a light smoked-salmon mousse. For entrees there are lamb chops, beef tenderloin, sauteed prawns, salmon, and, perhaps, an unusual East Coast fish such as cusk. Saucings are either light, as for fish, or of intense reductions, as for, say, sweetbreads. The thick chocolate mousse is justly celebrated.

★ **Nikko**	*D 5:30-10 Mon-Sat; closed Sun*
★ **1306 S King**	*Moderate; Full bar*
★ Res: 322-4641	*cc: AE, MC, V*

HH6 In the late '60s, Shiro Kashiba began the first sushi bar in Seattle. A decade ago he bought his own restaurant and, in proper Japanese style, has been presiding over the sushi bar there. Arguably (of course), it is the city's best. Just before opening time in the evening, the line begins forming, because to get a spot at Shiro's sushi bar is to not only enjoy good food but to witness a man of humor, knowledge, and charm perform his art with absolute mastery. (A second man works alongside Shiro with competence but in silence.) For those uncertain as to sushi-eating technique, Shiro will instruct. He'll also recommend what to taste and, with astonishing candor, what to avoid among his wide selection of ingredients. Though there are tables and tatami rooms, the way to get the most out of Nikko is to sit before Shiro and allow him to guide you. If you want food other than sushi, you can get it at the sushi bar also. Ask for the "small" or Japanese menu, which is actually more inclusive than the "large" menu of tempura, sukiyaki, and so on. From it you can get delectables such as   clam soup, fried chicken, spinach with sesame, broiled eel innards on a skewer (slightly bitter), and Spanish mackerel salad.

★ **1904 Restaurant/Bar**	*L 11:30-2:30 Mon-Fri; D 5:30-10*
★ **1904 Fourth Ave**	*Mon-Thur, 5:30-11 Fri & Sat; closed Sun*
I6 Res: 682-4142	*Moderate; Full bar; cc: AE, MC, V*

A starkly modern, long narrow room with a lively upstairs bar favored by the young and the restless, this downtown cafe features light fare and attentive, friendly service. Among many fine appetizers, one stands out: carpaccio with a smooth mustard sauce. Seafood, stew, and pasta specials generally are commendable. The wine list is first-rate, with many selections available by the glass.

FF8 **O'Leary's**	*L 11-3 Mon-Sat; D 5-10 Mon-Sat, 4-9 Sun*
5228 Ballard Ave	*Moderate; Full bar*
789-5558	*cc: MC, V*

A large-screen television in the bar, a long list of appetizers, and a menu of omelets, burgers, pasta, steaks, and a pretty good Irish stew mark this as a place for the young. It's also for the sports-minded since it's connected with the Olympic Racquet and Health Club in Ballard's historic Mathews Building.

★ **Original Ellen's**	*11-8 Mon-Fri, 8-8 Sat & Sun*
305 NW Gilman Blvd, Issaquah	*Moderate; Beer & Wine*
392-1209	*cc: MC, V*

Ellen Mohl built her reputation by serving simple food lavishly. Essentially, this is a burger-dessert place. The burgers are thick and nicely grilled, but the base price is high and the many condiments are priced individually, meaning the cost of a burger can mount alarmingly. The menu also has salads, excellent fries, a couple of dinner specials such as chicken fettucine, classic sandwiches such as Monte Cristos, cheese blintzes, and a long beer list. Its location, in Issaquah next to I-90, makes this a natural stop for those coming or going to the mountains, and there are hearty breakfasts served on weekends. Best of Ellen's fare are the desserts, most containing high-quality chocolate.

★ **The Other Place**	*L 11-4:30 Mon-Fri; D 5-11 Mon-Sat;*
★ **319 Union**	*closed Sun*
★ Res: 623-7340	*Expensive; Full bar*
★	*cc: AE, CB, DC, MC, V*
K6	

Restaurants

Warning: this is an extremely expensive place, and you can't escape at dinner since you pay for four courses whether you want them or not. (A three-course "theater menu" is about half the regular-menu price.) But it's also true that Robert Rosellini has put together the most ambitious restaurant in the city, sparing no effort in his search for fine ingredients. You enter a two-level dining room that is striking but not overpowering. The captain will be too fulsome in his description of the evening's offerings; the waiters will be too forcefully eager. The wine list, however, has no flaws; it's one of the finest in the country, wide and deep, particularly in French vintages. You begin with a soup, perhaps cream of carrot with a hint of cauliflower. Then a choice of a first course such as finely textured pheasant-liver pate. Then pear-and-rosehip sorbet or a salad of wild greens and edible flower blossoms. Then entrees vividly displaying Rosellini's hallmarks: fish done simply and ideally, and game birds and animals in inventive sauces, many including fruit and nuts. Fish choices might include rockfish with sorrel butter and salmon broiled with shallot butter. Meat choices might include sauteed veal liver with red pepper–apple chutney, roast pheasant with pears and red currants, and antelope with confit. There are sandwiches and salads for lunch as well as items from the dinner menu.

★ **Oyster Grotto**　　　　　　　　　　*L 11:30-5 Mon-Fri; D 5-10 Every day*
★ **5414 Sand Point Way NE**　　　*Expensive; Full bar*
FF5　**Res: 525-3230**　　　　　　　　　*cc: MC, V*

Original owner Tom Lee has reacquired this seafood place in northeast Seattle and restored its former quality. Oysters, naturally, head the menu and are served in several ways. Seafood generally is reliably well prepared. But there is also an excellent rack of lamb. Salads are superb: a variety of greens nicely dressed and topped by fresh croutons. And the standard accompaniments of potato slices topped with Parmesan, and mushroom caps stuffed with spinach, are excellent. The wine list is commendably varied in selection and price.

★ **The Palm Court**　　　　　　　　　　　　　　　*L 11:30-2:30 Mon-Fri; D 6-10:30 Sun-Thur,*
★ **Fifth Ave at Westlake (Westin Hotel)**　*6-11 Fri & Sat; Sun Brunch 10-2*
★ **Res: 624-7400**　　　　　　　　　　　　　　　*Expensive; Full bar; cc: AE, CB, DC, MC, V*

I5　The setting, in the Westin Hotel, is superb: four glass pavilions diminishing in size to one that holds a single table seating up to 12. All the glass and some imaginative lighting give the place two personalities: at night, intimacy with a certain sheen; for lunch, garden-like, with many potted palms and banks of pink-leaved caladiums bathed in outside light. Attention to detail—bottled water, silver crumb scoops, and so on—nearly unhinges some rough-and-ready Westerners who find it all pretentious. The cuisine is decidedly nouvelle and not always successful. A filet mignon with kiwi fruit and a blueberry sauce, for instance, seems silly. But other combinations are far more inviting: roast quail with goose liver in a juniper berry sauce; breast of duck stuffed with mushrooms and herbs, wrapped in grape leaves and served in a port sauce; roast loin of lamb with herbs and pink cherries. Salads at lunch are outstanding, and a fluffy seafood omelet comes in a perfect lobster sauce. Desserts are a disappointment, but the wine list is excellent.

★ **Panales**　　　　　　　　　*L 11:30-2:30 Tues-Fri; D 6-9 Thur-Sat;*
GG6　**2808 E Madison**　　　*closed Sun & Mon*
　　　Res: 325-7442　　　　　*Moderate; Beer & Wine*
　　　　　　　　　　　　　　　　　　cc: MC, V

Two friends who love to cook—one being Les Larsen, headmaster at The Bush School—and their spouses converted a house into a 30-seat country inn where they serve fixed-price dinners and light lunches. The fare is eclectic, an English mixed grill one week, for instance, and a Cajun jambalaya the next, and carefully done.

40

Homemade condiments, occasional live music, and spontaneous poetry from Nancy Larsen are special touches.

★ **Panchito's** N8 **704 First Ave** **Res: 343-9567**	*11-7 Mon-Fri; noon-7 Sat & Sun* *Inexpensive; Beer & Wine* *No credit cards*

It's hard to stand out from the general run of Tex-Mex restaurants, but this cafeteria in Pioneer Square does it by serving menudo, making its own chorizo and tamales, and preparing each dish with care instead of throwing things together and slopping sauce over the lot.

FF7 **Paul's Place** **4741 12th NE** **Res: 523-9812**	*L 11:30-2 Mon-Sat; D 5:30-10 Every day;* *Sun Brunch 10:30-2* *Expensive; Beer & Wine; cc: DC, MC, V*

This is a nouvelle cuisine Northern Italian place in the University District where the food is beautifully presented but has been disappointing in taste. Chef Paul Lee, nevertheless, is inventive and might improve with practice.

★ **Petit Cafe** EE6 **3410 NE 55th** **Res: 524-0819**	*5:30-10 Every day* *Moderate; Beer & Wine* *cc: MC, V*

Owner Abel Khemis, an Algerian, is moving to slightly larger quarters, which is unlikely to spoil the charm of his neighborhood French cafe. The menu here is surprisingly large, but Khemis copes by shortcuts such as offering duck in three sauces: peppercorn, raspberry, and chocolate. In addition to variations of French classics, there are North African touches such as couscous and Algerian wines.

★ **Phoenicia** ★ **4725 California Ave SW** JJ9 **Res: 935-8993**	*5-10 Tues-Thur, 5-11 Fri & Sat* *closed Sun & Mon* *Moderate; Wine; cc: MC, V*

A West Seattle storefront is an odd place for one of the best restaurants in the city. But owner-chef Hussein Khazaal has earned a solid reputation for his Middle Eastern cooking, with an accent on Lebanese. Kivvi (chopped raw lamb with bulgur), couscous with a lamb shank, a Balkan salad of greens, nuts, and bacon, and excellent desserts are among the items that lure diners here.

★ **The Pink Door** I8 **1919 Post Alley** **Res: 682-3241**	*L 11:30-2:30 Tues-Sat; 2:30-5:30 desserts;* *D 5:30-10 Tues-Sat; closed Sun & Mon* *Inexpensive lunch; Moderate dinner* *Beer & Wine; cc: MC, V*

This is a likeable trattoria, particularly at lunch, when it's packed with noisy patrons and the sunlight slants in from windows on Post Alley in the Pike Place Market. There are cheap Italian wines, pastas, a fountain burbling in the high-ceilinged room, a kitchen confident enough to serve polenta occasionally, and an owner, Jackie Roberts, brazen enough to protect her tablecloths with brown paper. But the food can be uneven in quality; the decor seems silly rather than eclectic; and there are only three entree choices available for candlelit dinners, when the menu is fixed-price for four courses. One of the choices always is cioppino, which, despite a thinness in taste, seems to be the house favorite. The others, which change weekly, generally are better. There are some good desserts and one great one: diplomatico, a chocolate-covered, rum-soaked cake surrounding chocolate mousse.

Restaurants

★ **Place Pigalle**
★ **Pike Place Market**
J8 **624-1756**

L 11:30-3:30 Mon-Fri, noon-3:30 Sat;
D 5:30-10 Mon-Thur, 5:30-11 Fri, 6-11 Sat;
Sat Brunch 10-noon; closed Sun
Moderate; Full bar; cc: MC, V

The kitchen is hitting its stride in this nicely styled Pike Place Market cafe with a great view of Elliott Bay. Menus at lunch and dinner are short and seasonal, with daily seafood and pasta specials and meat dishes such as lamb chops with applemint chutney and game hen with a skin stuffing of ricotta, Parmesan, and herbs. At lunch, the salads, such as squid and chicken-teriyaki, are understandably popular. Nice selection of beers and ales at the bar.

EE9 **Quinn's Fishmarket**
7001 Seaview Ave NW
Res: 784-4070

L 11:30-3 Mon-Sat; D 5:30-11 Mon-Thur,
5-11 Fri & Sat, 4-10 Sun; 10-2 Sun Brunch
4-10 Sun
Moderate; Full bar
cc: AE, MC, V

Overlooking the yacht basin at Shilshole Bay Marina, Quinn's offers a 41-foot salad bar, an in-house smoker for chicken, ribs, and salmon, overdone decor with lots of potted bamboo, and a bar-disco favored by the younger set. Stick with the smoked chicken and the simpler fish dishes. On Sundays, the salad bar is turned over to brunch.

★ **Quintana Roo**
303 Dayton St, Edmonds
Res: 778-9096

11:30-10 Every day
Moderate; Full bar
cc: AE, CB, DC, MC, V

This Tex-Mex house restaurant in Edmonds features a Texas-style beanless, tomatoless chili that won a state contest. Portions of most dishes are huge; a burrito, for example, will feed two. Care is taken with ingredients and preparation so that a chili relleno, say, is properly made with whipped eggwhites in the batter.

O7 **Rainier Pub**
210 S Washington
464-9773

11:30-2am Mon-Sat; closed Sun
Moderate; Full bar
cc: AE, MC, V

Music and a short menu of light fare attract the young to this small, modern tavern not far from the Kingdome. The food is limited to pastas, sandwiches, and steamed clams.

★ **raison d'etre**
★ **113 Virginia**
I7 **624-4622**

7am-1:30am Every day
Moderate; Wine; No credit cards

Service can be maddeningly inattentive and the light in some areas is insufficient for doing the crossword, but this still may be the best spot in town for a Europeanstyle breakfast. The room is done in gray and red, and sunlight floods the front. The espresso-machine operators are among the city's most skilled, brioche are big, fruits are beautiful, and egg dishes are outstanding. For lunch and dinner there are pates, salads, soups, and splendid desserts. In the evening, the menu includes hot specials such as game hen. A magazine rack invites lingering in the evenings.

★ **Rama House**
★ **2228 Second Ave**
G7 **624-2931**

11-10 Mon-Thur; 11-11 Fri; noon-11 Sat;
3-10 Sun
Inexpensive; Beer & Wine; cc: MC, V

Perhaps the best of the Thai restaurants in town, Rama House has excellent noodle dishes and a chicken curry in coconut milk that regulars order automatically. Thai salads can be disappointing, and Rama House's are no exception. But nearly everything else on the menu is delicious, especially the soups.

★ **Rasa Malaysia** *J8* **Pike Place Market** **624-8388**	*11-5:30 Mon-Sat; closed Sun* *Inexpensive; No alcohol* *No credit cards*
FF7 **4300 University Way NE** **545-7878**	*11-8 Mon-Sat; closed Sun*

The people you see in the Pike Place Market carrying steaming bowls of rice or noodles topped with Malaysian dishes such as five-spice chicken, vegetable curry, or sweet-and-sour pork have just come from this steam-table spot. There are a few tables, but many people take the food outside. Wansen Moore's simple but flavorful fare and her low prices took the Market by storm not long ago, and now she's opened a twin in the University District.

★ **Ray's Boathouse** *EE9* **6049 Seaview Ave NW** **Res: 789-3770**	*L 11:30-2:45 Mon-Fri; D 5-10:30* *Mon-Sat, 4-9:30 Sun* *Expensive; Full bar* *cc: AE, CB, DC, MC, V*

Probably as good a seafood place as exists in Seattle, Ray's takes care in selecting its fish and prepares them simply—broiled over mesquite charcoal, for instance. It also charges dearly for its superb Shilshole Bay setting. The upper bar, favored by sailors in their boating togs, is a great place to watch sunsets. The dining room is attractively done in polished woods and fabrics. There is a decent wine list, and salads and desserts are well prepared.

M8 **The Red Cabbage Restaurant** **75 Marion** **Res: 622-3822**	*L 11:30-3:30 Mon-Fri; D 5-10 Sun-Thur,* *5-11 Fri & Sat* *Moderate; Full bar* *cc: AE, CB, MC, V*

What's remarkable about this place is not its large and eclectic menu—Italian, French, Mexican, Russian, American, and so on—but its reasonably priced wine list that includes some true bargains on the French side. The large bar fills up in the evenings, particularly when there's a game on in the Kingdome.

II9 **The Restaurant Alki** **2716 Alki** **935-6550**	*9-10 Mon-Thur, 9-11 Fri, 8-10 Sat & Sun* *Moderate; Full bar* *cc: CB, MC, V*
GG7 **The Restaurant Queen Anne** **100 N Mercer (Hansen Baking Co)** **282-8558**	*11-midnight Mon-Fri; 9-midnight Sat; 9-9 Sun* *Moderate; Full bar* *cc: MC, V*

On the waterfront in West Seattle with a good view of Seattle's lights at night and of the passing parade in summer, this cafe serves breakfast all day as well as burgers, soups, and evening specials that lean to seafood. There's a companion place in the Hansen Bakery complex on Lower Queen Anne.

★ **Ristorante Pony** *GG7* **621½ Queen Anne Ave N** **Res: 283-8658**	*L 11-5 Tues-Fri, 11:30-5 Sat; D 5-midnight* *Tues-Sat, 5-11 Sun; closed Mon* *Moderate; Beer & Wine* *cc: MC, V*

Serving hearty, inventive dishes—not all of which are successful—this informal cafe attracts a regular clientele from its Lower Queen Anne neighborhood. Italian and Greek cooking predominate, although owner Lois Pierris includes dishes from other Mediterranean areas she has visited, including the Middle East and North

Restaurants

Africa. Daily specials, such as stuffed eggplant and sweet, fruity Turkish chicken borek, are the best bets, along with excellent homemade desserts. Among the latter, gelatabureko, a Greek confection of light custard flavored with cinnamon and baked in filo, should not be missed.

★ **Roanoke Exit** GG7 **2366 Eastlake E** **Res: 328-2775**	*B 7-11 Mon-Fri; L 11:30-2:30 Mon-Fri;* *D 5-10 Mon-Thur, 5-10:30 Fri & Sat,* *5-9 Sun; Sun Brunch 9-3* *Moderate; Full bar; cc: MC, V*

This has always been a nice spot for breakfast in the Eastlake area, especially since it may be the only place in town serving peanut-butter waffles. The lunch and dinner menus have been improved recently with the addition of pastas, steamed mussels, and a seafood special. Sunday brunch is served.

★ **Rosellini's Four-10** ★ **Fourth & Wall** E7 **Res: 624-5464**	*11-midnight Mon-Fri; 5-midnight Sat;* *3-8 Sun; Sun Brunch 11-3* *Expensive; Full bar* *cc: AE, CB, DC, MC, V*

Victor Rosellini is the dean of Seattle's restaurateurs, a superb host who skillfully arranges diners—most of them known to him—in his big restaurant on the edge of downtown. It is a lovely place, with a big bar favored by businesspeople for lunch, and the best waiter crew in town. The menu is continental: some Italian, some French, some indeterminate. The kitchen handles it unevenly, but you can't go wrong by ordering daily specials or the simpler preparations. Rosellini also arranges private lunches and dinners with skill and flair.

GG8 **Russets (unrated)** **2125 First Ave** **Res: 622-3663**	*L 11:30-2 Mon-Fri; D 6-10 Sun-Thur,* *5:30-11 Fri & Sat; Sun Brunch 11-3* *Expensive; Full bar; cc: AE, MC, V*

Opening too late to be reviewed, this large restaurant promises to be trendy but good. A spacious bar is on the street level; the dining room steps down in two levels toward Elliott Bay. Decor is all pastels and understated. The fare is light: pastas, salads such as olive-and-orange, grilled fish, duck in fruit sauce, fish stews, and rack of lamb with a sage hollandaise. Head chef Ted Furst once cooked at the late, lamented Manor House on Bainbridge Island, where the food occasionally was excellent.

★ **Saigon over the Counter** J8 **Pike Place Market** **622-6301**	*11-6 Mon-Sat; closed Sun* *Inexpensive; No alcohol* *No credit cards*

Pham Phuong is known, and loved, as "Lucy" in the Pike Place Market, where she and her delightful family serve simple, and simply delicious, Vietnamese food over-the-counter. The menu is short: a few salads such as bun bo sao (beef and noodles), a vegetarian special such as sauteed tofu and vegetables, entrees such as broiled sweet-and-sour chicken, and spring rolls.

★ **Saleh al Lago** ★ **6804 E Green Lake Way N** ★ **Res: 524-4044** EE7	*L 11:30-2:30 Mon-Fri; D 5:30-10:30* *Mon-Thur, 5:30-11 Fri & Sat; closed Sun* *(Light meals until midnight)* *Moderate; Full bar; cc: AE, CB, DC, MC, V*

Across the street from Green Lake, Saleh Joudeh, a Syrian who studied medicine in the central Italian city of Perugia, pays homage to the first of his two adopted countries by putting out some of the best Italian food in Seattle. The restaurant is small but nicely divided into a tile-floored cafe next to the windows and a raised, carpeted dining room. The former, ideal for a drink, snack, or late-night dessert and espresso, has white metal chairs. The latter has bentwood chairs with burgundy seats and is done in soft grays, blues, apricots, and off-whites. Over all there is a pink glow from the neon "cocktails" sign above the little bar. Joudeh says the cuisine from the theater kitchen is Central Italian—heavier and spicier than Northern. It's certainly done carefully and beautifully. The menu is short and includes veal with mushrooms or fresh sage that is unsurpassed in this city. Pastas are also exceptional. Saltimbocca is done Roman-style, with prosciutto and fresh sage. Among other delights is a flavorful fileto al piccantino, beef tenderloin with anchovies, capers, and tomato sauce. Service is attentive and the wine list decent.

★ **Santa Fe Cafe**	*L 11-2 Tues-Sat; D 5-10 Mon-Sat;*
EE6 **2255 NE 65th**	*Sun Brunch 9-2*
524-7736	*Inexpensive; Beer & Wine; cc: MC, V*

New Mexican cooking began with the Pueblo Indians. Its modern version, based on green and red chiles, is authentically prepared here. The menu is modest: try posole, a hominy-pork stew in red chile sauce, and the blue corn tortillas. On Sundays there's an extensive French-style brunch. The cafe is nicely done in blue and white, with track lights focused on paintings of Eastern Washington that are remarkably reminiscent of New Mexico.

Scandia Cafe	*8-2:15 Mon-Fri; 8-3 Sat; closed Sun*
Pike Place Market	*Inexpensive; No alcohol*
I8 **623-6422**	*No credit cards*

There's little of Scandinavia in this plain Pike Place Market cafe: pickled herring with boiled potatoes and Swedish pancakes with lingonberries and whipped cream are the only evidence, among the American breakfasts and sandwiches. But the pancakes alone bring people in.

BB6 **Seafood Shanty of Singapore**	*11-10 Mon-Sat; 4-9:30 Sun*
17549 15th Ave NE	*Inexpensive; Beer & Wine*
365-3474	*cc: MC, V*

There's an adult bookstore next door, and a menu that ranges from burgers to American-style seafood to Cantonese to Szechuan. But this small, cheerful place is noteworthy nonetheless because it has Singapore-style seafood dishes, including the famed chili crab. Spicing is overdone, so don't ask for too many stars.

★ **Settebello**	*D 5:30-11:30 Mon-Sat; closed Sun*
★ **1525 E Olive Way**	*Expensive; Full bar*
★ **Res: 323-7772**	*cc: AE, DC, MC, V*
★	

HH7 Italian-born Luciano Bardinelli, slender, handsome, and prematurely white-haired, managed restaurants in Las Vegas, Los Angeles, and San Francisco—including Hugh Hefner's exquisitely "in" club, Touch—before opening his own dazzlingly modern place on Capitol Hill. Immediately it became a magnet for the fashionable as well as for those longing to taste the cuisine of the '80s: Northern Italian. Some of the fashionable have faded away, and Settebello (the "beautiful seven" of the Italian card game scopa) is much the better. You won't have to wait 45 minutes for your reserved table, for instance. And, after shuffling through several chefs, Bardinelli again took control of the kitchen, with the aid of George V-trained Frenchman Patrick Sabourin. Now, with several imitators in town, Bardinelli is moving away from his set menu of pastas, grills, and sautes to nuova cucina dishes such as tiny Florida Bay scallops in a saffron-cream sauce, cold mussels in an orange mayonnaise, sweetbreads with peppers and cream, and veal stuffed with

Restaurants

fontina and prosciutto. He has not abandoned his superb homemade pastas. But even on that side of the menu, the specials—eggplant lasagna, for example, or linguini with white truffles and porcini—are the real treats. Bardinelli also serves heartier fare: osso bucco, say, and tripe. Gelati here, especially the fruits in their own skins, are the town's best. Though some carp about the wine prices, the list is extremely well chosen and particularly strong on Italian reds. Service is excellent. And there are other delights: espresso-chocolate-liqueur cappuccino, home-fried potato chips, zuppa Inglese. Dinner can be expensive, but pastas and salads are moderately priced.

★ **Shanghai**
HH3 **150 105th Ave NE, Bellevue**
455-3226

L 11:30-2:30 Mon-Fri; D 5-9:30
Mon-Thur, 5-10:30 Fri & Sat; closed Sun
Moderate; No alcohol; cc: AE, MC, V

The menu combines Shanghai, Mandarin, and Szechuan, but the real attraction in this Bellevue spot is the Shanghai fare. Baotze, for example, is an appetizer of steamed pastries filled with ground pork that is served nowhere else in this area. With a day's notice you can get yellowfish braised in soy and ginger. And there are other notable dishes available, such as crisp duck with butterfly rolls and shrimp with lobster sauce.

GG8 **Shortztop Cafe**
5109 Shilshole Ave NW
782-5539

B 6:30-11 Tues-Fri, 7:30-2 Sat, 8-2 Sun;
L 11-4:30 Tues-Sun; D 4:30-9 Tues-Sat;
closed Mon
Moderate; Beer & Wine
cc: MC, V

A large, clean, well-lighted place in an industrial section of Ballard, the Shortztop has a huge menu, a strong breakfast-and-lunch following, and a harmless baseball theme. Dinners are ordinary. But the many burgers, omelets, sandwiches, and salads are tasty and come in union-hall portions.

L6 **Shuckers (Four Seasons)**
Fourth & University
Res: 621-1700

L 11-2:30 Mon-Sat, D 5-11 Mon-Sat, 4-11 Sun
Moderate; Full bar
cc: AE, CB, DC, MC, V

This seafood bar, in the Four Seasons Olympic, changes its menu daily to reflect the fresh fish available. But its most notable items are two constants: Irish soda bread muffins and a slightly sweet geoduck stew. They get decent oysters on the half shell, but the fish preparations are inconsistent.

R6 **Silver Dragon**
421 Seventh Ave S
Res: 622-4141

L 11-3 Every day; D 4-11 Mon-Thur &
Sun, 4-1 Fri-Sat
Moderate; Full bar; cc: MC, V

A large, somewhat garishly spiffy Cantonese restaurant in the International District, Silver Dragon has a huge menu with many decent dishes—crab in black-bean sauce, for example. Oddly, for a Chinese place, it also has a large dessert selection, including Asian choices such as egg tart but also featuring Western selections such as cherries jubilee. For lunch, the menu is supplemented by a dim sum cart.

★ **Simon's**
OO5 **17401 Southcenter Pky, Tukwila**
Res: 575-3500

L 11-2:30 Mon-Fri; D 5:30-10:30
Mon-Thur, 5:30-11:30 Fri & Sat,
5-10 Sun
Expensive; Full bar; cc: AE, DC, MC, V

A snazzy place, but understated, Simon's is an updated version of the classic American steak-and-seafood house. Some of the seafood is frozen; what's fresh is done simply and well. The main attractions, however, are the large, classy bar and the dining-room decor, which includes a solarium with lots of greenery, copper light fixtures, dark wicker chairs, and pink linen.

★ I16	**South China** **2714 Beacon Ave S** Res: 329-5085	*11-2am Mon-Sat; 3-midnight Sun* *Inexpensive; Full bar* *cc: MC, V*

A non-greasy sweet-and-sour pork, fine almond chicken, and such daily specials as steamed rock cod with two types of ginger, including the sweet preserved type, are some of the dishes that make this large, neighborly Beacon Hill place one of the better Cantonese restaurants in town.

C6	**Space Needle & Top of the Needle** **Seattle Center** 447-3100	*L 11-3; D 4:30-10:30 Every day;* *Sun Brunch 10:30-3* *Expensive; Full bar* *cc: AE, CB, DC, MC, V*
C6	**Wheedle's** **Seattle Center**	*L 11-3; D 4-10:30 Every day;* *Sun Brunch 10:30-3* *Moderate; Full bar; cc: AE, CB, DC, MC, V* *(open Memorial Day to Labor Day only)*

Two and a half restaurants occupy part of this symbol of Seattle's World's Fair. On the mid-level is Wheedle's (named for a children's-book character), which is open from Memorial Day to Labor Day and serves sandwiches, salads, and desserts, mostly to tourists. The revolving top level contains the Space Needle Restaurant, which draws both tourists and locals celebrating special occasions. Salmon—broiled, poached, sauteed, and in two other forms as appetizers—is the principal attraction. Dinners are expensive, but there is a cheaper daily special. Finally, sectioned off from the Space Needle Restaurant by draped fabric, is the small Top of the Needle, which caters to business people with visitors, and better-heeled tourists. The fare here is a couple of dollars more than next door and includes lamb, veal, chicken, beef, and seafood. Quality is spotty.

★	**Streamliner Diner** **397 Winslow Way E, Bainbridge Island** 842-8595	*B 7-11 Mon-Fri, 8-3 Sat, 8-2 Sun;* *L 11-4 Mon-Fri, noon-4 Sat* *Moderate; Beer & Wine; cc: MC, V*

This steamy, noisy diner is the only culinary excuse for visiting Bainbridge Island. Located in the heart of little Winslow, within easy walking distance of the ferry terminal, the Streamliner is particularly attractive for weekend breakfasts. Lunches are soups, salads, and quiches. The breakfast fare is standard, too, but nicely done and served in ample portions: buttermilk waffles with real maple syrup are a special attraction. There are fresh baked goods, such as scones and muffins, homemade hot and cold cereals, huge omelets, fried potatoes with onions and lots of parika, and fruit-juice "smoothies."

EE9	**Stuart's at Shilshole** **6135 Seaview Ave NW** Res: 784-7974	*L 11:30-3 Mon-Fri; D 5:30-10 Sun-Thur,* *5:30-11 Fri, Sat; Sat, Sun Brunch 10-3* *Expensive; Full bar* *cc: AE, CB, MC, V*

The spectacularly beautiful failure of Stuart Anderson, of Black Angus steakhouse fame, to create a grand waterfront seafood place. The huge multi-level, Northwest-modern restaurant offers wonderful daytime views of Shilshole Bay and the Olympics. If you must dine here, stick to the steaks; the seafood isn't worth half the price.

GG7	**Sundays** **620 First Ave N** Res: 284-0456	*D 5-9 Tues-Thur & Sun, 5-10 Fri & Sat;* *Sun Brunch 9:30-2* *Expensive; Full bar* *cc: AE, MC, V*

A hushed atmosphere characterizes this palmy place in the Hansen Baking complex on Lower Queen Anne. It's no wonder; the building used to be a church. The menu is strictly up-to-date: many seafood sautes, some veal and chicken dishes, a rack of lamb, a steak, and a pasta. Sunday brunch is also served.

★ **The Surrogate Hostess** *6am-10pm Mon & Tues; 6am-11pm Wed-Sun*
GG6 **746 19th Ave E** *Moderate; Wine*
324-1944 *No credit cards*

Robin Woodward now serves late suppers of omelets, pastas, and pates at her busy Capitol Hill cafe. That means some of the regulars who love to linger at the long wood tables over a newspaper or a conversation can remain from dawn to nearly midnight. There are hearty breakfasts, lunches of salads, quiches, and hot specials, light dinners of mixed ethnic fare such as cassoulet and moussaka, baked goods and coffee, and suppers. It's a relaxed place, sort of a nutritional, no-smoking coffeehouse.

P7 **Swannie's** *L 11:30-5 Every day; D 5-10 Sun-Thur,*
222 S Main *5-1am Fri & Sat*
622-9353 *Moderate; Full bar; cc: AE, MC, V*

Professional athletes from the nearby Kingdome, especially baseball players, hang out here. The food is ordinary, but the jocks draw a young and noisy set to the bar.

R6 **Tai Tung** *10-3am Mon-Sat; 10-1:30am Sun*
655 S King *Inexpensive; Full bar*
622-7372 *No credit cards*

Try sorting through the array of daily specials and you might hit upon an exceptional dish. Otherwise, the Cantonese fare is only slightly above average, even though this huge place, with its lengthy menu and crack waiters, continues to be the busiest restaurant in the International District.

FF7 **Teriyaki Sagano** *L 11:30-2 Mon-Fri; D 5-9 Mon-Thur,*
4718 University Way NE *5-10 Fri & Sat; closed Sun*
Res: 525-1060 *Moderate; Beer & Wine*
  cc: AE, CB, DC, MC, V

Owner Yasuko Suzuki must be the nicest, gentlest restaurateur in town. She waits tables in her little University District cafe while the kitchen turns out simple Japanese fare such as teriyaki and tempura; there are also some worthy specials, such as sauteed spinach and squid.

★ **Thanh Lan** *11-9 Tues-Fri; 9-9 Sat & Sun; closed Mon*
I16 **2820 Empire Way S** *Inexpensive; No alcohol*
721-5067 *No credit cards*

Lan Di Hall, a woman of grace and good cheer, caters to the extensive Southeast Asian immigrant community in the South End. Thus, adjacent to the restaurant is a room of video games, pinball machines, and Vietnamese pool tables (no pockets). Her inexpensive Vietnamese country-style cooking is as authentic as the pool tables. Specialties are two rice-noodle soups, one of which includes pork liver and the other pork liver and heart, along with ingredients such as quail eggs and dried squid. For non-Asians, the cooks will automatically substitute chicken and shrimp for such exotica; so if you want to dine truly, insist on Vietnamese style.

F3 **Thirteen Coins** *Open 24 hours Every day*
125 Boren Ave N *Moderate; Full bar*
682-2513 *cc: AE, DC, MC, V*
O06 **18000 Pacific Hwy S (across from SeaTac)**
243-9500 *(same as above)*

Around-the-clock dining and classy short-order food have made these twin diners popular for many years. There are high-backed stools along the counters and private booths. Grill cooks work in the open, turning out sandwiches, salads, and a long list of pastas, fish, and meat dishes. Portions are huge, and some dishes—sweetbreads, for instance, and the daily special—can be quite tasty.

FF7	**Tien Tsin** **1401 N 45th** **Res: 634-0223**	*L 11:45-2 Mon-Fri; D 5-9:45 Mon-Thur,* *5-10:45 Fri, 4-10:45 Sat, 4-9:45 Sun* *Inexpensive; Beer & Wine; cc: MC, V*

Inconsistency in producing a mixture of Northern Chinese cuisines makes it risky to eat at this plain place. But some dishes can be quite good, and it's worth seeking the waiter's advice.

A5 008	★ **Toshi's Teriyaki** ★ **372 Roy** **282-0393** **9211 Holman NW** **784-0798**	*L 11:30-2:30 Tues-Fri; D 5-8:30 Tues-Thur,* *5-9 Fri & Sat; closed Sun & Mon* *Inexpensive; Beer & Saki; No credit cards* *(same as above)*

This drafty little place near the Seattle Center has the shortest menu in town: chicken and beef teriyaki and chicken curry. But the prices are low, the teriyaki is extremely well prepared, and it's served with a good sesame-oil-flavored salad and a heap of sticky rice.

H5	★ **Trader Vic's** ★ **1900 Fifth Ave (Westin Hotel)** **Res: 624-8520**	*L 11:30-2 Mon-Sat; D 5:30-10:30 Mon-Sat,* *5:30-9:30 Sun* *Expensive; Full bar* *cc: AE, CB, DC, MC, V*

This local outlet of the small national chain, located in the Westin Hotel, faithfully follows Trader Vic's formula: fancy bar concoctions, Oriental appetizers, and a peculiar mix of Polynesian, Chinese, and French cuisine. Meats from the Chinese ovens, such as lamb, beef, chicken, pork, and squab, are reliably excellent. But the best way to dine is to seek advice from maitre d'hotel Harry Wong, a master of his room, his regular guests, and the menu.

N8	★ **Trattoria Mitchelli** **84 Yesler Way** **Res: 623-3885**	*7am-4am Mon-Fri; 8am-4am Sat;* *9am-10pm Sun* *Moderate; Full bar; cc: AE, MC, V*

Opinions diverge widely about this Italian cafe, but there's no denying it's popular. And it's open until 4am, a service to people seeking a late supper, dessert and coffee, or just a spot to be among others. One opinion holds that the mediocre food—pastas, sauteed dishes, etc.—and the spotty, sometimes condescending service make "The Trat" intolerable. The other overlooks those shortcomings and finds the place lively and fun, full of interesting characters. Truth lies somewhere between.

H6	★ **Trattoria Pagliacci** **426 Broadway E** **322-3326**	*11:30-10 Mon-Thur, 11:30-11 Fri & Sat,* *4-10 Sun* *Inexpensive; Beer & Wine* *cc: AE, CB, DC, MC, V*

This spot caught on quickly with the young set that roams the Broadway District. Lunches are cafeteria-style, with pizza (by the slice, too), a daily pasta, and calzone. For dinner, the menu expands with the addition of several more pasta dishes, all prepared in a theater kitchen. You can sit at a counter or dine a touch more formally in the back. Service is quick and cheerful.

★ **Umberto's**
P9 100 S King
Res: 621-0575

L 11:30-2:30 Mon-Fri; D 5:30-11 Every day
Expensive; Full bar
cc: AE, MC, V

When Umberto Menghi, the pasta king of Vancouver, B.C. established his first south-of-the-border outpost near the Kingdome, the restaurant was jammed by eager diners. The response seemed to overwhelm the kitchen, for the fare here has not been at the level of Umberto's Canadian restaurants. Still, it's possible to have a decent meal by asking for fresh pasta dishes only, specifying what antipasti you want (avoid the odd selection of cold pasta salads), and sticking to the simpler veal dishes and the daily fresh fish.

FF7 **The Unicorn**
4550 University Way NE
634-1115

11:30-9 Mon-Sat; 12:30-8:30 Sun
Moderate; Beer & Wine
cc: MC, V

English pubs are appealing, English food is less so. But this University District place reverses those verities. The cold, boxy room is charmless, but the food—Scotch eggs, meat pies, curried shrimp, beef and Yorkshire pudding, and so on—is better than the setting. A good selection of bottled British brews is available, too.

★ **Union Bay Cafe**
FF6 3505 NE 45th
Res: 527-8364

L 11-2:30 Tues-Fri; D 5-10 Tues-Thur,
5-10:30 Fri & Sat; Sat & Sun Brunch
9-2:30; closed Mon
Inexpensive; Beer & Wine; No credit cards

Soups, salads, mixed ethnic specials, and a fish and pasta of the day mark this as another Northwest Modern lunch spot manned by earnest cooks with a concern for freshness and lightness. The menu expands a little at night, with specials such as breast of chicken in cashew and basil butter topped with fontina.

★ **Uruapan**
BB7 900 N 160th Ave
362-8725

11:30-10 Mon-Fri, 11:30-9 Sat, noon-8 Sun
Inexpensive; Beer & Wine
cc: MC, V

A little, family-run Mexican restaurant in the North End named after the hometown of owner Lupe Peach, this Mexican-Uruapan restaurant offers all the standard fare plus some good and unusual dishes. One, birria, seems unique to Seattle: it's a beef-and-tongue stew flavored with laurel. Others include menudo, posole (a hominy-pork soup), and a good chicken mole poblano.

★ **Vaersgo**
★ 2200 NW Market
FF8 782-8286

10-10:30 Tues-Sat; closed Sun & Mon
Moderate; Full bar
cc: MC, V

Lively at lunch, sober at dinner, this Danish-modern place lends distinction to Ballard, the center of Seattle's large Scandinavian community. There's a good selection of Scandinavian beers and akvavits, but the main attraction is the cooking of Ingeborg Kisbye, a cigar-smoking septuagenarian. The menu is bewildering but actually somewhat limited, with beautiful open-faced sandwiches, omelets, and such Danish classics as roast pork stuffed with apples, and prunes and meatballs in a silken mahogany sauce. The red cabbage and house cucumber-dill salad dressing are superb.

★ **Vietnam**
J4 914 E Pike
322-4080

11-11 Mon-Fri; 11-midnight Sat; noon-10 Sun
Inexpensive; No alcohol
cc: MC, V

Sadly, this small, family-run restaurant on Capitol Hill has never gotten the attention it deserves. The Vietnamese cooking, with its overtones of French cuisine, is quite good. And certain dishes, such as boned chicken wings stuffed with forcemeat, are outstanding.

M4 **Vito's**
927 Ninth Ave
Res: 682-2695

9am-12:30am Mon-Sat; closed Sun
Moderate; Full bar
cc: MC, V

This is a longtime hangout for Seattle's sporting crowd. The bar and dining room are comfortably done in dark wood and maroon banquettes. The menu has an Italian flavor, plus steaks and seafoods. Cooking is homestyle, and the waitresses greet regulars as family.

★ **Washington Post Cafe**
N8 **88 Yesler Way**
Res: 625-0696

L 11:30-2 Mon-Fri; D 5:30-10 Wed-Thur,
5:30-11 Fri & Sat; Sat & Sun Brunch 9-2
Moderate; Beer & Wine; cc: MC, V

A good spot for a weekend brunch—try the pecan waffles—this basement-level spot lets the Pioneer Square sun shine in through a street-level glass wall. It's busy at lunch, when salads, a soup, a quiche, a fish in, say, fennel-dill sauce, and pastas are served. Dinners are along the same line: light and with a Mediterranean touch.

★ **Woerne's European Cafe**
★ **4108 University Way NE**
FF7 **632-7893**

9-6 Tues-Wed, 9-midnight Thur-Sat;
closed Sun & Mon
Moderate; Beer & Wine; cc: MC, V

Three nights a week this University District lunch–pastry shop puts out excellent dinners with a German accent. Chef Beth Hammermeister changes the menu seasonally, but there are always beautiful cold plates such as chicken-and-ham pate, and spinach with oranges, mushrooms, fennel, pecans, and currants. The hot-dish side of the menu is short, but each dish is carefully prepared and served in the gentlest manner by soft-spoken waitresses. There will be two soups, a pasta, an omelet or two, and, say, sauerbraten and chicken paprika. Wines are inexpensive, and desserts are elaborately enticing but disappointing in taste.

★ **The Wok**
N2 **1301 Columbia St**
324-9488

L 11:30-3 Mon-Thur, 11-3 Fri; D 3-10
Mon-Thur, 3-11 Fri, 4-11 Sat; closed Sun
Moderate; Full bar
cc: MC, V

After establishing a reputation as perhaps Seattle's finest Chinese restaurant, The Wok's management broke up suddenly. The keys to The Wok's former reputation were the brothers Ma, cook Andy and frontman Jemmy. They're gone now, to their own place, Andy and Jemmy's Wok, near the Northgate shopping center. Still, the Szechuan-Hunan-Mandarin menu remains the same here, and Andy's second cook, John Yeh, is in the kitchen, so all is not lost.

★ **Yangtze Szechwan**
H1 **130 156th NE, Bellevue**
747-2404

L 11-2:30 Every day; D 5-10 Mon-Thur &
Sun, 5-11 Fri & Sat
Moderate; Full bar; cc: AE, CB, DC, MC, V

The kitchen, particularly at lunch, performs unevenly in this Eastside Chinese place that stands out amid a plethora of shopping-center fast-food spots. But a large party can dine well on Peking duck or other special dishes by ordering in advance and seeking the advice of owner Paul Yang.

J9 **Yung Ya**
4847 California Ave SW
Res: 935-9200

L 11:30-2:30 Mon-Fri; D 4:30-10:30
Mon-Thur, & Sun, 4:30-11:30 Fri & Sat
Moderate; Full bar; cc: MC, V

There are Cantonese, Shanghai, Szechuan, and American items on the menu here, indicating that this pleasant place in West Seattle has to cater to its neighborhood's

51

Restaurants

tastes. The room has a Spanish feel—brick and wood paneling, with hanging pots of dried flowers. Such dishes as Szechuan prawns are well prepared.

Other restaurants
Breakfast places in "Top 200"

A la Francaise	Hi-Spot Cafe	raison d'etre
Athenian	Julia's 14 Carrot Cafe	Restaurant Alki
Cafe Botanica	Lion O'Reilly's & BJ Monkeyshines	Restaurant Queen Anne
Cause Celebre		Shortztop Cafe
Costas	Madison Park Cafe	Streamliner Diner
Eggs Cetera	Malia's Northwest	Surrogate Hostess
Hector's	Maximilien	

Other breakfast places

O8 **The Bakery** 214 First S *622-3644*

If you are exploring Pioneer Square around breakfast time, drop into the Grand Central Arcade for the Bakery's popular crusty, honey-sweetened cinnamon rolls. Fruit, eggs, juice, and coffee are also served up cafeteria-style.

EE7 **Beth's Cafe** 7311 Aurora N *782-5588*

Open 24 hours a day, this little hole-in-the-wall cafe has developed a solid reputation for its gigantic omelets. Best time to go is with a large group at the end of a night's carousing—midnight snack, early breakfast?

GG7 **Burnie's Cafe** 8 W Boston *284-7081*

Burnie's Cafe is the sort of place that gives humble hashbrowns a good name: they're fried to a nice, crunchy crisp. Very fruity blueberry pancakes, home-style, thick-cut bread for toast, and omelets packed with fresh vegetables (watch out for raw onions) also say this is a place that cares about breakfast. And doesn't stop caring: the same breakfast menu is served all hours.

EE7 **Greenlake Jake's** 7918 E Green Lake Dr N *523-4747*

Blueberry muffin lovers swear by this short-order spot, which also serves the usual eggs and fries and such.

J8 **Lowell's** Pike Place Market *622-2036*

If you're in the Market early you may want to try their plain, solid breakfast served buffet style. You have a great choice of views: the second floor overlooks the Market stalls, the third commands a panorama of the Sound.

L8 **Mikado Fish & Tempura Company** Post Alley at Spring *622-0659*

Authentic Japanese-style breakfasts (noodles in broth, raw eel, raw-egg melanges, etc.) are served from 7:30; also American fare.

EE7 **Phinney Ridge Cafe** 6412 Phinney Ave N *782-1222*

Restaurants

A North End breakfast institution. A Phinney Ridge cinnamon roll and omelet, taken together in the morning, are like a "Godzilla Meets King Kong" flick, a collision of titanic forces. You can also nip the hair of the dog here over the Sunday papers.

EE7 **Val's Cafe**   6020 Phinney Ave N   *784-7666*

Down-home breakfast cooking on Phinney Ridge.

Selected brunch places from "Top 200"

JJ9 **Alaska Junction**   4548 California SW   *937-1800*

Quiches, omelets, crepes, pastas, in one of West Seattle's better restaurants. Moderate.

FF7 **The America's Cup**   1900 N Northlake Way   *633-0161*

A large fixed-price buffet including meat, fish, and egg dishes, with a view of Lake Union. Moderate.

EE3 **Anthony's Home Port**   135 Lake St, Kirkland   *822-0225*

Crepes, omelets, seafoods, at three waterfront locations. Moderate.

GG6 **Cafe Botanica**   4021 E Madison   *329-9015*

Superb espresso, fruit salad, salmon mousse, a special egg dish, home-baked goods in a garden-like Madison Park cafe. Moderate.

L6 **Georgian Room**   *621-1700*
411 University (Four Seasons Olympic)

A lavish fixed-price buffet of pates, lamb, fish, omelets, fruits, and fresh baked goods. Expensive. Reservations required.

FF9 **Hiram's at-the-Locks**   5300 34th NW   *784-1733*

Crepes, omelets, fruit plates, scones, plus a grand view of the yachting set negotiating the Ship Canal's locks. Moderate.

Le Bonaparte   *878-4412*
PP7 S 216th & Marine View Dr, Des Moines

Five French-accented courses plus champagne at a fixed price in a classy house-restaurant. Expensive.

Lion O'Reilly's & B.J. Monkeyshines
GG7 132 Broadway E   *322-1710*

A long menu, an omelet-crepe bar, and the Broadway District singles crowd. Moderate.

The Palm Court   *624-7400*
H5 Fifth Ave & Westlake (Westin Hotel)

Five courses at a fixed price, including egg dishes, steaks, and chops. Expensive.

EE9 **Quinn's Fishmarket**   7001 Seaview Ave NW   *784-4070*

A 41-foot fixed-price buffet, with a full view of the Shilshole Bay Marina. Moderate.

H8 **Russet's**   2125 First Ave   *622-3663*

Seafood souffle, mousses, omelets, fresh baked goods, in understated elegance with

53

Restaurants

a view of Elliott Bay. Moderate.

| EE6 | **Santa Fe Cafe** | 2255 NE 65th | 524-7736 |

Crepes, blintzes, quiches, fresh baked goods, and French-style specials, in a small neighborhood cafe. Moderate.

| GG7 | **Sundays** | 620 First Ave N | 284-0456 |

Prime rib hash, Belgian waffles, and other exotica, in a lovely converted church. Expensive.

| N8 | **Washington Post Cafe** | 88 Yesler Way | 625-0696 |

Omelets, pancakes, lovely waffles, in a sunny basement setting. Moderate.

Soup, salad, & sandwich restaurants in "Top 200"

brusseau's	*Elliott Bay Cafe*	Madison Park Cafe
Cafe Society	*J & M Cafe*	Wheedle's
Costas	*Last Exit on Brooklyn*	

Other soup, salad, & sandwich restaurants

| N7 | **Bakeman's Restaurant** | 615 Second Ave | 622-3375 |

Holder of the world record for the greatest turkey sandwich, Bakeman's is an institution well loved by Seattle's office workers, who form fast-moving lines there every day waiting for the delectable sandwiches (on homemade bread) made of big honest chunks of dark or light roast turkey, roast beef, or other delicacies. Fine soups, too. Eat in or take out.

| O8 | **The Bakery** | 214 First Ave S | 622-3644 |

A variety of filling sandwiches made on their own bread.

City Picnics
| L6 | 412 Spring | | 682-8183 |
| O8 | 117 S Main | | 682-2067 |

Tasty, fat sandwiches served on homemade breads. Also quiches, soups, and delicious bakery items.

| FF7 | **50th Street Deli and Cafe** | | |
| | 5000 University Way NE | | 525-3676 |

Offers a range of tasty soups, salads, and sandwiches in a sunny corner in the U District. Several hot dishes as well.

| FF7 | **The Fremont Cafe** | 3508 Fremont Pl | 634-2350 |

The Fremont Cafe is a semi-flashy incarnation of the longtime Tommy's Cafe; post-modern purple vinyl and neon wall-art mix surprisingly well with the basically all-American-lunchstand decor. Simple and inexpensive hearty burgers, good soup and salad, excellent carrot cake and pies.

The Nooner
| GG2 | 13804 NE 20th | | 747-1927 |
| HH3 | 233 Bellevue Way NE, Bellevue | | 453-1010 |

A pair of unpretentiously satisfying sandwich shops, these are good lunch-break places during a day of midweek mall shopping. Favored by business lunchers. Some breakfast items.

Olive's East	(3 locations)	

This used to be one of the very few places on the Eastside where one could get a decent cup of coffee and tasty pastries. It has since flourished in the Folgers-flooded suburbs and is turning into something of a chain, with sandwiches, quiches, and other light-meal dishes.

7 | **The Snug** | 1414 Second Ave | 682-4303

Tasty, large salads and thick sandwiches are some of the offerings served up at this friendly downtown spot—cozy in winter, and opened onto the street in summer.

8 | **The Soup and Salad** | Pike Place Market | 623-5700

A delightful luncheon spot tucked downstairs in the Market and overlooking the Sound, The Soup and Salad has a mouthwatering array of salads such as shrimp and spinach, marinated vegetables, and fruit and nut. Tasty homemade soup, quiche, and baked goods as well.

K7 | **Soupourri** | 216 University | 292-9184

Well-lighted little cafe serving delicious soups and salads at great prices.

EE7 | **Sunlight Cafe** | 6403 Roosevelt Way NE | 522-9060

Sprouty sandwiches and salads served by friendly counterculture types. They also offer delicious weekend brunches, including tasty sesame crunch, wholewheat waffles.

J8 | **Three Girls Bakery** | Pike Place Market | 622-1045

A Market institution, The Three Girls Bakery serves up very hearty soup and sandwich fare in addition to its pastries. If you're lucky, you'll get a seat at the crowded snack bar; otherwise you'll have to settle for takeout. Good prices.

FF6 | **Truffles** | 3701 NE 45th | 522-3016

Freshly made deli sandwiches, pates, and salads to go or to eat in the cheerful little cafe. Great place to stop for supplies along the Burke Gilman Trail. Also makes up a variety of delectable picnic baskets to suit every taste or pocketbook.

"Top 200" pizza places

Italo's
Trattoria Pagliacci

Other pizza places

J5 | **Abruzzi** | 604 Pike | 624-8122

Authentic, old-fashioned pizza for purists.

J8 | **Bugsy's** | Pike Place Market | 682-1673

Very thick, tasty pizza served up in an attractive Market cafe. Expensive. Lovely view over Elliott Bay (somewhat compromised by recent construction).

Restaurants

J8	**De Laurenti's**	**Pike Place Market**	*622-0141*

A quick slice of street pizza in the Market, good on the run.

FF7	**Godfather's** (plus six other locations)	**4524 University Way NE**	*633-0955*

Chicago-style deep-dish pizza—don't argue with the cook.

FF7	**Hungry U**	**5517 Roosevelt Way NE**	*524-7323*

Good pizza in something of a time capsule—an outpost of the '60s Berkeley culture. Heavy on the raw vegetables.

FF7	**Morningtown**	**4110 Roosevelt Way NE**	*632-6317*

Emma Goldman eats here. Whole-grain urban-collective pizzas and submarine sandwiches are the fare. Good selection of teas. Law students cram (the UW Law School is a block away) under "Eat the Rich" and "Question Authority" posters.

FF7	**Northlake Tavern**	**660 NE Northlake Way**	*633-5317*

An institution. A windowless tavern stuffed with behemoth pizzas and beer in quantity. Often a long wait, as phone-in orders are popular.

GG7	**Olympia Pizza & Spaghetti House**	**500 Queen Anne N**	*285-5550*

For lovers of thin-crust, New York-style pizza, this little place on top of the counterbalance on Queen Anne offers the best in Seattle.

FF7	**Piccolo's**	**5301 Roosevelt Way NE**	*522-8828*

Heavy on the sprouts. The decor is late-dungeon.

HH7	**Piecora's**	**1401 E Madison**	*322-9411*

Good new spot for New York-style, thin-crust pizza. Bring your own atmosphere.

G2	**Tony's**	**101 John**	*284-4878*

Chicago-style pizza. Goes down well with Chianti.

"Top 200" hamburger places

Original Ellen's
Deluxe Bar & Grill
Leschi Lake Cafe

Other hamburger places

GG6	**The Attic**	**4226 E Madison**	*323-3131*

Delivers the kind of solid, basic burger that more taverns should offer.

GG6	**Canterbury Ale & Eats**	**534 15th E**	*322-3130*

If you can ignore the styrofoam Tudor beams and the legendary inept service, the Canterbury offers big sloppy burgers at reasonable prices in a setting that is just bizarre enough that you can easily feel at home.

G7	**Daly's**	2713 Eastlake E	322-1918
G8		2201 15th W	283-7733

Juicy, cheap burgers and good fries.

FF7	**Dick's**	111 NE 45th	632-5125
	(plus four other locations)		

A local 1950s-style chain, they offer the best and among the cheapest fast-food burgers around—albeit heavy on the thousand-island dressing and preservatives. Real milkshakes and slim, crisp fries.

EE7	**Greenlake Jake's**	7918 E Green Lake Dr N	523-4747

Tasty grilled burgers for the active set at Green Lake.

GG7	**Harry's**	610 First Ave N	282-2002

Dining at Harry's is like going on safari in Disneyland. This doesn't really have much to do with the burgers themselves, which are big, sloppy, and satisfying.

	Kidd Valley Hamburger Company		
FF6	5502 25th NE		522-0890
GG1	15259 NE Bel-Red Rd, Bellevue		643-4165

Has developed a huge reputation made on bacon burgers, shakes, and fried mushrooms. It's a good spot—but don't expect thick patties or a place to sit. Time stands still after you order.

KK7	**Knight's Diner**	5717 Fourth S	762-9532

Down in industrial Seattle there's a former private rail car that now serves up some fine burgers—they even grind their own patties.

KK5	**One Stop Restaurant**	7315 Empire Way S	725-STOP

The Central Area's One Stop Takeout and its much-touted Suicide Burger with an enormous handmade patty have reappeared on Empire Way in the South End. It has new spiffy quarters and a variety of embellishments for the burgers such as hot links, avocado, bacon, and chili.

FF7	**Red Robin**	Eastlake E & Fuhrman E	323-0917
	(plus five other locations)		

A humble tavern on Eastlake becomes a major burger conglomerate offering everything from blue-cheese burgers to chicken teriyaki burgers. The circus burger format is wearing thin, especially at their prices. On a sunny day, though, it is still worth it to sit out on the deck at the original Eastlake spot and enjoy the views of passing boats.

O8	**2nd Avenue Extension**	201 Second Ave S	624-8071

Tucked away on Second and Washington in Pioneer Square, the 2nd Avenue Extension serves an inexpensive array of good-quality burgers, including one marinated in teriyaki sauce and several that use potato in with the meat.

FF7	**318 Tavern**	318 W Nickerson	285-9763

A local institution, the 318 is the kind of classic tavern every neighborhood deserves. Bill Dickerson serves up some of the finest burgers in Seattle there. With a draft or two and one of his specials under your belt—a succulent bacon burger with a secret sauce, and big, slim fries—all seems right with the world.

	William's	111 Sixth S, Edmonds	776-4900

This 1950s-looking family place serves the best truck-driver-pleasing burgers up Edmonds way. Tasty homemade fries, too.

Ethnic restaurants

Restaurants in **bold italics** are described in the "Top 200" Section.

Barbeque

Caveman Kitchen

GG7 **Funky Broadway East**   916 E John   323-8659

Definitely funky decor, and smoky atmosphere from the wood cooking. Table service is touted before takeout. Great sauce.

GG6 **Hill Brothers Barbecue**   608 21st   329-8070

Some say this smokehouse is the best in town.

DD6 **Lone Star Cafe**   11332 Lake City Way   362-9762

Texas hickory-smoked brisket, ribs, and chicken based on Angelo's of Fort Worth's legendary secrets.

Brazilian

Copacabana

Cajun/Creole

Burk's

Q7 **Franglor's Creole Cafe**   511 S Jackson   223-9763

From crab cakes to jambalaya in a funky cafe.

Chinese

Andy & Jemmy's Wok	House of Hong	Silver Dragon
China First	Inn Bin	South China
China Gate	Kau Kau	Tai Tung
China North	King Cafe	Tien Tsin
Concord Garden	Linyen	The Wok
Golden Palace	Louie's Cuisine of China	Yangtze Szechuan
Hong Kong	Shanghai	Yung Ya

Czechoslovakian

Labuznik

English

Mark Tobey   Unicorn

EE1 **British Pantry**   8125 161st Ave, Redmond   883-7511

Perfect little English tearoom serving tea, scones, and tarts. An adjoining deli offers meat pies, sausages, and canned goods.

Ethiopian

Kokeb

Filipino

| Alex's Cafe | Pike Place Market | 223-0292 |

Popular, inexpensive Market spot offering tasty dishes—spices are added according to your palate.

| Ponce's Pastelleria | 1600 First Ave | 624-5429 |

Good, cheap lunches—fixed-price menu with a choice of pork, chicken, or vegetable dishes. In summer, the meat is barbecued.

French

A la Francaise	Gerard's Relais de	Les Copains
Brasserie Pittsbourg	Lyon	Maximilien-in-the-
Cafe Casino	Le Bonaparte	Market
Chez Claude	Le Pigalle	Mirabeau
Crepe de Paris	Le Provencal	Mukilteo Cafe
French Invention	Le Tastevin	Le Petit Cafe

German/Austrian

| The Austrian | Woerne's European Pastry |

Greek

| Athenian | Costas | Costas Opa |

| Continental Restaurant and Pastry Shop | | |
| 4549 University Way NE | | 632-4700 |

Simple, light, and airy, it has the feel of a Greek storefront cafe. A range of appropriate specialties; the Greek fries are a must.

Indian

India House

| Maharaja | Pike Place Market | 621-9500 |

East Indian cooking in quiet surroundings.

Indonesian

Java Restaurant

Italian

Avenue 52	Italo's	Settebello
Bella Neapolis	Lofurno's	Trattoria Mitchelli
Cafe Juanita	Mama Lontoni's	Trattoria Pagliacci
D'Andrea	Paul's Place	Umberto's

Filiberto's	The Pink Door	Vito's
Il Bistro	Saleh Al Lago	

Japanese

Asuka	Kikuya	Nikko
Benihana of Tokyo	Mikado	Teriyaki Sagano
Chiyoko	Miya's	Toshi's Teriyaki
Hisago		

Korean

Han Il	Korea House	
FF7 East-West Garden	1624 N 45th	632-7818
Cha Kun Son's Korean home cooking.		

Kosher

Matzoh Momma

Malaysian

Rasa Malaysia	Seafood Shanty of Singapore

Mediterranean

Adriatica	Mediterranean Kitchen Kamalco
Alexis	Ristorante Pony

Middle Eastern

Al-Waaha	Karawan	Phoenicia
Avenue 52		
F6 Byblos	2311 Fifth Ave	682-9745
Mom and Pop Chapila's home-style Lebanese fare.		
D6 Lebanon	112 Fifth Ave N	624-6662
Belly dancers and shishkababs.		
I8 Sabra	Pike Place Market	682-1989
Arab and Israeli food, mostly pita sandwiches. Mainly takeout.		

Moroccan

Mamounia

Polynesian

Trader Vic's

Russian

Kaleenka Russian Cafe

Scandinavian

| Scandia Cafe | Vaersgo | |

Soul food

| Gene's Place | | |

Thai

| Bangkok Hut | Rama House | |

G2 **The Thai Kitchen**   14115 NE 20th, Bellevue   641-9166
Spicy home-cooked food for the Eastside.

'9 **Thai Taste**   3249 California SW   937-6099
Cheap home-cooked food and homelike hospitality.

Vietnamese

| Cafe Loc | Saigon Over-the- | Thanh Lan |
| Hon's | Counter | Vietnam |

Mexican

| Aurora's of Mexico | Panchito's | Santa Fe Cafe |
| El Puerco Lloron | Quintana Roo | Uruapan |

007 **Azteca**   15735 Ambaum Blvd SW,   243-2241
(plus four other locations) Burien

Azteca seems to have preserved its mainstream quality through its self-cloning. Chicken mole is a standout.

GG7 **Casa Lupita**
1823 Eastlake E   (plus two other locations)   325-7350

Casa Lupita mixes fern-bar and tropic ambience, hosted by cheerfully saucy waitresses. Prices are slightly higher than Mex-cafe-basic, but some dishes, including imaginative and tasty chiles rellenos, are well worth the difference.

F7 **El Cafe**   5020 Roosevelt Way NE   522-9805

El Cafe serves a one-of-a-kind Mexican/Mediterranean/eclectic cuisine, where familiar chili, etc., combines memorably with ingredients as unexpected as squid and coconut milk—with lots of varied veggies on the side, and surprisingly good prices.

KK6 **Flor de Mexico**   6302 Empire Way S   725-0191

Serves the standard Guadalajaran basics (enchiladas, burritos, tacos) at least as well as any other little family cafe, at very good prices. And it boasts what may be Seattle's wildest velvet painting.

Jalisco
B8   122 First Ave N   283-4242
GG6   1467 E Republican   325-9005

Jalisco does the Guadalajaran/Californian standards honestly, with a liberal blanketing of cheddar cheese.

| EE7 | **La Concha** | **1205 NE 65th** | *524-0717* |

Offers a family ambience, moderate prices, some seafood, and a penchant for sour-cream sauces.

| G7 | **Mama's Mexican Kitchen** | | |
| | **2234 Second Ave** | | *624-2640* |

A long-running Belltown favorite, Mama's Mexican Kitchen has a pleasantly funky atmosphere enlivened by freehanded murals. Food is hearty but underpeppered.

| EE7 | **Poquito de Mexico** | **8202 Greenwood Ave N** | *784-2150* |

Poquito de Mexico is as funky, and cheap, as any eatery in Seattle. But its homey atmosphere, complete with Jimmy Rogers memorabilia and a tree growing through the floor, and its rich, fiery chili and tamales are pure South Texas miraculously transported to North Seattle. Coup de grace is a strumming serenade from proprietor Hugh Pankey, when he can get away from the kitchen.

| EE7 | **Rosita's** | **7210 Woodlawn NE** | *523-3031* |

A mom-and-pop place verging on elegance, with chicken flautas a find, mole not so good.

| F6 | **Villa Real** | **409 Wall** | *622-6320* |

A pleasant drinking spot (ask any *P-I* staffer) and good stop for mainstream California-style dinners.

Dessert & coffee places in "Top 200"

A La Francaise	*Cafe Society*	*Karawan*
Apres Vous Cafe	*Cause Celebre*	*Last Exit on Brooklyn*
Belltown Cafe	*Elliott Bay Cafe*	*raison d'etre*
Cafe Botanica	*Gretchen's*	*Ristorante Pony*
		Woerne's

Other dessert & coffee places

| I8 | **American Pie** | **Pike Place Market** | *587-0531* |

Looks like a Norman Rockwell country kitchen and the pies themselves display fitting early American virtues: no-nonsense Crisco crusts and straightforward fillings that make liberal use of top-class ingredients.

| GG7 | **B&O Espresso** | **204 Belmont E, at Olive** | *322-5028* |

The B&O Espresso qualifies as one of the oldest of the "new-wave" dessert houses in town and is still very popular. Mouth-watering confections like sacher torte (apricot-filled chocolate cake with rich whipped cream), or almond-butter blueberry tarts are made on the premises daily.

| FF6 | **The Boiserie** | | *543-9854* |
| | **Burke Museum, UW campus, 45th Street entrance** | | |

With its hand-carved pine walls from an 18th-century French chateau and campus radio and collegiate disquisition in the air, the Boiserie is a fine place to enjoy espresso, croissants, carrot cake, and chocolate cream-cheese cupcakes. Nonstudents are quite welcome.

Cafe Allegro — 4214 University Way NE — 633-3030
FF7

Hidden away in the Campus Corridor on University Way is a long-established student hangout that most regulars get to through the door in the alley. The atmosphere is distinctly casual. Inexpensive desserts—croissants, cookies, brownies, a few pastries—and espresso drinks are the main fare.

Continental Restaurant and Pastry Shop
F7
4549 University Way NE — 632-4700

Tasty Greek pastries and coffee (in addition to full dinners) in a colorful streetfront cafe in the University District.

The Daily Grind — 2301 24th E — 323-0739
GG6

A charming coffee house in the Montlake area serving an ample range of coffees and espressos, Pacific Dessert cakes, Nook cookies, and Fratelli's ice cream. It's very peaceful and cheerful with blue-and-white-checked tablecloths, and newspapers and magazines for patrons to read.

The Dilettante — 416 Broadway E — 329-6463
GG7

"Dilettante" derives from the Italian verb "dilettare," "to delight"; and this dessert house, run by the grandson of the chief chocolate-maker to the Czar merits the name. It also very successfully caters to many Seattleites' chocolate fetishes with its large assortment of hand-dipped chocolates (eat-in or takeout) and extravagant chocolate tortes and coupes. Powerful espresso and gelati round out the offerings. The decor is chocolate brown.

Dominic's — 2114 N 45th — 545-7252
FF7

A shiny, spiffed-up little street-front cafe and gelati bar offering tasty ices—cantaloupe, date, hazelnut, kiwi fruit, licorice mint, and more—espresso, imported wines and beers, and port. An antipasto plate is there for the nonsweet tooths.

The Famous Pacific Dessert Company (no smoking)
GG7
2407 10th E — 325-9339

The original outlet, featuring an unbeatable 40 (or so) cakes, truffles, napoleons, including the notorious Chocolate Decadence. $3.50 is a typical tab for java and eats. Tiny seating area. Also at **429 E Denny** and **127 Mercer**.

Fortnum's — 10213 Main St, Bellevue — 455-2033
HH3

A pretty place with little tables, in keeping with Main Street's new look. An especially delicious chocolate Grand Marnier cheesecake, tasty pastries, and very little competition in the vicinity. The afternoon teas are also offered.

Gelateria Di Freddie — 2802 E Madison — 329-3838
GG6

Freddie Banks and Terri White opened this eight-table sweet shoppe in Madison Valley two winters ago. A delightful ambience is created with a hand-built brick chimney, overhead fan, and manual espresso machine named Lola. The homemade peach cobbler, pear pie, and warm chocolate cake are very tempting.

Geppetto's Gelateria — First & Yesler — 621-0000
N8

This splashy gelateria is owned by Danny Mitchell of Trattoria Mitchelli across the street. Lovely, muted rose-and-grey walls complement the tile floor, track lighting, and huge glass bar stocked with fancy ice-cream and soda glasses. The handmade ices and creams are among the best in Seattle (they have about 50 flavors but display only about 18 at a time) and include such novelties as muskmelon, nec-

Restaurants

tarine, and blueberry-lemon zest. Ices are available straight-up or in Italian sodas, along with a myriad of specialty concoctions.

FF7 **Grand Illusion**
50th & University Way NE   525-0573

An adjunct to the Grand Illusion Cinema, located in an old house with a cozy fireplace. Small but tasty home-baked dessert selection (flaky pastries and pies recommended), espresso, the Sunday *New York Times*. Occasionally overwhelmed by pre-show crowds.

Haagen Dazs   (seven locations)

On the forefront of the gourmet ice-cream parlor craze, Haagen Dazs still has most people's vote as the best place for creamy, rich scoops made with all natural ingredients and no preservatives. The coffee and strawberry flavors are the classics.

H6 **Kimberley's**   2004 Fourth Ave   622-7820

Ice cream, espresso, and a fine selection of classic American baked goods in a dandy cafe complete with mahogany bar.

FF7 **Primo Gelato**
4522 Brooklyn NE   634-2332
23818 Highway 99, Edmonds   776-2332

This little bit of high-tech in the U District opened last March, after the owners of the original Edmonds Primo Gelato went looking for foot traffic. They offer nine ice creams and fruit ices, rotating among 50 flavors (cappuccino's the popular favorite). Imported chocolates, fresh juices, and Dilettante ice-cream toppings. Best for takeout as there's not much room.

I8 **Procopio Gelateria**   Pike Street Hillclimb   622-4280

Seattle's original gelateria is surely responsible for the Italian-ice craze in the city. At least 14 flavors (seasonally rotated) of freshly made dolci de gelati are always displayed, and if you can get past these positively first-class ices, you can choose from an assortment of luscious desserts. Beverages include a great winter hot-spiced cider, a few Italian wines, and most espresso drinks. The white-tiled, rather stark, high-ceilinged gelateria is decorated simply with neon-look art signs.

FF7 **Roosevelt Bakery**   4759 Roosevelt Way NE   632-7977

Though its menu has expanded to include lunch and dinner, the rich-layered desserts are still popular here. (Try their fig-hazelnut flan, or an espresso float.) A range of espressos, herbal teas, and imported wines and beers make nice dessert accompaniments. A small corner stage in the large, airy room accommodates near-nightly performers, mostly classical and folk solo guitarists.

FF7 **Simply Desserts**   3421 Fremont Ave N   633-2671

A longtime supplier of local theaters, this tiny little bakery serves up a side selection of classic pastries: brandy cake, Kahlua cheesecake, sour-cream apple pie, and fudge pie, among a host of other calorie-laden goodies.

GG6 **Treats**   15th & E John   329-9191

The casual restaurant-confectionery has all the standards—pecan pie, carrot cake, cream-cheese brownies—and then some. A good bet is the purple berry pie (a combination of blueberries and blackberries). Relaxed atmosphere with lots of old books to read.

The Arts

Performing arts	65	Theater
	67	Movies
	68	Classical music
	69	Opera
	69	Dance
	70	Tickets
Visual arts	70	Museums
	72	Art galleries
	74	Craft galleries
	76	Glass galleries
	76	Galleries of Native American art
	77	Alternative spaces

Performing arts

Theater

Theater is Seattle's most lively art form. Not only are there a lot of theaters; most of those theaters perform lots of new plays along with the usual spectrum of classics, ancient and modern. During any given week of the year, you can usually choose from a roster including a touring Broadway musical, an avant-garde drama from Europe, a zany contemporary comedy, and a classic, either performed "straight" or duded up in modern dress. Consult the daily papers' Friday entertainment supplements and *The Weekly* for what's playing and promising. In Seattle biggest doesn't necessarily mean best, and the line between fully professional and gifted amateur is very vague, so don't be afraid to experiment.

A6 **The Seattle Repertory Theater** is the oldest and biggest show in town, with a six-play season running from October to June in its own striking, new, 800-seat Bagley Wright Theater at the Seattle Center. Under artistic director Dan Sullivan, the Rep's repertory is about one-third "classic" (Shakespeare, Shaw, Arthur Miller) and about two-thirds solid contemporary work from Broadway and England. Production values are invariably first-rate, and performances frequently hit as high a level as you'll find in the American regional theater. Call the box office (447-4764) for ticket prices and availability.

The 5th Avenue Theater isn't really a Seattle theater at all, but its presentations

The Arts

of touring Broadway musicals and plays add a welcome note of glitter and razzmatazz to the local scene. The theater is an architectural landmark, a classic old-time movie palace in flaming Imperial Chinese style. Its architectural virtue is its artistic vice: only the biggest musicals and stars can really fill the huge shoebox space. Straight drama is a disaster there, and don't buy back-of-the-house or balcony seats to *anything* unless you plan to bring binoculars. Hard times have sharply curtailed the number of big shows. Box office: 625-1900.

5K **A Contemporary Theater** opens up in May, when the Rep is about to shut down, and runs to October. Despite the name, ACT isn't any more contemporary in its play selection than the Rep, but its smaller (430-seat) auditorium and "thrust" stage make it a better spot for some intimate dramas. ACT's annual production of *A Christmas Carol*, running from Thanksgiving to New Year's, is a Seattle tradition. Box office: 285-5110.

GG8 **Intiman Theater Company** runs during the summer, too, but it's no "summer theater." At the Second Stage, the Company's freeway-side home downtown (plans are afoot to move to a new space), you'll see Sophocles, Ibsen, Chekhov, O'Casey, and Strindberg, performed by the closest thing to an ongoing ensemble company of professional actors that Seattle offers. Box office: 624-2992.

J4 **The Empty Space** recently celebrated its 12th birthday with its 100th production: quite a record for a 99-seat theater in a third-floor loft. Unpredictability is the only predictable thing about "The Space": the repertory includes far-out contemporary work, stripped-down classics, off-Broadway hits, and crazy homemade comedies. Despite its tiny size (the troupe is looking for a larger home), The Space is perhaps Seattle's most widely known and respected theater in the trade. Box office: 325-4443.

J4 **Tacoma Actors Guild** isn't in Seattle at all, but TAG's ambitious blend of American classics and Northwest premieres of important new plays and musicals commands respect and even some audience willing to make the 45-minute drive south. You'll find TAG's shows listed in all the Seattle theater listings. Box office: 1-272-2145.

FF6 **The Group**, though it operates out of a theater owned by the University of Washington, is scarcely a "college theater." On the contrary, with its multi-racial company and trenchant play selection, it could be called Seattle's only theater with a social and political point of view. Fortunately, that doesn't prevent its shows from often being great fun, too. Box office: 543-4327.

O8 **The Pioneer Square Theater** is the youngest of Seattle theaters and has compiled an enviable record of world premieres and original works in its two-year existence. Not yet professional (in the sense of hiring union actors) but on the verge, the PST has a faithful audience of younger Seattle theater fans who rather like the theater's bare-bones approach and pungent Skid Road ambiance. Box office: 682-2346.

EE7 **The Bathhouse Theater** stands on the shores of Green Lake, seating only 130 in a remodeled Parks Department building. Rarely employing professional actors, the Bathhouse still manages to demand serious attention through the work of its artistic director, Arne Zaslove, under whose direction young performers can do wonders. A totally personal theater, every production, from an Art Deco *Boy Meets Girl* to a Wild West version of *Macbeth*, bears the Zaslove stamp. Box office: 524-9110.

FF7 **The PONCHO Theater** near the Woodland Park Zoo is devoted to professional-quality productions of plays for children and families: check their current schedule at 633-4567.

The Arts

A6   **MusiComedy Northwest** is a semi-pro group that produces four Broadway-music revivals annually, some very satisfying. Their season runs from October to June at the Seattle Center Playhouse. A call to 325-3633 will let you know what they're performing.

A6   **The Gilbert and Sullivan Society** produces only occasionally but very professionally: its shows at the Seattle Center Playhouse are always well attended.

J4   **New City Theater**, not far from The Empty Space on Capitol Hill, books in lots of special shows, from improv comedy troupes to cabaret acts to straight plays. A call to 323-6800 will tell you what's up at the moment.

GG7 **Washington Hall Performance Gallery** is the local home of avant-garde dance and performance art, but it also presents a series of performances by touring big-time avant-gardists like Meredith Monk and Mabou Mines. Box office: 325-7901.

F7   The **Skid Road Theater** has been undergoing a period of reorganization and will reopen in the fall of 1983, under the new name of **CityStage** and in a new space, the second floor of a firehouse on Fourth and Battery. Call 622-0251 for information.

Movies

Over the past decade and a half, Seattle has won a national reputation as a lively movie town with conscientious exhibitors and discerning audiences. The film industry now regards the city as "a major market," so the first-run scene is always up to date. It's rare to look at the current movie listings and not find some offbeat, but often first-rate, film that has been brought to town by its producer or director for tender-loving-care showcasing by one of the local independent theaters; Seattle has helped many an "unreleasable" film prove its commercial viability, and a number of major filmmakers regularly preview early cuts of their films here.

G5   Among the many first-run houses, the **UA Cinema 150** (Sixth & Blanchard,
H6   624-6201) and SRO's **Cinerama** (Fourth & Lenora, 223-3983) are the prime locations for sink-into-your-seat, wrap-around-big-screen viewing. But the local independents have been coming on strong, not only offering the most consistently adventurous programming in the foreign and art-house line, but also treating major-studio releases with an intelligence and sensitivity that helps audiences discover the cream of the domestic film crop as well. The Seven Gables circuit started with one tiny store-front cinema in the early '70s, and has grown to a size (about a dozen screens around the greater Seattle area) and a commercial clout to challenge its national-circuit competitors in bidding for big films. The company prides itself on state-of-the-art presentation and—especially at its flagship theater,
FF6 the **Seven Gables** (NE 50th & Roosevelt Way NE, 632-8820)—offers the most congenial amenities to filmgoers.

K0   The **Egyptian** (Pine & Harvard, 32-EGYPT), in a grand old Masonic temple on Capitol Hill, is the new headquarters of Stage Fright, Inc., the brainchild of two enterprising Canadians who moved to Seattle in the mid-'70s and created the annual **Seattle International Film Festival**. (They also mount an estimable year-round schedule of art-house fare.) The Festival has become an indispensable fix for local film enthusiasts, bringing in more than 100 movies from all points of the cinematic compass, and an increasing number of film celebrities, each May. The
GG6 **Harvard Exit** (Harvard & E Roy, 323-8986), Seattle's first luxury art theater, concentrates on specialized programming; a pleasant second auditorium, the **Top of the Exit**, has recently been added to this charming moviehouse, located in a

The Arts

J8 former ladies' club headquarters. And the **Pike Place Cinema** (Post Alley, 622-2552) perseveres in offering esoteric foreign films and special revivals in its excellent auditorium "under the Market clock."

FF6
I7
FF6
GG7 Several repertory operations, theatrical and nontheatrical, further enhance the film taste of the Seattle audience. The **Neptune Theater** in the University District (NE 45th & Brooklyn NE, 633-5545) and the Seven Gables' **Moore Theater** downtown (Second & Virginia, 621-1744) recycle every type of vintage film, their respective programs changing daily and thrice-weekly. Premier among local institutional film programs are the **University of Washington Office of Cinema Studies Film Series** (3:30 & 7:30 Tuesdays, 130 Kane Hall; phone 543-2350) and the **Seattle Art Museum Film Series** (7:30 Thursdays, Volunteer Park Auditorium; 447-4710), offering imaginative retrospectives of national cinemas, key genres, and stars' and directors' careers. And entering its second decade, the nonprofit **Seattle Film Society** continues to showcase the many fine films everyone else manages to overlook; its schedule is less frequent than in the pre-Reaganomics era, but eminently worth keeping in touch with—phone 325-7632 for current projects, or pick up the lively SFS newsletter, *The Informer*, at most of the above-mentioned theaters.

Classical music

Seattle is not known as a particularly strong town for classical music, but it is a comer nonetheless. On a given night, there is a considerable range of music to be heard; the University of Washington has a fine music school that spawns concerts and performers and groups; the touring schedule is getting rich; and chamber music has recently come of age, filling out the spectrum.

A6 **Seattle Symphony Orchestra**, a greatly improved group over the past decade, is in another period of transition: it has a new general manager, financial difficulties aplenty, and is seeking a new music director after the loss of conductor Rainer Miedel to cancer. The 1983–84 season should be most interesting. The orchestra plays very well for guest conductors, and there will be a string of them this season, plus several attempts at new programs and venues. Regular subscription concerts are at the Opera House, with big-name soloists on Monday and Tuesday evenings; a Sunday-afternoon series presents younger soloists. There are also sold-out pops concerts of the usual variety, and an excellent Saturday-morning series of children's concerts conducted by resident conductor Richard Buckley. Call 447-4736 for ticket information.

FF6 The **Northwest Chamber Orchestra**, a most promising ensemble with a superb conductor, Alun Francis, at the helm, will be trying to restore some fiscal solidity this year. The concert season is condensed into a November–March interval, and performances will be at Kane Hall on the UW campus. With few guest soloists this year, the group will concentrate on the Baroque and chamber orchestra repertoire. For information call 343-0445.

Philadelphia String Quartet, lured here by the University of Washington many years ago, has been weaned from the U and is now making it on tours, performances at Meany Hall, and aggressive fundraising. A new violinist and cellist have joined the group this year: the ensemble is improved and the group seems very happy with each other, but the playing is technically shakier than in years past. They've started occasionally bringing in other players to join the quartet, to fine effect. Information: 527-8839.

Seattle Youth Symphony, one of the finest such ensembles in the country, is far more than a convincing demonstration of how well musicians from the age of

14-22 can play together: these concerts are memorable musical evenings, without qualification. Conductor Vilem Sokol presents demanding programs with very interesting pieces and dazzling young soloists. Call 623-2001 to see what concerts may be coming up.

CC7 **Seattle Chamber Music Festival** imports top international chamber-music players for three weeks of music-making in an elegant little theater on the Lakeside School Campus. The result is the city's one true *summer* festival: dining on the lawns (suppers can be purchased or brought), and gracious seasonal touches. The music is often of a very high order, conservatively programmed and played with brio. Music director Toby Saks, a UW professor of cello, attracts some of the top New York players for the festival. Information: 282-1807. 1983 dates: June 27-July 15.

FF6 **Santa Fe Chamber Music Festival** spends a concert-filled week in Seattle late each summer, with highly polished performances by some of the country's finest chamber players; the rousing programs are at Meany Hall. Tickets: 628-0888. 1983 dates: August 26–September 1.

Opera

A6 **The Seattle Opera Association** mounts five full-scale operas each season in the Opera House, with international casts in the original-language productions and many younger American talents in the English-language versions. The productions can be uneven, mixing excellent singers with has-beens, and usually cutting corners on sets, direction, and conductors. The repertoire for '83-'84 is much more interesting, however, and a new general manager from New York, Speight Jenkins, takes over this season; it should be one of the more intriguing years. In the summer, SOA presents its acclaimed production of Wagner's *Ring*, complete German and English cycles over two weeks. This *Ring* is done in the traditional, romantic style, with fine casts; it gets better each year, and next season the company will begin mounting new productions. Incidentally, acoustics in the cheapest seats, far back in the second balcony, are often better than the high-priced seats. Call 447-4711 for ticket information.

FF6 **UW School of Music** opera productions, at acoustically superb Meany Hall, are usually more interesting and less hackneyed. Recent performances of works by Stravinsky, Poulenc, Monteverdi, and Mozart have approached genuine excellence. Call 543-4880 for information.

Dance

A6 **Pacific Northwest Ballet**, the big show in town, is a classically-oriented company with regional aspirations. Now under the management of Kent Stowell and Francia Russell, two graduates of the New York City Ballet, PNB has a distinct Balanchine bias, with many of that master's works in its repertory and, thanks to Ms. Russell, his protege, Balanchine's spirit also is visible in the precision, coolness, and attack of the dancers.

PNB's season opens at the Opera House in December with the compulsory annual *Nutcracker*. There will, however, be a completely new production in 1983, designed by the imaginative children's-book illustrator Maurice Sendak.

Alternating in the spring are a very respectable *Swan Lake* and a *Coppelia*, both choreographed on traditional lines by artistic director Stowell. Three to four reper-

The Arts

FF6 tory evenings, each performed three to four times, fill out the PNB season between January and May, with some small-scale but interesting programs in summer at the University of Washington's Meany Hall, finances permitting. A call to the Ballet's box office at 447-4655 will tell you when and where the next program will occur.

A6
FF6 **Discover Dance** provides fine touring dance entertainment in town by bringing five or six of the continent's best companies to Seattle annually, either to Meany Hall or to the Opera House. The audience is enthusiastic and ferociously knowledgeable, and performances are consequently top-drawer, with many new works tried out here before New York gets to see them. Discover Dance performances are usually sold out, especially those at Meany, but persistence can pay off: try particularly for matinee or "student-performance" seats. The number to call for information is 282-1880.

HH6 Outside of PNB the classical dance scene in the area is artistically negligible, but there is a lively, constantly-changing modern dance scene. For the best of it, call **On the Boards** at Washington Hall Performance Gallery (325-7901), which presents half a dozen dance evenings and matinees a month, including Choreography, Etc., a series devoted to new dance and performance work by leading local artists.

Bill Evans, a highly individual exponent of modern dance, and Joan Skinner, founder of the widely praised Skinner Releasing (free improvisational) technique, are two Seattle-based teacher-choreographers with national reputations. They occasionally produce shows locally so keep an eye out for them in the entertainment sections of the papers.

Tickets

In addition to the box offices at individual concert halls, theaters, and sports centers, general ticket outlets are often good places to buy tickets. Some of the major ones are listed here:

A6 **BASS Seattle**, 220 W Mercer, 282-1880
I6 **The Bon Ticket Office**, Third & Pine, 344-7271
I6 **Fidelity Lane**, 1622 Fourth, 624-4971
K7 **Last Minute Tickets**, 1320 Second Ave, 623-8068. Half price, day-of-performance tickets to numerous performing arts events.
P8 **Ticketmaster**, 201 S King St, 628-0888
FF7 **U-District Ticket Center**, 4530 University Way NE, 632-7272

Visual arts

Museums

Seattle Art Museum	*10-5 Tues-Sat; until 9 Thur; noon-5 Sun*
Volunteer Park	*447-4710*
Seattle Center	*447-4796*

SAM still hasn't found its fancy new home downtown, but there's plenty else to

GG6 celebrate in its golden anniversary year. The Katherine White Collection, a bequest of African art so vast it will have to be exhibited serially, opens in spring 1984. There's the new department of photography; a beefed-up education department offering a growing program of film series, lectures, workshops, and performances; an art reference library anybody is welcome to use; the only lending slide library in the area. The museum's great strength is its Asian art collection. Starting July 1983, *Highlights of the Asian Art Collection* will share the Volunteer Park branch of the museum with 31 *Paintings from the Royal Academy*. The Art Pavilion, a vaulting glassed-in space at the Seattle Center, also houses the Rentaloft, which rents work by Northwest artists to museum members. Both museums have good gift shops.

FF6 **Henry Gallery** *10-5 Tues-Fri; until 7 Thur; 1-5 Sat & Sun*
University of Washington, 15th Ave NE *543-2280*

It used to be easy to walk right past the unassuming Henry, tucked cozily into a corner off the 15th Avenue University footbridge. Not so today: curator Harvey West has mounted a series of aggressive publicity campaigns. The showmanship is a bit much but the shows are generally good fun. Local artists are frequently exhibited.

FF6 **Burke Museum** *11-5:30 Tues-Fri; 9-4:30 Sat & Sun;*
45th St entrance to *closed Mon*
University of Washington *543-5590*

A natural history museum, the Burke covers the cultures of the Pacific Rim, focusing particularly on Northwest Coast Indian art. They've just gussied up the dinosaur exhibit (including a 12,500-year-old giant ground sloth found at the north end of Sea-Tac airport and, soon to be unveiled, the cast of a rhino buried alive in lava in ancient Eastern Washington, near Coulee City). *Puget Sound Basketry* and *American Indian Arts: Yesterday and Today* are the type of exhibits on show. Admission is free. The Burke is the only local museum with a topnotch coffeehouse downstairs, the Boiserie (see "Dessert & coffee places," page 62).

R6 **Wing Luke Memorial Museum** *11-4:30 Tues-Fri, noon-4 Sat,*
414 Eighth Ave S *and by appointment*
 623-5124

Wing Luke was a Seattle councilman killed in a plane crash in 1965; the museum is devoted not only to him but to the Asian experience in the Northwest. There are exhibits on everything from 19th-century pioneers who immigrated before the wave of anti-Chinese riots to Asian kites and how to make them. The permanent collection consists of historical photographs of the International District and unusual artifacts, foods, and costumes of its storied past. New Asian-American artists from the Puget Sound region are often displayed. Admission is free.

N3 **Frye Museum** *10-5 Mon-Sat; noon-5 Sun*
704 Terry at Cherry *622-9250*

The Frye is a modest anomaly among museums, crotchety and individualistic in taste and approach, and more than a little populist. As of August 1983, the enlarged and renovated Frye sports a new wing to house its Alaskan art collection, and about twice as much floor space. Exhibits range from the picturesque nature photography of Art Wolfe to a hoard of mid–19th century and Art Nouveau pieces.

HH3 **Bellevue Art Museum** *Noon-8 Tues-Fri; 9:30-6 Sat; 11-5 Sun;*
301 Bellevue Square, Bellevue *closed Mon; free admission on Tues*
 454-3322

Plucky BAM has outlived its humble former headquarters in a mortuary and has a new lease on life in the glassy, glitzy Bellevue Square Shopping Center. Its debut show in the new location, *5,000 Years of Faces*, was pretty impressive, with pieces contributed by the Seattle Art Museum, the Metropolitan Museum in New York, and prestigious museums elsewhere. The major touring shows will be joined by a series of shows in the smaller gallery leaning toward the local.

FF6	**Museum of History and Industry** 2161 E Hamlin	*10-5 Mon-Sat; noon-5 Sun* *324-1125*

The Museum, long an amiably underbudgeted place, has undergone a thoroughgoing facelift and has beefed up its exhibits considerably. There's a terrific archive of Seattleiana in the basement, open by appointment only (the public is welcome). Formerly free, the Museum must now charge an admission fee.

O8	**Klondike Gold Rush National Historical Park, Seattle Unit** 117 S Main	*Winter: 9-5 Mon-Fri; 9-6 Sat & Sun* *Summer: 9-7 Every day* *442-7220*

This little museum in Pioneer Square is actually part of a larger National Park in Alaska. It has exhibits of gold-mining artifacts and hardware, and photographic murals which show Seattle's role in the Klondike Gold Rush of 1897–98. Films and slides of the period are also shown in the auditorium. Admission is free.

Art galleries

J4	**and/or** 911 E Pine	*10-6 Wed-Fri; noon-9 Tues; noon-5 Sat; closed Sun & Mon 324-5880*

and/or, the godparent of experimental art in Seattle, administers the Focal Point Media Center, which is the city's only collection of video art, and an arts library called 911. Both offer an extensive schedule of video and film screenings, media performances, window installations, and lectures.

O9	**Carolyn Staley Fine Prints** 313 First Ave S	*11:30-5 Tues-Sat; closed Sun & Mon* *621-1888*

The specialty is old prints, including maps and Japanese woodblocks; historically or decoratively interesting and reasonably priced. Bibliophiles will appreciate Staley's dedication to the fine art of the book.

N8	**Davidson Galleries** 87 Yesler Way	*Noon-5 Tues-Sat; closed Sun & Mon* *624-7684*

The collection includes master prints, illuminated manuscripts, erotica, and contemporary prints representing several regional artists.

O8	**Diane Gilson Gallery** 209 Occidental S	*11:30-5 Tues-Sat; closed Sun & Mon* *628-9660*

This space represents contemporary American art with a strong showing from California and New York and a small stable of local talent.

HH6	**Equivalents Gallery** 1822 Broadway	*11-6 Tues-Sat; noon-5 Sun; closed Mon* *322-7765*

The focus is photography by local and international artists, with occasional shows in other mediums. Art-related books, postcards, and posters can also be found here. Located upstairs in a converted house on the southern edge of the Broadway shopping district.

The Arts

O9	**Flury & Co** 322 First Ave S	*11-5:30 Tues-Sat; 1-6 Sun; closed Mon* *587-0260*

Edward S. Curtis's photographs, goldtones, and photogravures of North American Indians are housed in one of the loveliest spaces in Pioneer Square, originally a beer-tasting room.

EE7	**Francine Seders Gallery** 6701 Greenwood Ave N	*10-5 Tues-Sat; 1-5 Sun; closed Mon* *782-0355*

Representing the more established Northwest artists—Mark Tobey, Guy Anderson—as well as mounting shows of young local artists and talent found outside the region.

O8	**Foster/White Gallery** 311½ Occidental S	*10-5:30 Mon-Sat; noon-5 Sun* *622-2833*

The major keeper of Northwest traditions (Callahan, Graves, Kenney, Tobey); also nurtures up-and-coming regional artists.

O8	**Jackson Street Gallery** 163 S Jackson	*11-4:30 Tues-Sat; closed Sun & Mon* *623-0435*

Each month there's a new show, coupling the works of a local artist with someone on tour. Occasional performance art is not to be missed. Leans toward the funky.

P8	**Linda Farris Gallery** 320 Second Ave S	*11:30-5 Mon-Sat; 1-5 Sun* *623-1110*

A major space for nationally represented artists and a stable of regional rising stars, represented with panache by a very public gallery owner.

N8	**Manolides Gallery** 89 Yesler Way	*11-5 Tues-Sat; closed Sun & Mon* *622-3204*

In this tiny Pioneer Square gallery resides a long-established tradition of high-spirited art. Schedule is irregular; call ahead.

I7	**Penryn Gallery** 1920½ First Ave	*11-5 Tues-Sat; closed Sun & Mon* *623-0495*

Paul Carkeek's 13-year-old gallery represents a wide spectrum of contemporary art with an emphasis on Northwest and West Coast artists.

O8	**The Silver Image Gallery** 92 S Washington	*Noon-5:30 Tues-Sun; closed Mon* *623-8116*

Devoted exclusively to fine photography by master and contemporary artists, including Edward Weston, one-time Seattleite Imogen Cunningham, Marsha Burns, Donn Leber, and Stu Levy.

N8	**Stone Press Gallery** 91 Yesler Way	*11-5 Tues-Sat; closed Sun & Mon* *624-6752*

The apex of contemporary printmaking in Seattle; original hand-printed lithographs and etchings at prices from modest to expensive.

H7	**Stonington Galleries** 2030 First Ave	*10-5:30 Tues-Sat; closed Sun & Mon* *621-1108*

A reliable source of contemporary Alaskan and Northwest artists.

H7	**Traver Sutton Gallery** 2219 Fourth Ave	*10-5 Tues-Fri; noon-5 Sat; closed Sun & Mon* *622-4534*

The Arts

G6	In the spring and fall, look for exhibits by painters and sculptors (both regional and national); each summer, a textile-arts show is mounted; and in December Traver Sutton hosts the annual Pilchuck glass show.	
I3	**Woodside/Braseth Galleries** 1101 Howell	*11-6 Mon-Sat; 1-6 Sun* 622-7243
	Strictly Northwest. Works by regional masters—Ivey, Horiuchi, Morris—and over a dozen young artists abide in this 24-year-old gallery, Seattle's oldest.	

Craft galleries

I8	**The African Gallery** Stewart House, 1906 Pike Place	*11-6 Mon-Sat; closed Sun* 292-9520
	The gallery contains items selected and purchased for import from the entire African continent by the owners Lois Jamieson and Harold Newman. Among the quality items at affordable prices are masks, jewelry, woven shoulder bags, baskets woven tightly enough to hold water, rugs, and wooden souvenirs, all of which are intriguing and beautiful. The staff is very knowledgeable, and a small library on Africa and African art is available.	
G7	**Bainbridge Arts & Crafts** Winslow Way, Bainbridge Island	*10-5:30 Mon-Sat; closed Sun* 842-3132
	Real gems (when available) are the Eskimo figurines produced at C. Allan Johnson's island studio. Also worthy of note are the batik wall hangings. Monthly shows feature exhibits by painters, potters, sculptors.	
G7	**Cerulean Blue Gallery** 119 Blanchard	*10-5:30 Thur-Sat; closed Sun-Wed* 625-9647
	A supply shop for textile artists and a gallery space for fabric arts that you're not likely to encounter elsewhere in the city. Workshops and classes in textile arts.	
I8	**The Clay Occasion** Stewart House, Pike Place Market	*10-5:30 Mon-Sat; closed Sun* 343-5992
	Functional and decorative forms with more artistic quality than one usually finds on the potters' tables along the Market's main arcade.	
GG6	**Conrow/Werner Studio** 1911 E Aloha	*1-5 Wed-Sat; closed Sun-Tues* 324-0734
	Ginny Conrow's delicate porcelain is most interesting in elegant copper-red glazes or with the soft detail of Sumi brushwork. Glass artist Loretta Werner also shows her wares in this space.	
O8	**FireWorks Gallery** Grand Central Arcade, 214 First Ave S	*10:30-5 Mon-Sat; noon-5 Sun* 682-8707
	Owner Steve McGovney, who manages the store while he hand-builds whimsical whistles of clay, regularly features functional and nonfunctional ceramics.	
O8	**The Flying Shuttle** 310 First Ave S	*11-6 Mon-Sat; 11-4 Sun* 343-9762
	More than 60 Northwest fiber artists are represented in weaving, knitting, felting, basketry, and surface design. The wearables are the showcase: superlative home-	

spun elegance in shawls, sweaters, silk dresses, and other apparel. Also, excellent rugs.

FF6	**Folk Art Gallery/La Tienda** 4138 University Way NE	10-5:30 Tues-Sat; until 9 Thur; closed Sun & Mon; 634-1795

In two decades, La Tienda's modest Mexican-import business has evolved into a one-of-a-kind gallery/shop for traditional folk arts from all over the world as well as contemporary American crafts. Of special note are the handmade instruments and the puppet room.

K1	**Form & Function Studio Gallery** 516 E Pine	11-6 Tues-Fri; 11-4 Sat; closed Sun & Mon 322-8175

Functional ceramics and large decorative pieces shaped by two potters.

FF7	**Fremont Architectural Pottery** 3504 Fremont Place N	10-5 Mon-Fri; noon-4 Sat; closed Sun 632-4848

Here's the place for hand-thrown stoneware bathroom sinks (from 12 to 19 inches) and pedestals (30 inches tall). Custom designs available.

O8	**Native Design Gallery** 108 S Jackson	11-5 Tues-Sat; closed Sun & Mon 624-9985

Ethnic imports, primarily African textiles and artifacts, selected by the very informative owners.

A7	**Northwest Craft Center** Seattle Center	11-6 Tues-Sun; closed Mon 624-7563

Displays by regional artisans, selected by jury. Excellent gift shopping.

O8	**Northwest Gallery of Fine Woodworking** 202 First Ave S	11-6 Tues-Sat; 11-5 Sun 625-0542

This cooperatively owned gallery is a showcase for some fine Northwest woodworkers who create fluid-lined, superbly crafted desks, chairs, sculpture, coffee tables, shelves, sideboards, screens, boxes, and other aesthetic woodcraft.

HH3	**Panaca Gallery** 133 Bellevue Square, Bellevue	9:30-9 Mon-Fri; 9:30-6 Sat; 11-5 Sun 454-0234

Panaca (Pacific Northwest Arts and Crafts Association) provides a shopping-mall storefront for regional fine arts and crafts. Art work can also be rented for up to six months, with fees applicable to purchase.

EE7	**Phinney Ridge Ceramics** 5914 Phinney Ave N	11-5 Tues-Sat; closed Sun & Mon 789-6410

One-potter studio that uses the storefront window to show hand-thrown functional ware.

GG6	**Polly's Wearable Art Gallery/Shop** 4105 E Madison	11-5:30 Tues-Sat; closed Sun & Mon 324-6124

Much needed outlet for 40 West Coast jewelers and textile artists whose clothes range from hand-woven separates and designer sweaters to studded t-shirts, silk jackets, and classic kimonos.

GG8	**Pottery Northwest** 226 First Ave N	Noon-5 Tues-Sat; closed Sun & Mon 285-4421

Ceramics produced by resident potters and their students.

The Arts

FF6	**The Running Stitch** 5251 University Way NE	*11-5 Tues-Fri; noon-5 Sat; closed Sun & Mon* *523-4367*

Custom interior textile designs (except drapery); made-to-order quilting with a special source for antique patchwork tops.

I8	**Southeast Asian Designs** 511 Mezzanine, Pike Place Market	*10-5 Mon-Sat; closed Sun* *343-0022*

A cooperative of Laotian women, refugees from the Mien and Hmong hill tribes, sells excellent embroidery, applique, and tie-dye handiwork. Traditional tribal designs dominate their craft, though fabric and color have been modified to suit American tastes.

J5	**Stewart & Stewart Pottery** 1510 Fifth Ave	*11-5:30 Mon-Sat; closed Sun* *622-7554*

Husband David runs the potter's wheel (the specialty is made-to-order electric lamps); wife Leanne manages the business.

Glass galleries

I8	**The Glass Eye** 1902 Post Alley	*10-5 Mon-Sat; closed Sun* *682-5929*

Formerly of the Pilchuck Glass School, Rob Adamson started both a studio and a gallery for hand-blown art glass. Mount St. Helens ash ornaments as well as limited-edition works by several glassblowers can be found here.

O8	**Glasshouse Art Glass** Grand Central Arcade, 214 First Ave S	*10-5 Every day* *682-9939*

Unique art-glass lamps are most notable. There's an ongoing demonstration of glassblowing.

GG7	**Glass Showcase** 2948 Eastlake E	*Noon-5 Mon-Sat; closed Sun* *329-1837*

Artist Michael Kennedy's studio/showroom exhibits the newer technology in contemporary art glass—fusing, etching, painting, and cast glass.

GG8	**Northwest Art Glass** 904 Elliott Ave W	*9-5:30 Mon-Fri; 10-5:30 Sat; closed Sun* *283-4990*

Blown-glass and stained-glass collectibles.

Galleries of Native American art

FF9	**Daybreak Star Gallery** Discovery Park	*9-5 Mon-Fri; closed Sat & Sun* *285-4425*

Inside the Daybreak Star Cultural Center you'll find outstanding, wood-carved murals and a small gallery which represents traditional arts and crafts of all Native American Indian tribes. Unfortunately Daybreak's only weekend hours are 10-4 on the second Saturday each month; call first.

L8	**Legacy** 1003 First Ave (Alexis Hotel)	*10-6 Mon-Sat; closed Sun* *624-6350*

Historic collections of Northwest Indian and Eskimo basketry, ivory carvings, beadwork, hunting and fishing implements, contemporary pottery, prints, and jewelry.

CC5 **Snow Goose Gallery** *11-5 Thur-Sat; closed Sun-Wed; by appoint-*
4220 NE 125th *ment only June to Sept; 362-3401*

A cozy display room filled with art and artifacts of Alaskan and Canadian Eskimos and Northwest Coast Indians. Worthy of note are the baskets and soapstone figures.

G6 **Sacred Circle Gallery** *10-5 Tues-Sat; closed Sun & Mon*
of American Indian Art *223-0072*
2223 Fourth Ave

Contemporary Indian art with a fresh view, flavored with tribal heritages. A profit-making arm of the United Indians of All Tribes Foundation.

N7 **Seattle Indian Arts & Crafts** *10-5 Mon-Fri; closed Sat & Sun*
617 Second Ave *623-2252*

This non-profit outlet for traditional American Indian crafts includes beadwork, basketry, Southwest pottery, Eskimo soapstone sculpture, and handmade Cowichan sweaters. Sponsored by the American Indian Women's Service League.

Alternative art spaces

Seattle has a number of alternative spaces that exhibit art from time to time. Here are the most conspicuous:

G8 **Belltown Cafe**
2309 First Ave *622-4392*

F7 **Two Bells Tavern**
2313 Fourth Ave *345-9203*

I7 **Virginia Inn**
1937 First Ave *624-3173*

FF6 **The Boiserie Cafe**
The Burke Memorial Museum
University of Washington Campus *543-9854*

GG7 **Julia's 14 Carrot Cafe**
2305 Eastlake E *324-1442*

HH6 **Hi Spot Cafe**
1410 34th *325-7905*

O6 **King County Arts Commission**
300 King County Administration
Building (Fourth & James) *344-7580*

P7 **Ground Zero (co-op gallery)**
202 Third S *223-9752*

HH6 **Nine One One**
911 E Pine *324-5880*

Nightlife

Drinks

- *78* Bars - Downtown
- *80* Bars - Other areas
- *82* Drinks with a view
- *84* Wine bars
- *84* Gay bars
- *84* Pubs
- *85* Taverns

Entertainment

- *87* Large venues
- *88* Clubs — Pioneer Square & Downtown
- *90* Clubs — University District & North End
- *92* Clubs — Other areas
- *93* Lounges, piano bars, discos — Downtown
- *95* Lounges, piano bars, discos — North End
- *95* Lounges, piano bars, discos — Other areas

Drinks

Bars — Downtown

L8 **Alexis Hotel Bar**
First & Madison   *624-4844*

A small and handsome bar located in one of Seattle's classiest new hotels. Good Spanish hors d'oeuvres. A working fireplace, too.

J8 **Il Bistro**
93-A Pike   *682-3049*

Tucked away under the clock at the Pike Place Market, Il Bistro is the last word in quiet elegance, and more than a bit European. Fine place to come for an after-theater drink.

Nightlife

K6 **Crepe de Paris**
Rainier Square *623-4111*

The smallish downtown location is sleek, smart, and angular to match its setting in the fancy urban complex of Rainier Square.

H5 **Fitzgerald's**
Westin Hotel lobby, Fifth & Virginia *624-7400*

A long, narrow alcove off the Westin lobby, sleek and formal; good-looking seafood.

P9 **F.X. McRory's Steak, Chop & Oyster House**
Occidental S at S King *623-4800*

Little brother to Jake's, McR's has less sophistication and Old World charm, more Gilded Age bravura, and more bourbon than you can well imagine. Definitely has the edge in pasted-together LeRoy Neiman paintings costing $100,000. Go with a Seattle Prep grad who talks sports—loud.

L6 **Garden Court**
411 University (Four Seasons Olympic) *621-1700*

For a little piece of *Masterpiece Theater* in the heart of Seattle, the Garden Court is the place to go. Also go for the spectacular skylight, 23-foot windows, and massive trees.

K5 **The Goose Restaurant & Bar**
1326 Fifth Ave *682-3066*

The dark wood and secluded booths of this basement bar near the 5th Avenue Theater give it a mellow atmosphere perfect for before- or after-theater drinks. The place is jammed with young professionals after work.

I7 **Labuznik**
1924 First Ave *682-1624*

A fine restaurant with a well-stocked bar and exceedingly low lights giving it a hushed atmosphere.

M7 **Malia's Northwest**
820 Second Ave *624-3287*

An attractive, casual bar, looking out onto the street. The large round table in the middle of the bar is a nice place to meet people, and a goodly crowd gathers each day after work.

N6 **McCormick's**
722 Fourth Ave *682-3900*

Dark woods, brass, stand-up counters—it's the model of a classy San Francisco-style bar. The large tables are conducive to putting together business deals or meetings of the office clan. McCormick's attracts a smart young professional crowd relaxing after work, waiting for lunch in the fish-house restaurant, or gathering before a game at the Kingdome.

J6 **Oliver's**
Mayflower Park Hotel, Fourth & Olive *623-3363*

Oliver's is furnished in glass and chrome, but without any sacrifice in friendliness. A nice little streetscape view, with just enough bustle.

M7 **The Price Is Right**
308 Marion *624-7190*

Nightlife

Home of the 78-cent highball and the 1½-pound baked potato, $1.99–5.99, depending on which of the 30 toppings you want.

M8 **Red Cabbage**
75 Marion   *622-3822*

A hit with Federal Building employees and ferry-boat passengers. A tasty selection of free hors d'oeuvres at 5, 75-cent beer 4:30-6:30 weekdays.

E7 **Rosellini's Four-10**
Fourth & Wall   *624-5464*

A gathering place for admen, politicos, and business types of megabucks status. The bartenders are great, the drinks are always stiff and well mixed, and the air is full of important-sounding conversation. After work, singles and Regrade office workers move in.

L6 **Shucker's**
411 University (Four Seasons Olympic)   *621-1700*

A dark, cozy place which mixes excellent drinks and offers fine happy-hour hors d'oeuvres and tasty seafood dishes.

H5 **Trader Vic's**
Fifth & Westlake (Westin Hotel)   *624-8520*

Poly-poly decor, cutesy drinks, and other excesses, but the room is comfortable, the service is experienced, and the drinks are honest.

P9 **Umberto's**
100 S King   *621-0575*

An attractive, large upstairs bar above this popular Italian restaurant is a good spot for an after-Kingdome drink.

I7 **Virginia Inn**
1937 First Ave   *624-3173*

The Virginia Inn is an intriguingly schizoid place: by day it's for confirmed drinkers of a certain age (some look as if they've been there since the doors opened in 1901); by night, it's a refuge for the up-to-the-second hip, with avant-garde art on the old brick walls (the Inn is in the Pike Place Market Historical District). Three beers on tap, 17 in bottles, eight aperitifs, sake, pasties, and apple-and-cheese plates.

Bars — Other areas

GG6 **Boondock's, Sundecker's & Greenthumb's**
611 Broadway E   *323-7272*

Gerry Kingen is an important figure in Seattle bar history, the first to aggressively orchestrate atmosphere. Now Boondock's, the first big scene bar, looks 1973 on a street that's unforgivingly au courant. Kingen's Lion O'Reilly's down the street works better.

GG6 **The Broadway**
314 Broadway E   *323-1990*

It is no accident that the long stand-up bar at the Broadway looks like a display window: the patrons *are* on display, and dressed to kill. Valet parking.

Nightlife

GG6 Deluxe One Bar & Grill
625 Broadway E   *324-9697*

Formerly utilitarian, the time-honored Deluxe is now beferned and spiffy for the upscale, youngish Broadway boulevardiers. There is also a Deluxe Two north of University Village.

HH7 Duke's
236 First W   *283-4400*
10116 NE Eighth, Bellevue   *455-5775*

A snug singles bar with John Wayne memorabilia on the walls. It's a flashy, crowded scene on Friday and Saturday nights. Tasty snacks in the bar and a pretty good little restaurant adjoining.

HH3 The Fireside Room
900 Madison (Sorrento Hotel)   *622-6400*

This clubby little bar evokes the stately elegance of a leisurely world dominated by hearthside chats in overstuffed chairs, the day's news, or perhaps a hand of whist. A pleasant place to drop by for an after-theater drink; the appetizer menu is also available late. Service can be slow at times.

M3 Henry's Off Broadway
1705 E Olive Way   *329-8063*

"Her voice," said Scott Fitzgerald, "was full of money." She could've been a customer at Henry's, the spacious, posh watering spot on Capitol Hill. Watch for one-upsmanship out front: the valet parks the highest-status car in the place of honor (a Mercedes bumps an Audi, a Rolls a Mercedes, etc.). It's good fun.

HH6 Jake O'Shaughnessey's
100 Mercer (Hansen Baking Company) *285-1897*

In a town where ethnicity means an "Uff da" sticker on your Volvo, Jake's is truly Irish. It was built to look like an old bar with heart, and felt like one almost on opening. The unequalled array of Scotches and the fine Irish coffee are known far and wide, as is the bartender tenor, who ain't just singin' in the shower.

HH7 Lion O'Reilly's
132 Broadway E   *322-1710*

It's really "Lion O'Reilly's and B.J. Monkeyshines Eating & Drinking Establishment," to be precise, which should tell you something. Concept Albums of the 1960s, perhaps. The concept here is mahogany and mirrors, a shotgun wedding of Irish and Old West shticks. Preppy singles scene.

GG6 Morgan's Lakeplace
2 Lake Bellevue Drive, Bellevue   *455-2244*

Located on little Lake Bellevue, Morgan's is a place to see and be seen on the Eastside. It's a popular place to come after work and is especially crowded on Friday and Saturday nights. Lunch and dinner can be served in the bar if you're so inclined.

GG7 Settebello
1525 E Olive Way   *323-7772*

One of the best bartenders in town resides in this spiffy uptown Northern Italian restaurant. Crackling homemade potato chips are a nice touch, too.

Nightlife

FF7 **University Bar & Grill**
4553 University Way NE   *632-3275*

It's a little chilly in the decor department, but its proximity to the U assures a constant throng of lively customers. Besides the hard liquor, 22 wines are offered.

FF7 **University Tower Hotel Bar**
4507 Brooklyn NE   *634-2000*

The only place in the immediate vicinity that can qualify as a neighborhood haunt without also being a student haunt. Low-ceilinged and smoky.

Drinks with a view

EE9 **Acapulco y los Arcos**
6017 Seaview NW   *789-7373*

This northern outpost of the Californian gourmet-Mexican restaurant chain boasts spectacular Soundward views, especially at sunset, amusingly outlandish interior architecture (bulbous colored plaster formation that evokes mushrooms or volcanic eruptions), and a Baskin–Robbins theory of margaritas—21 flavors, ranging from peach and raspberry to banana and coconut.

I8 **Athenian Inn**
Main Arcade, Pike Place Market   *624-7166*

The only authentic place left in the Market, the modest Athenian is open early, has a beer list that will break your arm, and commands a superb view over Elliott Bay.

HH3 **Benjamin's**
Top of Seattle Trust Building   *454-8255*
10655 NE Fourth, Bellevue

This is the place Eastsiders bring out-of-towners for a view of Bellevue and Mount Rainier. Intimate with low lighting and comfortable modular seating, this is a popular spot for YPs. Tasty happy-hour hors d'oeuvres.

GG7 **Canlis'**
2576 Aurora N   *283-3313*

Perched high on the northeast corner of Queen Anne Hill, Canlis' offers a stunning view of Lake Union and the Cascades beyond. Canlis', a dignified old name in Seattle restaurants, has one of the city's most elegant bars; an evening here entails dressing up and spending some real money.

K9 **The Fisherman's**
Pier 57, Alaskan Way   *623-3500*

Another fine place to catch the sunset over Puget Sound, especially if you don't have time to go out to Shilshole Bay. Located at the end of Pier 57, near Waterfront Park, The Fisherman's restaurant has a delightful little dimly-lit upstairs bar which commands superb views over Elliott Bay and the docking ferries.

GG7 **Franco's Hidden Harbor**
1500 Westlake N   *282-0501*

A place to sit alongside the bobbing boats on Lake Union. It's usually jammed, jolly, and loud, as regulars table-hop or josh the waitresses. A pretty good bar lunch, too.

Nightlife

Girvan's
2701 First Ave   621-9313

Standard drinks, knockout view of the Sound.

Hiram's at the Locks
5300 34th NW   784-1733

A nice place to sit and sip and watch the nautical world go by (to or from the Hiram M. Chittenden Boat Locks to the south—hence the name). There's a grassy patio outside for toasting Seattle's occasional fair weather.

Horatio's
1200 Westlake N   284-2535

Happily, the management has deep-sixed the *H.M.S. Pinafore* decor and waitress attire, leaving unobstructed the beautiful water's-edge view of Lake Union.

The Lakeside
2501 N Northlake Way   634-0823

Formerly Gasworks, redecorated but still a sailor's paradise—you can tie up at the pier, quaff daiquiris, and sail off without touching dry land. Delightful Lake Union view.

Leschi Lakecafe
102 Lakeside Ave S   328-2233

Another of Tim Firnstahl's incarnations, this one is in sleepy Leschi on the shore of Lake Washington and caters to the local sailing and preppy community. Good beers on tap.

Mirabeau
46th Floor, Seafirst Building   624-4550
Fourth & Madison

The most elevated (700 feet up) spot for a drink in Seattle, with prices to match. The spectacular aerial views of the bay make it worthwhile.

Ray's Boathouse
6049 Seaview NW   789-3770

A fisherman's hangout recently invaded by three-pieced YPs, and the more interesting for it. Ray's affords the best view of the sunset over Shilshole Bay and the Olympics, and everybody knows it—so it's apt to be packed of a nice weekend evening. You can rent boats downstairs (783-9779), or dock your own and saunter up for a grog.

Red Robin
Eastlake E & Fuhrman E   323-0917

Originally Seattle's collegiate Algonquin Club, it is now part of the flashy Red Robin burger-and-cocktail chain. Still, this branch overlooking Portage Bay has the advantage of being one of the few restaurant bars in the city with a deck offering a fine view of the water and passing boats. Elaborate and exotic cocktails flow freely too.

Space Needle
Seattle Center   447-3100

"Seattle's most overlooked restaurant," say the ads, and for years it was with good reason. They're trying to upgrade the fare; at last report, the specialty drinks

Nightlife

resembled Sno-Cones, but the view took the sting out of the $2.50 elevator ride. (Free ride for restaurant patrons, not bar patrons.)

EE9 **Stuart's At Shilshole**
6135 Seaview NW   *784-7974*

Much roomier than neighboring Ray's, and with an essentially similar view. Ray's is more of a scene, however.

GG7 **Sundays**
620 First N (Hansen Baking Company)   *284-0456*

Dimly lit, but with the best available view of the Space Needle by night.

Wine bars

J5 **Enoteca**
1522 Fifth Ave   *624-9108*

About 30 wines by the glass in a wine-cellar setting. Good prices. There are informal tastings on Saturdays, often featuring winemakers.

I6 **1904**
1904 Fourth Ave   *682-4142*

A noisy, modern upstairs full bar, with some 15 wines by the glass.

H5 **Shampers**
1900 Fifth Ave, Westin Hotel   *624-7400*

Upholstered elegance and comfort, and 55 wines by the glass at the full bar.

GG8 **Le Tastevin**
19 W Harrison   *283-0991*

GG7 About 30 sherries and 20 ports are served by the glass in this top-notch French restaurant. Exquisite happy-hour hors d'oeuvres are also offered.

Gay bars

Gay bars and discos sprout and fade with the speed and unpredictability of mushrooms in the spring. Those listed here have both longevity and stylistic predictability, and you can find out what's new and hot by a visit to one of them. **Tugs**
G8 **Belltown Tavern** (2207 First Avenue) is *the* social, see-and-be-seen spot; lots of straight trendies drop in for the new-new new-wave music and dancing on
I2 Wednesday nights (The Scene). Incredibly crowded on weekends. **The AxelRock Saloon** (1114 Howell), is a Levi's-and-leather men's dance bar, catering to a late-20's, early-30's crowd. An elaborate sound system produces rock on weeknights and disco (with live DJs) on weekends.

Pubs

HH6 **Canterbury Ale & Eats**
534 15th Ave E   *322-3130*

Nightlife

A cozy place to drink in quasi-olde-English-pub musty splendor.

FF7 **College Inn Pub**
4006 University Way NE   *634-2307*

Since the state's antediluvian liquor laws prohibit one on-campus, the closest thing to a Rathskeller at the UW is the College Inn: dark, rough-wood decor, dartboards, and a private room or two for student symposia.

L8 **Mark Tobey**   *682-1333*
First & Madison (Alexis Hotel)

A stylized English pub, with English lunches and suppers, a crowd of city and arts activists, and an extensive collection of beers and fresh ales.

FF7 **Murphy's, A Pub**
2110 N 45th   *634-2110*

A little bit of Hibernia in the heart o' the Great Northwest. Entertainment nightly, tending to the Irish and country/bluegrass. More beers than even a Dubliner could get through in an evening.

Taverns

FF7 **Blue Moon Tavern**
712 NE 45th   *545-9775 (pay phone)*

If the Blue Moon's scarred old wooden tables could talk, they'd reminisce about bibulous visits by Kerouac and Ginsberg and Tom Robbins. The Moon's restroom walls can talk a sailorly blue streak, but we can't reprint it. Despite a recent facelift, the place retains its somewhat seedy charm, and a whiff of its colorful history.

FF7 **The Buckaroo**
4201 Fremont N   *634-3161*

Fremont is Seattle's sole remaining funky neighborhood, and the Buckaroo belongs here. Good pizza.

O8 **Central Tavern**
207 First S   *622-0209*

The Central is a haunt for government and Pioneer Square types.

HH6 **Comet Tavern**
922 E Pike   *323-9853*

The Comet isn't as countercultural as it used to be, but just as funky. Thanks to the Empty Space across the street, it's *the* place for theater gossip. As corporate symbol and perennial Presidential candidate Ed Comet asks: "Where else can you go and drink beer like a normal person?"

FF7 **Dante's**
5300 Roosevelt Way NE   *525-1300*

UW student haunt, with incessant pool, video, and air-hockey games. Widescreen TV upstairs.

GG7 **Fat Albert's**
2245 Eastlake E   *322-9000*

A rowdy rec room for the post-hippie houseboat crowd.

Nightlife

O8 J&M Cafe
201 First S 624-1670

In a district festooned with tavs, this is the largest and one of the most energetic. What it is, pretty much, is one big brick room with a very long bar at the entrance.

FF7 Northlake Tavern & Pizza House
660 NE Northlake Way 633-5317

The reason to drink beer here is to complement the famous pizza—thick and multiply bedecked.

II4 Roanoke Inn
1825 72nd SE, Mercer Island 232-0800

This rustic old Mercer Island country tavern is a fine place to relax over a cool beer after a bike ride round the island. Locals often stop here on their way home from work, too. You'll find it near where the island meets the bridge on the west side.

FF7 Roanoke Park Place
2409 10th E 324-5882

Gone is the pool table; video games are unheard of; soon to come this summer is a beer garden out back. The Roanoke's new owners have made the old tav into a badly needed hangout for North Capitol Hill's new gentry (the ones who still own a pair of bluejeans). Tasty snacks include hamburgers on French rolls, steamed clams, and oysters baked in the shell over the fireplace. There are seven draft beers, 20 bottled, and a dozen wines by glass or bottle.

GG8 Targy's Tavern
Sixth Ave W & Crockett 285-9700

Targy's is the unofficial, multi-generational Upper Queen Anne Community Center. Perhaps it's its consummate ordinariness, or funny mix of friendliness and exclusivity, that sparks Targy's reputation as Seattle's quintessential neighborhood tavern.

FF7 318 Tavern
318 Nickerson 285-9763

Hot and packed of a warm summer night, the 318 is just the place to welcome you to funky Fremont (just across the orange bridge). Beer is the main order of the evening, but the chef's piece de resistance—the Fries and Burger Basket—features a secret grease with a hint of mayo. A strangely satisfying repast. Enjoy it at the long narrow bar or over a game of pool in the back.

G8 Watertown Tavern
2301 First Ave 624-8436

Aggressively urban artsies, opponents to US policy in El Salvador, plus a few sailors, oldtime riffraff, and vestigial sproutheads, mingle in the roomy confines of the Watertown. The tav is part of the trend toward a new Soho-ified Belltown, still a distant dream.

Nightlife

Entertainment

Seattle nightlife has improved dramatically in the last decade. No longer a sleepy town of Puritan homebodies, Seattle has discovered the pleasures of eating out, dancing, and listening to music. The tavern rock scene is especially strong, with scores of watering holes to choose from. Though the imported new wave and new jazz action is sometimes wanting, there are plenty of energetic homegrown experimentalists. The city sports two jazz clubs, one featuring major traveling acts, the other, nationally-known pianists. The Northwest folk and folkdance scene runs deep, too, with several regular outlets and an annual Folklife Festival that attracts 100,000 people. Seattleites tend to be blase about it, but there are few nightlife districts in any city as lively as Pioneer Square, where ten clubs may be all going at once on a Friday night.

Large venues

H6 Broadway Performance Hall *587-3806*
Broadway & Pine

A fine little theater with excellent acoustics, associated with Seattle Central Community College.

G7 Cornish Theater *323-1400*
710 E Roy

A center for the avant-garde since the '30s, Cornish students and faculty present unusual creations here regularly.

K4 Hippodrome *628-0434*
Seventh & Union (entrance on Union)

Formerly an Eagles ballroom, this huge, neoclassic auditorium downtown now hosts teen dances and rock shows. With its square pillars, hardwood dance floor, chandeliers, and two-seat-deep balcony surrounding the entire floor, it is indeed grand.

Q9 Kingdome *628-3311*
201 S King

This squat concrete nob, an urban echo of Mount Rainier on a clear day, occasionally tries to present music, on the order of the Rolling Stones, with very little success. Nobody who goes cares.

EE8 Monroe Center *782-0505*
1810 NW 65th

A dream come true for the Seattle Folklore Society, this scuttled Ballard junior high school is now headquarters for major folk acts, national and international.

I4 Music Hall Theater *621-8822 or 282-1880*
Seventh & Olive

Seattle just doesn't seem to want a supper-club theater, but various promoters keep trying to give the idea new life. It's a swell place, with tiers of cocktail and dining tables and a large stage in the grand manner of nightclubs of yore.

J3 Paramount Theater *682-1414*
901 Pine

This lavish old moviehouse, established in 1927, hosted rock acts through the '70s. In 1981, they scrubbed the marijuana smoke off the chandeliers and generally gave a facelift to the old gal. She really shines. Everything from soft rock to Vegas acts.

Nightlife

B6 **Seattle Center**	*625-4234*
Bounded by Mercer, Denny, Fifth Ave, and First Ave	

Home of the Opera House, where the Seattle Symphony and Seattle Opera perform, the Arena, where the acoustics are okay at large concerts by the likes of Miles Davis, and the Coliseum, which hosts dinosaur rock artists. The Center House also books a regular series of concerts by local acts; the Seattle Center itself is the scene of musical festivals such as Bumbershoot and the Folklife Festival.

G2 **Seattle Concert Theater**	*624-2770*
1153 John	

The most pleasant, intimate concert venue in town, this little theater with one balcony used to be a Lutheran church. Owned by the Seattle Times across the street; it would be a sacrilege if they ever chose to tear it down.

Showbox Theater	*633-5005*
142 First Ave	

Scene of Seattle's first major new-wave rock concerts, the Showbox has had mixed fortunes, with its all-ages (no alcohol) policy and rundown First Avenue location. When it's on, though, there's not a nicer place to be.

FF6 **University of Washington**	*543-2100*
Bounded by 15th NE, NE 45th, Pacific, and Montlake	

Chamber music and other musical events at acoustically superb Meany Theater; Kane Hall hosts more modest crowds; HUB Ballroom, in the student union building, has rock dances and other concerts. The basketball court and bleachers of Hec Edmundson Pavilion, named for UW basketball coach (1921-47) Clarence S. "Hec" Edmundson, occasionally provide better-than-reasonable acoustics for rock concerts.

HH6 **Washington Hall Performance Gallery**	
153 14th	*325-7901*

This small theater with the funky balcony has hosted some of the finest performance art in the country.

H5 **Westin Hotel Ballroom**	*447-5000*
Fifth Ave & Olive Way	

The new Westin Hotel sports a third-floor ballroom that can host a 1,200-person event that isn't even noticed within the labyrinthine new complex.

Clubs — Pioneer Square & Downtown

H6 **Astor Park**	*625-1578*
415 Lenora	

The jumpy new-wavers get their choppy music and hard drinks in tall doses here. A young, hip dancing crowd that ranges from students to stewardesses. The volume's high, so you're not going to talk; you're going to dance to the top draws in town, as well as new-wave nationals graduating from the club to concert scene. The video screen offers a variety of contemporary rock visuals. Snappy, trashy, and fashion-conscious, Astor Park has its thumb on the pulse of the '80s.

P8 **Blarney Stone**	*624-5928*
323 Second Ave S	

Pioneer Square spot features light jazz, not Irish music; closes early.

Nightlife

Central Tavern　　　　　　　　622-0209
207 First Ave S

Large, funky, and comfortable Pioneer Square establishment that features local rock and rhythm and blues; Guinness on tap.

Comedy Underground　　　　　628-0303
222 S Main

The best in national and local comedy is featured at this Pioneer Square cabaret beneath Swannie's tavern. Be prepared for some audience involvement with the entertainment.

Doc Maynard's　　　　　　　　682-4649
610 First Ave

The long Pioneer Square bar, bluegrass music, and country rock have been packing them in for years.

Ernestine's　　　　　　　　　　624-2389
313 Occidental Mall

Formerly Parnell's, this venerable Pioneer Square jazz club is now owned by a quartet of investors that includes namesake Ernestine Anderson, Seattle's internationally famous vocalist. As comfortable as a living room, but thankfully not as casual, Ernestine's only serves beer and wine and the food isn't much. Nevertheless, people come back again and again for the solid mainstream jazz (national as well as local acts) and the friendly, low-key atmosphere. Jazz is a tough business. Let's hope Ernestine's can keep the faith.

Golden Crown　　　　　　　　622-5304
1608 Times Court (across from The Bon on Fourth Ave)

Up a long flight of stairs above the Chinese restaurant of the same name, the dark, low-ceilinged cocktail lounge consists of a large dance floor and a great expanse of square formica tables. The Crown features little-known experimental rock bands, unusual national acts, and reggae.

Hibble & Hyde's　　　　　　　623-1541
608 First Ave

Young professional rock musicians. Hard dancing, beer-drinking; open 'til 4am.

Merchant's Cafe　　　　　　　624-1515
109 Yesler Way

Music is mostly local lounge acts in Seattle's oldest restaurant, which is a spectacular example of Pioneer Square's turn-of-the-century appointments.

Michael J's　　　　　　　　　　623-7767
114 First Ave S

Hard liquor, hard rock.

Mint　　　　　　　　　　　　　624-1365
Pike Place Market

Long, narrow room located upstairs in the Sanitary Market building, featuring local blues and rhythm-and-blues acts. Homey.

Pier 70　　　　　　　　　　　　624-8090
Foot of Alaskan Way & Broad

Nightlife

Top 40 bands, singles. Great view of the harbor through plate glass, big dance floor, video games, and pool.

O8 **Pioneer Square Tavern** *223-9051*
111 Yesler Way

The PST is literally on Skid Road: back in the early days, Yesler Way was steep enough to skid logs down to the water, and the name stuck when the neighborhood went downhill with the timber. But this funky tavern has a sparkle in its eye, and the management keeps the real undesirables on the sidewalk. Unpredictable, but often rewarding, local jazz and rock musicians. No cover.

E7 **Rio Cafe** *622-6613*
Fifth & Denny Way

Folk-rock, Latin, and light jazz for the chi-chi Western set. Don't forget your cowboy boots and turquoise bracelet.

O9 **Tijuana Tilly's** *682-9095*
309 First Ave S

Formerly Juan Miguel's, this okay Mexican restaurant features a real Latin nightclub downstairs, with salsa and rhythm bands that have the authentic touch and a crowd to match.

Clubs — University District & North End

GG8 **Back Court Tavern** *282-9982*
1524 15th Ave W

A little out of the way, the Back Court features solid local folk acts in an intimate environment. When weather permits, musicians perform outside in the garden amphitheater.

FF8 **Backstage** *789-6953*
2208 NW Market

The Scandinavian owners of the Ballard restaurant Vaersgo recently reopened this languishing ballroom, hidden inside the Eagles building that also houses their eatery. A wonderful, huge place with a real hardwood dance floor and full bar, plus a bar in the foyer, the Backstage features the top rock acts in town.

FF8 **Buffalo Tavern** *782-9754*
5403 Ballard NW

A longstanding favorite hippie–redneck tavern, the Buffalo has had its ups and downs, but remains an outpost for new bands and boogie-down dancing.

FF7 **College Inn Pub** *634-2307*
4002 University Way NE

Local folk and bluegrass acts make merry as you sip your locally brewed Red Hook Ale. Rooms in the back are just right for solving the world's problems in this underground U District tavern.

B5 **Dez's 400** *283-5825*
400 Mercer

Unpretentious tavern across the street from the Seattle Center, featuring local rock.

Nightlife

CC7 Flame   *364-0370*
10815 Roosevelt Way NE

The big horseshoe bar used to host cowboys and country music; now it's country rock. Large dance floor.

DD8 G-Note Tavern   *783-8112*
Third & NW 85th

The gigantic G-Note features rock and folk acts on the "granola" circuit, but on Tuesdays and Wednesdays something special happens when local bands call and teach square and contra-dances. The atmosphere is warm and open, non-competitive, nothing like those Western dress-ups sponsored by the Square Dancing Federation. Sunday features the Seattle Independent Comedy Co-op's standup comic laff-offs. A real relief from the rest of the nightlife scene, the G-Note is a family affair, with a cheerfulness special to the thriving Northwest folk scene. Beer and wine only.

FF7 Hall of Fame   *633-5500*
4518 University Way NE

Cocktail rock and the best in local new wave. Similar to Astor Park: jumpy, young, fashion-conscious.

FF7 Jazz Alley   *632-7414*
4135 University Way NE

It's taken a while for this U District jazz club to find its niche, but the frequent line-ups at the door argue that it's one of the most pleasant packages in town. It's certainly the nicest-looking, a pleasure to sit in: an airy, open spot, stripped down to the pipes and painted over with an understated coat of white. Jazz Alley presents the finest in national jazz pianists, from Tommy Flanagan to Dave McKenna. Because it's also a pretty good Mediterranean restaurant, the crowd often comes to eat and not to listen; but on a good night, the aficionados hover around the piano and the talkers sit in back. No cover.

DD6 Jolly Roger Roadhouse   *524-7479*
8721 Lake City Way NE

A speakeasy in the 1920s, with a lookout turret above and prostitution cribs below to prove it, this rococo roadhouse was granted status as an historic monument in 1981. Since then, the new owners have established the place as a rhythm-and-blues spot, featuring local and national acts, and have restored the basement to its original speakeasy decor. Dancing upstairs in the biscuits 'n' gravy ballroom, drinks below.

GG8 Lofurno's   *283-7980*
2060 15th W

The excellent Italian restaurant downstairs features a piano bar with good Seattle talent; upstairs, in an old ballroom, the Mickey Martin Orchestra plays authentic swing and the irrepressible Vonne Griffin takes you down memory lane with her gutsy vocals.

FF6 Longhorn Bar & Grill   *523-8856*
4530 Union Bay Pl NE

Enormous, low-ceilinged country'n'western spot, the only one even close to downtown. All-you-can-eat ribs, Lone Star beer, countless photographs of Hopalong Cassidy and other "Western" paraphernalia, plus solid local country bands make this a shonuff country spot. Large dance floor.

Nightlife

FF7	**Medieval Cellar** 400 NE 45th	*632-2231*

Dress up and dance to disco-tinged Top 40. Sleek as a Camaro.

FF7	**Murphy's** 2110 N 45th	*634-2110*

Irish theme, with folk music, imported Irish musicians, and Guinness on tap, served at room temperature. Crowded, and for good reasons. Darts.

FF7	**O'Banion's** 5220 Roosevelt Way NE	*523-3463*

Local rock, pitchers of beer, and 10-foot TV screen upstairs.

FF8	**Owl Cafe** 5140 Ballard Ave NW	*784-3640*

As comfortable a spot as you'll find in Seattle, the Owl is located in the old Scandinavian district of Ballard, and still retains a homey, neighborhood flavor. Seattle acts change every night, there's a good dance area, and the crowd is lively and friendly.

BB7	**Parker's** 17001 Aurora N	*542-9491*

This enormous ballroom north of town with the spectacular latticed ceiling and chairs to match has an illustrious history that goes back to the '20s, when it was a dance-band roadhouse. Everyone from Tommy Dorsey to Ray Charles has played Parker's. During the '50s, it hosted Seattle's early rockers, like the Kingsmen and Wailers, then in the '70s it was the major rock emporium, The Aquarius. For the '80s, it's a Top 40 dinner-and-dance place when it's not hosting national touring acts.

FF7	**Rainbow Tavern** 722 NE 45th	*632-3360*

This huge U District tavern, as comfortable as an old workboot, has hosted the best of the long-haired local and national rock and blues acts. The audience drinks beer by the pitcher and boogies 'til it drops.

EE8	**Rainy Town Folk Music Club** 1810 NW 65th	*323-2838*

Seattle waited a long time for a specialty folk music club, so it was a bit of a disappointment that one opened in an old junior high school, the Monroe Center, purchased by the Seattle Folklore Society. Nevertheless, they've done up the old classroom rather nicely, and the music's excellent. No alcohol.

Clubs — Other areas

GG2	**Ad Lib Tavern** 23803 104th Ave SE, Kent	*854-3059*

Young crowds of suburban longhairs pack this hard-drinking tav and dance to heavy metal.

HH6	**Gatsby's** 12700 Bel-Red Road, Bellevue	*455-0666*

A young drinking crowd with a lot of nervous energy dances here to the top acts in the area, under a post-and-beam barnroof amid "sailing" decor of rough-cut lumber and ropes.

HH6 **Gene's Place** 323-6006
2304 E Union

Soul food and light soul music. A mellow spot.

GG7 **Matzoh Momma's** 324-MAMA
509 15th Ave E

A Jewish deli by day, Matzoh Momma's features live music by night. Two nights a week, Seattle favorite Joni Metcalf hosts the very popular Singer's Showcase, a sign-up sort of affair that attracts everyone from rank amateurs to topnotch pros. Other nights there's comedy, light jazz, vocal groups, etc., to accompany your chopped-liver sandwich. The folksy yet upscale audience is supportive and generous. No cover.

AA1 **Silver Spoon** 788-2734
Main & Stella, Duvall

The tiny country-hippie town of Duvall is one of the area's folk-music hubs. The Silver Spoon, an excellent restaurant, hosts national and local acts of distinction in its upstairs concert hall. Folding chairs; no booze.

Lounges, piano bars, & discos — Downtown

I4 **The Cloud Room, Camlin Hotel**
1619 Ninth Ave 682-0100

As warm and pleasant as Rob and Laura Petrie's living room on *The Dick Van Dyke Show*, the Cloud Room looks out over Lake Union to the north, and the city skyline from downtown to Queen Anne on the west. The drinks are well-mixed, and Gil Conte will sing your request gladly if you pass him a Queen's 1886 cigar. This is the closest you'll ever get in Seattle—if you want to—to authentic East Coast gloss in a nightclub.

F5 **Dog House**
2230 Seventh Ave 624-2741

Rivaled only by the Tropics for enthusiasm, the patrons at this piano bar do carry on. Be prepared to let your hair down.

F8 **Edgewater Inn**
2411 Alaskan Way 624-7000

Gloria Jean holds forth at the piano bar—a real one, the type with a counter circling the grand piano—as customers request, and sometimes even sing, their favorites. In a city that ought to have more spots where you can have a drink with a view, the Edgewater will have to do.

L6 **Garden Court, Four Seasons Olympic Hotel**
411 University 621-1700

Spacious and grand, with 40-foot trees, high French windows, and upholstered, high-back chairs, the formal but friendly Garden Court is the *piece de resistance* of the newly remodeled Olympic Hotel. The patrons' pearls and basic black set off the marble planters and gold banisters nicely. There's dancing on a small parquet floor to a society combo (piano bar during the week). Have lunch, high tea, a

Nightlife

drink and hors d'oeuvres, or a torte and coffee. You may overhear a good commodities tip from the table next door.

J5	**Goose**	
	1326 Fifth Ave	*682-3066*

Piano bar beneath the 5th Avenue Theater is a popular dining spot. The Old Seattle decor—paneling and brass—was retrieved from the old White Henry Stuart Building across the street.

J5	**Green's, Seattle Sheraton**	
	Sixth & Union	*621-9000*

Long and low lounge in the brand-new Sheraton Hotel features top local acts, with dancing. No one is sure why it's called Green's, but maybe the seaweed-looking stuff hanging from the ceiling (or the waterfall behind the bar) has something to do with it.

L5	**Morilles, Park Hilton**	
	Sixth & Seneca	*464-1980*

High-tech, two-tiered bar in the Park Hilton features piano music and a spiffy downtown atmosphere.

M8	**Red Cabbage**	
	75 Marion St	*622-3822*

Not a bad place to wait for the ferry: there's a real piano bar (the kind with wraparound seating), varnished natural-wood decor, imported beer, and connoisseur wines by the ounce, glass, or bottle.

E7	**Rosellini's Four-10**	
	Fourth & Wall	*624-5464*

Lush, rich wood paneling surrounds the triangular piano bar that accommodates both diners waiting for a table in the restaurant and locals in for a couple of martinis. Tends to be a neighborhood hangout for media types, pols, and other offices in the area.

D9	**Smuggler**	
	Pier 70, Foot of Broad & Alaskan Way	*623-8343*

Nice view of the water from this bar featuring variety shows of local lounge entertainment.

H5	**Tally Ho, Sixth Avenue Motor Inn**	
	2000 Sixth Ave	*682-8300*

Average lounge with above-average acts.

K5	**Top of the Hilton, Hilton Hotel**	
	Sixth & University	*464-1980*

Top 40 lounge trios and quartets. Singles and couples. Nice view.

H7	**Vogue**	
	2018 First Ave	*625-9739*

Formerly the punk/new-wave club Wrex, this high-tech tavern, with the prices written in white lipstick on the mirror behind the bar, features local new-wave art, video, and loud recorded dance music. Ultra-chic.

Nightlife

Lounges, piano bars, & discos — North End

F7 America's Cup 633-0161
1900 N Northlake Way

Primarily a restaurant for Seattle's nouveau quiche, this spiffy spot with the sailing motif overlooking Lake Union features Jack Brownlow, far and away the best piano-bar pianist in the city. The late Paul Desmond, who played with Dave Brubeck, once declared, "If I could play piano, I'd want to play like Jack Brownlow." The piano nook off the main bar is a little exposed, but features comfortable living-room furniture.

GG7 Latitude 47 284-1047
1232 Westlake N

The diners have a view of Lake Union; lounge patrons view the diners. Dance floor, quality Top 40 lounge acts.

EE9 Quinn's 784-4070
7001 Seaview Ave NW

Top 40 bands have kept the singles hopping at this waterside wateringhole, formerly known as the Windjammer, for over five years. The formula seems to work: romance by the water, with sailboats out the window. And when it doesn't, you can always hop over to one of the other Shilshole nightspots. Disco Monday nights.

F7 Simonetti's 632-0848
4312 Aurora N

Piano bar upstairs at this Italian restaurant features opera singers Tuesday through Saturday, emceed with verve by Howard Bulson. Sunday and Monday it's jazz and pop favorites at the piano.

EE9 Stuart's at Shilshole 784-7974
6135 Seaview NW

Piano bar by the water with booth seating and a spiffy crowd. Disco in the lounge.

HH7 Sundays 284-0456
620 First Ave N (Hansen Baking Company)

Best in local comedy, weekends; disco during the week at this active Lower Queen Anne spot located in an old brick church.

GG7 Tropics 624-6789
Aurora N at John

Tucked in behind the parking garage at the Tropics Hotel is a campy little grotto with red booth furniture and a velvet painting behind the piano. Lyric sheets are provided for the singalong crowd, which sometimes gets quite crazy.

FF7 University Tower 634-2000
NE 45th & Brooklyn NE

Best lounge in the U District.

Lounges, piano bars, & discos — Other areas

Q6 Chiyoko 623-9347
610 S Jackson

Q7 Japanese open mike draws an astonishing array of interesting amateur performers in the back room of this popular sushi bar.

Nightlife

OO5 **Doubletree Plaza** *575-8220*
16500 Southcenter Parkway

The Boojum Tree lounge features live trios for dancing and listening; across the highway, the Doubletree Inn has disco in the Infinity Lounge.

HH6 **Henry's Off Broadway** *329-8063*
1705 E Olive Way

The piano music here is mainly a sonic backdrop for the scene at this spats'n'spiff Capitol Hill singles spot, but the music is usually good, for anyone who cares to listen. Oysters Rockefeller flame up behind the wraparound bar as the customers sip popsicle drinks and strike movie poses.

HH3 **Jonah and the Whale** *455-5240*
11211 Main, Bellevue

Lounge serves the Bellevue Holiday Inn and the Eastside with the top local acts.

MM4 **Sheraton Renton Hotel** *226-7700*
800 Rainier Ave S, Renton

Comedy on the weekends in Brandy's piano lounge (during the week it's just piano) and Top 40 rock upstairs in The Penthouse.

Shopping

Shopping areas	98	
Department stores	99	
Fashion	101	Accessories & luggage
	103	Children's clothes
	105	Fabric, sewing, and knitting
	107	Jewelry
	109	Large, tall, maternity, petite
	110	Lingerie
	110	Men's and women's wear
	117	Rainwear
	118	Vintage clothes
Food & drink	120	Bakeries
	122	Butchers
	123	Candies & chocolates
	124	Catering & gourmet take-out
	127	Cheese
	127	Coffees and teas
	128	Consumer food cooperatives
	129	Delis
	132	Health food stores
	133	Pasta
	133	Produce markets
	134	Seafood
	135	State liquor stores
	135	Wine
Home	138	Antiques
	141	Auctions
	141	Hardware
	143	Home furnishings
	146	Kitchenware
	148	Rugs
	148	Stereo equipment
Other	149	Books
	152	Camera

97

Shopping

154	Computers
155	Florists and nurseries
158	Gifts
161	Imports
163	Magazines & newspapers
164	Outdoor equipment
168	Records
170	Toys
173	Graphic art shops

Shopping areas

Here's a brief orientation to the shopping districts in the Seattle area.

K6 **Downtown.** There are two main centers, one around the large **department stores** on Pine between Third and Sixth, and the other around the elegant and expensive **Rainier Square** at Fourth and Union. Most of the department stores are open seven days a week (and Monday and Friday evenings), Rainier Square Monday through Saturday.

H8-J8 **Pike Place Market.** This is the spot for food-related stores, as well as secondhand goods and hand-crafted wares. Located on First between Pike and Virginia and west to the Waterfront, the Market is open Monday through Saturday.

N8-P8 **Pioneer Square.** Around First and Yesler, this is the locale for galleries, plus antique, clothing, and gift shops. Many are open seven days.

GG6-7 HH6-7 **Capitol Hill.** From Denny to Roy on Broadway, there are boutiques and a major collection of home-furnishings shops. Some stores have extended hours to accommodate evening strollers.

EE7-FF7 **University District.** "The Ave" has a concentration of book stores and shops catering to students, plus interesting boutiques and restaurants; NE 40th to NE 55th along University Way NE. Most shops stay open Thursday evening.

FF6 **University Village.** The city's one close-in shopping mall, with fine specialty food stores. Most shops are also open Thursday and Friday evening, and Sunday afternoon. At the intersection of 25th NE and NE 45th, just north of UW's Husky Stadium.

DD7 **Northgate.** One of the first malls in the nation, now modernized and quite complete; Interstate 5 at Northgate Way (about NE 110th). Most stores are also open Monday-Friday evenings, and Sunday afternoon.

AA7 **Aurora Village.** Really suburban—at Highway 99 (Aurora) and N 205th—and runs the full gamut of stores and services. Open also Monday through Friday evening and Sunday afternoon.

OO5 **Southcenter.** A comprehensive covered mall; many furnishings stores cluster in the area just to the south. Close to Sea-Tac airport, just off I-5 at the Renton-Southcenter exit; most stores are also open Monday-Friday evening, and Sunday afternoon.

05 **Pavilion Outlet Center.** 7900 Southcenter Parkway, south of Southcenter. A huge array of discount shops. Also open weekday evenings and Sunday afternoon.

H3 **Bellevue Square.** On the Eastside: the most glittering shopping mall, with a full range of goods, though not much in the way of home furnishings. You won't notice. In Bellevue, NE Eighth at Bellevue Way; also open Monday-Friday evenings, Sunday afternoon.

H3 **Olde Bellevue.** Traditional shops catering to the Eastside carriage trade. Open Monday through Saturday, hours vary. Main St at Bellevue Way.

J2 **Factoria Square.** Yet another suburban shopping mall; family-oriented shops. Also open weekday evenings and Sunday afternoon.

H1 **Crossroads.** A handsome Eastside shopping center, ringed with fast-food places, carriage-trade clothing shops. In Bellevue at NE Eighth at 156th NE; also open Monday-Friday evenings, Sunday afternoon.

Gilman Village, Issaquah. A novel idea: taking old houses, moving them to a boardwalk complex, and filling them up with shops, mostly housewares and gifts. Take I-90 east to Issaquah. Hours vary; it's best to call and check.

Department stores

The retail core of downtown Seattle is alive and well, due to the long-time presence of four major stores within a three-block area on Pine Street. The stores are large and prosperous, the merchandise abundant, varied, and attractively presented. The Bon offers selection and good value; Frederick & Nelson has well-priced quality merchandise in attractive surroundings; Nordstrom displays its upbeat apparel in a seemingly endless choice of dynamic departments; and I. Magnin pitches serene elegance in a luxurious setting. All have beauty salons which may open earlier than regular store hours.

6 **The Bon** *Open every day*
Third & Pine *344-2121*

The Bon is big (nine floors on a city block) and offers a full complement of services: tire center, pharmacy, babysitting, ticket office, shoe repair, optometrist, engraving, three restaurants, travel service, post office, liquor store, and a bakery (noted for its blueberry muffins).

Good-looking, moderate-priced merchandise, and lots of it, is The Bon's specialty. They also carry some of the more expensive lines found at Nordstrom and Frederick's: for instance, Anne Klein and Albert Nipon are two of the labels in the Northwest Room, and Baccarat crystal is stocked in glassware.

Particularly noteworthy are the women's sportswear department, and the large and attractive linen and fine furniture departments.

I5 **Frederick & Nelson** *Open every day*
Fifth & Pine *682-5500*

Frederick & Nelson has made some dramatic changes in recent years while retaining many of the grand traditions which have made it a Seattle institution: a doorman to assist with packages; Frango chocolates made in the store; spring and fall international fashion shows; children's breakfasts at Christmas and Easter; the Steuben glass shop, a Northwest exclusive; the Wide World Shop featuring antiques and collectible porcelains, and a small art gallery.

Designs by Blass, Beene, Halston, St. Laurent, Missoni, Hermes, Givenchy, Chanel, and others are stunningly showcased, along with original jewelry and accessories. But don't stop here. Four floors are devoted to apparel so there is much more, representing a wide range in prices. The men's department is very large, with good selection. Leave the children in the store's kindergarten, enjoy lunch at one of the five restaurants, and explore all 10 floors.

New and not to be missed is the spectacular Arcade, the completely refurbished basement housing a wine shop, fresh pasta shop, and a good bakery, plus a great deli selling sausage, hundreds of cheeses, fresh seafood, salads, dairy products, a variety of imported delicacies, and many items prepared in Frederick's own kitchens. Also in the Arcade: a newsstand with over a thousand publications, a cafe, espresso bar, pipe and tobacco shop, shoe repair, chocolate dipping, cake decorating, cooking demonstrations and a cooking school, a housewares section, cameras, and an outstanding book department.

Christmas at Frederick & Nelson is a local tradition. The holiday season brings out gorgeous decorations, amusing animated window displays, strolling minstrels in Dickensian costumes, and wide-eyed children waiting to see Santa.

J5 | **I. Magnin** | *Open Mon-Sat*
| **Sixth & Pine** | *682-6111*

This small and tasteful store is the most northern branch of its California parent company. From the clean-lined marble facade to the dignified and spare designer floor, it exudes calm and class. The first floor is the most lively, with a well-appointed men's store carrying sportswear by Valentino, Armani, and Polo. There is a large leather department with some fine things from Louis Vuitton. Also on this floor are cosmetics, jewelry, accessories, gifts, and in the accessories area, are imaginative blouses, sweaters, and jackets less expensively priced than clothing elsewhere in the store. Magnin's carries many of the lines found at Frederick's and Nordstrom but a couple of exclusives found on the designer floor are Adolfo and Hanae Mori. The small children's department is particularly good for gift-giving grandparents.

J6 | **Nordstrom** | *Open every day*
| **Fifth & Pine** | *628-2111*

This locally owned success story owes much of that success to the Nordstrom emphasis on service. The extremely helpful sales staff is very well informed about current fashions and their store's merchandise, and they dress to emphasize the point.

Shoes are the Nordstrom specialty; in fact Nordstrom started business as a shoe store. Today, its shoe departments are the best stocked in the city with tremendous choice in style and price. Well-designed, well-priced "fashion forward" clothes are displayed in a series of shops with names like Savvy, Collectors Library, Brass Plum, Point of View, and Individualist Sportswear. For good bargain shopping check out the Shoe Rack and the Clothes Rack on the lower levels. Watch also for the excellent sales throughout the store.

There are three men's departments: sportswear, suits and sportcoats, and young men's. Much of this merchandise has a Northwest Ivy League look to it. The sandwich shop is fast and convenient. The gift shop has some nice country items and novelties for the home.

The building itself is strikingly clean-lined, with antiques and dark floors inside, and some vestiges of the original architecture still visible in the contemporary facade.

Shopping

Fashion

Accessories and luggage

L6	**Bally of Switzerland** 1218 Fourth Ave (Four Seasons Olympic)	*Open Mon-Sat* *624-9255*

The ultimate specialty store for shoe hounds, this plush-carpeted, cleanly displayed shop is stocked only with the Swiss leathered finery of the Bally brand. Shoes, handbags, a few accessories, and even some leatherwear are available at stiff prices.

J5 HH3	**The Bag Merchant** 1518 Sixth Ave 1026 Bellevue Way SE, Bellevue	*Open Mon-Sat, 682-0143* *Open Mon-Sat, 454-9193*

Exclusively eelskin.

FF7	**Bench Leathers** 4223 University Way NE	*Open Mon-Sat* *633-5367*

Specializes in Frye Boots and Van's sneakers—an interesting mix of the Western look and new-wave—in an effort to keep up with the times. Also stocks leather jackets and a range of packs.

GG1 H6 OO5	**Bergman Luggage** 1930 Third Ave 15116 NE 24th, Bellevue 17900 Southcenter Parkway	*Open Mon-Sat, 622-2354* *Open Mon-Sat, 643-2344* *Open every day, 575-4090*

Bergman Luggage, with its three massive stores stretching throughout the Greater Seattle area, is a local institution when it comes to luggage. The knowledgeable sales staff is friendly and more than willing to guide you through the wide selection of suitcases, attache cases, carry-ons, tote bags, and wallets at all price ranges. They also repair all luggage; it doesn't have to be bought there.

K6 HH3	**Biagio** Rainier Square Bellevue Square	*Open Mon-Sat, 223-0469* *Open every day, 455-3583*

Biagio carries some of the finest lines in luggage, wallets, and handbags, including the Hartmann, French, and Land and Wings labels, all displayed beautifully in their two elegant stores.

K6	**Byrnie Utz Men's Hat Store** 310 Union	*Open Mon-Sat* *623-0233*

Hats, hats, and more hats. The endless variety of size and style has made Byrnie's a downtown landmark over the years. Fedoras, berets, Stetsons, Borsalinos, and Panamas are just some of the finds in this little store popular with both sexes. Byrnie and his wife are helpful and patient, even with the customers who love trying on *all* the hats.

O8	**The Clog Factory** First & Main	*Open every day* *682-2564*

If clogs are your choice for footwear, don't overlook the largest selection in the world. Some 2,200 pairs from all over Northern Europe, Switzerland, and Germany come in an incredible abundance of style and color, for adults and children.

101

L6 The Coach Store
417 University
(Four Seasons Olympic)

Open Mon-Sat
382-1772

The specific craftsmanship of Coach leathers has created a demand large enough to merit its own specialty corner in the Four Seasons Hotel. Belts, purses, and accessories in thick-leathered, trademark-simple quality are here in every available color and shape.

J6 Florsheim Shoe Shop
1432 Fourth
(also at suburban shopping malls)

Open Mon-Sat
624-8782

High-quality brands of men's shoes. Good service.

FF7 Footware (formerly Roots)
4519 University Way NE

Open Mon-Sat
634-2382

Once Washington State's sole outlet for the exquisitely made shoes and boots by Roots of Canada, this store has recently branched out into other well-known footwear brands. Socks and bags, too.

J5 Frank More Shoe Store
511 Pine

Open Mon-Sat
623-4554

An established landmark for downtown shoppers, this store stocks quality shoes for men and women, and smart handbags, all in familiar high-end brands.

Joyce-Selby's Shoes
Alderwood Mall

Open every day
771-7808

This only branch north of its San Francisco outlet carries a wider selection of its brand than can be found in general shoe stores around Puget Sound.

FF7 / J8 MJ Feet
4334 University Way NE
Pike Place Market

Open Mon-Sat
632-5353
624-2929

The local outpost for Birkenstock footwear, designed for people who are serious about freedom for their feet. Other accessories include Indian cotton shirts, socks, and even handmade kids'-stuff.

K5 Simms & Marchesi
520 Union

Open Mon-Sat
623-1676

Simms & Marchesi's exquisite selection of handbags, carry-on cases, wallets, belts, and tote bags is one of Seattle's finest. The workmanship and leather quality is superb, with correspondingly high prices. While Simms is here in Seattle running the shop, Marchesi lives in Italy buying the merchandise. Hence, the store carries lines not normally found in the US.

HH3 LeSportSac
Bellevue Square, Bellevue

Open every day
455-5588

Lightweight travel bags, purses, and suitcases—mainly synthetic.

O8 Star Design Company
214 First Ave S

Open every day
622-4840

Downstairs in a basement corner of the Grand Central Arcade in Pioneer Square is where you will find unusual luggage. Hanging on the walls are all varieties, shapes, and sizes of bags. From India there is an extremely durable water-buffalo bag which already looks as though it has been around the world twice. There are

Shopping

pigskin bags from Afghanistan, the Woodsaw line from New Jersey, and a variety of pieces from Colombia. They also carry the more traditional types of luggage with a good selection of carry-ons.

I7	**La Valise**	*Open Mon-Sat*
	1919 Third Ave	682-0528

Just across the street from Bergman's is another excellent luggage shop with a smaller, more specific selection. Hard-sided, soft-sided, and semi-soft pieces are all available. The service is good, and the selections meet the needs and budgets of executives or students.

N8	**We — Hats and Vests**	*Open every day*
	105 First S	623-3409

A favorite try-on-a-hat shop for tourists and locals alike. Many of the items are made upstairs in the mini-factory, while others are imported. The late-night hours on weekends attract Pioneer Square's night-hoppers.

FF7	**The Woolly Mammoth**	*Open Mon-Sat*
	4303 University Way NE	632-3254

This U District shop has reasonably priced shoes, some fine briefcases, and a range of day packs and overnight bags.

Children's clothing

FF7	**Chickabiddy Trading Company**	*Open Tues-Sat*
	1720 N 45th	633-5437

This children's clothing shop deals in several lines of new clothes and in used clothes in reasonable shape that moms can bring in and trade for credits. An occasional used Gerry pack may turn up, and there are also some good handmade clothes and baby items.

FF6	**Fine Threads**	*Open every day*
	2660 University Village Mall	525-5888

With its fine selection of good quality tweeds, flannels, and other preppy accoutrements for young boys to adolescents, Fine Threads is an excellent place to outfit those would-be Ivy Leaguers.

OO5	**Kid's Mart**	*Open every day*
	Pavilion Outlet Center	575-8585

A factory outlet that carries a good selection of children's clothes from infant sizes through girls' 14 and boys' 20. Quality and styling are good; you can find labels like Izod, OshKosh, Rob Roy, and Pierre Cardin. Prices are below retail.

	Le Petit Bateau	
GG7	705 Broadway E	*Open Mon-Sat,* 325-9543
K5	1324 Fifth Ave	*Open Mon-Sat,* 625-9643
HH3	Gelati Place, 10630 NE Eighth, Bellevue	*Open Mon-Sat,* 453-0708

Le Petit Bateau carries well-designed, expensive, and irresistible clothing from Europe, as well as such top-quality domestic lines as Florence Eisemann.

OO5	**Little Foxes**	*Open every day*
	Pavilion Outlet Center	575-3797

Carries pants and tops for girls in pre-teen sizes 6 to 17/18, junior sizes 00 to 15; some boys' pants are also available. Calvin Klein, Esprit, Normandee Rose, Levi Strauss, and Britannia are among the labels available. It's a factory outlet, so prices are well below the usual retail.

005 **Me and My Baby**　　　　　　*Open every day*
Pavilion Outlet Center　　　　　*575-8557*

Specializes in factory-outlet maternity wear, but also has devoted space to children's clothes and toys for infants and toddlers. The clothes range from practical playwear to some very fussy flounced long dresses in impractical fabrics.

Merry Go Round Baby News
HH3 **11111 NE Eighth, Bellevue**　　*Open every day, 454-1610*
18905 33rd Ave W, Lynnwood　　*Open every day, 774-2797*

It has a *huge* selection of quality clothes for infants through size 14. Furnishings such as cribs, dressers, highchairs, and changing tables are also to be found here, as well as coordinating accessories to dress them up with.

DD7 **Me 'N Mom's**　　　　　　　*Open Mon-Sat*
8414 Fifth NE　　　　　　　　*524-9344*

Middle-class Seattle's original answer to the thrift shop. You'll find secondhand children's clothes here, mostly in very good condition and quite reasonably priced, sizes infant through 14. Several lines of new clothes (OshKosh, Pete's Jeans) are also available, usually at a slight discount over department-store prices, and there's usually a small selection of attractive handmade clothes as well. Expectant moms will find used maternity clothes, plus a modest selection of new clothes.

GG7 **Pacific Trail Seconds Dept (Sportswear)**
1310 Mercer　　　　　　　　　*Open Mon-Fri, 682-8196*

A factory outlet for jackets and parkas mostly; seconds and overruns are available from size 0-6-months and up, and at bargain prices.

GG6 **Punch & Judy**　　　　　　　*Open Mon-Sat*
413 15th Ave E　　　　　　　*324-4409*

This is a sample shop specializing in children's clothes from infants through size 12 or so. Items tend to be available in only one size and one color. This is a particularly good place to find Polly Flinders hand-smocked dresses for babies and toddlers.

HH7 **REI**　　　　　　　　　　　*Open Mon-Sat*
1525 11th Ave　　　　　　　　*323-8333*

Carries children's outdoor wear such as parkas, ragg sweaters, and slickers in sizes 6 and up. Quilted ski jackets start at 0-6 months, and are available in the basement along with ski pants, bibs, and caps. Several ski-equipment packages are available for both cross-country and downhill.

HH1 **Sassafras Children's Clothiers**　*Open every day*
Crossroads Mall, Bellevue　　　*881-8558*

An exclusive kids' clothing shop, infant to size 14, Sassafras is for doting friends and relatives.

T.J. Waugh, Junior Expeditioner　*Open every day*
Gilman Village, Issaquah　　　*392-7547*

A combination of Eddie Bauer and Brooks Brothers—for kids (and moms). Year-round sportswear is available in sizes 6 to 20 tops, 4 to 20 pants, for any outdoor activity. The clothes themselves are unabashedly preppy. Downhill and cross-country skis and ski boots for age 2 and up, gloves, vests, parkas, caps, hiking boots, backpacks, and other outdoor gear are all scaled down for young people; everything is of the highest quality.

HH3	**Tyke Place Market** Bellevue Square, Bellevue	*Open every day* 453-1629

A combination clothing and toy store, with an emphasis on handmade, imaginative items. You might find rain slickers appliqued with clouds, overalls embellished with E.T., custom-knit personalized sweaters, an all-wood wagon, a piggybank to rock on, or even hand-painted baby bottles.

Fabric, sewing, and knitting

FF6	**Acorn Street Yarn Shop** University Village	*Open every day* 525-1726

Acorn Street stocks a special Canadian worsted wool that is a favorite for outdoor wear because of the water-repellent feature of its natural lanolin. It also keeps patterns to go with this yarn as well as a wide supply of needlepoint, embroidery, and other knitting materials.

HH3	**Calico Corners** 210 105th NE, Bellevue	*Open Mon-Sat* 455-2510

Discount seconds in upholstery fabrics, plus a good selection of canvas. They will recommend workrooms if you need one.

GG8	**Cloth Art** 317 W Galer	*Open Mon-Sat* 284-1262

For the home or boat decorator who wants to be surrounded by the luxury of natural cottons, silks, linens, and wool. You select the fabric from their many catalogues, and they make up shades, bedspreads, or slipcovers to order.

Cottage Weaving Limited Gilman Village, Issaquah	*Open Mon-Sat* 392-3492

With its old Fisher Feed sign on the false front of the store, the feed store makes an intriguing home for the upstairs loom and spinning wheels.

HH1	**Designer's Fabrics** Crossroads Mall, Bellevue	*Open every day* 747-5200

A marvelous playroom keeps kids happy while you appreciate a superb selection of cords, wools, specialty, and children's fabrics.

EE7	**In the Beginning** 6414 Roosevelt Way NE	*Open Mon-Sat* 523-8862

This store has possibly the largest selection of calicos and cottons in Seattle. Quilts, quilting fabrics, and wearable art are highlights; the huge Amish coverlets are especially beautiful. You'll also find folkwear and other craft patterns. Call to be placed on their mailing list for classes.

HH3	**Magnolia Weaving** 820 102nd NE, Bellevue	*Open Mon-Sat* 454-9665

You step back into another era when you enter this store. Wools and yarns for

Shopping

knitting, spinning, weaving, and basketry; natural fibers and bone buttons; many classes available.

II4 **Mercer Island Fabrics Inc**
7811 SE 27th
Open Mon-Sat
232-8641

In addition to a good range of fashion goods, they offer what may be the largest selection of outerwear fabrics, patterns, and notions on the West Coast.

GG8 **Nancy's Sewing Basket**
2205 Queen Anne Ave N
Open every day
282-9112

The place to go to find out what makes a French seam or a gored pleat, Nancy's likes to take time with its customers. Apart from offering classes in sewing, knitting, and crocheting, a knitting expert is at the store twice a week to answer questions. Specialty fabrics include calico prints, silks, and wools. They also sell Bernina sewing machines at low prices.

Patty's Place
515 Fifth Ave S, Edmonds
Open Mon-Sat
774-6446

An amazing find right on the approach to downtown Edmonds, this small house contains room after room of great quilting fabrics, supplies, and oddments: wooden needle holders, needlepoint specimens, tatted goods, and truly attractive post cards of quilts.

FF6 **Plenty of Textiles**
2909 NE Blakeley
Open every day
524-4383

If you know what you're looking for, you'll probably find it here, and at some of the best prices in town.

Rumpelstiltskin
HH7 **112 Broadway E**
(and outlying areas)
Open every day
329-8750

Upmarket outlets for the Pacific Fabric World chain; the Broadway store specializes in fashion fabrics and an exclusive line of Swiss wool blanket fashions.

J4 **Shamek's Button Shop**
709 Pine
Open Mon-Sat
622-5350

Possibly the best button shop in Seattle: bone, wood, plastic, glass, pewter and other metals, shell, and tusk designs can all be found.

FF7 **The Stitch**
4302 University Way NE
Open Mon-Sat
632-1101

Just about everything you might need: Marimekko and other large cotton prints, a huge range of braids and buttons, and some great herringbone wools. Sewing classes, too.

Stitch 'N Time
HH3 **707 112th NE, Bellevue**
FF6 **University Village**
Open every day
454-4444
524-4444

A good selection of fabrics and patterns plus classes, machines, and machine repair.

Unicorn Textiles Ltd
K6 **Rainier Square**
HH3 **10218 NE Eighth, Bellevue**
Open Mon-Sat, 292-9941
Open every day, 451-9612

Imported and unusual fabrics, pure silks, fabric sculpture, gifts, baskets, upholstery

106

fabrics, wallpapers to order, and Vogue sweater kits help make this eclectic collection fun to browse. Classes, too.

| F7 | **The Weaving Works**
5049 Brooklyn NE | *Open Mon-Sat*
524-1221 |

There's a loom set up to get you in the mood, plus walls of wonderful wool in all textures and thicknesses. Everything you need for dyeing, spinning, and weaving, and all the advice you could want, including classes.

Jewelry — Downtown

| J5 | **Allen's Fifth Avenue Jewelers**
1518 Fifth Ave | *Open Mon-Sat*
622-4780 |

Allen's Fifth Avenue Jewelers is a small, intimate shop that carries gold pieces, designer pieces, and a distinctive selection of jade and lapis lazuli.

| J6 | **Azose & Son**
2018 Third Ave | *Open Mon-Thur*
622-5323 |

Azose & Son, a small jeweler, has some of the most striking designer pieces in Seattle. All of the jewelry in this light, comfortable shop was made in the rooms adjacent to the display area. The family business has established itself for quality work in gold, silver, and platinum.

| J6 | **Ben Bridge**
409 Pike (and outlying areas) | *Open Mon-Sat*
628-6800 |

The best place for diamonds is Ben Bridge, in the same downtown location since 1912. Mountings are fairly traditional, but custom design work is offered, and service is very informative.

| K6 | **Carroll's**
1427 Fourth Ave | *Open Mon-Sat*
622-9191 |

Carroll's Fine Jewelry, a family-managed business since 1895, features rings, watches, and necklaces; a small selection of silver—baby presents, for instance; a few choice art objects; and an unusual assortment of gemstones: kunzite, blue topaz, golden sapphire, and Cat's Eye.

| J6
HH3 | **Daniel Louis at Nordstrom**
1501 Fifth Ave
Bellevue Square, Bellevue | *Open every day*
623-2277
455-5800, ext. 112 |

This small shop is probably Seattle's best for contemporary jewelry.

| J6 | **Dobson Jewelers, Inc.**
1425 Fourth Ave, Joshua Green Building, Suite 909 | *Open Mon-Fri, 624-6088* |

Seattle's "upstairs" jeweler, Dobson is located on the ninth floor of the Joshua Green Building, freed of higher overhead expenses. The shop houses a selection of jade, diamonds, silver objects, and watches. Individual service and excellent prices on engagement settings.

| K6 | **Fox's Gem Shop**
1341 Fifth Ave | *Open Mon-Sat*
623-2528 |

A family business in Seattle for 70 years, Fox's is noted for the quality and selection of its fine jewelry. The diamonds are spectacular, and Fox's jade collection,

Shopping

with a design range from traditional to contemporary, is one of the best on the West Coast. The staff is helpful and expert.

J5	**Friedlander & Sons** Fifth Ave & Pike	*Open Mon-Sat* *223-7474*

Established in 1886, Friedlander & Sons ranks as an institution among Seattle jewelers, the largest of the downtown jewelry stores, and one of the best. Along with the usual selection of rings, pendants, and watches, Friedlander has a fine selection of collectors' items, some of which are estate pieces and true works of art. The range is extensive: china, silver, crystal, and pewter are all available in one downtown store.

J5	**Lillian's Pearl Shop** 504 Pike	*Open Mon-Fri* *682-1043*

Lillian's carries only cultured pearls, mainly from Japan, in all sizes and colors. The shop can string pearls to any length, make necklaces, bracelets, and rings.

J5	**Philip Monroe Jeweler** 527 Pine	*Open Mon-Sat* *624-1531*

This small, elegant store on Pine Street is the creme de la creme of fine custom jewelers.

	Pike Place Market	*Open Mon-Sat*
H8- J8	If you are looking for craft or folk-art jewelry, Pike Place Market is the best place to shop. Artisans from the Seattle area and beyond, like the farmers, rent stalls to display their work. There is a large selection—both in choice and quality, while many of the artists are willing to fulfill any whimsy if you cannot find exactly what you want. The jewelry at the Market is generally silver, copper, and brass with semi-precious stones. There is a sprinkling of leather and wood jewelry as well. The designs are contemporary and the prices are excellent.	

O8	**Robin's Jewelers** 220 First Ave S	*Open Mon-Sat* *622-4337*

A small shop in Pioneer Square, Robin's Jewelers specializes in custom jewelry and original design work, mostly in gold. The handsomely displayed selection of one-of-a-kind pieces is reasonably priced, considering the excellent design quality.

I8	**Tama** 1904 Post Alley	*Open Tues-Sat* *624-1935*

Tama means jewel in Japanese, and this store is a jewel of jewelry stores. Simple and handsome, the store offers an excellent selection of contemporary and sculptured jewelry, most of which is done in gold, using semi-precious and precious stones. For custom work, Tama works closely with the customer, taking you from a drawing, to a wax casting, to the final product. Careful attention, kind service, and design ability are the store's hallmarks.

Jewelry — Other areas

	Benders Creative Jewelers	*Open Mon-Sat*
FF8	2314 NW Market	*784-3298*
FF7	4534 University Way NE	*633-4812*

Classical jewelers in traditional surroundings, Benders will design and handcraft special pieces for you. Check out their fine display of antique jewelry in the University District store.

F7	**Benton's University Jewelers**	*Open Mon-Sat*
	4333 University Way NE	*632-0730*

This family-owned business (since 1909) operates a quiet shop in the midst of University Way's more trendy stores. A parrot perches in his cage in a corner overlooking counters of rings, watches, and necklaces.

F7	**Expressions in Gold**	*Open Tues-Sat*
	4232 University Way NE	*632-7639*

Offers individually sculpted fine jewelry, most of which is exclusively designed for the store. The look is contemporary.

F7	**Kendall's Original Jewelry**	*Open Mon-Sat*
	4309 University Way	*634-3648*

Kendall's is primarily a creative design and manufacturing store. A wide selection of unset stones is available for you to choose from, and your vaguest specifications can be made into a beautiful final product. Most of the work involves precious and semi-precious stones in contemporary designs. For an unpretentious store with personal attention, Kendall's is the place to visit.

Large, tall, maternity, petite

	Court Fashions for the Petite Woman	
A7	Seattle Trust Court	*Open Mon-Sat, 623-7474*
A7	Aurora Village	*Open every day, 542-8900*
JH1	Crossroads Mall, Bellevue	*Open every day, 643-1530*

The shop selectively specializes in small sizes (0–9) for shorter women (5'5" and under). A cross-section from blue jeans to working suits is available. Prices are slightly higher than average.

K5	**Fifth Avenue Maternity**	*Open Mon-Sat*
	518 Union	*343-9470*

Flattering, fashionable maternity clothing: styles are often selected for easy belting and attractive wear after the baby is born.

	La Mamina Maternity Shop	
OD7	2121 N Northgate Way	*Open every day, 362-0183*
JH3	10210 NE Eighth, Bellevue	*Open every day, 454-4443*

These shops stock a good supply of maternity underthings and outerwear.

H7	**Mich's Clothiers**	*Open Mon-Sat*
	2122 Third	*682-7364*

Specializing in short and small men's sizes in casual and professional clothing, Mich's carries such brands as Cricketeer, Cardin, and St. Laurent.

	Pacific Big & Tall Shops	
K7	1303 Third	*Open Mon-Sat, 622-2936*
A7	Aurora Village	*Open every day, 546-3333*
JH3	Bellevue Square, Bellevue	*Open every day, 455-2150*

Shopping

	Menswear clothing store that caters to larger size needs; wide selection and many labels.	
005	**Prager's High & Mighty Store** **Alderwood Mall** **Southcenter**	*Open every day*, 771-5115 *Open every day*, 246-6060
	Expert, personalized service and good brands such as Ratner and Cassini mark this menswear shop for tall and large men.	
GG2 NN4	**Queen Size Boutique** **2102 140th NE, Bellevue** **Renton Shopping Center, Renton**	*Open every day*, 747-8881 *Open every day*, 271-6570
	Tasteful, fashionable clothes for the larger-size woman.	
HH3	**Short Story** **Bellevue Square, Bellevue**	*Open every day* 454-2224
	This specialty-size women's store stocks petite models of Breckenridge, Gordon of Philadelphia, Jones of New York, and other labels.	

Lingerie

L8	**Bella Notte** **First at Madison (Alexis Hotel)**	*Open Mon-Sat* 343-9536
	Located in the newly renovated Alexis Hotel, this special lingerie boutique carries a wonderful variety of sizes and styles. The store itself is elegant and the inventory can be decadent or straightforward.	
II2	**Satin Lady** **Factoria Square, Bellevue**	*Open every day* 643-1640
	This tantalizing little lingerie shop, while not as elegant as downtown's Bella Notte or Susan Barry, follows the trend toward exclusive frivolity in underthings.	
K5	**Susan Barry** **1318 Fifth Ave**	*Open Mon-Sat* 625-9200
	This eclectic shop has about as much square footage as the walk-in closets of some of its customers, but the inventory doesn't take up much room. Indeed, the delightful brevity and tasteful luxury in this lingerie shop have made it a local favorite for the physically and fiscally fortunate.	

Men's and women's wear — Downtown

I7 J6	**Baby & Co** **1936 First Ave.** **417 Pike**	*Open every day*, 622-4077 *Open Mon-Sat*, 621-8388
	One of the favorite stores for clothing in Seattle is this oh-so-on-the-fringe, fashion-bold store just above the Public Market. Too often pigeonholed for new-wave clothing, Baby also carries excellent linens, sportswear, shirts of silks, rayons, and cottons in sizes that comfortably cover both sexes. Silhouettes are short or extra long, tight or oversized; prices are moderate and up.	

Shopping

K6	**Brooks Brothers**	*Open Mon-Sat*
	1401 Fourth Ave	624-4400

Offers its famous conservative lines of men's fashions, well geared to Seattle's climate, amid sedate surroundings. Tremendous depth of inventory, a fine special-order system, and gracious service are some of the store's trademarks. Also stocks some good women's and children's lines.

	Brotman's	
M7	823 Third Ave, Seattle Trust Court	*Open Mon-Sat*, 623-3866
O03	Bellevue Square, Bellevue	*Open every day*, 454-9611

The first Brotman's, located in the Seattle Trust Court, was welcomed by women customers in the surrounding offices. A dress-for-success approach governs most of the inventory selection with some fun, non-traditional items as well. The inventory in the Eastside mall is more recreational.

K5	**Butch Blum**	*Open Mon-Sat*
	1408 Fifth Ave	622-5760

Long a high-fashion haven for men, Butch Blum has recently opened a section of their shop for women. Clothing and jewelry is all designer chic, much of it from European lines.

O8	**Design Products Clothing**	*Open Mon-Sat*
	208 First Ave S	624-7795

Beautifully tailored slacks, silk shirts, and sleekly designed suits for women can be found here, plus a scattering of men's items and leather accessories. The hand-knit sweaters and Italian trouser line are recently popular.

M7	**Frugalman's**	*Open Mon-Sat*
	823 Third Ave, Seattle Trust Court	622-9499

This shop is a favorite for its reliably good brand-name menswear at discounted prices. Popular brands from suits to shirts to socks are priced dollars below the average. An abundance of good products—Cricketeer, Botany, John Henry—in relatively small square footage.

K5	**Gallen Matti**	*Open Mon-Sat*
	517 Union	682-6054

This specialized store imports exclusively from West Germany and Austria both the high-fashion contemporary and ethnic dressing of that part of the world.

K5	**Helen's (Of Course)**	*Open Mon-Sat*
	1302 Fifth Ave	624-4000

This plush shop carries a good cross-section of designer wear at Fifth Avenue prices. Employees are helpful and the dressing rooms spacious. Helen's carries Perry Ellis, Anne Klein, Calvin Klein, Nipon, as well as some less conventional imports.

G4	**Jana Imports**	*Open Mon-Fri*
	2126 Westlake Ave	624-6265

This is a low-overhead outlet for the Jana label, which has been popular in many retail stores. Trademarks of the line are the prevalent Indonesian batiks on simply designed cotton dresses or quilted jackets. The fabric quality is good and a beauty of color and print distinguish the Asian-flavored clothing.

J5	**Jay Jacobs**	*Open every day*
	1530 Fifth Ave (and other areas)	622-5400

Shopping

Larger than the shops and smaller than the major department stores, this busy store is popular with the younger shoppers. Most of the inventory is casual, trendy, and affordable. Clothing and accessories are carried for both men and women, featuring some of the more popular designers.

K6	**Jeffrey Michael** Rainier Square	*Open Mon-Sat* *625-9891*

An eclectic mix of casual wear and suits for younger, professional men. Shoes, sweaters, and slacks for play are especially sharp. Prices are competitive.

J5	**Klopfenstein's Inc** **600 Pine** (and outlying areas)	*Open Mon-Sat* *622-2360*

Standard lines of the better American brands, plus some good bargains in European-cut clothes.

L6	**Laura Ashley** **405 University** (Four Seasons Olympic)	*Open Mon-Sat* *343-9637*

Women who have had to content themselves with ordering Laura Ashley fabrics and clothing from catalogues or making long-distance trips to London or New York to pick up the signature white eyelet petticoats, now have a local outlet in the newly remodeled Four Seasons Hotel. Racks of corduroy, velveteen, and prints, along with tiles, wallpaper, and sundries.

K6	**Little Daisy** Rainier Square	*Open Mon-Sat* *382-0266*

A more adventurous attitude toward retailing dictates the collection at this store. Working women's suits are shown in conventional styling with offbeat colors or basic colors in unpredictable patterns. Small sections for shoes, lingerie, and accessories encourage total outfit purchases.

K6	**Littler Inc.** Rainier Square	*Open Mon-Sat* *223-1331*

Littler has long catered to and taken pride in its mature, upper-income clientele, mixing conventional styling and top-quality fabrics with dressy evening wear. The Jaeger line is exclusively available in Washington in its own shop within Littler's Women's Section.

I5	**Mario's/Ragazza** **1513 Sixth Ave**	*Open Mon-Sat* *223-1461*

Italian-fashion worshippers have a required stop at this store. The Mario's portion of the store caters to men in the fashion vanguard, while Ragazza offers the same high quality in women's wear. Fashion choices range from perfectly proportioned wool gabardine to outlandish silks and suedes. The prices are heady, but the personnel are very friendly.

K5 N8	**Maxims** **510 Union** **155 Yesler Way**	*Open Mon-Sat, 624-0670* *Open Mon-Sat, 622-3542*

Selective and somewhat conservative choices of quality clothes for the working woman can be found in both locations. Although the square footage is small, the selection is reliable.

J5	**The Mediterranean** **515 Pine**	*Open Mon-Fri* *622-2949*

This conservative alternative for imported fashion is popular with slightly older

Shopping

women. The atmosphere is staid, and the prices are high. It has a very loyal following.

K6	**Michael's Bespoke Tailor** **Rainier Square**	*Open Mon-Sat* *623-4785*

This shop has established itself as one of the premier suppliers of custom-made shirts and suits for men. Bolts of richly woven, conservative wools in pinstripes and herringbone, good quality cottons and blends, are all available and ready to be tailored to your needs.

K5	**Nubia's** **522 Union**	*Open Mon-Sat, 622-0297*
GG6	**4116 E Madison**	*Open Mon-Sat, 325-4354*

An eclectic selection of well-displayed designer items from the US and all over the world. The focus is on clean-lined natural fabrics with some especially interesting pieces from Latin America.

K5	**Pino's** **521 Union**	*Open Mon-Sat* *623-8107*

Italian imports of top-shelf caliber. The choices are fashion-forward, continental, elegant, innovative, and expensive.

K6	**Polo—Ralph Lauren** **Rainier Square**	*Open Mon-Sat* *587-0200*

Lauren's storefront in Seattle carries solely the polo-playing seal of approval and, though predominantly stocked for men, has the latest in the designer's creations for women. Items here are not the department-store, mass-produced lines but the more select and therefore more expensive pieces from the Lauren collection.

K6	**Puella** **Rainier Square**	*Open Mon-Sat, 682-2638*
HH3	**Gelati Place, 10630 NE 8th**	*Open Mon-Sat, 451-3363*

A good selection for middle-of-the-road dressing with a mix of play and working wear for women. Items can be bright for recreational duds, but wearable, no-nonsense basics at competitive prices are emphasized here.

L6	**Richard Ltd** **1208 Fourth Ave (Four Seasons Olympic)**	*Open Mon-Sat* *621-8650*

Wall-to-wall classics for men and women are the offerings at this new hotel address. Immaculate finishings like scarf ties for women, casually creased corduroys, and conservative working wear for the downtowner are the trade here.

K5	**The Satin Goose** **519 Union**	*Open Mon-Sat* *682-6014*

A smaller downtown boutique carrying the common-sense designs of Joanie Char, Ellen Tracy, John Henry, and the like. Atmosphere is comfortable, and the quality is dependable.

	Sbocco	
G7	**100 Mercer St (Hanson Baking Company)**	*Open every day, 285-2140*
K6	**Fifth & Union**	*Open Mon-Sat, 624-9900*
HH3	**602 Bellevue Way NE, Bellevue**	*Open Mon-Sat, 455-9930*

Diverse and bold clothing: evening wear is especially glitzy and the pizazz of some of the more radical designs is refreshing. The spectrum from sporty to slinky is well represented.

Shopping

K6	**The Star Store** Rainier Square	*Open Mon-Sat* *624-0354*

A contemporary general store for urbanites: high-fashion clothing, yard goods, yarns, shoes, dishware, knickknacks, jewelry, and decorator items. Prices, though usually steep, can be as diverse as the offerings.

K7	**T & N** 1220 First Ave	*Open Mon-Sat* *622-0516*

A few blocks south of the Public Market, this exotic shop carries a potpourri of clothing, jewelry, even a few furnishings, all from the Orient. Cloisonne earrings and combs, some antique and valuable necklaces, comfortable cottons, rayons, and silks in Mandarin-collared tops are all available.

K6	**Totally Michael's** Rainier Square	*Open Mon-Sat* *622-4920*

For exceptional quality in suit fabrics and easy elegance in silk dresses, this shop for women offers some of the best lines and fit available for the young professional. Prices are justifiably high.

Men's and women's wear — Other areas

GG6	**Bagatelle** 4110 E Madison	*Open Tues-Sat* *329-2524*

Nice little neighborhood boutique with many of the major name brands at prices and styles to suit its wealthy, young professional clientele in Madison Park. Some interesting belts, scarves, and purses.

FF7	**Bluebeards** 4241 University Way NE	*Open Mon-Sat* *633-1769*

Leaning toward the new-wave look for the fashion-conscious student, Bluebeards also has a good range of casual gear, hats, and plaid jackets at good prices.

FF6	**Bronka** University Village	*Open every day* *523-0450*

An excellent selection of clothes for the career woman, whether she is at work, yachting, or at a cocktail party. Coordinates are a specialty and there is a rack for petites.

GG7	**Dita Boutique** 603 Broadway E	*Open every day* *329-2777*

Striking and distinctive high-fashion women's clothing for the would-be model. A little overpriced but excellent quality.

FF7	**Europa** 4507 University Way NE	*Open Mon-Sat* *633-3737*

An oasis of high fashion for men in the U District, Europa has a fine selection of European-cut suits and jackets (mainly from Italy), Pierre Cardin and Nino Cerruti shirts, designer ties, and cotton-knit shirts.

FF7 HH1	**Leg Room** 4546 University Way NE Crossroads Mall, Bellevue	*Open every day, 634-3763* *Open every day, 746-7293*

Levi's galore!

The Limited
O5 Southcenter   *Open every day, 244-8222*
H3 Bellevue Square, Bellevue   *Open every day, 454-9672*
Alderwood Mall   *Open every day, 771-8348*

This Ohio-based chain has become popular locally for its Hunter's Run label of dressy women's casuals and sportswear.

Nelly Stallion
F7 1311 NE 45th   *Open Mon-Sat*
    633-3950

With its striking array of fashion separates, Nelly Stallion has become an institution in the U District. Its colorful range of handknit sweaters, many directly imported from England and Ireland, are a special attraction, as are its small but distinctive selection of shoes, including a new line by Perry Ellis.

Opus 204
G7 204 Broadway E   *Open Mon-Sat*
    325-1782

In the heart of Capitol Hill, this delightful store reflects the striking tastes of its owner, Vija Rekevics, who is originally from Latvia and has lived in Rome, Bagdad, and London. Heavy Indian ivory bracelets, ornate Pakistani slippers, African musical instruments, and antique bowls from Southern China are only a few of the items stocked. Opus has its own distinctive line of loose-fitting clothing made of natural fibers and with a clean, simple design. Their hand-knit sweaters are also exclusive.

Peck & Peck
Alderwood Mall   *Open every day*
    771-7250

The only Seattle-area branch of this exclusive national women's fashion company stocks a slightly higher proportion of casual clothes among its classic dresses, coats, slacks, and blazers.

Up Front Boutique
F6 University Village   *Open every day*
    522-6526

A hip little boutique with unusual sweaters, dressy separates like wool skirts and sequined tops, and a small selection of exquisite silk lingerie. Great window designs.

Village Lady
O5 Southcenter Mall   *Open every day*
    242-3000

This high-quality women's wear shop carries one of the best selections of Pendleton woolens and tailored clothes in the area.

Yankee Peddler
G6 4218 E Madison   *Open Tues-Sat, 324-4218*
F7 1409 NE 45th   *Open Tues-Sat, 633-1409*

Catering superbly to the needs of the classic dresser, these stores exude an air of tradition and order. High-quality tweed jackets, Oxford shirts, corduroy pants, and Shetland sweaters are just some of the accoutrements they stock for this very East Coast look. The stores focus on menswear, with a good depth of inventory, although they have a small women's section as well.

Shopping

Men's and women's wear — Eastside

HH1	**Accolade**	Open every day
	Crossroads Mall, Bellevue	643-0584

This small, neutral-toned clothes shop caters to mature tastes: women's suits and casual wear, reasonably- to higher-priced.

HH3	**Albert Ltd**	Open every day
	Bellevue Square, Bellevue	455-2970

Fine (mainly English) men's and women's clothes—tweedy, traditional, and very well chosen.

HH3	**Ann House Ltd.**	Open every day
	Bellevue Square, Bellevue	454-5567

Well-displayed racks and piles of such designer labels as Adrienne Vittadi, Jones, and Dior ensure a pleasant browse through this low-key shop.

HH3	**Apropos Boutique**	Open Mon-Sat
	832 102nd NE, Bellevue	453-0918

Another good little "updated classics" vendor on the Eastside, this one carries lots of gabardine, silks, and linens. Misses' sizes.

HH3	**Babe's**	Open every day
	Bellevue Square, Bellevue	451-0095

A seductively youth-oriented clothing shop, the decor comprises at least half its charm. Babe's is one of the most talented of the youth-market performers in the Square.

Calico Cat	Open every day
Gilman Village, Issaquah	392-3302

Spread throughout the first-floor rooms of an old farmhouse, this tasteful women's clothing store carries excellent brands, well arranged, and caters to young professional and mature styles.

II4	**Carol Gilmour**	Open Mon-Sat
	Mercer Island Square	232-9255

A salon of particular and professional, yet energetic, women's clothing.

	Classic Clothes	
HH1	Crossroads Mall	Open every day, 643-1190
HH3	Bellevue Square	Open every day, 454-2632

The Crossroads branch of this classy women's clothier is more spacious and less frazzling. Many good standard brands at the higher end of the price and quality scale.

HH3	**Country Gentleman**	Open Tues-Sat
	10116 NE Eighth, Bellevue (QFC Village)	455-2969

This good, traditional clothing store stocks classic brands for men and women.

HH3	**La Croisette**	Open every day
	Bellevue Square	453-2800

A surprise in the middle of Bellevue is this high-fashion importer of European labels (85 percent French) such as Synonyme, Roger Nahr, and Guy Laroche.

HH3	**La Difference European Fashion**	Open Mon-Sat
	10020 Main, Bellevue	455-4414

Shopping

This store carries imported, mainly French, designer clothing for women; not too flamboyant, inclining toward the casual.

H3 Ducks and Drakes **Bellevue Square**	*Open every day* *453-1274*

A rare combination: a small, high-quality apparel store that stocks women's, preteen, and children's clothing. David Brooks and Nantucket labels are plentiful.

2 Loehmann's **3620 128th Ave SE, Bellevue**	*Open every day* *641-7596*

Don't let the bag checks at the door put you off: this store offers some of the best women's fashion bargains around. Designer, professional, and casual clothing at discount prices, and a back room of "discounted discounts" keep customers coming back for cheap clothing thrills. Across from Factoria Square.

H3 Margeo's **10042 Main, Bellevue**	*Open Mon-Sat* *451-9100*

Silks and suits for women of all ages.

2 Michael Patrick's Men's Wear **Factoria Square**	*Open every day* *747-5877*

A good menswear store, with some women's tailored and professional clothing, Michael Patrick's sells house-label imported shirts and suits, in addition to other brands.

H3 Nicole Dante **Bellevue Square, Bellevue**	*Open every day* *453-9990*

The only Seattle-area outlet of this continental men's clothier, Nicole Dante carries many imported and domestic labels in both professional and casual clothing.

H3 Papillon **608 Bellevue Way NE, Bellevue**	*Open Mon-Sat* *454-7324*

An excellent women's apparel and accessories store, catering to both professional and designer wardrobe shoppers.

H3 Sarah Chapman **10020 Main, Bellevue**	*Open Mon-Sat* *455-4987*

One of Bellevue's very best women's clothing stores, combining style with solidly comprehensive wardrobe selections, Sarah Chapman's twin apparel and shoe salons cater to the demanding social and professional dresser.

H3 Sheep Shack **602½ Bellevue Way NE, Bellevue**	*Open Mon-Sat* *454-2240*

Most of this small store's stock is made up of unusual and unique woven, knit, and fur items: just the place to buy a gift for someone who already has every bag, sweater, or coat on the market.

Rainwear

K6 Partly Cloudy **Rainier Square**	*Open Mon-Sat* *622-4147*

Determined to free Seattleites from tan trenchcoats, this outerwear boutique stocks a full selection, for men and women, in higher style (and at higher prices) than the usual department-store offerings. Umbrellas and brightly colored rubber rain boots are also sold.

M7	**Rain or Shine** 814 Second Ave, Seattle Trust Court	*Open Mon-Fri* 625-9998

This small corner in the SeaTrust Court is full of tasteful options in rainwear. The emphasis is on raincoats, classic trench or trendy, but accessories, umbrellas, and other fun wear can also be found.

	Weatherbeaters, Inc.	
FF6	University Village	*Open every day, 527-3033*
EE1	7875 Leary Way, Redmond	*Open Mon-Sat, 881-9565*

Good selection of comfortable and practical outerwear and accessories from raincoats and umbrellas to jackets, scarves, and water-repellent sweaters.

Vintage clothes — Downtown

J8	**Donna's This Place** Pike Place Market	*Open Mon-Sat* No phone

1940s and '50s general clothing for men and women in a casual, warm atmosphere. A specialty is *old* leather jackets, including 40-year-old original Army Air Corps jackets.

J8	**Fritzi Ritz** Pike Place Market	*Open Mon-Sat* 683-3163

This store's motto is "Classic Clothing from the Past with a Future" and that means turn-of-the-century to the late '50s, with a '40s emphasis. There are lots of silk, crepe, and beaded dresses, silk and rayon lingerie, Hawaiian shirts, and, during the winter months, Scandinavian wool sweaters from the '40s and '50s.

J8	**Grandma's Attic** Pike Place Market	*Open Mon-Sat* 682-9281

Focusing on the '20s through the '60s, this store has a strong line of vintage menswear. They have '50s long wool overcoats, tweed jackets, men's and women's hats from the '20s to the '50s, and occasionally alligator handbags.

N8	**Jasmine Room** 109 First Ave S	*Open Mon-Sat* 624-0853

This store stocks quality women's and men's garments from Victorian times to the '50s, with more '40s apparel than anything else. This is the place to find lots of handworked lace and linens, including handmade lace collars, in addition to costume jewelry, cashmere sweaters, and silk aviator scarves.

O8	**Madame & Co.** 117 Yesler	*Open Mon-Sat* 621-1728

Designers/buyers come from all over the country to purchase the very high quality vintage (almost exclusively women's) clothing and yardage assembled here by owner Carol Winship and her daughter Deborah. The inventory, including some genuine museum-pieces, spans the 1800s to the 1940s, but concentrates largely on the Edwardian era to the '20s. The mint-condition blouses, evening wear, fur coats, capes, etc. are all carefully restored on the premises, and there is a generous collection of fine lace yardage, collars, buttons, and other sartorial goodies.

Market Space-31 Pike Place Market	Open Mon-Sat No phone

Focusing mostly on elegant women's attire from the 1890s to the 1940s, this store has such items as Victorian dresses, beaded dresses, long chiffon dresses, wide belts, and glitter tops.

RetroViva 1511 First Ave	Open Mon-Sat 624-2529

Women's and men's wear from Victorian era to present day. Emphasizing '50s clothing, they have a good collection of hats (including men's '50s fedora-type felt hats) and furs (muskrat, fox, raccoon, squirrel).

Vintage clothes — Other areas

F7	Deluxe Junk 3518 Fremont Place N	Open every day 634-2733

Located in what used to be a funeral parlor, this shop is a gold mine for inexpensive and ever-changing men's and women's clothing. (It also carries a lot of older furniture and dime-store collectibles.) The merchandise (covering the '30s through the '60s) changes with the seasons—handmade sweaters and woollens in winter, straw hats in summer.

GG7 7 8	Dreamland 619 Broadway E 1905 Third Ave Pike Place Market	Call for hours 329-8044 343-0101 624-6137

Vintage garb for hipsters. Some of their merchandise, including Eisenhower jackets, skinny slacks, and sport shirts, was manufactured in the '40s and '50s, but was never sold and so still bears the original tags. They also carry narrow and square-edge wool ties, tweed jackets, new and old sunglasses, some contemporary clothes.

GG7	Isadora 1502 E Olive Way	Open Mon-Sat 323-7702

Isadora features classy, tasteful attire from the Edwardian period to the '50s. Fashionable coats and suits, fabulous furs, elegant silk lingerie are all specialties.

GG7	Out of the Past 219 Broadway E	Open Tues-Sat 329-2691

This reasonably priced store has a variety of women's and men's wear from the '40s, '50s and '60s, with some contemporary used clothes. Hard-to-find fabrics (silks, rayons, woollens, etc.) from the '40s and '50s are also a specialty.

GG7	That's Atomic 1504 E Olive Way	Open Tues-Sat 325-4994

A highly specialized shop dealing in the period from 1945-1962 (the Atomic Age), it is a definite "must visit" if you're looking for capri pants, pedal pushers, bowling shirts, cocktail dresses, or chiffon party/prom dresses. About half of the merchandise is women's and men's apparel the rest is collectible glassware, TV lamps, '50s kitsch, etc. Hours extremely variable.

Shopping

EE7	**Vintage Clothing** 6501 Roosevelt Way NE	*Open Mon-Sat* 522-5234

Best known for its sophisticated 1940s dresses, Vintage Clothing has Victorian through 1950s apparel, including lots of beaded cardigan sweaters, ladies' silk nightgowns, and bed jackets. The staff is particularly friendly and helpful.

Food & drink

Bakeries — Downtown

F7	**A La Francaise** 2325 Fourth Ave	*Open every day* 447-1500

A charming French bakery and cafe in the Denny Regrade, with some of the best croissants around; also fine French breads and pastries.

J8	**Au Gavroche** Pike Place Market	*Open Mon-Sat* 624-2222

This French patisserie occupies a stall near the staircase in the Sanitary Market. Filled croissants, brioche, Viennese pastries, and crepes are the daily fare, all of them extremely good.

K7	**John Nielsen Pastry** 1329 Third Ave	*Open Mon-Sat* 622-1570

A marvelous downtown bakery and coffee shop with authentic Danish pastries, petit fours, and specialty cakes at very reasonable prices.

Bakeries — Other areas

DD7	**La Baguette** 620 N 85th	*Open every day* 789-5610
FF7	**La Baguette Universite** 4141 University Way NE	*Open every day* 547-3070

The Greenwood bakery is among the newer of the French boulangeries in Seattle, and it occupies a cavernous space that was formerly a roller rink. Baguettes, round boules, croissants, brioche, quiche, and assorted pastries fill the bakery case along with imported French oils, mustards, jams, and candies. The new University branch is located downstairs in a smartly refurbished building on the same block as Jazz Alley.

HH3	**La Battelle** Bellevue Square Mall, Bellevue	*Open every day* 455-2060

The only branch in the Puget Sound area of this nationally known bakery chain, La Battelle bakes crusty baguettes that are in steady demand all week. Expensive, but delicious products.

FF7	**Boulangerie** 2200 N 45th	*Open Tues-Sun* 634-2211

Located in the Wallingford district, this authentic French bakery serves up excellent crusty loaves, buttery croissants, and brioches. The place is always busy and parking can be a bit difficult.

Borrachini's Ginger Belle Bakery
2307 Rainier Ave S

Open every day
325-1550

An Italian bakery with good, chewy country breads. Popular for wedding and birthday cakes.

Fran's Patisserie
2805 E Madison

Open Tues-Sat
322-6511

This shop features a small selection of ultra-rich tortes and cakes for the chocolate purist, plus handmade chocolates and country truffles.

Larsen Brothers Danish Bakery
8000 24th Ave NW

Open Mon-Sat
782-8285

Arguably the best Scandinavian bakery in town, Larsen Brothers offers moderately priced Danish coffee cakes, Kringler, and assorted pastries and cookies, plus great breads.

Madison Park Bakery
4214 E Madison

Open Mon-Sat
322-3238

One of the best sources for cinnamon rolls and good rye breads. The small coffee shop is locally popular.

Mama Reuben's Bakery
7660 SE 27th, Mercer Island

Open Mon-Sat
232-4000

This combination bakery-delicatessen on the Eastside has some of the best bagels in these parts, in addition to a fine selection of cookies, pastries, and pies.

Marcel's Pastry Shop & Tea Room
1603 14th Ave

Open Wed-Sat
329-7000

Swiss pastries in a gingerbread setting. The bakery has a large tea room (they also serve lunch), many specialty tortes, cakes, and hand-dipped chocolates.

Mon Hei Chinese Bakery
667 S King
4224 University Way NE

Open Wed-Mon, 624-4156
Open Mon-Sat, 632-3359

With a new University district branch, it's even harder to resist the temptation of the curried beef buns, Chinese chicken crisp, sweet red bean crisp, cream rolls, fortune cookies, and lotus seed cakes—at very reasonable prices.

The Quicherie
2302 24th Ave E

Open Tues-Sun
329-9680

This gourmet bakery has the best quiche in the city, marvelous seasonal fruit tarts, and unsurpassed cheesecake.

Schumacher's Bakery & Croissanterie
2112 NE 65th
(also in Rainier & Bellevue Squares)

Open every day
527-4046

A large kitchen and full retail bakery with plenty of table space (adjoining a delicatessen). Select from a huge assortment of European pastries, cakes, and breads.

Sivertsen's
100 Mercer

Open Tues-Sun
283-3797

This picturesque little bakery in the Hansen Baking Co. features Scandinavian delicacies and nice party cakes.

Shopping

GG7	**Standard Bakery** 2 Boston	*Open Tues-Sat* *283-6359*

Queen Anne hilltop's larger starch stop draws loyal pastry lovers from other districts for a full range of sweet concoctions, cake decorations, and such offbeat specialties as a French Boule with crackling Dutch crust.

GG2 GG7	**Sunshine Bakery** 14625 NE 20th, Bellevue 518 Broadway E	*Open Mon-Sat, 641-6121* *Open every day, 329-6121*

With a solid reputation for some of the best croissants and sourdough French bread on the Eastside, and deliveries all over the Seattle area, Sunshine is popular on weekends for its cinnamon rolls and apple strips.

FF7	**Woerne's European Pastry Shop** 4108 University Way NE	*Open Tues-Sat* *632-7893*

Guenter Woerne has been serving up sweets in the University District for 23 years, and his Black Forest cherry cake is renowned all over the UW campus. Many traditional European pastries and a nice assortment of butter-cream cakes.

Butchers

GG8	**A & J Meats** 2401 Queen Anne N	*Open Tues-Sat* *284-3885*

A & J Meats has a wonderful selection of specialty items as well as top-quality basic cuts. They make all their own weiners and lunch meats (both pure beef), chicken cordon bleu, chicken Kiev, stuffed pork chops, meat loafs, and sausages of all types including blueberry, apple, cranberry, strawberry, apricot, and, of course, plain.

AA8	**Arctic Merchant Food Fancies** 1443 NW Richmond Beach Rd	*Open every day* *542-6816*

In addition to their full range of basic cuts of meat, the Arctic Merchant also carries seafood: lobster tails, prawns, shrimp, and cod fillets, as well as poultry specialty items, including chicken a la cordon bleu, chicken a la Kiev, chicken rice and mushroom, and boneless chicken breast. Other unusual items include Polynesian kabobs, tropis steaks, teriyaki steaks, and stuffed pork chops.

J8	**Bavarian Meats** Pike Place Market	*Open Mon-Sat* *682-0942*

A large selection of sausages (bratwurst, knackwurst, etc.)

DD3	**Blue Ribbon Meats** 125 Lake St S, Kirkland	*Open Tues-Sat* *822-1522*

"You can live on the Eastside and never go to Pike Place Market with places like this," says one longtime Bellevue resident about this excellent butcher shop.

HH3	**Bud's Select Meats and Deli** 202 106th Place NE, Bellevue	*Open Mon-Sat* *454-1777*

A fine butcher shop and quality delicatessen, all in one small shopping area: try it as an alternative to mall lunching.

J8	**Don and Joe's** Pike Place Market	*Open Mon-Sat* *682-7670*

The best in the Market from whole chickens to steaks to lamb. Their smoked ham, fresh turkeys, and lamb chops are superb.

NN7	**Hans' Sausage** 717 SW 148th	*Open Mon-Sat* *244-4978*

A very good German deli in the South End: game sausage along with the usual German sausages and meats, most made on the premises.

FF8	**Jones Brothers** 5404 22nd NW 8220 238th SW, Edmonds	*Open Mon-Sat* *783-1258* *775-5623*

Three generations of one family have operated these two butcher shops and it is a tradition of which they should be justly proud. The leanest of ground beef, prime rib roasts, New York cut, tender top sirloin, and a good selection of sausages are among the specialties served up in these friendly neighborhood shops, and with complimentary coffee to boot.

EE7	**The Meat Shop, Inc.** 6522 Fremont Ave.	*Open Mon-Sat; Co-op every day* *789-5438*

A workers' cooperative, the Meat Shop is the most complete supplier of organic meats in the Pacific Northwest. Their beef, pork, lamb, and poultry are raised without hormones, antibiotics, and other additives. All ham, bacon, lunch meat, weiners, and sausages are produced without sodium nitrate or other preservatives.

HH7	**Torino's Sausage** 700 S Dearborn	*Open Mon-Sat* *623-1530*

A family-run company that specializes in freshly made sausages (no preservatives) that you can watch being made.

Candies and chocolates

K6	**Au Chocolat** Rainier Square	*Open Mon-Sat* *624-5365*

Imported candies, at stiff prices. French and Swiss plus some domestic chocolates, including Godiva.

CC6 B7	**Baker's Old Fashioned Sweet Parlour** 12534 Lake City Way NE also at Seattle Center House	*Open every day, 365-1888*

Longtime makers of handmade chocolates run this good family place, with every type of soda-fountain offering imaginable.

EE7	**Boehm's Candy Kitchen** 559 NE Ravenna Blvd **Boehm's Edelweiss Chalet** 255 NE Gilman Blvd, Issaquah	*Open every day* *523-9380* *Open every day* *392-6652*

A great selection of homemade Swiss chocolates and other fine candies at decent prices. The more modest Ravenna shop has been there more than 40 years; now all the candies are made at the distinctive Swiss chalet in Issaquah.

Shopping

GG7	**The Dilettante** **416 Broadway E**	*Open Mon-Sat* *329-6463*

Sinfully rich and expensive buttercream- and truffle-filled chocolates, which also are carried by many area gourmet shops. You'll also find a variety of dessert selections —specialty tortes, cakes, ice cream concoctions, and espresso. The chocolates are delicious, many made from old-fashioned recipes.

HH6	**Dilettante Factory** **2306 E Cherry**	*Open Mon-Fri* *328-1530*

The small retail outlet at the candy factory sells mostly "seconds" and broken chocolates at much reduced prices.

L6	**Elegant Edibles** **Four Seasons Olympic**	*Open Tues-Sun, 621-1700*

An elegant little shop in the newly restored Four Seasons Olympic Hotel, featuring delectable chocolates, cakes, and pastries, all made by the hotel pastry shop.

GG6	**Fran's Patisserie** **2805 E Madison**	*Open Tues-Sat* *322-6511*

Outstanding hand-dipped chocolates and country truffles. In addition to being a skilled chocolatier, Fran makes many fine Swiss pastries.

I5	**Frederick & Nelson** **Fifth & Pine** **(plus Southcenter & Aurora Village)**	*Open every day* *682-5500*

Frederick & Nelson's distinctive Frango Mints are well-known in the Northwest. The generous, individually wrapped truffles are popular gifts, boxed in attractive cylinders and available in five flavors: mint, rum, almond, mocha, and a new lemon mint.

FF8	**Sutliff's Candy Co** **910 NW Leary Way**	*Open Mon-Fri* *784-5212*

In Seattle for 44 years, Sutliff's has some of the best chocolate truffles around. Now primarily a wholesale business (they supply Nordstrom and Hilton Hotels), the factory has a modest retail counter and unbeatable prices (plus broken chocolates).

Catering and gourmet take-out

N8	**Brasserie Pittsbourg** **602 First Ave**	*Catering and takeout: 8-5 Mon-Sat; closed Sun* *623-4167*

Elegant French cuisine, with a light touch and seasonal variations. Flowers, china, and linen are particularly well cared for by the chef, Francois Kissel, who has a genius for unusual touches on grand occasions. A classically trained chef who grew up in Vietnam, Francois can mix the world's cuisines like a master.

	brusseau's **117 Fifth S, Edmonds**	*Takeout and catering: 7:30-7 Every day,* *By appt; 774-4166*

Reasonably priced, with excellent French-accented cuisine for nearly any occasion.

KK9	**Cynthia's Lincoln Park Catering** **7301 Fauntleroy Way SW**	*Catering by appt. Takeout: 10-7 Mon-Wed;* *10-8 Fri & Sat; 11-7 Sun; 937-2905*

Shopping

From chicken breasts in puff pastries to full dinners, this cosmopolitan caterer custom-designs your party.

| FF6 | **Eleanor's Catering**
3234 NE 45th | *By appt, including takeout*
522-1613 |

Hors d'oeuvres, buffets, *lots* of weddings. China, silver, and flatware are provided.

| | **Flamenco Guitar** | *By appt; 322-0908* |

This caterer combines Spanish victuals, music, and dance plus excellent personal service; the cook entertains at your home.

| GG7 | **Gourmet To Go**
819 E Thomas | *11-8 Mon-Sat; closed Sun*
329-6997 |

Just opened in March, this newcomer to the take-out food business in Seattle serves soups to nuts. Entrees like roast chicken, salads, fresh pastas and sauces, pates, and tasty desserts are all available.

| I8 | **Gretchen's Of Course**
94 Stewart | *Catering: By appt. Takeout: 9-4 Mon-Thur;*
8-4 Fri & Sat; closed Sun; 621-9133 |

Gretchen's elegant array of hearty desserts, luscious quiches, main dishes, salads, and other meals are all available for catered affairs. The menus are imaginative and quite up-to-date.

| EE6 | **International Kitchen**
2201 NE 65th | *By appt*
524-4004 |

International Kitchen is also a cooking school and so it is well equipped to prepare for nearly any meal arrangement.

| | **Kim's Breakfast in Bed** | *By appt; 634-0789* |

High-end breakfasts: $45-$55 for two (less during the week). The menu provides fresh fruit, crab-and-scallop crepes, coffee, champagne, and flowers.

| JJ8 | **La Bonne Femme**
3520 SW Genesee | *Catering: By appt. Takeout: 10-5 Mon-Sat;*
closed Sun; 932-4597 |

Excellent continental fare with individual touches, for catering and takeout: buffets, appetizers, soups, sandwiches, desserts.

| FF7 | **Les Copains**
2202 N 45th | *Catering: By appt. Takeout: 3-11 Every day*
633-5753 |

Nouvelle cuisine Northwest—for gourmet takeout or catering: call ahead for both. The chef is one of the most creative and daring in Seattle, so this is a good place to use for impressive occasions. Closed at press time. Call for possible reopening.

| J8 | **Market Place Caterers**
94 Pike Place | *By appt*
682-2208 |

One of the best: comprehensive (accommodates any size party), thorough (every detail of service and menu accounted for), and wonderful, cosmopolitan food. Joe McDonnell can do breakfasts at 5am, after-theater dinners, intimate groups, and large productions. He specializes in novel combinations, beautifully presented.

| | **Original Ellen's**
305 NW Gilman Blvd | *9-8 Mon-Fri; 8-8 Sat & Sun*
392-1209 |

All of Ellen Mohl's famous pastries, candies, and full meals are available for customers' personal catering requirements: she'll even whip up her "best hamburgers in the world." She can handle very large events, and the range is extensive.

Shopping

The Famous Pacific Dessert Company
GG7   2407 10th E, 325-9339   Noon-11 Mon-Thur & Sun; noon-midnight Fri & Sat
HH7   420 E Denny, 328-1950   7:30am-11pm Mon-Thur; 7:30am-midnight Fri & Sat; 9am-11pm Sun
GG7   127 Mercer, 284-8100   7:30am-11pm Mon-Thur; 7:30am-midnight Fri & Sat; 9am-11pm Sun

Besides a wonderful dessert and light-meal gourmet takeout service, Pacific Desserts caters charming dessert parties (great for kids of all ages) and light buffets.

The Quicherie
GG6   2302 24th E, 329-9680   Catering: By appt. Takeout: 7am-9pm Tues-Sat; 10-2 Sun; closed Mon

A wonderful bakery and gourmet takeout on the premises provide the base of operations. Full meals, good service, and all the accoutrements.

Rex's Delicatessen
I8   Pike Place Market, 624-5738   7:30-7 Mon-Fri; 10-6 Sat; closed Sun
GG7   428 Broadway E, 329-9001   7-8 Sun-Thur; 7-9 Fri & Sat

Rex's is one of the city's best delis, with its own baked goods and many fine salads and soups. It also provides full-line catering, at high prices.

Rosellini's Four-10
E7   Fourth & Wall   Catering: By appt; 624-5464
E7   Gourmet Kitchen: Fourth & Vine   Takeout: 9-5 Mon-Fri; 622-1970

The gourmet takeout kitchen offers nearly all the continental delicacies as the regular full-service catering outlet; 24-hours notice is required for larger orders, but soups and sandwiches are available immediately.

Smith–Glaziere Caterers, Ltd.
HH6   1123 34th Ave, 329-3880   Catering: By appt. Takeout: 10-6 Fri; 9-5 Sat; 9-1 Sun; closed Mon-Thur

This caterer combines the excellent service of a hotel caterer with the exquisite food of a skilled private small-scale chef. Weddings (chocolate hazelnut torte), complete party planning, flower arrangements, wine selection, hors d'oeuvres (rosemary walnuts to spanakopita), entrees (veal saltimbocca to roast lamb), vegetarian dishes, desserts, and lovely breakfasts. The takeout menu is selective, so it's often best to call ahead for something special.

Travelling Kitchen
Catering and takeout: By appt. 784-9569

This one specializes in Mediterranean cuisine, including Italian breads, hearty salads, and main dishes, and has a takeout service of hot and cold food at reasonable prices.

Westin Hotel
H5   1900 Fifth Ave   Catering: 624-7400

This year's competitive hotel spirit has encouraged the growth of the Westin's food and beverage industry, to draw local business. The catering department offers an in-house and your-house "French service"—warmed plates, individual silver trays of food, formal waiters, etc.—for lunch and dinner. Theme parties have also increased in size and number. Prices vary. With Westin's ability to mobilize dozens of waiters, large parties are the hotel's specialty.

William's Catering
111 Sixth S, Edmonds   11-8:30 Mon-Fri; 11-7:30 Sat; closed Sun 776-4900

This hamburger joint has full-service gourmet catering for a wide range of meals

Shopping

and palates: hors d'oeuvres, buffets, French, Italian, German, and American dinners, all prepared from scratch. Reasonable prices.

F7 **Yak's Deli & Catering** *Catering: By appt. Takeout: 10:30-8:30*
3424 Fremont N *Mon-Sat; 5-8:30 Sun; 632-0560*

This interesting Japanese caterer offers a wide range of Japanese and Western dishes, at very reasonable prices.

IH6 **Your Place or Mine** *Catering: By appt. Takeout: noon-8 Tues-Sat;*
1131-A 34th *closed Sun & Mon; 329-2966*

From sesame chicken with cucumber on Fridays, to hummus and pita with antipasto on Tuesdays, to beef salad dijonnaise on Saturdays, this new spot is one of the nicest gourmet places around. It is designed for quick pickup dinners for the busy Madrona residents, but you can also eat here. Menus change monthly.

Cheese

4 **C'est Cheese** *Open every day*
2448 76th SE, Mercer Island *232-9810*

Mercer Island's fine cheese, wine, and gourmet take-out shop, C'est Cheese, also caters.

GG6 **The Cheese Shop** *Open Mon-Sat*
4122 E Madison *323-6110*

The Cheese Shop carries a very large selection of domestic and major European cheeses with French and Italian being the specialties. Also offered are pates, meats, breads, crackers, mustards, and a wine selection—great picnic fixings.

8 **Pike Place Cheese** *Open Mon-Sat*
Pike Place Market *622-3055*

Over one hundred different varieties of cheeses can be found here. Norwegian, Swiss, Danish, English, and a well-stocked French selection.

F6 **The Wedge** *Open every day*
University Village *523-2560*

The Wedge specializes in local products, offering Cougar Gold cheese, made at Washington State University, and their own smoked Monterey Jack and herbed cream cheese. Three hundred varieties of cheeses are carried in all. Meats, fresh breads, pates, wines, and imported beers are also stocked and make great picnic combinations.

Coffees and teas

M8 **The Good Coffee Company** *Open Mon-Fri*
911 Western, #412 *622-5602*

This small business roasts its own coffee and can offer custom service.

Pegasus
131 Parfitt Way SW *Open every day*
Winslow, Bainbridge Island *842-3113*

Shopping

Sells its own freshly ground beans. You can also relax with a cup of coffee and a pastry in the little cafe.

J8	**Specialty Spice Shop** **Pike Place Market**	*Open Mon-Sat* *622-6340*

Home of the aromatic Market Spice tea, the Specialty Spice Shop also stocks a good selection of coffees (some of which they roast themselves), other herb and black teas, spices, and herbs. They also offer salt-free seasonings.

	Starbucks	*Call for hours*
I8	Pike Place Market	*622-8762*
FF7	4555 University Way NE	*634-1390*
FF6	4520 University Village	*522-5228*
GG7	507 Broadway E	*323-7888*
HH3	10214 NE Eighth, Bellevue	*454-0191*

One of the finest coffee stores in the nation, with its own roaster, a broad line of beans, and lots of brewing equipment, kettles and teapots, spices, imported teas, and Guittard's and Nestle's chocolate.

	Stewart Brothers – Wet Whisker **Coffee Company**	*Call for hours*
HH8	Pier 70	*624-8858*
FF7	4518 University Way NE	*634-3766*
HH3	Bellevue Square, Bellevue	*451-8102*
B7	Seattle Center House	*624-4785*

They offer a good selection of their own roasted beans. Also stocked are coffee makers, espresso machines, and imported teas as well as ice cream, espresso, and cappuccino to go.

Consumer food cooperatives

There are about a half-dozen storefront food co-ops in the Seattle area, a bastion of the co-op movement, as well as dozens of food buying clubs. **The Puget Sound Cooperative Federation** (2407 First Ave, 292-8313) acts as a clearinghouse and referral service for area co-ops, and publishes a directory of Puget Sound cooperatives (which, incidentally, includes categories other than food—such as housing, arts, child-care, and various collectives).

J8	**Bulk Commodities Exchange** 1408 Western Ave (Pike Place Market)	*Open Mon-Sat* *447-9516*

A farmer-consumer cooperative created to provide direct marketing of Washington produce, although it now purchases out-of-state produce to round out its line. Membership is $8 per year, which includes a weekly price report. BCE sells only in bulk quantities on a pre-order basis, but has a small storefront where you can buy fruit baskets, jams, and the like. There are 12 neighborhood delivery points.

HH6	**Central Co-op** 1835 12th Ave	*Open every day* *329-1545*

Bulk grains, flours, nuts, fresh produce, and raw dairy products. Members pay a $5 membership fee and contribute up to $60 as a loan investment to the co-op (refundable). Working members get price breaks; non-members pay a 15-percent surcharge.

Shopping

F7	**Phinney Street Co-op** 400 N 43rd St	*Open every day* *633-2354*

Operating since 1974, the co-op is run entirely by volunteer workers who receive price breaks for hours worked. Members pay $3 per month as a loan to the co-op (refundable). In addition to bulk grains and such, this friendly, laid-back co-op carries produce, dairy, bakery products, and bulk soaps. Prices are all marked at wholesale; nonmembers pay an additional 30 percent.

E6	**Puget Consumers Co-op/Ravenna** 6504 20th NE	*Open every day* *525-1450*
E7	**Puget Consumers Co-op/Green Lake** 6522 Fremont N	*Open every day* *789-7144*
E3	**Puget Consumers Co-op/Kirkland** 10718 NE 68th	*Open every day* *828-4621*

As the area's leading food cooperative (15,000 members), Puget Consumers Co-op (PCC) currently has three stores, all featuring wholesome, natural foods, but with some product variation at each location. The Green Lake and Kirkland stores include organic meat and deli items (they even make their own sausages) and sell beer and wine. The Ravenna store has a mercantile department—tools and hardware—and books. PCC members pay $2 per month toward a $60 full membership, which is refundable if you drop out. Non-members can shop at PCC but pay a 13.8-percent surcharge on purchases.

Delis — Downtown

	DeLaurenti's	
J8	Pike Place Market	*Open Mon-Sat, 622-0141*
HH3	317 Bellevue Way NE, Bellevue	*Open Mon-Sat, 454-7155*

This international deli has been an institution in the Market since 1944. People swarm through the narrow aisles in pursuit of unusual canned items, outstanding cheeses, olives, imported pasta (their fresh pasta is not up to the store's usual standards), wines, and deli meats. Service is cheerful and expert, which helps with the long lines. It's more international than Italian, but the Mediterranean lines are the specialty.

O8	**Estoa** 116 S Washington	*Open Mon-Sat* *623-4164*

Greek and Mediterranean lines, as part of a small restaurant and espresso bar in Pioneer Square.

P8	**Mekong Oriental Foods** 318 Second Ave S	*Open every day* *624-2476*

This Vietnamese store is jammed with fresh greens, prepared dishes, and extensive lines of fish sauces and rice noodles.

I8	**Mexican Grocery** Pike Place Market	*Open Mon-Sat* *682-2822*

Fresh tortillas and chips arrive thrice weekly from their factory, and you can find many rare herbs and dried chilis.

Shopping

I8	**Rex's**	
GG7	**Pike Place Market**	*Open Mon-Sat, 624-5738*
	428 Broadway E	*Open every day, 329-9001*

This high-tech deli makes its own excellent croissants, salads, soups, pates, and sandwiches, along with some takeout meals of European accent; they stock jams, vinegars, beers, and mustards in profusion, along with some of the better local offerings in smoked fish and other delicacies. Prices are a shade high.

J8	**Scandinavian Delicatessen**	*Open Mon-Sat*
	Pike Place Market	*223-0998*

An outpost of Vaersgo restaurant, this deli has a good selection of smoked herring, pastries, salads, and the makings for fine open-faced sandwiches.

	The Souk	
J8	**Pike Place Market**	*Open Mon-Sat, 623-1166*
EE7	**7825 Lake City Way NE**	*Open every day, 527-5332*

These outlets have an excellent selection of Middle Eastern and Indian delicacies: bulghur in varying coarsenesses, spices, teas, orange and rose waters, olives.

Delis — Other areas

II6	**Beacon Market**	*Open every day*
	2500 Beacon Ave S	*323-2050*

An impressive array of Chinese and Japanese produce, plus hard-to-find canned and dried specialties.

FF7	**Bodega Latina**	*Open Mon-Sat*
	901 NE 45th	*545-3502*

A store catering to Latin and Mexican cooks, with unusual Brazilian oils, frozen banana leaves, bitter orange concentrates, dried beans, and much more.

II6	**Borracchini's**	*Open every day*
	2307 Rainier Ave	*325-1550*

Famed as a place for making individual birthday cakes, Remo's spot also makes fresh pasta, a variety of country breads, and stocks Italian canned goods and wines.

GG3	**Brenner Brothers**	*Open every day*
	12000 NE Bellevue–Redmond Rd,	*454-0600*
	Bellevue	

It's a deli verging on supermarket, with kosher meats and sausages, cheeses, baked goods, rye breads, lox, and salads.

FF7	**Continental Store**	*Open Tues-Sat*
	5014 Roosevelt Way NE	*523-0606*

A German deli, with excellent cheeses, sausages, mustards, sauerkrauts, breads, pastries, chocolates, and pickled everything.

FF7	**House of Rice**	*Open Mon-Sat*
	4112 University Way NE	*633-5181*

One of the largest selections of Japanese and Chinese goods, plus spices and foodstuffs for Indonesian, Indian, and Pakistani dishes. The House is known for its excellent cooking classes and expert advice.

Husky Delicatessen	*Open Tues-Sun*
4721 California Ave SW	*937-2810*

West Seattleites come here for the large selection of deli regulars; the whole city flocks here for its wonderful homemade ice cream.

Johnsen's Scandinavian Foods	*Open Mon-Sat*
2248 NW Market	*783-8288*

A mecca for Ballard Scandinavians, noted for its baked goods, imported Baltic herring, rolled meats, and lefse (a flat potato bread).

King Chong Lung	*Open Mon-Sat*
707 S King	*622-2896*

Here is an extensive stock of Chinese and Thai foodstuffs, fresh, frozen, tinned, and dried; good prices, too.

New York Style Deli	*Open every day*
2801 E Madison	*328-0750*

It's more Russian than New York, but they have nice lunches, the usual deli salads, egg creams, their own cheesecake, and tasty piroshkis. It's a cheerful place for lunch.

Norwegian Sausage Co.	*Open Mon-Sat*
8539 15th Ave NW	*784-7020*

An admirable Ballard outpost: salted lamb, fish balls, lingonberries, cloudberries, cheeses, potato sausage, lutefisk, and other authentic fare.

Pasta & Co.	
University Village	*Open every day, 523-8594*
Bellevue Square, Bellevue	*Open every day, 453-8760*

The leading fresh-pasta emporium also has some fine deli offerings: sun-dried tomatoes, olive oils (from Italy, France, and Napa Valley), antipasto plates, aponat, heavenly caramels, and sauces for the pasta. We favor the smoked-salmon sauce, the matricciana sauce, and the current hot item: a garlicky veal-and-cheese-filled tortellini with a gorgonzola sauce. Owner Marcella Rosene is a reliable dispenser of foods and advice.

Sanelli's	*Open every day*
3700 128th SE, Bellevue	*644-3354*

Steve Sanelli makes his grandfather's recipe for Italian sausage (pork, beef, and fennel), and has added a large deli-full of Italian and Greek specialties. Fresh breads come from Puget Sound Baking Co. in Issaquah; good pastries; fresh pasta; nice desserts like cannoli; and sandwiches, subs, and soups to eat on premises or take out.

Surrogate Hostess	*Open every day*
1907 E Aloha	*328-0908*

Deli items are drawn from the restaurant and catering business that founder Robin Woodward runs. The cooking is correct and a la mode, though a shade bland in the seasoning; desserts are particularly fine.

Truffles	*Open Mon-Sat*
3701 NE 45th	*522-3016*

This many-owned institution in the University District has been improving smartly since Bobbi Smyth took it over in 1980: fine breads, salads, pates, and special orders of all sorts are made on the premises; on the shelves are excellent assortments of packaged foods. You can have a nice lunch or early supper here, made from deli items. Best place for truffles, not surprisingly.

Health food stores

QQ6 **Federal Way Health Foods**   *Open every day*
2012 S 320th (Across from Sea-Tac Mall) *839-0933*

This place is a nutritional gold mine, with a large book section, vitamins, herbs, bulk grains, spices, raw dairy products, and produce. A natural-foods lunchroom is attached to the store.

FF7 **Garden Grocer**   *Open every day*
4217 University Way NE   *634-3430*

A virtual health-supermarket that's been on "The Ave" for 12 years. Besides a wide selection of natural groceries, vitamins, and bulk foods, the store has added a delicatessen—salads, sandwiches, pates, imported cheeses, premium beers, and wines.

OO7 **The Grainery**   *Open Mon-Sat*
13629 First Ave S, Burien   *244-5015*

The Spendloves have been in business in Burien for eight years. They market their own honeys, grind their own flours, and carry a large selection of grains and beans including many hard-to-find items. In their central kitchen they frequently demonstrate milling and grinding, dehydrating, juicing, and such.

GG7 **Kernels Natural Foods**   *Open every day*
621 Broadway E   *323-8900*

This Capitol Hill store has a whole-grain bakery, organic foods, bulk grains, and vitamins.

J8 **Market Whole Foods**   *Open Mon-Sat*
Pike Place Market   *223-9582*

A great place for bulk buying of pasta, rice, beans, flours, grains, nuts, coffees, teas, and spices. Their bulk olive oil is a real bargain.

J8 **Pike Place Natural Foods**   *Open Mon-Sat*
Pike Place Market   *623-2231*

The only place in the Market where you can buy natural vitamins. They also have bulk sunflower seeds, spices, and herbs.

I8 **Scotty's Juicery**   *Open Mon-Sat*
Pike Place Market   *623-2500*

A small, open-air health bar in the Pike Place Market with a variety of fresh-squeezed natural juices, including such flavors as watermelon and their ultra-healthful "green" drink.

I5 **Seattle First Natural**   *Open Mon-Sat*
1629 Sixth Ave   *622-5090*

This 11-year-old "all-natural eating establishment," located next door to Frederick & Nelson, features baked goods, vitamins, and health supplies, but is best known for its luncheon salad bar (served from 11 to 4 daily).

Pasta

GG6	**Spadaccini Pasta-Deli** 1131 34th Ave	*Open Tues-Sat;* 325-9828 *(Your Place or Mine next door)*

The shop supplies fresh pasta (semolina plus plain white flour) to many restaurants, and it is invariably good; even better are the zesty sauces like a spicy meat sauce, a garlicky gorgonzola, and a tart marinara. Spadaccini is a wholesale outlet, but you can get their pasta and sauces next door at Your Place or Mine, a gourmet take-out restaurant.

J8	**La Coppa Pan** Pike Place Market	*Open Mon-Sat* 623-8166

Eggy, rich pasta, including tomato pasta, plus a line of red and white sauces, seafood salads, home-cured olives, their own pates, and some Italian desserts.

	Pasta & Co	
FF6	University Village	*Open every day;* 523-8594
HH3	Bellevue Square	*Open every day;* 453-8760

An outstanding fresh-pasta shop (see also Delis). The pasta is made to absorb sauces and is a shade thinner than usual, so the cooking time is more critical, but the pure semolina taste is wonderful. They do their own tortellini and the sauces are extremely good.

Produce markets

J8	**Pike Place Farmer's Market** First and Pike, Seattle	*Year round* *9-6 Mon-Sat; closed Sun*

This has to be the finest and most varied source of fruit and vegetables in the entire Northwest. *The Weekly* newspaper publishes a column on the seasonal specialties on sale at the Market on a week-by-week basis. The best way to buy fruit and vegetables there is to first look at the farmers' tables. Although their range is not as extensive, their produce is always fresher and cheaper as there is no middleman involved. Continue your shopping at the high stalls, which have a fine selection but which are essentially middlemen just like Safeway. Several of the high stalls have developed solid reputations over the years for their consistently good produce and personal service; they include Hasson Brothers, Manzo Brothers, and the Genzales.

Other farmers' markets (which are administered by the King County Farm Extension Office) in the area include the following. The official hours are listed but try to visit at opening time. Some markets consist of only a few farmers. Once they sell out, the market closes.

HH6	**Inner City Farmers' Market** 24th and Yesler, Seattle	*June-Sept* *9-2 Sat*
NN7	**Burien Saturday Market** (Metro Park & Ride lot) SW 148th and Fourth SW, Burien	*July-Sept* *10-4 Sat*
EE1	**Redmond Saturday Market** 85th NE, Downtown Redmond	*May-Sept* *9-2 Sat*
	Kent Saturday Market First Ave & Meeker St, Kent	*May-Sept* *9-2 Sat*

Shopping

| Vashon Saturday Market | *June-Sept* |
| 99th Ave SW, Downtown Vashon | *10-1 Sat* |

Seafood

NN4 **Center Seafoods** *Open Mon-Sat*
Renton Shopping Center, Renton *228-0971*

A large, good, and unlikely find next to Sears; they do their own custom smoking and carry hard-to-find items like fresh squid.

I8 **City Fish** *Open Mon-Sat*
Pike Place Market *682-9329*

Jack Levy's place always does a brisk business and has many steady customers; if you're a regular, you'll get fine quality, but a one-time customer might want to stare the fish in the unclouded eye first, a good test of freshness.

Jack's Fish Spot
GG6 2701 E Madison *Open Mon-Sat, 324-2041*
I8 Pike Place Market *Open Mon-Sat, 622-3727*

Small and smart, this shop has excellent products in a modest selection, plus a few deli items from Gretchen Mather's restaurants—she being the sister of the owner. Another outlet, with a much larger selection, has recently opened in the Pike Place Market.

HH3 **Johnston's Seafoods** *Open Mon-Sat*
210 106th Pl NE, Bellevue *454-6502*

This is the favorite seafood spot on the Eastside, with a substantial selection of quality goods and expert help.

I16 **Mutual Fish Company** *Open Mon-Sat*
2335 Rainier Ave S *322-4368*

This outstanding place, lovingly run by the Yoshimura family, gets some of the widest selection and freshest seafood in the city. Prices are good, they will slice raw fish for sashimi, they know all about packing for air freight or carry-home, and they take great care to keep live products fresh and pure.

Pacific Fish House *Open Mon-Sat*
HH7 617 S Dearborn *382-4632*

Pacific is a mammoth supplier to restaurants, so they always have tons of seafood on hand, of all levels of quality. This retail outlet is a bit overwhelming, but you can find excellent fish here if you are skilled at spotting quality.

J8 **Pike Place Fish** *Open Mon-Sat*
Pike Place Market *682-7181*

Often considered the best in the Market, with a wide selection of scrupulously fresh fish, plus smoked and kippered seafood. They are likely to have some local rarities, and they know how to pack for the traveler.

FF8 **Port Chatham Packing Company** *Open Mon-Sat*
632 NW 46th *783-8200*

Julia Child discovered the satiny, cool-smoked salmon this place has been turning out for years, and they've done land-office business ever since. They handpack salmon, slice their extraordinary lox, and offer some new lines like smoked black cod. It's hard to find in Ballard, but it's a fascinating old-fashioned place to visit, and it might take care of your gift needs for the next decade.

FF7 **University Seafood & Poultry** *Open Mon-Sat*
1317 NE 47th *632-3900*

A dandy store, with an owner who loves to find delicacies that no other shop has managed to get (like fresh halibut). Everything is fresh and top-of-the-line, which means pricey by Seattle standards but a bargain compared to inland prices.

Q7 **Uwajimaya** *Open every day*
Sixth S & S King *624-6248*
(also at Bellevue & Southcenter)

An extraordinary Japanese supermarket in the International District, with some of the finest fish you can find in the city. The specialty is cutting raw fish for sushi or sashimi, and they have many rarities used in Japanese cuisine.

FF8 **Wild Salmon Fish Market** *Open Mon-Sat*
1800 W Emerson Pl *283-3366*

The wild salmon is being replaced by hatchery-raised salmon, alas, and you cannot be sure of catching the former, healthier species. Even so, this shop does a decent job of getting fresh salmon, and the location by Fishermen's Terminal helps whet the appetite.

State liquor stores

For stronger stuff than beer and wine, Washingtonians must still call on their liquor stores. There are 60 or so stores in the greater Seattle area, some more accessible (longer hours, parking facilities, etc.) and with larger selections than others. Other stores operate more as a convenience to specific neighborhoods. The
A7 three state liquor stores with the largest selections are on Lower Queen Anne Hill,
I6 515 First N (464-6092), in the University Village (522-5434), and downtown in
N7 The Bon (464-6744). Other downtown stores are located at Second and James,
G5 Sixth and Lenora, and Seventh and Pike. Store hours vary, so it's best to call if
J4 you intend to shop after 5 p.m.

Wine — Downtown

J8 **De Laurenti's** *Open Mon-Sat*
Pike Place Market *622-0141*
317 Bellevue Way, Bellevue *454-7155*

As befits an Italian deli, the strong suit here is Italian wine. The wine department, on a mezzanine overlooking an atrium in the Market, has professional service and good prices.

II7 **Esquin Wine Merchants** *Open Mon-Sat*
1516 First Ave S *682-7374*

135

Shopping

The location is a bit out-of-the-way and, at street level, Esquin looks like a little brick bunker. The treasures, however, are in the catacombs below, where owner Rand Sealey cellars some of the finest vintages in the city. The shop specializes in outstanding wines to be bought early (at lower prices) and "put down" for years.

I8	**Pike and Western Wine Merchants** Pike Place Market	*Open Mon-Sat* *623-1307*

Managing partner Ron Irvine comes as close as any retailer to being *the* authority on Northwest wines; he is frequently called on as a speaker or judge in wine competitions, and he stays in close touch with the leading Northwest winemakers. The shop carries an excellent selection of classic French and German wines, in addition to the best Northwest bottlings. Prices are a tad high.

Wine — Other areas

	The Cellar	
CC7	14411 Greenwood Ave N	*Open every day, 365-7660*
GG2	14603 NE 20th Ave, Bellevue	*Open Mon-Sat, 644-1512*

Joe Marleau is one of the city's best-established wine merchants, and his stores carry a marvelous collection of wine-making and beer-making equipment in addition to wine.

C8	**Champion Cellars** 108 Denny	*Open Mon-Sat* *284-8306*

Partly owned by Emile Ninaud, owner of Le Tastevin. Long regarded as a fine wine shop.

	The Cork Shop Winslow Mall, Bainbridge Island	*Open Mon-Sat* *842-6428*

The Island's only wine shop (excepting the state liquor store down the street), and a good one at that. The Bainbridge Island Winery hasn't produced enough wine yet to supply the shop, but other Northwest wineries are represented.

FF7	**European Vine Selections** 318 N 36th	*Open 5-8 Wed & Thur; 11-5 Sat;* *633-5752*

Glenn White of the University of Washington started this little shop (in a Fremont district basement) in order to provide low-overhead, low-cost wine to connoisseurs. The Liquor Board originally balked at the store's short hours, but has since relented. Selections are good, quality is high.

	La Cantina	
FF6	University Village	*Open every day, 525-4340*
HH3	104 Bellevue Way SE, Bellevue	*Open Mon-Sat, 455-4363*

Harry Alhadeff's stores employ some of the region's most informative sales people, and regular classes are offered on topics from champagne to port. Wide range, with an excellent selection of Northwest wines.

EE6	**McCarthy & Co., Wine Merchants** 6500 Ravenna NE	*Open Tues-Sat* *524-0999*

Dan McCarthy, a young veteran of Seattle's wholesale wine business, opened his small shop with the intention of finding the very best wines on the market, then

Shopping

selling them at low prices. It's a tribute to his expertise, as well as his pricing, that the shop is such a success. The owner is particularly knowledgeable about Northwest wines.

II5 **Mercer Point Wine**   *Open every day*
Factoria Square, Bellevue   *747-7557*

Two dozen Northwest labels are represented here, plus meats, cheeses, and breads from the Sunshine Baking Company.

JJ5 **Mondo's World**   *Open Tues-Sat*
4223 Rainier Ave S   *725-5433*

Scores of faithful customers come here to order (and pick up) caseloads of wine at the best prices in town; proprietor Jerry Banchero presides over the cramped quarters with great enthusiasm.

Safeway   *Open every day*
FF6 **University Village (3020 NE 45th)**   *522-7821*
(and other locations)

Safeway stores have awakened to the fact that people are buying more and more wine, and are increasingly interested in finding out more about wine. Safeway now puts out its own wine newsletter, and some two dozen Safeway stores around Puget Sound have at least one full-time wine steward. The University Village Safeway has the largest wine selection in Seattle; here, the wine section is guided by Richard Kinssies (a wine educator, wine columnist for the *P-I*, and commentator on KING-FM). Special attention is paid to Northwest wines. Prices are as good as you'll find anywhere.

A Northwest Wine Sampler
Suggested wines for a gift pack

White Wines
Gewurztraminer
    1981 Associated Vintners
        "Centennial" release
    1981 Mont Elise
Riesling
    1981 Tualatin Vineyards
    1981 Knudsen-Erath
    1981 Elk Cove
Chardonnay
    1980 Ste. Chapelle
        (Idaho or Washington)
    1980 The Eyrie Vineyards
    1981 E.B. Foote
Fume Blanc/Sauvignon Blanc
    1981 Preston Wine Cellars
    1981 Chateau Ste. Michelle
    1981 Worden's Washington Winery
    1981 Daquila Wines

Red Wines
Cabernet Sauvignon
    1976 or 1978 Chateau Ste. Michelle
        Reserve
    1978 or 1979 Leonetti Cellar
    1978 Hinzerling Cabernet-Merlot
        (blend)
Pinot Noir
    1978 or 1979 Salishan Vineyards
    1978 Scott Henry/Henry Estate
    1979 Knudsen-Erath
    1979 Ponzi
    1979 Elk Cove
Merlot
    1980 Associated Vintners
    1980 Sokol Blosser

Shopping

Other Wines of Interest
1976 Chateau Ste. Michelle
   Blanc de Noirs (sparkling)
Amity Vineyards Pinot Noir Nouveau
Paul Thomas Crimson Rhubarb
Arterberry Cider (non-vintage)

Best Bets among the "open" wines
Hinzerling "Ashfall White"
Henry "Umpqua Red"
Neuharth "Dungeness Red"

Home

Antiques — Downtown

F7	**Antiques & Art Associates** 2113 Third Ave	*Open Mon-Sat* 624-4378

The front room, presided over by George Harder, contains a fine collection of rare books, prints, and maps. Lucinda Harder runs the back, which has a general line of china, glass, and silver.

D2	**Antique Liquidators** 503 Westlake Ave N	*Open Mon-Sat* 623-2740

Without a doubt the largest store in town, with 20,000 square feet of sales and storage space. Unpretentious, too, with hundreds of pieces of practical furniture, mostly English. High turnover; if they don't have what you're looking for, try again next week after the next containerload comes in. Good prices.

P7	**Charles & McClain, Ltd.** 210 Third Ave S	*By appointment* 623-6090

Spacious, classy showroom of Chinese and Japanese antiques for collectors of very rare objects.

K6	**The Crane Gallery** 1326 Sixth Ave	*Open Mon-Sat* 622-7185

Fine Asian antiques and artifacts such as paintings, ceramics, bronzes, ivory, jade, and furniture from around the Orient: China, Japan, Korea, India.

J5	**Globe Antiques** 529 Pine	*Open Mon-Sat* 682-1420

Betty Balcomb's shop on Sixth Avenue is a downtown treasure: 18th- and 19th-century European and American furniture, Georgian silver, very fine Oriental porcelain, Oriental rugs. You won't find bargains here, but you will find good value and fair counsel.

I8	**Post Alley Antiques** 1926 Post Alley	*Open Tues-Sat* 464-1407

Collectors of old maps will find their hearts' desire here (or Mary Morgan and Ann Barker will find it for them). There's the usual 18th- and 19th-century furniture, of course, but the specialty is 16th- and 17th-century antique maps: everything from the earliest (1580) woodcut of Alaska, to early (1626) maps of Virginia, to a map showing California as an island, to hand-engraved and hand-colored maps of France and Britain.

Shopping

J7	**Royal City Antiques** 2313 Third Ave	*Open Mon-Sat* *587-3711*

A wide variety of British and Danish furniture, in a big store; free parking next door.

J6	**Wm. L. Davis & Co.** 1300 Fifth Ave	*Open Mon-Sat* *622-0518*

Since its founding in 1890, this has been one of Seattle's most respected (and expensive) importers of 18th- and early 19th-century antique furniture and accessories. Originally limited to English antiques, the shop now features Italian and Oriental pieces as well. Bill Bowden, one of the owners, gives lectures illustrated with his own slides upon request. The firm also offers interior design services to buyers.

G9	**Vanity Fair Antiques** Pier 70	*Open every day* *622-9240*

Proprietor Karen Lorene is perhaps Seattle's leading authority on antique jewelry. She also offers appraisals, classes, tours to England. The store stocks choice Victorian gift items in all price categories.

Antiques — Other areas

F6	**Anita's** University Village	*Open every day* **524-0070**

A small space below Ken's Suburban Furniture filled with expensive, high-quality merchandise: small furniture pieces, fine glass and china, baskets and pottery, sterling and jewelry.

	Antique Appraisal & **Estate Sales Service** 160 Gilman Blvd NW, Issaquah	*Open Wed-Sat* *746-3793*

Despite its formidable name, this antique shop across the street from Gilman Village is open to the public, and sells art glass, sterling silver, fine furniture, and porcelain.

P6	**Barker's** 22456 Pacific Hwy S	*By appointment only* *878-4161*

Barker's is the grande dame of the local antique community. Art glass, jewelry, silver, reference books.

F6	**Chelsea Antiques** 3622 NE 45th	*Open Mon-Sat* *525-2727*

Furniture, lamps, and porcelain are sold here, but the main attraction is the Georgian silver. Owner Suzanne Ries is perhaps among the most knowledgeable in town about sterling.

H7	**Connoisseur Antiques** 713 Broadway E	*Open Mon-Sat* *322-1222*

Located in the charming Loveless Building, complete with parquet floors and a fireplace, this shop could be in the English countryside: 18th- and 19th-century English and French furniture and decorative accessories, porcelain, silver, glass,

Shopping

and ceramics. Proprietor John Yaconetti is most helpful, and prices are very fair.

HH6 **David Weatherford**
　　　Antiques & Interiors　　　*Open Mon-Sat*
　　　133 14th Ave E　　　　　　　329-6533

Quite possibly the largest selection of museum-quality period furniture in town, thanks to the staff of over a dozen interior designers who use the inventory for residential and commercial assignments. The collection of 18th-century English and French furniture is exquisite. Oriental art is another specialty. The setting is one of Capitol Hill's most elegant mansions, with additional treasures tucked away in warehouses.

HH3 **The Golden Box**　　　　　*Open Tues-Sat*
　　　10020 Main St, Bellevue　　 453-8853

Jewelry, objets d'art, and decorator accessories, all nicely displayed.

O4 **Honeychurch Antiques**　　　*Open Mon-Sat*
　　　1008 James St　　　　　　　622-1225

John Fairman runs this excellent shop, which is supplied in part by his parents, antique buyers who live in Hong Kong. He has the largest selection of 19th-century Japanese furniture in the Northwest, but the store's attraction lies in its blend of Asian fine art, folk art, and furniture. Occasional shows of very high quality (Asian scrolls, for instance).

GG8 **Oak Parlor**　　　　　　　　*Open Tues-Fri*
　　　5405 Ballard Ave NW　　　　783-2327

Straightforward collection of American oak pieces.

EE7 **Old Seattle Antiques**　　　*Open Tues-Sat*
　　　308 NE 65th　　　　　　　　522-7229

A big shop, loaded with "primitives": early American kitchen implements, woodenware, washboards, and other miscellany. There's also a big collection of antique jewelry.

　　　Pelayo's　　　　　　　　　　*Open every day*
DD6 3236 NE 45th　　　　　　　525-1444
DD7 8421 Greenwood Ave N　　　789-1333

Pedro Pelayo specializes in European furniture, mostly English, from the 19th- and 20th-centuries. Brass and copper accessories, too. The Greenwood store has more oak, the 45th store more pine furniture. Reasonable prices.

HH3 **Second Story Antiques**　　　*Open Tues-Sat*
　　　10220 NE First Pl, Bellevue　 455-9636

Specializes in European furniture: walnut, mahogany, rosewood, and English oak.

GG8 **Third Hand Shop**　　　　　*Open every day*
　　　11 W McGraw　　　　　　　 284-3011

Here's a great place to browse: a three-story, chocolate-brown Queen Anne home that's been stuffed with ornate brass beds, beveled glass, stained glass, armoires, bits of copper, and what-have-you. Dale Rutherford has been in business here since 1967.

EE8 **Tipton & Richardson**　　　*Open Wed-Sat*
　　　5959 15th Ave NW　　　　　782-2814

Shopping

Interesting old woodworking handtools among an inventory of American country antiques and quilts.

Mapbook of Antique Shops
Box 501, Snoqualmie, WA 98065   *(206) 888-0647*

Many of the better (or at least more prosperous) antique shops in Washington, Oregon, and California are listed in this handy volume, compiled by Theodore Crane. It's available at many antique shops (or by mail) for about $6, and is particularly useful for "antiquing" in unfamiliar territory.

Auctions

7 **Bushell's Auctions**   *Hours: 8-5 Wed-Fri; Previews: noon-5 Fri,*
  2006 Second Ave   *8-7 Mon;   Auctions: 10-3 or*
                                    7:30pm-9:30pm Tues; 622-5833

Mary Bushell's auction house is open to all, with auctions on most Tuesdays in the daytime or evening (depending on what's being sold; there are more antiques in the evenings). The merchandise consists of a great variety of household items, some antique, some contemporary: dishes, glassware, rugs, bedroom sets, etc. Real treasures are to be found here, but you have to know your stuff because there's little help from "salespeople." The merchandise comes from estate liquidations and private sales. Rummage around, then bid what you think the item is worth.

04 **Renton Auction**   *11-8 Mon pickup; 10-10 Fri pickup, preview;*
   7721 S Longacres Way, Renton *10-? Sat preview, auction   255-7122*

Every Saturday night starting at 6:30 it's auction-time in this big barnlike building near the Longacres racetrack. Container-loads of antiques and secondhand furniture from Great Britain—drop-leaf and draw-leaf tables, armoires, desks, dressing tables, occasional tables, dining-room chairs, bowls, plates, clocks—go under the hammer at a brisk pace, so there are some bargains to be had. They also auction appliances and new (garish) furniture after the antiques. It's a marathon affair, often going into the wee hours, but it's a lot of fun watching the colorful auctioneer, and the crowds of auction hounds. Dress warmly and bring a pillow—it's spartan.

6 **Satori Fine Art Auction**   *9:30-5 Mon-Fri; Auctions normally 7pm*
  2305 Fifth Ave   *every third Tues. Call 223-9505 for details*

An auction at Satori's is a very civilized affair albeit in a warehouse-like room. The European-style auction house operates in a low-key, refined manner with Satori Gregorakis, the auctioneer, calmly describing the antique furniture, coins, fine art, porcelain, Oriental rugs, and other collectibles that are all on consignment from private estates. Complimentary desserts (from B&O Espresso) and coffee are also served. If you're interested in the international market, Satori's has offices in the UK and Singapore, too.

Hardware

F8 **Ballard Hardware and Supply**   *Open Mon-Sat*
   5229 Ballard NW   *783-6626*

141

Shopping

A hardware store for the hard-core: if you need pipe fittings, this is the place to go, but there's nothing to touch up the kitchen. You'll get professional service, if you know what you want.

GG6	**City People's Mercantile** 1463 E Republican	*Open every day* *324-9510*

This aptly named cooperative carries basic hardware on the first floor and attractive, inexpensive kitchen ware on the second floor; natural-fabric clothing and imported items are also stocked.

FF7	**Hardwick's Swap Shop** 4214 Roosevelt Way NE	*Open Tues-Sat* *632-1203*

Your best bet to beat the high cost of tools, this hardware store offers just about anything, new and used, to stock and run a home, from furniture and fire irons to sinks and toilet seats.

EE7	**Gowan's Greenwood Hardware** 7201 Greenwood N	*Open every day* *783-2900*

This excellent store features ceiling fans, sleds, cast-iron stoves, an extensive line of garden tools, paint, insulation, fittings, and fixtures. The salesman who says, "If you don't see it, it's somewhere," is right on the mark.

GG6	**Madison Park Hardware** 1837 42nd E	*Open Mon-Sat* *322-5331*

No ordinary hardware store, Madison Park Hardware is the center of life in this single-family, YP community. Proprietress Lola knows Madison Park like the back of her hand, is very active in its politics, and her shop caters well to its needs. In addition to providing a solid range of standard hardware goods, she stocks a good selection of kitchen and gift items, decorator baskets, toys, and pet supplies, all in a friendly atmosphere and at prices that reflect the neighborhood. The store is closed for the month of January every year.

DD6	**McVicar's** 8507 35th NE	*Open Mon-Sat* *523-1400*

Seeds, bulbs, baskets, candles, cookware, and cleaning supplies are just a few items among McVicar's comprehensive inventory. The store also has a mile-long selection of catalogues to order from.

II7	**Pacific Iron Building Materials** 2230 Fourth S	*Open every day* *628-6222*

It's eclectic: cork, chicken-wire, doors, rope, ladders, styrofoam, insulation, and lumber plus a bin of discounted oddities. But if you've taken on some serious remodeling, you'll get excellent help with your specifications.

EE6	**R & R Hardware** 6512 15th Ave NE	*Open every day* *522-7810*

A neighborhood store with a wood stove, Coke machine, and kids out front makes a fine place to browse, watch the game, or pick up a few yard tools. There's not much in the way of cookware, but it's a well-stocked, friendly store.

Q6	**Tashiro's Japanese Tools** 618 S Jackson	*Open Mon-Sat* *622-8452*

As its name denotes, this store specializes in high-quality Japanese woodworking tools and cooking knives—elegant saws with high-carbon stainless-steel blades, files, carving chisels, fine sashimi knives, and much more.

142

Shopping

| FF7 | **Tweedy and Popp's Ace Hardware**
1916 N 45th | *Open Mon-Sat*
632-2290 |

The only touch of whimsy in this compulsively well-organized store is the Yankee Clipper sleds hanging high on the wall. For the suburbanite with an impeccable house and garden, this store has everything, including kitchen sinks and bright red lawn mowers.

| FF7 | **University Tru Value Hardware**
4713 University Way NE | *Open Mon-Sat*
523-5353 |

Parking this close to the University is no cinch, but if it's low-cost sturdy cookware and kitchen supplies you want, University Hardware *is* a true value. A fine store with friendly service.

Home furnishings — Downtown

| K8 | **Abodio**
1223 Western Ave | *Open every day*
587-0516 |

Marketing themselves as "the total home store," Abodio stocks the full gamut of contemporary home furnishings with everything from couches, tables, beds, and linens downstairs to cookware, kitchen accessories, dinnerware, and knicknacks upstairs. There is a good selection of mainly US-made furniture in their large showrooms, but the kitchen and dinnerware items are limited. By buying stock in large quantities, the store can offer good prices and special discounts.

| G8 | **Egbert's**
2231 First Ave | *Open Mon-Sat*
624-3377 |

Egbert's stands out among modern-furnishings stores, with its one-of-a-kind furniture, accessories, dinner services, and kitchenware imported directly from Europe by the owner, Jim Egbert. You'll find some of the best examples of Scandinavian furniture design, from light oak Danish tables to superb Finnish lighting fixtures and wall units, a large selection of European glassware, unusual dinnerware sets, and selected kitchen accessories effectively displayed in room ensembles. Soft Irish floor rugs, whimsical French tiles, and Finnish mohair blankets in rich, warm colors are more of the delightful finds.

| J8 | **Habitat**
Pike Market Hillclimb | *Open every day*
623-7795 |

Habitat stocks furniture, glassware, lighting, storage containers, kitchenware, and all manner of accessories with an eye to the modern apartment dweller. Much of the furniture is of the assemble-it-yourself type, to help keep prices moderate.

| M7 | **Houseworks**
823 Third Ave, Seattle Trust Court | *Open Mon-Fri*
622-6328 |

Located in the heart of Seattle's downtown business district, Houseworks is a convenient place for office workers to shop for designer household goods. The store stocks selected kitchen and living-room items, many of which it imports directly from Europe, like the softly colored Italian ceramic crock pots, old Danish pine furniture, Finnish shelving and storage units, and Marimekko fabrics.

| K6 | **Just Designs**
Rainier Square | *Open Mon-Sat*
623-3301 |

Shopping

Another sleek-lined, Scandinavian-influenced home-furnishings store, Just Designs is located in equally sleek surroundings in Rainier Square. The store is strong in Scandinavian and German glassware while it also stocks a broad range of European and US furniture, with some fine Norwegian pieces.

K6	**The Linen Store** Rainier Square	*Open Mon-Sat* *622-9372*

Superior-quality, all-cotton towels and sheets, linen tablecloths, wool and cashmere blankets, and goose-down pillows and comforters make The Linen Store a superb place to shop for the home. It also stocks all manner of bathroom accessories and provides an excellent monogramming service.

	Masin Furniture Co., Inc.	
O8	220 Second Ave S	*Open Mon-Sat, 622-5606*
GG2	14024 Bellevue–Redmond Rd, Bellevue	*Open every day, 746-5606*

A full-service, traditional furniture store, Masin's has extensive showrooms of designed interiors with selected items from the full range of classical furniture styles (there are some particularly interesting Oriental pieces). Carrying the top name brands in furniture and furnishings, Masin's also stocks floor and wall coverings and draperies, and offers free in-home consultation services.

N8	**Sitka Design — The Butcher Block Shop** 113 First Ave S	*Open every day, 622-4446*

Reasonably priced, quality modern lightwood furniture and accessories are the hallmarks of Sitka Design, which directly imports much of its merchandise from Europe. The owners got their start building and selling butcher-block furniture (hence the other name), and they have now expanded into furniture and wall units which have the mix-and-match, modular feel appropriate for apartment and condominium living.

Home furnishings — Other areas

FF7	**The Basics** 4536 University Way NE	*Open every day* *634-2221*

Jumping on the bandwagon of design living, this store has all the basics for apartment dwellers—brightly colored plastic storage containers and dishes, glasses, kitchen utensils, picture frames, and a few basic couches. The color-coded displays are attractive but you can find most things elsewhere at lower prices.

	Bel Square Furniture and Interiors	
HH7	211 Broadway E	*Open every day, 324-6220*
II2	3550 128th SE, Bellevue	*Open every day, 643-6844*
GG9	2454 33rd W	*Open Mon-Sat, 283-0221*

A well-stocked furniture store with a distinct suburban look, Bel Square offers more traditional lines by several notable makers.

GG7	**Current** 815 E Thomas	*Open every day* *325-2995*

A newcomer to the designer home-furnishings scene, Current stocks some interesting European items new to the Seattle market. Its strong suit is lighting in all shapes and sizes; it also has some white Italian deck furniture and a special-order

Italian couch line. Along with its sister store, Houseworks, it also offers a bright line of Finnish organizers, trays and bins, etc., and a selection of imported glassware.

HH7 **Del Teet Furniture Company** *Open Mon-Sat*
127 Broadway E *323-5400*

With its three floors of showrooms on Capitol Hill, Del Teet stocks an extensive range of modern furniture with an emphasis on oak and pine, and natural-looking fabrics. The store offers an interior-design service and can custom-make furniture to any specifications.

HH7 **Fabrik Seconds Store** *Open Mon-Sat*
321 Broadway E *329-2110*

This tiny Capitol Hill store serves as an outlet for factory seconds of Fabrik dinnerware, a local ceramic company that markets its stoneware nationally. The store also stocks other items such as wooden bowls, glassware, dishcloths, wrapping paper, and ribbon.

H3 **Interior Concepts** *Open every day*
Bellevue Square, Bellevue *454-7042*

This outlet features Finland's fine screened and printed fabric (Marimekko) and accessories to match.

H7 **Keeg's** *Open Mon-Sat*
310 Broadway E *325-1771*

Located in the heart of Capitol Hill, Keeg's is a very popular home-furnishings and gift store stocking modern, lightwood, Danish-flavored furniture that is sometimes a little pricey, plus a good selection of dinner- and flatware, cookware, kitchen accessories, rugs, and sundry gift items. It also offers a good range of wrapping paper, cards, and other paper products.

Miller–Pollard Interiors, Inc.
F7 **4538 University Way NE** *Open Mon-Sat, 633-1277*
G6 **4218 E Madison** *Open Tues-Sat, 325-3600*

Good-quality lines of oak and pine furniture, comfortable couches, a selection of dinner- and glassware, silver, brass, and wooden pieces, dinner mats, aprons, and a range of cards and paper goods are all tastefully displayed. The store also offers in-store design consultation and a free delivery service in the Greater Seattle area.

H7 **McBreen, Inc.** *Open Mon-Sat*
905 E John *323-2336*

Stocking the major name furniture brands, McBreen's lends a distinctive Oriental tone to its interiors. The store is well known for its design services.

Murphy's
F8 **2242 NW Market** *Open Tues-Sat, 789-3970*

In a home-furnishings and collectibles store that grew out of a lucrative interior-design business, Murphy's has an interesting and eclectic collection of selected antiques and gift items, such as rag dolls, linen table mats, Dilettante chocolates, baskets, glassware, and a tantalizing array of gourmet delicacies from Maxims de Paris.

H3 **Scan Design** *Open every day*
10515 NE Sixth, Bellevue *454-7200*
H3 **Scan Import** *Open every day*
12130 Bellevue-Redmond Rd, Bellevue *454-4220*

Shopping

This elegant Scandinavian furniture dealer carries the best rosewood, teak, and walnut available. Scan Import has somewhat cheaper items, many for assembly by the customer; teak only.

005	**Woodpeople** 16600 Southcenter Pky, Tukwila	*Open every day* 575-3900

Just south of the main Southcenter Mall is this back-to-basics (gracefully) furniture store. Plenty of oak, maple, beech, and ash butcher-block tables and chairs.

Kitchenware — Downtown

K9	**A Cook's Tour** Pier 56	*Open every day* 623-7277

An attractively designed and spacious kitchen store located behind Trident Imports on the waterfront, A Cook's Tour stocks all the ingredients for a gourmet kitchen. Cuisinarts, copperware, pots and pans (and the racks to hang them on), glassware, place settings, storage containers, and every conceivable kitchen utensil and knickknack can be found here.

08	**Grand Central Mercantile** 316 First Ave S	*Open every day* 623-8894

This long, narrow store in Pioneer Square is a gold mine of mainly imported kitchenware, cooking accessories, and dinnerware. There is a good selection of knives, some tempting specialty food items, and other unusual knickknacks. The basement warehouse in the Grand Central on the Park Building has some great buys in discontinued and overstocked items.

I8	**Sur La Table** Pike Place Market	*Open Mon-Sat* 622-2459

Nestled in a warm, peach-colored building in Pike Place Market, Sur la Table is packed with all the essential equipment and utensils for the gourmet cook. Every conceivable type of baking pan and mold crams the shelves, copper pots and saucepans hang from wire racks, while Cuisinarts and their countless accessories abound. The store also stocks many cookbooks and has periodic cooking demonstrations. The knowledgeable sales staff helps with all sorts of questions.

Kitchenware — Other areas

DD7	**Addison's** Northgate	*Open every day* 362-0707

Not quite a kitchenware store, not quite a gift shop, Addison's has plenty of usual, slightly expensive housewares, plus cards, books, some toys, and knickknacks.

	The Berry Patch and Contents Winslow, Bainbridge Island	*Open Mon-Sat* 842-3593

Fine accoutrements for the kitchen and bathroom, many of them imported. A good selection of pricey cooking pans, utensils, and gadgets.

Shopping

HH3	**Domus**	*Open every day*
	Bellevue Square, Bellevue	*454-2728*

The best of the Bellevue Square kitchen gift shops, Domus carries generally exclusive brands in linen, plates, flatware, food preparation tools, and hundreds of gadgets.

	The Kitchen Cupboard	*Open every day*
	Gilman Village, Issaquah	*392-7284*

Located at the tree-shaded western end of Gilman Village in the old Court House, this shop offers the expected display of pricey but attractive gift items for the kitchen, including Asta Ware, cute utensils, and lots of copper items.

EE8	**Kitchen 'N Things**	*Open Mon-Sat*
	2322 NW Market	*784-8717*

Russian porcelain and a wide range of Scandinavian home accessories, including woven runners and braid, are highlights in this Ballard shop, which also stocks a good general selection of kitchen items.

FF9	**Magnolia Kitchen Shoppe and**	*Open Mon-Sat*
	Cooking School	*282-2665*
	2416 32nd W	

A warm, inviting interior welcomes visitors to this well-stocked kitchen-supplies and gift store, with a cooking school in operation.

HH3	**Mr. J's Kitchen Gourmet**	*Open Mon-Sat*
	Gelati Place, 10630 NE Eighth, Bellevue	*455-2270*

One of Bellevue's best kitchen-supply stores: a veritable warehouse of tasteful domestic and imported pots, pans, glassware, plates, flatware, cooking aids, processors, and trendy gadgets. Also, a full-fledged cooking school.

FF6	**The Mrs Cooks**	*Open every day*
	University Village	*525-5008*

A neighborhood kitchen store which concentrates on top-quality, useful cookware and accessories as well as gift items for the home. A good range of practical baskets.

	Seattle Design Store	*Open every day*
GG7	**406 Broadway E**	*324-9700*
HH3	**10222 NE Eighth, Bellevue**	*455-4300*
I5	**1621 Westlake**	*625-0500*
FF6	**2943 NE Blakeley**	*523-7500*

Seattle Design Store has been very successful in marketing "designer" goods for the home. Cooking pots and utensils, colorful storage jars, baskets and racks, picture frames, flatware, and glassware are well chosen and displayed. Its four convenient locations and generous hours add to its popularity.

	Yankee Kitchen	
HH3	**10108 Main St, Bellevue**	*Open Mon-Sat, 454-2377*
	Old Milltown, 201 Fifth Ave S,	
	Edmonds	*Open every day, 774-6787*

The Yankee Kitchen sells pots and pans with panache. A chic clutter of gift gadgets on several tables, good cast-iron and porcelain tureens, jams, coffees, and

147

Shopping

table linens are just some of the offerings. Both outlets have cooking schools as well.

Rugs

O8	**The Golden Horn** 214 First Ave S, Grand Central Arcade	*Open Tues-Sun* 464-0578

Owned by the Bozatli family, the Golden Horn is the finest local importer of Turkish rugs and kilims. Using no middlemen, the Bozatli family selects rugs from homes and villages with which they have an established association. The rugs are exported from Istanbul directly to the United States, and prices reflect this direct merchandising. The rugs are exquisite in design and colors, and Janice, the manager of the store, knows her rugs and is happy to answer any questions.

EE7	**Oasis Antique Oriental Rugs** 5655 University Way NE	*Open Mon-Sat* 525-2060

Doug Barnhart uses his gallery setting to maximum advantage, displaying a large collection of original, antique tribal rugs—some room-size, some smaller. Showcases and shelves of pottery and porcelain as well, with paintings and prints also displayed.

J4	**Pande Cameron** 815 Pine	*Open Mon-Sat* 624-6263

Mostly new rugs from India, Pakistan, Romania, Turkey, Iran, Morocco, China, and Afghanistan. Machine-made rugs from Holland and Belgium, too, and a new section devoted to high-quality carpets. One of the three Andonian brothers is always on hand. The store also has its own service department.

J2	**Rosen-Colgren Gallery** 1207 Pine	*Open Mon-Sat* 623-3230

A wide variety of antique, Oriental rugs, particularly Caucasian tribal pieces, with a few unusual items, such as Persian silks, also on hand. Ralph Rosen and Monte Colgren also use their shop to display a large collection of antique furniture, porcelain, and paintings.

Stereo equipment

EE7	**Definitive Audio** 6017 Roosevelt Way NE	*Open Tues-Sat* 524-6633

Seattle's oldest dealer in high-end systems, Definitive Audio emphasizes straightforward component matching and system adjustment to achieve the best performance with some of the latest innovations in audio.

FF7	**Optimum Sound** 4730 University Way NE	*Open every day* 525-1903

Don't be put off by the casual approach and small selection. Optimum Sound offers good value in mid-priced systems at somewhat lower prices.

Shopping

E7	**Magnolia Hi-Fi** 6322 Roosevelt Way NE	*Open every day* 525-0080

Magnolia Hi-Fi stocks several durable brands and the attentive sales people can put together systems for the uninitiated. Well known for service long after the sale, Magnolia wants your business for life.

E7	**Speakerlab** 6414 Roosevelt Way NE (also at Parkway Plaza, Lynnwood, & Bellevue)	*Open every day* 525-2202

A Seattle institution, Speakerlab carries several lines of well-engineered components that virtually sell themselves. They also make their own speakers, which they sell as a kit or individually.

)05	**The Stereo Shoppe** 17790 Southcenter Parkway	*Open every day* 575-8282

The Stereo Shoppe has the area's most knowledgeable and cooperative sales staff who are acquainted with a broad range of equipment, including the more esoteric gear. All decks and turntables are extensively tuned at purchase and every six months thereafter.

E7	**Great American Stereo Warehouse** 6220 Roosevelt Way NE	*Open every day* 524-9090

The closest thing to a discount stereo store in Seattle, Great American Stereo Warehouse is a good place to buy styli, cartridges, car stereos, and accessories.

Other

Books — Downtown

F8	**Art in Form** 2237 Second Ave	*Open Wed-Sat and by appointment* 623-6381

Located in Belltown, the heart of Seattle's artists' district, Art in Form has the largest and most in-depth selection of art books and magazines west of New York. The store also runs a well-connected international mail-order business.

K6	**B. Bailey Books** Rainier Square	*Open Mon-Sat* 624-1328

An uptown bookstore to match its location, the most dramatic block in the business district. The stock leans toward business, economics and travel titles.

J6 M8	**B. Dalton Bookseller** 1533 Fourth (and outlying areas, plus new store at First & Marion)	*Open every day* 223-1364

A large chain store with sections devoted to computers, local maps, and cookbooks.

H8	**DeGraff Books** First & Virginia	*Open Mon-Sat (in summer, Sun)* 292-9477

This attractive bookstore is across the street from the main Pike Place Market complex, in the new Market Place North building. General titles with a section devoted to Oriental books.

O8	**David Ishii** 212 First S	*Open every day* 622-4719

Ishii, the learned and most helpful owner, is an explorer for fine editions of scarce out-of-print and secondhand books, with a little treasure trove in the Grand Central Arcade in Pioneer Square. Since he's also a fly fisherman, he's got a fair stock of nature and fishing titles.

O8	**Elliott Bay Book Company** First S & S Main	*Open every day* 624-6600	

Pioneer Square's wood-toned, rustic-looking Elliott Bay Book Company, with its excellent selection and relaxed atmosphere, is a splendid place to browse. The kids' book nook upstairs, complete with mini-castle, is a marvelous feature, while the cozy, book-lined underground cafe serving tasty snacks, espresso, and imported beers is another big draw. Open late, when it attracts many interesting bookpeople.

J8	**Fix-Madore Book Company** 1503 Western	*Open every day* 682-5444

Nestled on the Hillclimb between the Pike Place Market and the waterfront Aquarium, Fix-Madore can be easily located by its trademark elephant banner flying outside the building. Inside, it offers probably the city's best selection of Penguin classics and prompt personal service. Strong in fiction and cookbooks.

I5	**Frederick & Nelson** Fifth & Pine	*Open every day* 682-5500

An exceptionally fine department-store book department, located in expanded quarters in the fancy new Frederick's Arcade. It carries a considerable range of general and regional books.

J5	**J. K. Gill** 1422 Fifth Ave (and outlying areas)	*Open Mon-Sat* 623-8870

A major stationery store with a good general book department.

J8	**Left Bank Books** 96 Pike	*Open Mon-Sat* 622-0195

Tucked in the elbow of the Pike Place Market (not far from the clock), this is a bookstore where politics of a reddish hue is the order of the day.

E6	**M. Taylor Bowie Bookseller** 2613 Fifth Ave	*Open Mon-Sat or by appointment* 682-5363

A trove of out-of-print and antiquarian books; Bowie has particular interests in literary first editions and books on travel, exploration, and the arts.

I7	**Peter Miller Books** 1909 First Ave	*Open Mon-Sat* 623-5563

With far and away the most extensive collection of architecture and design books in the area, this fascinating specialty store is dazzling to browse through. Excellent cards, children's items, and some magazines. The owner is extremely knowledgeable. It is nicely complemented by the American Institute of Architects/Seattle Branch one door north, which often mounts interesting design exhibits—from paper cutouts of the Empire State Building to portfolios of Frank Lloyd Wright.

K7 P8	**Shorey's** 110 Union (main store) 119 S Jackson	*Open Mon-Sat* 624-0221 622-8720

Perhaps Seattle's most famous bookstores, they are the first- and second-largest used bookstores in the city. Both are massive storehouses of used books of varying degrees of obscurity. Particularly strong in titles about the Pacific Northwest.

8	**J. Spencer Books** First & Madison (Alexis Hotel)	*Open Mon-Sat* *621-0026*

A branch of the Fix-Madore Book Company, quite in keeping with its elegant surroundings. The stock is similar to Fix-Madore, though with somewhat greater emphasis on magazines, literary, travel, and large-format books.

6	**Waldenbooks** 406 Pine (and outlying areas)	*Open every day* *624-3419*

A high-volume chain bookstore, with a good selection of regional books and tourist guidebooks.

Books — Other areas

FF7	**Arbur Books** 4505 University Way NE	*Open every day* *632-4204*

A snug and friendly bookshop on the University District's "Ave," Arbur also has one of the finest magazine sections in the area.

GG7	**B. Bailey Books** 408 Broadway E	*Open every day* *323-8842*

This Capitol Hill branch of B. Bailey concentrates on art, architecture, and left-ish lifestyle books in its general bookstore format.

GG7	**Cinema Books** 701 Broadway E	*Open every day* *323-5150*

Located in the corner of a classy little brick-and-ivy building across the street from The Harvard Exit, dowager empress of Seattle's cineaste theaters, Cinema Books stocks the region's largest selection of film-related books and magazines. Screenplays, technical books, plays, posters, and stills can all be found here.

GG7	**Counterbalance Books** 8 W Roy	*Open Tues-Sun* *282-2808*

A small but roomy general bookstore with particular interests in children's and computer books. The service is usually instantaneous.

GG7	**A Different Drummer** 420 Broadway E	*Open every day* *324-0525*

A selective general bookstore on Capitol Hill, it has a good selection of current titles, especially paperbacks, and a modest array of first editions of notable books. Open late.

HH7	**Fillipi Book and Record Shop** 1351 E Olive Way	*Open Tues-Sat* *682-4266*

If you get in an argument about an Eartha Kitt record or an Earnest Thompson Seton (out-of-print) nature book, Fillipi's would be a good place to settle it. They carry a fine selection of old books and records, antiquarian finds, memorabilia sheet music, back numbers of Collier's and so on.

FF7	**45th Street Books** (formerly Montana Books) 1716 N 45th	*Open Mon-Sat* *633-0811*

The new management at this neighborhood bookshop emphasizes literary titles, Northwest literature in particular—from the University Press to the various small-press imprints. They're compiling an extensive mail-order catalog.

GG6 **International Books**   *Open Tue-Sat*
1506 E Denny   *323-5667*

Six years ago, UW grad student J.P. Gagnon was frustrated when he couldn't find a French/Spanish dictionary at the library. So he started his own store, stocking everything from dictionaries to novels to kids' books in the seven major Western languages.

FF6 **Kay's Bookmark**   *Open every day*
University Village   *522-3989*

A pleasant little shop offering much personal attention.

GG7 **Quest Bookshop**   *Open every day*
717 Broadway E   *323-4281*

An occult bookstore/library that feels like one. Also has a natural-medicine shelf.

GG6 **Red and Black Books**   *Open every day*
524 15th Ave E   *323-7323*

This leftist bookshop has changed somewhat since it moved from its old quarters on University Way. A contingent of the old collective split off to start Left Bank Books; the original group has shifted focus to accommodate its less academic new clientele with gardening, self-reliance, and children's books. But most titles are intensely political.

GG7 **Tower Books**   *Open every day*
20 Mercer   *283-6333*

A high-volume book supermart, very strong in current bestsellers, often discounted from list price.

FF7 **University Book Store**   *Open Mon-Sat*
4326 University Way NE   *634-3400*

The nation's largest bookstore under a single roof, the University Book Store has a vast selection (the textbook, arts, and children's departments are particularly distinguished), a knowledgeable sales staff, and an efficient, computerized inventory system for quick information. There is an extensive stationery department with all manner of file folders, notebooks, graphics and writing supplies, and, in what may seem a surprising diversification to the uninitiated, well-stocked camera, computer, record, sporting goods, clothes, and gift sections.

FF7 **Wide World Bookshop**   *Open Mon-Sat*
401 NE 45th   *634-3453*

A specialty store for the globetrotter and armchair traveler alike, Wide World Bookshop imports many travel books that you will not find elsewhere in Seattle. Among other titles for the budget-traveler it carries the Lonely Planet Series from Australia, which covers Southeast Asia, USA West, and parts in between.

Camera

I6 **Cameras West**   *Open every day*
1908 Fourth Ave   *622-0066*

Shopping

Some of the best prices in Seattle for cameras. Virtually no darkroom equipment, but a good supply of video equipment.

K6 **Clyed's Camera Store** *Open Mon-Sat*
1410 Fourth Ave *624-4090*

An excellent selection of cameras, including hard-to-find Leicas and Hasselblads. You'll also find 16mm movie equipment and video tapes, decks, and cameras.

Five-Day Camera *Open Mon-Sat*
E3 **411 Westlake N** *583-0324*
HH3 **309 105th NE, Bellevue** *454-0277*
CC2 **Totem Lake Shopping Ctr, Kirkland** *821-1300*

Cameras at a good price, but not much in the way of other photo equipment.

I7 **Glazer's Camera Supply** *Open Mon-Sat*
1923 Third Ave *624-1100*

A very helpful, knowledgeable staff purveys a good selection of darkroom supplies and cameras; camera rentals, too.

O8 **Ivey-Seright Photo Lab** *Open Mon-Sat*
83 S Washington *623-8113*

The best full-service photo lab in Seattle. They do excellent black-and-white work, but color is their forte with a wide range of services including display transparencies and huge murals. Service is fast, professional, and expensive.

EE7 **Moonphoto** *Open Mon-Fri*
7704 Greenwood N *783-3377*

Professionals go here for black-and-white lab work by meticulous craftsmen.

F6 **Moon's Camera Repair** *Open Mon-Sat*
2307 Fifth Ave *624-5113*

Many professionals have their repair work done here: good solid service.

F3 **Photo-tronics** *Open Mon-Sat*
223 Westlake N *682-2646*

This is the place where many of the camera stores send their cameras to be repaired: good factory-authorized repair work, but they can be expensive.

FF8 **ProLab** *Open Mon-Sat*
4353 Sixth NW *784-9100*

A good full-service lab specializing in work from slides, plus the fastest Ektachrome service in Seattle (two-hour normal processing time).

FF7 **University Bookstore** *Open Mon-Sat*
4326 University Way NE *634-3400*

The best prices in town for most darkroom supplies.

M8 **Warshal's** *Open Mon-Sat*
First & Madison *624-7303*

The best selection of darkroom supplies and equipment at some of the best prices.

153

Shopping

Computers

09	**Anchor Computer Systems** **323 First Ave S**	*Open Mon-Sat* *621-9307*

The only full-service computer store in Seattle that rents its wares by the hour, day, week, and month. Anchor offers seminars, custom programming, and sales and service of the computers it rents: Apple, Eagle, Epson, KAYPRO, Osborne, Otrona, and Zenith. Printers and modems are also available for sale or rent.

H6	**Byte Shop** **2030 Fifth Ave**	*Open Mon-Sat* *622-BYTE*

Complete systems for the cost-conscious beginner (Atari), small-business user (Apple and Northstar), and those in between (Osborne and Zenith); plus a good selection of software and peripherals.

EE	**Compu-lab** **6414 Roosevelt Way NE and other locations**	*Open every day, 525-2202*

The computer branch of the Speakerlab stereo equipment chain. Computer brands include: Commodore, Eagle, Franklin, KAYPRO, and TDP (manufactured by Tandy, makers of Radio Shack computers).

08 GG2	**ComputerLand** **119 Yesler Way** **14340 NE 20th, Bellevue** **18415 33rd Ave W, Lynnwood**	*Open Mon-Sat* *223-1075* *746-2070* *774-6993*

The local stores of this international chain emphasize computer systems for the professional and the serious hobbyist. Complete sales, service, and training for IBM PC, DEC, Apple, Fortune, and COMPAQ. A wide assortment of software and computer-related books are also stocked.

DD7	**Creative Computers** **10732 Fifth NE**	*Open Mon-Sat* *365-6502*

A new store (its counterpart in Kent is two years old) with a select line of computer systems: Atari, Commodore, Epson, Franklin, and KAYPRO. Offers a full-range of software and accessories, and a well-chosen stock of computer books and magazines for the general reader.

J7 OO5 AA7	**Radio Shack Computer Center** **1521 Third Ave** **17360 Southcenter Pkwy** **18407 Aurora Ave N**	*Open Mon-Sat, 447-1959* *Open every day, 575-4099* *Open every day, 542-1220*

They stock only one brand, Radio Shack, but if that's what you are looking for you'll find the entire line here along with classroom training in programming and software applications, and professional sales and service.

FF7	**University Book Store** **4236 University Way NE**	*Open Mon-Sat* *634-3400*

Tucked in among the cameras, stationery, record albums, and Husky sweatshirts is a well-stocked and staffed computer department. They carry the full line of Hewlett Packard computers for the scientist and engineer, plus several other personal computer systems including Atari, Commodore, Franklin, and Timex-Sinclair. Also every calculator you'll ever need.

Florists and nurseries — Downtown

I8 **R. David Adams** *Open Mon-Sat*
89 Virginia *622-5325*

This spacious nook of green and blooming plants and exotic cut flowers could make your next party or remodel an unusual affair. R. David Adams is as much a designer as a florist, and the shop prides itself on individual service. It's pricey, but there's no minimum fee for delivered arrangements.

Crissey Flowers and Gifts
H6 **Fifth & Lenora** *Open Mon-Sat, 622-1100*
K6 **Fifth & University (Rainier Square)** *Open Mon-Sat, 624-6661*

From office bud vases to exotic custom arrangements of alstroemeria, Crissey's is a chic urban florist. Definitely not a budget shop; no buckets of carnations clutter the floor. It's a full-range vendor with a good supply of gifts, silks, and "drieds" for all occasions. And their flower compositions have a clean-lined European look, skipping the bows and frills.

Pike Place Flowers
J8 **1501 First Ave** *Open Mon-Sat, 682-9797*
I5 **Frederick and Nelson, Fifth & Pine** *Open every day, 382-8221*

Pike Place Flowers carries the widest range and best overall quality of blossoms at the Market, and its newer indoor outlet at Frederick and Nelson's has made possible a larger display of warmth-loving plants.

O8 **Pioneer Square Gardens** *Open Mon-Sat & by appointment*
100 S Main *622-4429*

This cool flower shop at the corner of Pioneer Square's Grand Central on the Park complex leans to the exotic. "I try to avoid too many carnations and mums," says manager Laura Stocker; instead, such Northern European and tropical blooms as freesia, heather, daffodils, ginger, and anemones dot the store. Delivery is free around the Square.

L7 **Plantes & Fleurs** *Open Mon-Fri*
1111 Third Ave *583-0110*

Located in an attractive plaza on the corner of Third and Spring, Plantes & Fleurs caters well to the downtown business community with its stock of cut flowers. A relative newcomer to the field, the shop now carries annuals and perennials in summer, as well as a healthy supply of houseplants.

I8 **Seattle Garden Center** *Open Mon-Sat*
Pike Place Market *624-0431*

Recently purchased by Molbak's in Woodinville, this Pike Place Market garden shop (no cut flowers) and plant vendor retains its name, but will probably expand its merchandise.

Florists and nurseries — Other areas

GG6 **Environmental Design** *Open Mon-Sat*
342 15th Ave E *322-5279*

This Capitol Hill florist concentrates on unusual subtropicals, tropicals, and exotic blooms that form the backbone of the fluid "European" trend in flower arranging,

155

Shopping

free of gewgaws and grosgrain ribbons. Sample lilacs and lilies from Holland, protea, birds of paradise, and Washington tulips. A simple yet sophisticated gift is a single "flower by the stem."

	Furney's Nursery	*Open every day*
PP6	**21215 Pacific Hwy S**	*878-8761*
GG2	**13427 NE 16th, Bellevue**	*747-8282*

This is the place to buy trees and shrubs: 17 planted acres on Pacific Hwy S (and another 40 in Oregon), plus some stock from wholesalers, make the nearly 50-year family business a mainstay of Seattle gardens. Bare-root fruit trees, balled and burlapped deciduous trees, field-grown evergreens, shrubs, and shade and flowering trees are all stocked here in abundance. A second, fully-stocked retail outlet, three acres in the heart of Bellevue, curves around a picturesque water wheel, and offers an item not found at the southern center—bonsai. Delivery charges are $7.50-$20.

KK5	**Holly Park Greenhouse & Nursery**	*Open every day*
	4031 S Willow	*722-2000*
KK5	**G. Mizuki Nursery & Garden Store**	*Open every day*
	6033 Empire Way S	*722-8802*

These two South End stores are best sources for Oriental seeds and plant specimens. Mizuki's sells a multitude of the fast-growing starting seeds: Chinese parsley, coriander, pea pods, bok choy, takana (Japanese mustard), Japanese onions and cucumbers, and Chinese cabbage. Also stocked are bonsai, bedding plants (including vegetables), some apple trees, and a variety of shrubs and non-fruit trees. At Holly Park (just east off Empire Way S) you'll find such delicacies as Japanese eggplant and bitter melon, plus several Asian trees and shrubs, such as Japanese laceleaf maples and Japanese pear trees.

BB2	**Molbak's Greenhouse and Nursery**	*Open every day*
	13625 NE 175th, Woodinville	*483-5000*

The showplace of Seattle area nurseries, Molbak's has 28 greenhouses crowded with bedding and flowering plants and foliage; a tropical plants conservatory; and even an aviary. Flowering plants (10 greenhouses full) are this nursery's forte. The gift shop is well-stocked with crystal and fine glassware. Deliveries are $5-$10 but there's no charge for deliveries of purchases over $50 on Saturdays, or over $150 on weekdays.

AA8	**MsK Rare Plant Nursery**	*By appointment only*
	20066 15th Ave NW	*546-1281*

Come spring, how many local gardeners make plans for putting in a few pellaeas, dwarf maidenhairs, polystichums, catsuras or idesias? Yet these are all native Washington ferns and trees. For 13 years, the MsK Rare Plant Nursery has grown these and 3,000 other forgotten shrubs, ground covers, and rock-garden plants from seeds and cuttings. This unique one-acre growing area will send you away dreaming of saxifrages, penstemons, and evergreen oaks.

FF7	**Ness Flowers**	*Open every day*
	4247 University Way NE	*632-7733*

This bustling corner in the U District is a traditional neighborhood florist. Since 1936, the Ness family has arranged flowers for weddings, proms, and funerals and this generational story is told in the array of merchandise: standard flower settings and green houseplants, novelty gifts and hospital vases, some tacky and some tasteful.

QQ6	**Prentice Nursery & Decorating Co.**	*Open Mon-Fri*
	24955 Frager Road S, Kent	*859-0040*

This new arrival to the South End is a mecca for home landscapers. Prentice's specialties are rhododendrons and other large plants that are bred carefully for sale, often nurtured for years, at correspondingly higher prices. After 50 years in Seattle, Prentice recently moved to the 18-acre Kent site. Landscape designing and installation are offered and Prentice does a thriving trade in Christmas tree sales, fire-proofing and decorating. Bedding plants and vegetables are extensive. Delivery rates vary.

EE6	**Saxe Floral & Greenhouses** **2402 NE 65th**	*Open every day* *523-3646 or 523-4415*

This traditional florist and nursery just north of the U District in Seattle's Ravenna neighborhood tucks 11 greenhouses of tropical blooms, cacti, and flowering plants into two-and-a-half acres of space—a real find in the middle of the city. Saxe has big container planters of marigolds and petunias for the patio and garden, lovely hanging baskets of geraniums, bonsai shrubs, and some trees. The gift section boasts one of the largest basket collections of any florist.

GG8	**Sherwood Forest Plant Shoppe** **1835 Queen Anne Ave N**	*Open every day* *284-1077*

Here's a pleasing combination—a generously stocked plant shop and full-service florist at reasonable prices. Opened nine years ago as a hip houseplant boutique, Sherwood went into flowers two years later and has worked hard to maintain its innovative style. There are winter pansies and live evergreens at Christmas time. Though tropical flower sales are modest, Sherwood strives to keep its exotics in good supply. Bedding plants go on sale in spring and summer, and house plants can be rented.

AA7	**Sky Garden Nursery** **18528 Aurora Ave N**	*Open every day* *546-4851*

Deceptively compact Sky Garden Nursery is one of the better bargains. With only four greenhouses, this North End vendor packs into just two-and-a-half acres 6,000 rose bushes, 10,000 rhododendrons, fruit trees, shade and flower trees—but, most importantly, annuals, exotic perennials, landscape plants, and the hardware to tend them. Sky is also one of the best sources of bedding plants and garden supplies. All in a comfortable setting, with helpful advice, and at good prices. No cut flowers. Delivery charges vary.

DD8	**Swanson's** **9701 15th Ave NW**	*Open every day* *782-2543*

This wonderful garden of annuals, perennials and yard plants is perched at the northwest corner of the city. For a treat, stop here on a Sunday drive along the Sound. Delivery charges vary.

FF6	**Taylor Nurseries** **4647 Union Bay Place NE**	*Open Mon-Sat* *523-7437*

Not for the general nursery shopper, Taylor's deals entirely in ornamental bedding plants and trees, with a specialty of acclimatized rose bushes and black bamboo. Landscaping and consulting are also available.

GG7	**Venetian Gardens** **1416 E Olive Way**	*Open Mon-Sat* *328-0211*

This attractive newcomer to the Seattle floral scene has an unusual touch: an antique and gift shop complements the flowers (dried, silks, and potted plants, too). Potpourri, crystal vases, candles, flatware, and porcelain dolls compete with the blooms for room. Its seasonal specialty is a boggling variety of Christmas orna-

Shopping

ments and fully decorated live trees.

006	**Washington Florist**	*Open Mon-Sat*
	16445 Pacific Hwy S	*243-2383*

Better than the usual floral offerings available at Sea-Tac is this cozy verdant bandbox. Across from ample flower coolers are ceramics, brass, copper, and antiques. Annuals are sold during the warm months, and bedding baskets at Easter.

GG3	**Wells-Medina Nursery**	*Open every day*
	8300 NE 24th, Bellevue	*454-1853*

This fine Eastside nursery draws home gardeners with its wide variety of unusual plants, especially shrubs. Houseplants, vegetable and fruit plants are also available. Delivery charges vary.

Gifts — Downtown

08	**Country Brunch**	*Open every day*
	109 S Main	*622-2165*

As classy a novelty shop as you'll find anywhere. Also has a good selection of cards.

H7	**Elements of Northwest Living**	*Open Mon-Sat*
	2032 First Ave	*587-0120*

This one's *for* Northwest living, not necessarily *made* here. A wide assortment of special "household items" that go far beyond that designation.

I6	**Exclusively Northwest**	*Open Mon-Sat*
	415 Stewart	*622-9144*

A relaxing place to browse for a tasteful souvenir of the Northwest, this little gift shop in the Times Square Building specializes in work by Northwest artists, designers, and craftspeople—photographs, paintings, an array of wooden, woven, and knitted items, select Northwest books, intricate scrimshaw, and specialty food items are just some of the offerings.

08	**Iris Fine Gifts**	*Open Mon-Sat*
	110 S Washington	*623-3173*

A delightful store with domestic and imported handmade gifts: ceramics, macrame, some wearables, glassware, dolls—all on a small scale and beautifully arranged.

L8	**Neville et Cie**	*Open Mon-Sat*
	1007 First Ave, Alexis Hotel	*343-9404*

Much more than just an average hotel gift store, Neville arranges lovely flowers and sells superb chocolates.

N8	**On the Square**	*Open Mon-Sat*
	614 First Ave	*622-1730*

Located right on Pioneer Square, this store has a great mixture of cards, curiosities, and "nice items."

J9	**Sandpiper Gifts and Books**	*Open every day*
	Seattle Aquarium, Pier 59	*624-2835*

One of the best tourist outlets on the Waterfront, with interesting nature and marine-related books as well.

Shopping

M7	**The Soap Box**	
	Seattle Trust Court	*Open Mon-Fri, 623-1795*
J8	Pike Place Market	*Open Mon-Sat, 623-5680*
FF7	4340 University Way NE	*Open every day, 634-2379*

This fragrant emporium of cleansing bars, herbals, lotions, potpourri, cards, calendars, and footsie rollers now has two branch stores, but the original University District shop is still the most fun.

G6	**UNICEF Gift Shop**	*Open Mon-Fri*
	2217 Fourth	*622-5352*

Sure, you think of cards, and they are wonderful, but check out the other attractive domestic and imported gifts here.

	William Ernest Brown Stationery	
K6	Rainier Square	*Open Mon-Sat, 292-9404*
HH3	10630 NE Eighth, Bellevue	*Open Mon-Sat, 455-3665*

A wide range of custom-made and monogrammed cards and writing paper are this store's hallmark. There are also delightful accessories such as cloth-covered diaries, bookmarks, and even an inlaid wooden clipboard to match the elegant stationery.

MM9	**Ye Olde Curiosity Shop**	*Open every day*
	Pier 51	*682-5844*

A traditional souvenir seller that most Seattle natives put off visiting until relatives come to town.

Gifts — Other areas

GG7	**All That Jazz**	*Open every day*
	233 Broadway E	*324-9877*

All That Jazz, an aptly titled emporium located on Broadway in the heart of Capitol Hill, features a vast assortment of merchandise varying from risque greeting cards to New Wave wearing apparel. The brightly colored, well-stocked notepaper section is impressive. Especially notable are the seasonal displays. Open late for Broadway promenaders.

EE7	**The Back Room**	*Open every day*
	7200 Greenwood N	*782-7002*

Catty, comical, creative, sometimes salty cards.

K6	**Caswell–Massey**	*Open Mon-Sat*
	Rainier Square	*292-9483*

Too chic just for soap, this pretty little place at first glance resembles a perfume shop. Well-stocked and organized, with many accoutrements for the bath.

	The Country Mouse	*Open every day*
	Gilman Village, Issaquah	*392-1050*

Perhaps the best gift shop in the Gilman Village complex, this one stocks an ample supply of knits, toys, pottery, wooden knickknacks, and cards—all somewhat unusual and of good quality.

HH3	**Crabtree & Evelyn**	*Open every day*
	Bellevue Square, Bellevue	*451-8457*

159

Shopping

The Seattle-area branch of the famed London soap-and-sundries vendor. Jams, savories, water biscuits, and other delectables can be found next to the soaps, brushes, and potpourri.

FF7	**Encore Gift Gallery** **4514 University Way NE** **Factoria Square**	*Open every day,* 633-5566 *Open every day,* 746-4466

Despite the plethora of hanging prisms, scattered jewelry, and marvelous large-faced clocks, this is basically a desk-accessory store: blotters, pens, cloth-covered diaries, cards, sturdy mugs, etc.

	Fox Paw **Lynwood Center, Bainbridge Island**	*Open Mon-Sat,* 842-7788

This little shop has a wonderfully eclectic selection of collectible items: hand-knit sweaters and hand-painted T-shirts, some imported clothes, unusual gifts, and even wallpaper.

GG7	**Great Things** **414 Broadway E**	*Open every day* 325-3200

Great things abound, from glassware to bodywear. This establishment offers a limited selection of gifts, a tad expensive but all good quality. Although some merchandise duplicates what you can find elsewhere, careful searching can lead to exquisite finds. To complete your purchase, there is a wide selection of gift wrap and note cards.

FF6	**Henry Art Gallery Book and Gift Shop** **University of Washington**	*Open Tues-Sun,* 543-2280

Opening soon under new management, so worth checking out for any changes in the book–card–objet d'art merchandise.

FF6	**Mr. Peepers** **University Village**	*Open every day* 522-8202

Somehow one always thinks of Christmas in connection with this lavish, not-quite-out-of-control display of just about every toy, card, knickknack, dollhouse assembly, doohickey, and you-name-it imaginable. All tasteful. Now there's a second shop, called Mr. Peepers Miniatures, in University Village that carries only dollhouses and their accessories.

HH3	**Northwest Discovery** **Bellevue Square, Bellevue**	*Open every day* 454-1676

Carries a marvelous array of wooden items: oak boxes, butter dishes, clocks, even a telephone. Also inlaid furniture, Northwest jewelry, scrimshaw, and brass and copper accessories. Not inexpensive.

HH3	**San Francisco Paper World** **Bellevue Square, Bellevue**	*Open every day* 451-8035

Tasteful selection of cards, stationery, and invitations. Custom orders are a large part of the business in this attractive shop.

B7 GG6	**Seattle Art Museum Gift Shops** **Seattle Center** **Volunteer Park**	*Open Tues-Sun,* 447-5596 *Open Tues-Sun,* 447-4674

The Seattle Art Museum's Pavilion gift shop at the Seattle Center carries books, cards, some interesting jewelry, and theme gifts that match current exhibits, while

Shopping

the gift shop at Volunteer Park has a large and reasonably priced selection of posters and prints.

F6	**Thomas Burke Memorial Museum Shop**	
	University of Washington	*Open Tues-Sun, 543-5590*

Located at the northwest corner of the campus, the gift store is a good shop after a tour through the artifact and dinosaur exhibits. Northwest art theme in the cards, jewelry, and other gifts.

GG8	**Village Gallery**	*Open Tues-Sat*
	621 W McGraw	*285-1619*

The Love Israel Family outlet at the top of Queen Anne. A fair assortment of arts and crafts, good pottery, paintings, jewelry, pillows, and some clothes, at reasonable prices.

	Weed Lady	*Open Tues-Sat*
	122 Fourth S, Edmonds	*775-3800*

Perhaps the most sweetly fragrant gift shop on Puget Sound, the Weed Lady's potpourri, dried grasses, soaps, scents, and complementary gifts—set in an old-fashioned, arbor-guarded house off Edmonds' main street—entice customers without a whiff of cloying incense.

	The Yankee Trader	*Open Mon-Sat*
	117 Fifth N, Edmonds	*771-5811*

A piece of fine china resting on an antique bureau, beautiful "conversation pieces," unusual cards—hard to describe the merchandise, but somehow it all works together. A peaceful yet stimulating shop to wander in.

Imports — Downtown

J8	**Cibol**	*Open Mon-Sat*
	Pike Place Market	*682-5640*

Cibol has quality imported clothing at great prices. Shirts, hats, skirts, and dresses are mostly from Latin America, but other countries are also represented and there are nice imported artifacts.

J8	**Hands of the World**	*Open Mon-Sat*
	Pike Place Market	*622-1696*

Hands of the World is an import store tucked into a corner of the Pike Place Market. Cindy Hope and Valerie Smith, the owners and buyers, buy crafts and textiles directly from artisans in aid and development projects in Southeast and South Asian countries thereby supporting the craftspeople and eliminating middleman costs. The store is filled with a fine array of textiles, belts, crafts, jewelry, and miscellaneous contemporary and traditional objects.

O8	**Hanuman**	*Open Mon-Sat*
	210 First Ave S	*622-4560*

In Pioneer Square you can step off the street into a transplanted piece of Southeast Asia. Charles and Carolyn Cox, owners and managers, were in the Peace Corps in Thailand for years and the store reflects their knowledge of and attachment to the culture and crafts of this part of Asia, particularly Thailand. The Coxes travel twice a year to Southeast Asia to purchase the textiles and artifacts.

161

Shopping

Everything is exquisite. Small cards identify and explain the history, techniques and traditions connected to the pieces.

08	**Nordic House**	*Open every day*
	218 First Ave S	*682-5684*

The Nordic House in Pioneer Square has a small selection of objects from Scandinavia. Highlights are Norwegian yarns (Peer Gynt and Fritidsgarn) at reasonable prices, Bastad Clogs, amber jewelry from Denmark, and Royal Copenhagen porcelain.

	Pier One Imports	*Open every day*
HH7	Pier 70, Alaskan Way	*622-4072*
FF7	4345 University Way NE	*545-7397*
HH3	905 Bellevue Way NE, Bellevue	*451-8002*

Imports from China, Japan, Thailand, Norway, France, and many other countries at three stores. Good prices on simple cotton clothing, bamboo blinds, and wickerware.

K5	**Pierre Deux**	*Open Mon-Sat*
	603 Union	*382-0745*

Everything in the store is made with Souleiado hand-blocked fabric from Provence. Picture frames, dresses, ties, nothing-books, placemats, and Kleenex holders fill the store with a beautiful, but expensive, selection. Souleiado yardage and trims are also available.

I7	**Prasad's**	*Open Mon-Fri*
	210 Terminal Sales Building	*624-4809*
	1932 First Ave	

Devi Prasad, the store's owner and buyer, is from India, and she fills her shop with an excellent selection of Indian imports which she imports directly. Rosewood boxes with brass inlay deserve particular attention.

08	**Rose & Thistle**	*Open Mon-Sat (in summer, every day)*
	301 Occidental Ave S	*624-2757*

The Rose & Thistle is Seattle's British Isles import store. While most of it is cluttered with knickknacky gift items, inexpensive china, and small toys, their huge selection of tartan ties is admirable; see if your name is on the clan chart.

	Trident Imports	*Open every day*
K9	Pier 56, Alaskan Way	*622-2838*
GG3	11838 Bellevue-Redmond Rd, Bellevue	*455-2920*

Trident Imports, a vast warehouse on Pier 56, displays goods from all around the world. As with many import stores, you have to look hard for the quality pieces amid the clutter of candles, mugs, rice bowls, straw mats, and cane furniture. They do have a good basket selection, however.

P8	**Wee Bit O' Ireland**	*Open every day*
	400 Occidental Ave S	*622-9111*

Wee Bit O' Ireland is a delight to visit. Classic cream Irish fisherman's sweaters, mohair shawls, mittens, caps, linen handkerchiefs, posters, and Irish memorabilia are all beautifully displayed in a cozy little store in Pioneer Square.

Shopping

Imports — Other areas

PP5 Aussie Woolies   *Open Mon-Sat*
12606 Interurban Ave S, Tukwila   *248-3584*

A factory outlet store, Aussie Woolies carries Australian sheepskins at excellent prices: simple sheepskin, sheepskin seatcovers, coats, wall decorations, and steering wheel covers.

FF7 Folk Art Gallery/La Tienda   *Open Tues-Sat*
4138 University Way NE   *632-1796*

The Folk Art Gallery/La Tienda is one of the most exciting places in Seattle to shop for imported goods; it has an extensive selection, all of the highest quality. The emphasis is on crafts from South and Central America; however, pieces from numerous other countries as well as the United States are also on show. Textiles, jewelry, pottery, puppets, musical instruments, and clothing are all beautifully displayed, and the staff is very knowledgeable about all the store's treasures.

FF7 Inca Palace   *Open Mon-Sat*
4544 University Way NE   *632-3300*

There's a good choice in clothing and fabrics, but the rugs make this store better than many other import stores. India, South America, and Afghanistan are best represented.

FF7 Khan's of Morocco   *Open Mon-Sat*
4518 University Way NE   *633-4360*

The University District has an overabundance of import stores with Indian clothing, imported silver jewelry, baskets, and assorted knickknacks; among the best of these is Khan's of Morocco, slightly more expensive than the others, but carrying a more interesting and diverse selection of goods. Of note are a few elegant and truly beautiful dresses, Turkish copper pieces, some jewelry, and handcarved wooden boxes.

FF7 Scandia Imports   *Open Mon-Sat*
4517 University Way NE   *632-3296*

Knickknacks at the front of the store, but the back has a nice selection of Holmegaard Crystal from Denmark and other glass and crystal selections. Upstairs there is a good yarn store.

OO7 The Scottish Shopper Corporation   *Open Tues-Sat*
14202 First Ave S, Burien   *242-1768*

What began as a supply store for Seattle's resident Scottish bagpiping community is today also a national mail-order business supplying anyone who ever wanted anything from Scotland. Tartans, bagpipes, traditional pottery, clan pins, sheet music, memorabilia, tartan socks, mohair tams and scarves are to be found at this South End store at reasonable prices.

Magazines & newspapers

HH3 City News   *Open every day*
10116 NE Eighth, Bellevue   *455-9683*

Stocks domestic, national, and foreign papers, general interest books, and over

Shopping

1,000 magazines. Strong travel section includes Hallwag and Michelin maps and guides.

K7 **Magazine City** Open every day
   1315 Third Ave 624-6084

Do not let the anatomy books embarrass you out of the store: this is a magazine mart, with everything from *Gray's Sporting Journal* to *Film Directors* and *High Times*. Newspapers from across the country, across the waters.

J7 **Read All About It** Open every day
   Pike Place Market 624-0140

Has a wide selection of local, national, and international papers and magazines, all displayed on a colorful newsstand in the Pike Place Market (right across from De Laurenti's).

Outdoor equipment — Downtown

Eddie Bauer Open every day
K5 **Fifth & Union** 622-2766
HH3 **Bellevue Square** 453-0450

The Abercrombie and Fitch of local outdoor stores, Eddie Bauer is a posh place to eye the best in outdoor wear. Bauer, now a national chain, made its reputation with fine goosedown products. You'll glide across plush carpets from rack to rack of men's and women's field garb and dressy outdoor wear and on to its fine selection of down bags, comforters, and pillows. Eddie Bauer also stocks water-sports accessories (but no boats or paddles); cross-country skis; backpacking gear; fishing hardware, knives, and hunting goods (except firearms). Be sure to check the bargain basement for some great deals on equipment and clothing. Cross-country ski rentals are also there.

H8 **Early Winters** Open every day
   2001 Western Ave 622-6011

Unique designs and imported outdoor accessories are the hallmarks of this manufacturer, which is one of the Northwest's pioneers in the use of Gore-Tex, the fabric that breathes while repelling water. Early Winters markets its products internationally but has a spacious new catalog showroom in Downtown Seattle. With everything from Gore-Tex tents and Chinese silk to sushi campfood, knife and fork penknives, and lights to attach to pens for campsite writing—Early Winters lines are esoteric, yet strangely desirable.

Osborn and Ulland Sports Open Mon-Sat
L7 **1123 Second Ave** 624-6954
I6 **1926 Third Ave** 624-8999

This good general sports store carries tennis, golf, racquetball, and similar sporting gear, downhill and water skis, and a full line of professional swim apparel, but no camping or hunting gear. The Second Ave. location, the original store, now offers only first line discontinued items at bargain basement markdowns of 40-50 percent off.

G4 **Ski Rack Sports** Open Mon-Sat (in winter Sun)
   2118 Eighth Ave 623-7318

If you're trading up for better skiing equipment, or know how to pick out good used gear, the Ski Rack is a good value. Seattle's largest dealer in used equipment has a liberal trade-up program—so anyone can sell their old equipment here on consignment. Beginners should bring a knowledgeable friend along for advice in the purchase of used equipment. Ski Rack also sells ski apparel, foul-weather marine gear, and active sportswear, as well as renting ski equipment.

	Sportcaster/Mountain Products	
O8	160 S Jackson St	Open Mon-Sat; 624-2748
OO5	Pavilion Outlet Center	Open every day; 575-3394
O8	Occidental Mall	Open Tues-Sat; 628-0728

This factory outlet for a nationally distributed line of skiwear, jackets, and outerwear has a no-frills bargain basement crammed with sweats and t-shirts, Dacron comforters, down pillows, packs, and ski gloves. Samples, discontinued items, and irregulars priced at wholesale plus 30 percent.

L7	Warshal's Sporting Goods 1000 First Ave (at Madison)	Open Mon-Sat 624-7300

A convenient place to shop for virtually any sporting goods need, Warshal's also offers good unadvertised buys in swimsuits and name-brand running shoes, because it serves as an outlet for factory closeouts and irregulars. In fact, most of the stock is attractively discounted. The sales staff can be counted on for good advice as well. In-house repair service is available on fishing reels and firearms. The large camera department stocks only professional-quality equipment.

H4	The Yak Works 2030 Westlake Ave	Open every day 623-8053

A chalet atmosphere with friendly advice, the Yak Works caters to bicyclists, sailors, kayakers, backpackers, climbers, and cross-country skiers. They make their own line of backpacking gear, clothing, and related soft goods right on the premises—some to custom specifications. They're the nation's largest manufacturer of frameless packs, and the price of pack rentals may be applied to purchase of backpack products.

Outdoor equipment — Other areas

	Cal Marine	Call for hours
EE9	6317 Seaview Ave NW	789-4640
HH3	1100 Bellevue Way NE, Bellevue	455-5510

This store has a well-established reputation as a sailing-equipment supplier and is now expanding into the sailboard market stocking boards, sails, wetsuits, harnesses, and car racks.

	The Crow's Nest	Open every day
FF7	1900 N Northlake Way	632-3555
K9	Pier 55	623-4462
EE9	6010 Seaview NW	783-6262

The largest marine hardware store in Seattle, The Crow's Nest specializes in yachting hardware, accessories, clothing, and rain gear.

OO4	Easy Rider 15666 W Valley Hwy, Tukwila	Open Mon-Sat 228-3633

The biggest West Coast manufacturer of canoes and kayaks, Easy Rider offers its

Shopping

complete line of 34 different styles factory-direct to the public here. Factory pick-up offers savings of 15 percent on first quality vessels, 25 percent on seconds. There are whitewater, lake, saltwater, all-purpose, family, or hunting styles, designed in fiberglas or the stronger, lighter hi-tech Kevlar 49, in 13- to 18-foot lengths.

GG2 **Fast Lady Sports**
14310 NE 20th, Bellevue   *Open Mon-Sat; 641-9696*
Gilman Village, Issaquah   *Open every day; 392-1098*

As its name implies, for women only. A good place to get encouragement and strokes, as well as special fit requirements. It has the most complete selection of women's accessories for running, racquetball, tennis and aerobic dance, and clinics catering to women.

FF7 **Fiorini Sports**
4720 University Village Pl NE   *Open every day*
   523-9610

Stocking a good selection of top brand sporting goods for all four seasons, Fiorini Sports has informed and helpful clerks, and good sales.

EE7 **Gregg's Greenlake Cycle**
7007 Woodlawn NE   *Open every day*
   523-9610

Located close to Green Lake, a hub of activity for skaters and bicyclists, Gregg's taps a ready market with sales, rental, and repair of bikes and roller skates, plus seasonal rental of downhill skis. Also: men's and women's bicycling apparel, all-purpose rain gear, touring and racing cycling shoes.

MM3 **Lighthouse Dive & Ski**
350 Sunset Blvd N, Renton   *Open every day*
   228-7332

Owned by an enthusiastic and experienced diver, Joe Liburdi, Lighthouse Dive and Ski is a hub of local diving activity. Its free "buddy" service makes it an excellent resource for scuba enthusiasts without partners (and out-of-towners). In addition to scuba equipment sales, underwater photography classes, and full-service repairs, the shop sells and rents water skis and stocks wet suits for surfboarding, sailing, and waterskiing.

The North Face
FF7 4560 University Way NE   *Open Mon-Sat; 633-4431*
L8 1023 First Ave   *Open every day, 633-4111*

The North Face gave the world the first geodesic dome tent—and has come up with innovative designs ever since. A well-known name in back-packing-equipment design for more than 15 years, it now offers down clothing and bags, outdoor apparel, and downhill skiwear. The Seattle stores offer a climbing school, and rentals to meet virtually any mountaineering equipment need.

FF7 **R & E Cycles**
5627 University Way NE   *Open Mon-Sat (in summer Sun)*
   527-4822

Nationally known as a prestigious custom frame-building shop, R & E is run by partners Angel Rodriguez and Glenn Erickson, who are well-known in competitive bicycling circles. The emphasis is on competition cycling, so the shop could be a bit intimidating for recreational or novice cyclists. The shop builds singles, tandems, and racing bicycles. Overnight repair services are available on any make of bicycle; painting and wheel-building are also offered.

HH7 **Recreational Equipment,
      Inc. (REI)**
1525 11th Ave   *Call for hours*
   323-8333

Founded in Seattle in 1938 to provide equipment for the serious mountaineer, and presided over for years by Everest-conqueror Jim Whittaker, REI has now grown to gargantuan proportions and supplies the needs of outdoor types all over the world through an outstanding mail order service and several stores in different states. No wonder there are 1.2 million members when memberships cost only $5 and members get a 10 percent annual rebate on their purchases. (Of course, nonmembers can also shop here.) The warehouse-like emporium on Capitol Hill is stocked to the rafters with equipment for climbers, backpackers, downhill and cross-country skiers, kayakers, canoeists, and bicyclists. The young, conservation-minded, and knowledgeable sales staff can answer almost any question. With the store's extensive rental services, "try before you buy" is part of its philosophy of buyer satisfaction. In addition to its specialist equipment, the store has a huge range of reasonably priced outdoor clothing and shoes, trail food, and a well-stocked map and outdoor book section.

GG7	**The Runner's Place** 321 Broadway E	*Open every day* *324-6537*

This compact Capitol Hill store offers all the top brands of runners' clothing and shoes, and the knowledgeable staff is a good source for local running information.

A8	**Second Wind** 300 Queen Anne N	*Open Mon-Sat* *283-4658*

This is a factory outlet for seconds and discontinued items manufactured by Early Winters. You'll find the same high quality outdoor goods available at the showroom, but at a substantial savings if you're willing to sort through a supply that varies daily.

GG8 OO5	**The Strapped Jock** 410 Elliott W **Pavilion Outlet Center**	*Open every day* *283-1179* *575-4400*

Closeouts, samples, special buys, and irregulars in footwear and apparel for running, tennis, racquetball, basketball, soccer, and track, with savings that average 20-40 percent below manufacturer's suggested retail price. Well-stocked in women's styles; no athletic hardware.

EE7	**Super Jock 'N Jill** 7210 E Green Lake Dr N	*Open every day* *522-7711*

This full-line running store emphasizes sports medicine and injury prevention; much of its clientele is referred by leading sports medicine practitioners. Super Jock 'N Jill works with runners who have foot structure problems or injuries, to be certain of the right fit. They stock all major brands and will special order. Evening clinics feature podiatrists and doctors.

FF7 GG1	**The Swallows' Nest** 3320 Meridian N 15155 NE 24th, Redmond	*Open every day* *633-0408* *644-1666*

A specialty climbing shop, the Swallows' Nest also outfits backpackers and cross-country skiers, and has everything but skis for ski mountaineering. It manufactures its own line of Gore-Tex rainwear, well-suited for Northwest backcountry use. Rentals are available for cross-country skiing, backpacking, and mountaineering.

	The Velo Stores	*Call for hours*
FF7	**U District Cycle Shop**	*1307 NE 45th; 632-3955*
GG6	**Velocipede Bike Shop**	*3101 E Madison; 325-3292*
JJ9	**West Seattle Bike Shop**	*4800 California Ave SW; 932-2920*
HH7	**Pine Street Cycle**	*611 E Pine; 325-1958*

Shopping

Being owned by one corporation, these four neighborhood bike stores have the inventory advantages of a large store, while each can offer very personal service possible only in a small store. They have a good selection of Japanese and French bikes and excellent post-purchase servicing, as well as servicing on any make and model of bike.

EE7	**White Water Sports** **307 NE 71st**	*Open Mon-Sat (in summer Sun)* *523-5150*

Conveniently located at the edge of Green Lake, White Water Sports is a good place to go for sailboards and accessories, a windsurfing demonstration, or a private lesson. It also stocks canoes and kayaks which are special-ordered from Northwest manufacturers. Rentals are available in the water-sports section and the small ski department, which sells cross-country skis and related hardware.

Records — Downtown

Seattle is a record-buying town, some say, with the highest per-capita consumption of records and tapes of any region in the country. To service that demand, there are, in addition to the rock-dominated chains, some cozy specialty shops with knowledgeable personnel and reasonably well-stocked bins.

O8	**Bud's Jazz Records** **102 S Jackson**	*Open every day* *628-0445*

Seattle's first and only all-jazz, whole-jazz, and nothing but the true-jazz store was established in 1982 by Chicago refugee and jazz buff Bud Young. Rivaling Tower Records at Mercer in stock, Bud's is not only the place to look for records, it's the place: musicians argue here over the unlisted sidemen on old Charlie Parker records. Bud's also features an exhaustive jazz library to settle the argument. Spend the afternoon.

K6	**Fifth Avenue Record Shop** **Rainier Square**	*Open Mon-Sat* *624-6507*

Classical is the tune of this posh, large shop, and the stock is comprehensive. The clerks are very informative, particularly in the store's specialties: opera and chamber music.

J7	**Musicland** **215 Pike**	*Open every day* *624-9910*

Soul supermarket, from Aretha to Grandmaster Flash: very current, largest stock in town in recently renovated store.

Records — Other areas

FF8	**Ballard Record Shop** **5512 20th NW**	*Open Tues-Sat* *782-8616*

Best selection of country and western and bluegrass is at this Ballard disc depot.

OO7	**Bop Street Records & Books** **8524 Greenwood N**	*Open every day* *784-4631*

Off-the-wall specialty shop run by a charming, eccentric young man who likes Northwest rock and sci-fi. Great vintage rock, good conversation, some jazz.

Cellophane Square Open every day
1311 NE 42nd 634-2280

Closest thing to Berkeley's Telegraph Avenue selection in used jazz and rock. Lots of stock, vintage and new, fast turnover, quality merchandise, friendly, knowledgeable staff.

Easy Street Open every day
15251 Bel-Red Road, Bellevue 643-1433

Best Eastside selection of new-wave rock, imports, and heavy metal.

Everybody's Record Company Open every day
10640 NE Eighth, Bellevue 455-9380

Best general outlet, especially for new rock, on the Eastside, and it's not even in a shopping mall.

Fillipi Book & Record Shop Open Tues-Sat
1351 E Olive Way 682-4266

Musty old place run by an eccentric couple in the manner a New York friend once described thus: "A rare book or record shop is a place where you get on your knees and beg to pay too much money for something you really don't need." Here's where you'll find that old Wardell Gray 78, or the old-timey sheet music you lost last time you moved.

Golden Oldies Open every day
4530 Roosevelt Way NE 634-0322

Enormous selection of singles and albums, fastidiously organized and stocked at this wonderful U District shop. Even if you don't pop for the original Buddy Holly ($90) or a "butcher cover" Beatles ($150), you'll gape at the wallpaper of pop charts from 1952 to the present and the rare rock photos. These historians will search for your seventh-grade favorite record, nationwide.

Music Menu Open every day
2101 Rainier Ave S 324-1800

Good selection of current 12-inch singles, as well as the latest soul albums at this neighborhood outlet, a good alternative to downtown Musicland.

Peaches Open every day
811 NE 45th 633-2990

This record supermarket used to be owned by a chain, but is now the best independent store for folk and women's music. Bargain cut-outs in soul, jazz, and rock. Local rock. Large selection of audio paraphernalia, displayed with a sense of fun.

Record Library Open Mon-Sat
4518 University Way NE 634-3959

This concept caught on fast: record rental. Borrow an album for seven days (membership fee, plus per-record charge), take it home, and...well, there's a bill pending in Congress to eliminate this and other home-taping activities. Check it out while it lasts. Strong on chart-action rock and new wave.

Reggae City Open Sat only
5240 Leary Way No phone

Tiny store-front live-in shop specializes in Jamaican beat music. New singles,

Shopping

albums, posters, etc.

HH3 **Rubato Records**
10672 NE Eighth, Bellevue
Open every day
455-9417

Owner/musician John Rogers pulled the name out of a music dictionary, but after years of being greeted as "Mr. Rubato" gave in and changed his name to Johnny Rubato. Excellent used new-wave, jazz, and experimental selections in this suburban second-floor shop, plus a good used classical section.

EE7 **Standard Records**
1028 NE 65th
Open Mon-Sat
524-2933

This 50-year-old Mom 'n' Pop has everything. And if you remember record stores before shrink-wrap, the old bins and personal service will warm your heart. Standard excels in international, ethnic, local jazz and rock, and classical.

EE7 **Stewart & Sullivan/Platters**
8064 Lake City Way NE
Open every day
523-9900/523-8888

Two stores in one, here's where to search for oldies singles (all unused) and also current and back stock of 12-inch singles, the largest stock in Seattle. Also country. Special orders and searches.

Tower Records
B4 500 Mercer (corner Taylor)
FF7 4321 University Way NE
Open every day
283-4556
632-1187

One side is classicial, the other pop and jazz (or in the U District, upstairs-downstairs). Supermarket-style, but staffed with at least one informed clerk at all times. Classical side is extremely good and well priced. Popular side has a 10-foot-long wall of jazz. Good first-look place for folk, country, children's, and women's music; strong local, old, and new-wave rock. Jazz cut-outs.

FF7 **University Bookstore**
4326 University Way NE
Open Mon-Sat
634-3400

The best selection of children's records in town.

FF7 **Urban Renewal**
4548 University Way NE
Open every day
634-1775

In the rear of a trendy gift shop called Peachy Keen, Urban Renewal features immaculate copies of used new wave and jazz; also new new wave. Some finds, lots of expertise.

Toys — Downtown

J8 **City Kites**
Pike Place Market Hillclimb
Open every day
622-5349

O8 **Great Winds Kite Shop**
166 S Jackson
Open Mon-Sat (in spring and summer, Sun)
624-6886

N8 **Sound Winds/Air Arts**
108 First S
Open Mon-Sat
622-6652

For kids of all ages, these stores carry kites of all shapes, sizes, and levels of sophistication, plus variations on the ubiquitous Northwest windsock.

Champion Display & Costumes
Pike Place Market — *Open Mon-Sat, 623-1925*
Pavilion Outlet Center — *Open every day, 575-1925*
17900 Southcenter Pky

Has lots of neat stuff: party favors, masks, theatrical makeup, costumes, and novelties.

Christopher House
7010 35th NE — *Open every day*
Fourth & Stewart — *523-9600 / 292-9600*

Christopher House carries a dazzling assortment of toys. Many are imported from Europe and available nowhere else in town; all have been chosen with an eye to quality, durability, and appeal.

Golden Age Collectables
Pike Place Market — *Open Mon-Sat, 622-9799*

This store will catch and hold the attention of any kid old enough to read. Comic books old and new.

Learning World
500 Westlake N — *Open Mon-Sat, 464-1515*
(Also at Bellevue Square, SeaTac Mall, and Lynnwood Square)

A large selection of such lines as Fisher Price, Playskool, and Gabriel. They shine in the areas of craft supplies, and educational aids and materials.

Magic Mouse
217 First Ave S — *Open every day, 682-8097*

Run by a self-proclaimed Professional Child, this store crams a lot into a little. The selection is big on quality stuffed animals, imported toys, puppets, and small knicknacks.

The Orphanage
Pike Place Market — *Open Mon-Sat, 622-0501*

Carries small handmade-only toys for children, mostly inexpensive.

Pippin
Pike Place Market — *Open Mon-Sat, 625-9634*

Has many small, inexpensive, and whimsical toys, including wind-up types. Also nursery prints.

The Wood Shop
402 Occidental S — *Open every day, 624-1763*

Carries exceptionally well-crafted wooden toys both small and large; many are handmade. There's also some pottery, a large collection of stuffed animals and dolls, and nice hand-spun yarn in soft colors.

Shopping

Toys — Other areas

II2 **Arthur Bird Toys**
3610 128th SE, Bellevue *Open every day, 747-7940*
(Loehmann's Plaza)

One of the best toy stores in the area. In addition to an outstanding selection of the usual lines, it also specializes in model trains, Steiff animals, dolls for kids and collectors, dollhouses, doll furniture and furnishings of every description, models, and kits and tools for hobbyists.

GG6 **The Cheshire Cat** *Open Mon-Sat*
3109 E Madison *325-2866*

The Cheshire Cat has a handsome inventory of toys both classic and contemporary, many of them imported.

Children's Corner *Call for hours*
Northgate Mall, Alderwood Mall, Renton Shopping Center, SeaTac Mall, Southcenter, 4306 SW Alaska

A chain store that features a big selection of Carter and Health-tex, among others. It's a good place to look for a winter coat, a baby's layette, or everyday playclothes.

FF6 **Dow's University Village Hobbies** *Open every day, 525-7700*

A veritable gold mine for the hobbyist—train sets, model airplanes, and assemble-it-yourself dinosaurs and skeletons galore.

Kids R Special *Open every day*
201 Fifth Ave S, Edmonds *775-0085*

In addition to cloth and board books for infants and quality hardbound children's books, you will find book-related stuffed animals, posters, classic games like checkers and backgammon, and *lots* of stickers. The Sweet Dreams line of first-love romances, aimed at pre-teens, is here in force, as well as some of the Judy Blume books, but the owner steers clear of anything explicit ("no smut"), and reads each book before it goes on the shelves.

FF7 **Pastimes** *Open Mon-Sat*
4239 University Way NE *632-9840*

What this small toy shop lacks in size, it makes up for in its high quality and imaginative stock. There's a good selection of stuffed animals, mostly by Dakin; baby toys by Ambi and other European makers; educational toys that a child will actually *want* to play with; a few carefully chosen books; and some boutique-type items that will please adults too.

EE7 **The Secret Garden** *Open Mon-Sat*
7900 E Green Lake Drive N *524-4556*

The Secret Garden deals exclusively with books for children, from infants up through junior high. The store is warm and cozy, the books enchanting and wide-ranging, and there are occasional story hours or singalongs for the youngsters (get on the mailing list for advance notice).

Thinker Toys *Open every day*
Gilman Village, Issaquah *392-2020*

A toy store's toy store; the intelligently chosen inventory has a little bit of everything—kites, games, trains, dolls, books, puppets, and so on.

Shopping

Toys R Us	*Open every day*
16700 Southcenter Pky	*575-0780*
Alderwood Mall	*771-4748*

Overwhelming for kids and adults, the gimmick is hard to beat: take a warehouse and fill it with what seems to be every toy, game, bicycle, sporting good, and electronic gadget ever made. There's also children's furniture, party supplies, car seats, clothing, baby supplies, swing sets, and even some home computers.

raphic art shops

Somewhere between fine art and posters there exists a growing market in "graphics" —prints of exceptional quality yet reasonable price. Four of the leading outlets in town are: Elliott Bay Graphics, First S & S Main, 223-0241; Market Graphics, 1935 First Ave, 682-7732; Signatures, 601 Queen Anne N, 282-9801; and Nancy Teague Gallery, 1512 Fifth Ave, 447-9166.

Touring Seattle

**Touring Seattle with a native son
by Emmett Watson** *174*

Other Seattle tours	*187*	Blue Seattle
	189	Built Seattle
	192	Green Seattle — parks
	198	Green Seattle — gardens
	199	Indian Seattle
	201	Kidstuff
	203	Commercial tours
	206	Neighborhoods —
		International District
		University District
		Capitol Hill

By Emmett Watson

If I were you, I wouldn't visit Seattle at all in November, December, January, February, March, or maybe even April. I wouldn't trust May or June much, either. Frankly, if I had my way, you wouldn't be here at all, since I happen to lead a determined band of anti-growth, anti-tourist, anti-progress guerrillas who sabotage so-called good works under the tattered banner of Lesser Seattle. Our active provocateurs, who try to undermine visitor relations, are known as KBO agents after their underground motto: Keep the Bastards Out.

But since you are here, and plan to stay a few days, I'm willing to make the best of it. Let us hope you are here in June, July, August, September, or October. Otherwise, we will all get surly under the constant cloudiness and frequent drizzle that turns Seattle into a sort of urban car wash for much of the year.

Hell, you look like pretty good folks, so I will even introduce myself. I am an overweight, underpaid, rain-soaked native of Seattle and for all the guff I give visitors about the place, I wouldn't live anywhere else. That KBO slogan is not to be feared. I don't rummage through your luggage. It's just that I hope, after a civil visit, you all go back to East Lansing or Green Bay, or whatever heavenly place you came from.

A lifetime in Seattle has shaped within me certain values, which I hope you will endure. And you must understand that I have locked out a lot of information that is best found in slick, skim-the-surface travel stories you may be accustomed to seeing.

Moreover, if you want to find the most perfectly sauced salmon in town, you are keeping company with the wrong tour guide. I am weak on quiche and sundry other anti-foods. When I float the city alone, I avoid the fern-and-chrome spots, the kind where the proprietors are too cheap to install carpets and thus raise the noise level to a chattery din that could compete with a Pittsburgh iron foundry. I can't tell you where to find the best examples of Northwest paintings, or Indian and Eskimo art, and if you intend to plunder the city of its collectibles and imported antiques, you don't need me. It's your VISA card. But if you came here to sort of schlep around and take things as they come, I think we can have a pretty good time together.

At the extreme west end of Pike Street in downtown Seattle there is a clock, a huge clock that can be read a block away. I suggest we meet under that clock at 7:30am tomorrow. Or the next day. Or the next. As long as it isn't Sunday, the day isn't important. You see, this clock sits smack above the north end of the Pike Place Market where every day is just like any other day, except for Saturday, which is more so.

Day 1

In some ways, this is the best time to visit the **Pike Place Market**—and a splendid place to begin your first day in Seattle. The Market is really coming alive at this early hour. Produce trucks clog Pike Place, which is the artery of the Market, and guys are yelling at each other, often obscenely, as they stack fruit, vegetables, fish, meat, and more damned good-smelling stuff than your senses can stand. Bakeries are all over the place and the smell of these, along with the aroma of coffee and early-morning cookery in a half-dozen languages, would drive a stoic off his 1,500-calorie diet.

You see, the Market is for real. It is about the closest thing to the old Les Halles in Paris that America has produced—a genuine food brokerage center for an entire city. It is a good place to have breakfast on your first day in Seattle. After 20 minutes of goggling around and just smelling, you will eat the way you used to eat before a lot of nitwit nutritionists told you that most of what you eat is lethal.

We can do a sit-down breakfast at the Athenian, Lowell's Cafeteria, or Maximilien's, all with great views of Elliott Bay. Personally, I like to make the Market into a moveable feast, especially at breakfast and lunch. We start with an orange, maybe, from one of the dozen or so stalls. We get our orange and go lean against a post and peel it. Most of the Market posts have garbage cans right next to them, so you can eat your orange standing up and throw the peel in the garbage can. If it's the right time of year, you can get the Mineola oranges, which are the best, although the Royal Mandarins are close up there.

There is a potpourri of pastry places. The offerings range from croissants to old-fashioned, love-it-or-leave-it American cinnamon rolls. You can buy a single banana, or a small handful of grapes, maybe one of 38 different species of doughnut, or a Bosc pear. The best pears are the Comice, but you can only get them in winter. Incidentally, don't squeeze the fruit, unless you want to get yelled at. In their hearts of hearts, the fruit and vegetable vendors hate tourists, because tourists, who are more ill-mannered and untrained than natives, have a berserk desire to pinch and pluck and squeeze the merchandise.

The best coffee, I think, is found at Rex's Deli at the north end of the Market. We'll eat our way down there in about half an hour. Here and there we can find a place to sit down as we eat our way into mid-morning. The Market has its fair share of junk shops, funky clothes stores, old poster galleries, used books, and import shops featuring stuff from countries that are still trying to catch up with the Rand-McNally Atlas updates. We'll work through the Market's crannies on three levels until about noon, and then take what we call "the Market Hillclimb" down to the waterfront.

Pike Place Market at a glance

The Market was started in 1907 as a way for farmers to circumvent middlemen in getting produce directly to the customers; it was built around a switchback road leading up from the waterfront. After falling into decline and disrepair through the 1950s and '60s, it was saved by a citizens' referendum and massive federal funds.

Market hours are 9-6 Mon-Sat, closed Sunday; a few restaurants stay open in the evening. The local farmers sometimes take off Monday and Tuesday, and Saturday in the summer can be mobbed: hence the best visiting days are Wednesday-Friday. The local farmers display their produce in the "low stalls" along the main arcade; operators of the more elaborate "high stalls," with devices to secure the vegetables overnight, are not required to grow their own produce. The farmers, in the main arcade on the west side of Pike Place, are the main attraction in the entire Market.

When visiting the Market, you will find certain things take getting used to. There are no shopping carts, so you can quickly get overloaded; shopping bags (available from any merchant) work best. Parking is tough along the main drag, but it is easier to find in the lots along Western Avenue (and it's a downhill walk with your bundles after shopping). The main arcade gets jammed with people, but you can amble out in the brick-paved main street for faster progress; cars are slowed to 5 mph.

Finally, a few tips on food shopping at the Market. Price shopping should not be your main incentive, although it is wise to compare prices; often produce on sale is that way because it is overripe. If you are going to shop at the Market often, the best approach is to find a merchant you like and keep on dealing with him or her. A few merchants will slip a tourist some fruit a shade too soft, so it is wise to keep your eyes (and nose) open.

The Market is divided into three main parts. The main arcade is the home of the farmers and high stallers, with craftspeople located at the northern part. East of Pike Place are the newer shops, with specialty gourmet items concentrated here. Lastly (and often overlooked) are the lower floors of the main market building, underneath the farmers' stands: here are the shops with used goods, bargains, and all sorts of oddities. These lower floors are a good place to turn the kids loose for an hour.

We'll be gone quite a while, so I hope you stuffed enough dollar bills into the orange-colored parking gizmo on the Joe Diamond lot up by the Market. Joe Diamond has a virtual monopoly on Seattle's parking lots, and if you shortchange him, one of his operatives will attach a barrel to your car with a cable. But don't worry. If it comes to that, I know a guy with a pair of bull-snippers who'll cut you loose from the barrel when nobody's looking.

Let me clear up one thing about the waterfront. This isn't the "real" waterfront. It used to be the real waterfront, maybe 30 years ago, and it was a lot more interesting then than it is now. It had taverns and fights and greasy-spoon joints and freight cars which spurred off into the docks and blocked traffic on what was then known as "Railroad Avenue." Now we call it "Alaskan Way," but I forget why. It had a lot of sailors, civilian and Navy, and longshore gangs working the holds of ships that docked at the piers that fingered out to face into the prevailing winds off the bay.

The old waterfront, the real one, had its own special charm for visitors. The visitors were sailors off the freighters and the battleships that used to anchor out in Elliott Bay. One particular appeal for these visitors was its proximity ("a short little stroll," as the tourbooks put it today) to a plethora of rather splendid whorehouses that abounded in the skid road, along with illegal saloons and some alley-entrance gambling joints. The skid road, as such, is long gone; we call it Pioneer Square now, but I won't confuse you with further explanations until we get there.

Waterfront at a glance

In the spring of 1792, Captain George Vancouver sailed his ship *Discovery* into these waters, naming Puget Sound after Peter Puget, a lieutenant aboard. About 100 years later, Seattle was dominating the Sound's commerce from piers at her central waterfront. The piers were built here because the water is so deep and the tall ships could come in close to shore. Later, however, the "finger piers" could not be extended outward, so the shipping moved to the southern and northern parts of the harbor and the old piers were recycled into a tourist strip.

You can have a very nice stroll here, and many of the piers afford access to the outer portions, where the view is unobstructed and the fishing's good, too. Parking gets tougher down by the ferry terminal, and the crowds on the narrow sidewalks get too much on a sunny Saturday. Treat both the shopping and the dining along this strip with caution.

Some highlights: Pier 48 (foot of Main), home of the Alaskan ferries, has a nifty new observation platform on the southwest portion, with giant periscopes to view the busy port traffic; Ye Olde Curiosity Shop (foot of Yesler), a zany emporium of oddities pushed well into the far side of camp; Fisheries Supply Company (foot of Spring) is a genuine nautical supply house with more interesting souvenirs than most shops; Waterfront Park (foot of Union) has good fishing on its southern flank and lots of intricate walkways with great views of the harbor; Aquarium (foot of Pike) is small but exceedingly well conceived, with informative displays and odd-angle views of the finny world leading up to a great topside view at the end. A fine way to end the day here is to relax over a drink in the upstairs bar of the Fisherman's Restaurant. Located on Pier 57, just south of the Aquarium, it commands a fine view of the sun setting over Elliott Bay.

Anyway, you are not on the "real" waterfront. The real waterfront is further south and over on Harbor Island, and the old longshore gangs have largely been replaced by huge, box-like ship containers, brought in by rail and truck. These containers are put aboard the ships by cranes so tall they are a hazard to low-flying aircraft. Quite dull, actually.

The waterfront we are on now is quite safe unless you are a spendthrift. The old working docks, or many of them, have been refurbished and turned into waterfront shopping malls. We could spend a whole day just poking through these places. Some of the stuff, the memorabilia you might take home, is quite good. For example, there is a "senior store" on Pier 70 at the north end that sells some fine, imaginative handicrafts made only by elderly citizens. The restaurants range from Rolaids-deep-fried to posh-and-pricey. The big import shops have cutesy

177

names like Pirate's Plunder and Trident and Pier 1 Imports, which isn't on Pier 1, but on Pier 70. Pier 1, if it still exists, is about two miles south, since the numbers get bigger the further north you go.

If your feet hurt, it's easy to "do" the waterfront. For 60 cents we can ride the "waterfront trolleys," these being a monument to the stubbornness of an ex-druggist named George Benson. George is a city councilman who pushed through this idea of importing some ancient Australian streetcars and running them along the railroad tracks that were already there. George's idea was originally supposed to cost about $300,000 but it ballooned to $3.2 million before he finally jammed it through. I hear the Pentagon is trying to hire George to improve its cost overruns.

But the trolley is great, and we can work the whole waterfront with it. Right now, I'd suggest a Harbor Tour. It's easy, comfortable, takes only about an hour, and the spielers can tell you more about Seattle's piers, docking facilities, tonnage, shipyards, and such than possibly you care to know: a nice break in the afternoon, however, and a great view of the city's skyline. Sometime this afternoon we will pass Pier 54, where presides one of Seattle's durable landmarks, Ivar Haglund. There is no need to genuflect, but you have to admire a man who is the world's champion fish hustler, bar none, a congenial mollusk merchant who made a fortune off clam nectar alone, by slyly hinting that clam nectar is probably an aphrodisiac. I think he came here before Alki Point.

The easiest way to get back up to your car near the Market is to mosey over to First Avenue and catch one of the free buses going north. North is that way. I'll meet you under the Market clock again tomorrow morning. We'll do our walking breakfast number again, but this time we'll take a bus back down to Pioneer Square. Try to find one of the all-day garages, and forget about taking your car into Pioneer Square. Joe Diamond is just as deadly there as he is uptown.

Day 2

Well, folks, here we are in **Pioneer Square**. Isn't it lovely? This is the so-called "old" part of town, and the brick you see is genuine, having been laid when they rebuilt Seattle after the big fire that almost leveled the city. I forget when, but it was a long time ago: 1889, I think. As I mentioned before, Pioneer Square was really known as "the skid road," because they used to skid logs down what is now Yesler Way to the sawmill. Henry Yesler owned the sawmill and he was a tightwad and one of the early pioneers, which I guess is how you get streets named after yourself.

We're on the west side of First Avenue where Marion Street ends. If you look right behind you, there's a doorway and some stairs. Those stairs now lead to some offices, but they used to lead to a wax museum. It had wax figures, in glorious colors, of men's private parts, and these wax images purported to show what terrible, scaly diseases you would get if you frequented the whorehouses in the skid road. You were supposed to have second thoughts about going to those places, but most of us never got beyond the first thought. By the way, we never capitalized "skid road." It was just part of our language.

Anyway, Pioneer Square went through a sandblasting and modernization renaissance, and it now has more restaurants and boutiques than seem absolutely necessary. In these few square blocks you can spend yourself silly on designer dresses, decorator lamps, custom-made leather clothes, fine linens, gourmet cookware, and knit sweaters from Ireland that go for $175. Maybe the centerpiece of all this restoration is the Grand Central Arcade, First South and South Main. It is loaded with galleries, food places, pricey shops, and a great used bookstore, presided over by David Ishii, who may be wearing a Seattle Mariners baseball cap. David is a hopeless baseball fan.

Every Pioneer Square building has its colorful history, but the Grand Central appeals to me. It was once owned by a Japanese family named Yoshida when it was a skid-road hotel. Jimmy Yoshida used to tell me how he'd have to make the beds and clean the rooms and mop the throw-up on the stairs left by the treetoppers, loggers, and sailors who stayed there after drinking too much rotgut whiskey in the speakeasies I told you about. Born not far from the Grand Central, Jimmy went over to visit his forebears in Japan and got himself conscripted into the Japanese army, thus becoming, when World War II ended, a man without a country. He was the subject of a best-selling book called *The Two Worlds of Jimmy Yoshida*, and is now a wealthy contractor in Honolulu.

Pioneer Square at a glance

In February, 1852, the small band of pioneers who had settled on Alki Point (present West Seattle) abandoned that windswept spot and moved to the area now called Pioneer Square. This became the center of town until the 1920s, when the action moved north and east. It was rebuilt, in a rush of consistent architecture, after the Great Fire of June 6, 1889; most of the old buildings you see here date from within a few years of 1889.

One way to tour the Square is the Underground Tours (tickets at 610 First Avenue, 682-1511), which takes you one flight down, where the old street level was before the Great Fire (poor drainage made a higher level necessary); the tour is corny but informative.

If you are walking around on your own, you'll want to see several things. There are two main squares (though one is a triangle): the original Pioneer Square is at First and Yesler, with totem pole, statue of Chief Seattle, and wrought-iron pergola; the new park, called Occidental, is along Occidental between Washington and Main. From Occidental there is an attractive pedestrian mall leading south toward the Kingdome; along this mall were the art and decorator galleries that spurred the rediscovery of the Square in the 1960s. The district abounds in good galleries today, along with bookstores, gift shops, restaurants, bars, and nightclubs; lawyers, architects, and mediafolk dominate the workforce. There are plenty of parking lots (as long as a Kingdome event is not on), but be sure to lock your car.

A good walking route is a lazy figure eight: start at Pioneer Square and go west on Yesler to the waterfront; turn south past antique shops to Washington; head east a block and a half to Occidental Park and Mall; go south for three blocks to King Street; turn west for one block; then walk all the way back on First Avenue, heading north four blocks until you return to Pioneer Square itself. Saturdays and Sundays are particularly good days for browsing in the Square.

Just poking around Pioneer Square can blow a whole morning quite easily, but I'm going to cut out now. You can go uptown on your own and I'll see you tomorrow under the Market clock again. Just to help you along, here's a daffy saying about our city: "Jesus Christ Made Seattle Under Protest." You might memorize this, in case you get lost.

You just take this saying, "Jesus Christ Made Seattle Under Protest," and read it in a northerly direction, so to speak. The "J" stands for two streets, Jefferson and James, which are really part of the old Seattle. The "C" stands for the next two streets, Cherry and Columbia. This gets you into what passes for our erstwhile financial district, Second and Third Avenues. The "M" in the saying stands for Marion and Madison streets. Spring and Seneca, as in the "S" part, get you fairly well uptown; the southwest corner of the Four Seasons Olympic Hotel, in fact, is at Fourth and Seneca. From there on, everything is downhill. After "S" comes "U," so your next two streets are University and Union. University and Union between Fourth and Fifth avenues, put you in the high-rent district, what we now call Rainier Square. This is elegant stuff, in terms of quality clothing, good dining, "name" shops, and jewelry stores. The area bounding Rainier Square isn't exactly Hooverville, either; in fact, much of Union Street, starting with Brooks Brothers on Fourth Avenue and moving east to Seventh and Union, has become a shopping mall that adds up to a minor-league Maiden Lane.

Downtown at a glance

One of the great attractions of Seattle's downtown is its walkability. It is compact, with all its attractions well within the reach of the average pedestrian. Being built on a sidehill, it affords terrific and frequent views of the harbor and mountains. It is clean and prosperous, with few run-down areas to depress or frighten the pedestrian. One other thing: taxi fares are too high, so if you insist on motorized aid, remember that the buses running through town are all free in the downtown Magic Carpet zone.

The retail core is in the uptown district, roughly between the Westin and Four Seasons Olympic hotels and connected by Fifth Avenue. The major department stores face on Pine Street, with the carriage-trade boutiques tending to cluster toward Rainier Square and Sixth Avenue. The stores to the north of the core, in the Denny Regrade, have more bargains and more of the feel of the old Seattle.

The midtown area, along Fourth Avenue from Seneca to James, is the office core, giving way in the south to the governmental complex. There's less for the browser here, so you might want to head down to Second Avenue, the old heart of the financial district, where the buildings are more attractively scaled and the shops more interesting. By the way, many of the buildings have east-west interior escalators to assist pedestrians coming uphill: it's a nice route to sniff out in rainy weather or if you want to see the interiors of the buildings. Just ask.

The other major downtown area is toward the waterfront, ranged along First Avenue from Yesler to Virginia. First Avenue itself, rapidly changing now, is the best reminder that Seattle was a salty, earthy town once. A half block waterward is Post Alley, being turned into a pedestrian way lined with shops and eateries: it's worth a look in the Madison-Seneca portion where an old warehouse district is becoming a new Georgetown.

A good city presents layers of its history for the orientation of its inhabitants. You can experience this trip back into time by walking south through the uptown retail core, past the Fourth Avenue skyscrapers, down into the old Second Avenue and its terra-cotta offices, and then back north along First Avenue ending at the Public Market. You've gone from modern glitter to frontier Gold Rush in eight easy decades.

Your next two "P's" are Pike and Pine. This is the core of retail downtown. It is where the fashion-wise stewardesses shop, because they don't have much time between flights. Once you hit Pine, between Third and Sixth, you are in Consumersville, USA. It is an area that includes the Big Four—Frederick & Nelson (Marshall Field), I. Magnin, Nordstrom, and the Bon Marche. For reasons best known in soft-goods circles, they cut off the "Marche," so that it's now officially known as

"The Bon." Forget it. We still go on calling it the Bon Marche, the same way we call the Hiram M. Chittenden Locks just "the government locks." We will not be intimidated. Nordstrom was once a mom 'n pop shoe store that grew into one of the most prosperous and largest retail clothing outlets in America. But the Nordstroms also own the Seattle Seahawks football team, so life isn't all smiles.

Day 3

Anyway, here we are, back under the Market clock for our third day of soaking up Seattle, and maybe vice versa. Since this is not your usual glass-sided Trailway Bus excursion, we'll take a Third Avenue Metro bus (almost any bus will do) out to **Seattle Center** for the morning. I'll do my Charles Kuralt number as we drift along, telling you about the Denny Regrade on the way.

Maybe a dozen high-rise hooligan developers would like to come up with a new name for this district, but we natives resolutely call it the Denny Regrade. That's because many years ago there was a high hill here known as Denny Hill. Those early mouth-breathers thought it would be a swell idea to do away with that hill. They sluiced it down with millions of gallons of water, so Denny Hill is now down in Elliott Bay on our left. The whole hill is in the bay. The idea was that downtown Seattle would grow north, once they got that hill out of the way, and a chosen few of these early developers would come down rich. But downtown Seattle didn't move north, not for a long time. It tended to grow up, as in high, instead of out; or it tended not to grow much at all.

Seattle Center at a glance

This 74-acre park is the legacy of the 1962 World's Fair, one of the few to turn a profit and leave a permanent facility behind. The site was once a ceremonial grounds for Indian gatherings; now it's a gathering place for the culture crowd, sports fans, people-watchers, couples, elderly folks, and tourists. It's open all hours, no admission.

Parking can be a problem, particularly in the hour before evening curtains. The best and cheapest lots are located to the north side. To beat the crush, you can go early and either dine downtown and take the Monorail or eat at the good restaurants lying to the west of the Center. The parking garage to the north affords easy access, but the egress can be maddeningly long on busy nights; a post-event drink at one of the watering holes lying north of the Center might solve that problem.

The Center holds many special events, like music and crafts festivals, to serve as draws for the many shops, restaurants, and exhibits on the grounds: call 625-4234 to see what's cooking. The rental facilities for special meetings are extensive and very flexible: call 625-4254 for details.

A few other tips. The food in the Center House is not exactly inspiring, but the Oriental fare is the most reliable. The Fun Forest has a number of enjoyable rides, but check to see if it's open before you disappoint your brood: it closes during the winter months. One of the lesser known delights of the Center is its collection of fountains and statues. A splendid fountain is James FitzGerald's "Fountain of the Northwest" in the Playhouse courtyard; one of the silliest statues is "Doughboy Bringing Home Victory" between the Opera House and Memorial Stadium.

Well, for a whole lot of years, this was a no-good, unattractive, flattened-out area that didn't amount to much of anything. It was what you had to go through to get to Queen Anne Hill. It had a few service shops, some low-rise apartments, a few low-rent prostitutes, a great old dance hall called the Trianon Ballroom, and some other businesses that ran a losing race with their creditors. Over by *The P-I* (that's a newspaper) at Fifth and Battery, there used to be a tabernacle run by a character named Brother Ralph. He was a 1950s-style Oral Roberts who shook up the folks with visions of hell-and-damnation if they didn't pony up for his crusades. He exhorted his troops in person at his tabernacle and also on radio, and for my money Brother Ralph ran a pretty good soul-recycling shop.

Across the street at *The P-I*, where I worked, we drank a lot, bet on horses and ball games, and ran a few scams like "Lucky Bucks" to increase circulation, but Brother Ralph never came across the street to get us right with the Lord. He worked his side of the street and we worked ours. His old tabernacle is now a *P-I* parking garage.

Anyway, since the World's Fair of 1962, the Regrade has had a mild—well, you can't call it a renaissance, because the Regrade never was much in the first place. But they built the Monorail to the Fair along Fifth Avenue and what with all the people going through the Regrade, by Monorail, car, and bus, I guess it started to get noticed. Anyway, a few more businesses went in and a tree-planting crusade in the 1960s made Second, Third, Fourth, and Fifth look halfway respectable. Lately, some high-rise condos have popped up and now the Regrade (to the surprise of us natives) is taking on a few characteristics of a nice neighborhood. That was the Regrade we just passed.

So this is your first view of the Space Needle from close up. You are now in Seattle Center. The Space Needle has become Seattle's symbol and rightfully so, I guess. If you want to spend the $2.50 it takes to ride the elevator to the top, the view is worth it. If you want to eat at the Space Needle restaurant, which I don't right now, the place revolves a full 360 degrees each hour, which gives you a panoramic idea of Seattle and Puget Sound. Incidentally, "the Sound" is anything salty between Port Angeles and Olympia. So from the Space Needle, you can really get an overview of the city, so to speak. Any first-class city should have an overview, which is precisely what you're not getting from me.

The original owners of the Needle were a low-key bunch who kind of let Seattle people think the Needle was "theirs." They ran it the way it has become—a city institution. Then some new owners came along. They looked in the Yellow Pages and found that restaurant listings only took up about a third of the pages. So they decided that Seattle desperately needed yet another restaurant. After a lot of fighting and City Council hearings, they beat the zoning and built that thing you see about 100 feet up. What it does, mainly, is make the spindly-legged Space Needle look like it has dropped its drawers.

As we walk though the Center itself, I'll tell you about it. Off to your left the Seattle Art Museum has a branch with a nice gift store. Near there is the Science Center, which cost about $15 million to build back in 1962. It was designed by Minoru Yamasaki, the guy who built the inverted-pencil building in Rainier Square, and for a long time it was run by a lady named Dixy Lee Ray, a zoology teacher from the University of Washington. Dixy got a lot of fame from running the Science Center and putting programs on Channel 9. She parlayed that into heading up the Atomic Energy Commission and came home to run for governor. Damned if she didn't make it. But after one term the voters decided she ran a better Science Center than a state government, and Dixy has more or less dropped out of sight.

The squeals on your right (we're kind of angling through the Center from the southeast corner to the northwest corner) come from what we call the "Fun Forest," a sort of permanent carnival that gets a big play from the kids. The big building right next to it is the Food Circus, or the Center House, I think they call it now. A lot of natives still call it "the Armory," because that's what it once was when the Washington State National Guard had it. It is quite a place, although it's had financial problems. In the Center House you can buy everything from a Belgian waffle to a $5,000 glass galleon. They hold senior-citizen dances, square dances, and Big Band dances in there. The Center House is full of shops and restaurants on three levels; on the whole, not bad for eating, although I always get the feeling that I'm eating in the middle of an echo chamber, or one of those old high-domed train stations.

The funny-looking building on our left, the one that looks like a collapsed teepee, is the Coliseum, good for basketball, hockey, flat shows, and exhibits; very big on rock concerts, too. To the right of us are the Opera House and the Arena, and as we come out here on the northwest corner, you can see the new Bagley Wright Theater. Bagley is one of the original Space Needle fellows and, along with his wife, Virginia, strong on culture. They collect paintings and civic tributes. Bagley is the guy who helped found the Seattle Repertory Theater Company, and this building is the Rep's new theater, named after him. A large chunk of money to build it was put up by some anonymous donors. Rumor has it that they wanted to remain anonymous to escape being prematurely cast in bronze by a grateful populace. We take our culture seriously in Seattle.

As we come out of the Center, on your right you will see Seattle's newest QFC store. You may think I'm kidding, but the architecture of QFC stores is a lot better than some of the glass boxes we get from downtown developers. Furthermore, they put plantings and trees around their parking lots, which is more than we get from Joe Diamond. Seattle, it must be added here, is a city of real neighborhoods. We won't have time to hit them all, but my own favorites run about as follows, in no particular order:

Madison Park, which fronts on Lake Washington, has a semi-resort flavor about it, especially in summer, for resort area is what Madison Park used to be when people built "summer homes" out there. These summer homes, furbished and refurbished and added on to, bring good prices today; some of the condominium prices blow right off the real-estate charts. But the heart of Madison Park still is the "village," and the heart of the village is Madison Park Hardware, owned by Lola and Bud McKee. It is the nerve center, the gossip mecca, for not only the subdued commercialism of the village and Madison Park itself, but for such adjoining neighborhoods as Canterbury Shores, Broadmoor, and Washington Park.

The **Wallingford** district, out on N 45th, is another good one, but in my book hasn't quite made it. Maybe it's because the Wallingford Precinct cop shop takes away some of its charm, or it could be the garish Food Giant store. But the neighborhood does have a good theater, the Guild 45th, and a variety of shops, plus a French restaurant, Les Copains, that some say is one of the best in town.

Green Lake is more of a playground than a neighborhood, because people come from all over the city to fish, or jog, or ride bikes, or roller skate. They have crew races and assorted boat races on Green Lake in summer. Green Lake is really one big park and it's the best hot-weather girl-watching area in the Northwest, possibly excepting the "apartment strip" near Kirkland, across Lake Washington. Not to digress, but I've always thought the Pike Place Market is the best day-in, day-out girl-watching place in the city. The Market has girls for all seasons, and they come in all sizes and colors, which is more interesting, and they aren't there to be seen so much as to shop or browse, the same way everyone else is. On this subject, I would like to hereby nominate Delores Greenblat as the most beautiful butcher in America, possibly the world. Delores, who has spectacular skin color, black hair, and a smile that makes guys come unglued, works at Crystal Meats in the north end of the Market. Her husband owns Crystal Meats.

Let's see, where was I? As I said, we can't hit all the neighborhoods, so I'll just talk about a couple more.

Greenwood, which is thought of more as a "district" than a neighborhood, gets its name from being out on 85th and Greenwood. It is an interesting blue-collar area. Like all such working-class areas, it has a heavy sprinkling of "antique shops," whose authenticated antiques (some of them) go back as far as 1938. Greenwood is a quaint mixture of Col. Sanders, McDonald's, and Fred Meyer, if you get the idea.

The U District blew it a long time ago as a real neighborhood but it's fun to go there. This is the strip by the UW, running north and south, called "The Ave," although its official name is University Way NE. In the old days it had more of a "college village" flavor than it has now; a lot of the apartments are a bit seedy, and major-league commercialism has taken over The Ave. To give you an idea, the old University Book Store, which was a true trade-'em-in textbook store, is now a department store that could service a small midwestern city. But its book section is still the largest you'll find this side of Harvard Yard.

Anyway, back to where we are now, just west of Seattle Center. We are now smack in the middle of my favorite neighborhood in Seattle, which is known by the unpoetic name of **Lower Queen Anne**. It sits at the bottom of Queen Anne Hill, which is old Seattle, real old Seattle. Up there is the "counterbalance," a term which even puzzles our younger natives. It is really Queen Anne Avenue N, the main street that goes up that steep hill. It is called the "counterbalance" because when we had streetcars, they couldn't make it up that hill without tying onto a counterbalance, or counterweight, attached to cables under the street.

What makes Lower Queen Anne great is its street life. The Center attracts a lot of people here on event nights at the Coliseum, the Rep, the Exhibition Hall, or the Opera House. But it has a fine street life of its own. The mixture is a good cross-section of Seattle: a lot of older, retired people; young professionals who live on the south slope of Queen Anne; business types who work in the low-rise office buildings nearby. Because of the Center, some eight or ten good restaurants have cropped up in a four-block-square area. A small neighborhood-style grocery, Sinnett's, goes on prospering despite QFC and Safeway nearby, both of them mercifully out of sight of the main street. Sinnett's has a first-rate deli called Beba's. Both Sinnett's and the Uptown Florists, a couple of shops away, seem to compete on who can put the most flowers for sale on the sidewalk. We need more competition like that. The one block of the main "village," from Mercer Street down to Republican, has a theater (the Uptown), a variety store, a gift shop, a top-cabin fish-and-chips stand, a clothing store, a TV store, a cleaners, a barber and beauty shop, and a Chinese restaurant. If your spirit and your feet hurt, there's also a Christian Science reading room. The tight little area surrounding the main corner of Mercer and Queen Anne Avenue has everything you could want—a big bookstore, a drugstore, a variety of neighborhood restaurants, some dress shops, a shoe-repair store, a couple of picture-framing places, a state booze shop, and, of course, the Mecca Cafe. The Mecca, a working-class place, draws a mix of blue-collars, newspaper people, professionals, and real "regulars"—the residents nearby. The Mecca is about 900 years old, or at least it's one of the oldest such places in Seattle. It is one of the few places left which makes its own old-fashioned tapioca pudding and custard.

That's it for today, folks. We'll meet under the Market clock tomorrow morning, same time, but before we split I'll give you a little homework to do. Pencils ready? Cultural anthropologists will probably tell you that there is no such thing as a Puget Sound accent, but we do have some peculiarities of speech and habits. Natives like me, for no reason I can understand, seem to put an "s" after Boeing, as in "Boeings." Natives rarely bother to call it "Mount Rainier." To us it's just "The Mountain," but all other mountains (Baker, St. Helens, Pilchuck) are referred to by name.

As I said earlier, we will not be intimidated by names imposed on us. A true Seattle person would not be caught dead referring to Seattle as "The Emerald City." It is faintly embarrassing to us, just as the last bit of tourist hokum was. An earlier generation of tourist-hustlers "officially" christened us "The Queen City." My friend Don Duncan, on *The Seattle Times*, once compiled a whole list of peculiar traits about us, the main one being our refusal to use officially mandated names.

So the Lacey V. Murrow Memorial Bridge is the "old bridge" or "the Mercer Island Bridge." The other floating bridge, further north, isn't really the Evergreen Point Bridge, as it's supposed to be called. It's just the "new bridge." The George Washington Bridge is simply the Aurora Bridge to us; it crosses the canal that connects downtown Lake Union with Puget Sound, and it's the only one high enough for serious suicide attempts. Discovery Park is still Fort Lawton to us, and the "Space," as in Needle, is superfluous, and that theater I showed you earlier is just "the Rep," nothing more. "The Valley" is Rainier Valley, once known as "Garlic Gulch," and First Hill is "Pill Hill." That last name comes because of all the hospitals up there. If you are planning to have a gall-bladder attack, or something, do it on Pill Hill. You can walk into emergency entrances like they were branch banks.

Anyway, I'm signing off for now, and I'll see you in the morning under the Market clock. This time we'll somehow jam into one car and go out to "Snoose Junction" and other uplifting places.

Day 4

Yes, here we are, stalled on the Ballard Bridge. You see, the **Ballard** district is what we call "Snoose Junction," because for many years this was a community, made up of lumbermen and fishermen. A few of the old "Swede taverns" remain, and without checking, I suspect there are a lot of Johnsons, Johansens, Swenssons, Swansons, and so forth still concentrated out in the Ballard area. If you just scan through the phonebook and see how many names end in "son" or "sen" or "berg," you can get a good handle on our heritage.

The reason we are stuck here is because Ballard Bridge is "up," as we say. We have a lot of drawbridges like this. As long as we are stuck here, I might give you a little more travelogue about Seattle. Off to your left, where you see a zillion boats tied up, is what we call Fisherman's Terminal. These are the boats that bring back the salmon you pay $3.99 a pound for in the Market. They go off to Alaska for months at a time. They also go out and catch halibut. In fact, this may be the only city in the world that has a Halibut Fishermen's Wives Association. The tour brochures tell you that one of the charms of Salmon Bay is "watching the fishermen repair their nets." You go watch if you want to, but I find it a bit too exciting for my taste.

We are more or less suffocated by nature around here. We get water from above and from all sides, which is why you see that idiot parked just in front of us with a bumper sticker that says, "I'd Rather Be Sailing." That other car has one that says, "I'd Rather Be Skiing." Seattle is peculiar in a lot of little ways. For example, a lot of the men resist carrying umbrellas, even though it's six, two, and even on any day that you're going to get rained on. If you've noticed the colors of the city, you've noticed they are kind of muted, like the underside of a mushroom. In Nova Scotia, where it's cloudy and overcast, they paint their houses and buildings in wild, bright colors; here we stay pretty drab and conventional.

Residents of Seattle get resigned to some certainties about the city. They know that at least once a year, maybe twice, a ferry will get out of control and ram a dock, causing "an estimated $1,283,411.32 worth of damage." They know the Mariners will finish last, or near there, in the American League. They know that jaywalking is probably sinful, but not as sinful as taking a three-hour lunch. They also know that drawbridges, like this one that's up now, always stall traffic to allow a 38-foot sailboat to go through.

Well, the traffic has cleared and here we are in Ballard. In Seattle, we don't have Polish jokes, we have Ballard jokes. Like: "How do you get a one-armed Swede out of a tree?" "Wave." And: "Why aren't there any pharmacists in Ballard?" "Because they can't figure out how to fit those little bottles into the typewriter."

For all its quaintness as the city's "snoose" center and the home of taverns that drew half-baked intellectuals looking to soak up "the real color," Ballard was quite scruffy for a long time. But of all the Seattle neighborhoods, I think, Ballard came the longest way to where it is now—a clean, decent neighborhood which even has one of the city's 9,852 gourmet cookware places. I'm honor bound not to tell you exactly where he lives, but one of Ballard's citizens is the late Clark Gable's half-brother. I visited him once. He's the spitting image of The King and he has a fine collection of family photos. Like a lot of veteran Ballard citizens, he just wants to be left alone.

Ballard serves another good purpose. It's what you go through to get to the government locks. The locks really add up to a big city park. People come here with picnic lunches, watch the boats go through the locks, everything from dinghies to ocean-going freighters. You can also take in the underwater viewing gallery where the salmon, steelhead, and trout make it up the fish ladders.

On the way back, I'll take you past the canal that runs from the Ballard Bridge to Lake Union. For my money, this is one of the nicest places to be in Seattle on a sunny day, of which we have several. The canal is a lengthy mini-park on either side. You can pack a lunch and spend a pleasant hour or two watching canoes and kayaks and yachts and all the bigger boats pass through.

On our way back downtown I haven't said much, but I would like you folks to know that you have been a good group. Not one of you asked me how many inches of rain we get, or where you can meet an Eskimo, or how you can find a restaurant that serves "good seafood," or where the "real live action is," and stuff like that. We'll end our tour here in the Market, under the clock, where we began.

This is your last chance to send a salmon home packed in ice. It's also your last chance to walk across Pike Place and see if what I said about Delores Greenblat isn't true. As you can tell, the place is closing up. The canvas shields are rolling down over the vegetable stalls, and the Market regulars are heading for the Athenian or Lowell's or the Mint for a couple of quick day-enders. I would suggest you might have your last Seattle supper at Il Bistro, which is right down those stairs here under the clock, the end of Pike Street. Il Bistro has great food and it's got a sort of out-of-the-way, alley-entrance European style that I like. Another thing I like about it is that it doesn't have a view of anything. I'm not putting you on, but in Seattle we actually do get a little tired of having so many views. Sometimes.

Nice to have met you all. And by the way, don't pronounce it See-attle the way I've heard some of you do. Drop a bit harder on the "a" and you've got it right. Come back again, maybe, but don't bring a lot of relatives with you. We half mean that stuff about KBO.

Other Seattle tours

Blue Seattle

Seattle's heart, in spirit as in history and commerce, has always been the deep, lovely harbor around which it grew, **Elliott Bay**. When Captain George Vancouver's ship *Discovery* sailed into Puget Sound in the spring of 1792, Vancouver noted "a landscape almost as enchantingly beautiful as the most elegantly finished pleasure grounds of Europe," and thereby discovered one of the world's noblest and most navigable major ocean inlets. Since that time, Seattle's growth, and its perennial dreams of even greater commercial grandeur, have been built on its maritime access: first as a shipping point for logs, followed by wheat and coal; then as the staging point for the Alaskan and Yukon gold rushes; and today as the city hustles to cash in on emerging trade with the Pacific Rim countries.

Other waterways surround Seattle as well, some natural, some carved by its citizens. The 17-mile-long **Lake Washington** forms Seattle's eastern border and joins the city to Bellevue and the other Eastside towns that comprise the Greater Seattle area. Lake Washington is one of Seattle's big urban environmental success stories. Back in 1958, when 28 primary sewage treatment plants were releasing their effluents directly into the lake, the beaches had to be closed. Giant algae blooms floated on the water and visibility was two feet. Today, the water is sparkling clean and the lake is ringed with numerous parks, thanks to an aggressive cleanup program and treatment plan.

Little **Lake Union**, almost at the city's center, opens up between the Montlake Cut from Lake Washington and the Ship Canal from the Sound. It's markedly and fascinatingly different from its bigger neighbors: largely devoted, especially on its south and west shores, to boat-building, ship repair and other traditional industries. The Eastlake strip is a beguiling village-within-the-city of houseboats, from floating shacks to designer boxes complete with security gates. Washed with salty spill from the Locks, Lake Union remains warm and clean enough to swim in (at Gasworks Park).

Green Lake, a little patch of aqua paradise in the heart of a residential area, is the center of the city's jogging, roller-skating, and summer beach cultures.

When the weather is clear, some of the best ways to view the city are from its waters, or walking its shorelines. Here are some ways to get launched.

Downtown waterfront. There are interesting attractions, plus plenty of food for snackers, in the strip from the Alaska Ferry Terminal at Pier 48 to Pier 70, and northward to Myrtle Edwards Park. See Emmett Watson in the Touring Seattle chapter for more details.

Harbor Tours. Boat tours run daily from May through October, departing Pier 56. These tours are quite good, since you see both a beautiful bay and a very busy world harbor. Seattle Harbor Tours, 623-1445; see Commercial Tour section in the Touring Seattle chapter for more details.

Tillicum Village. Four-hour lunch- and suppertime excursions take you across the Bay from Pier 56 to an Indian-style salmon roast on Blake Island. Seattle Harbor Tours, 623-1445; see Commercial Tour section for more details.

Ferries. This is the easiest way to take in the skyline and inhale the fresh breezes. Simply board a boat at the Seattle Ferry Terminal, Pier 52, and go to Winslow on Bainbridge Island. You can make the round trip in about an hour and a half. Best advice is to bring your own lunch and eat it on the sundeck, but there is routine food in the ferry cafeterias. A longer trip goes to Bremerton and back. See Transportation section in the Services chapter for more details.

Gray Line Tours. Two-hour Adventure Water Cruises (April-October) run between Fisherman's Terminal, through the Ballard Locks, and Pier 57 downtown. The starting point alternates between Fisherman's Terminal and Pier 57 on different days, so it's best to pick up the tour at the Westin Hotel. Call 343-2000 for details.

Princess Marguerite. Leave at 8 in the morning and sail to Victoria, see the sights, and arrive back at Pier 69 around 9:45 that night. This is the long, expensive, and civilized way to challenge the waves. (See Transportation section or Out of Town Tour chapter for details; reservations at 623-5560 are usually essential.)

Puget Sound. Several small companies offer tours of Puget Sound. You can choose between cruising in style on the old *Virginia V* steamer (624-9119), or on a luxurious sailboat (Seahawk Sailing Tours, 343-9480, or Wind Works Sailing Charters, 784-9386), and taking an educational tour with Anchor Excursions (282-8368). See the Commercial Tour section in the Touring Seattle chapter for details.

Fishing. If you prefer a tiny boat for getting offshore, there are some good rentals available, along with advice on where to find the salmon. One of the best is Ray's Boathouse, to the north of the city (789-4130 or 783-9679). Fishing piers are another fine public amenity in Seattle. See the section on fishing in the Sports chapter for more details on rentals and fishing piers.

Canoes. You can rent canoes from the University of Washington Waterfront Activities Center (543-2217 or 543-9433), and then paddle around the marshes and freeway posts at the north end of the Arboretum. Paddleboats are available at Green Lake. (See Boating and Canoeing sections of the Sports chapter for information.)

Lake Washington and Green Lake. There are lovely walks along the groomed parklands that adjoin these two lakes, and the kids will like feeding the ducks. See Parks section for details.

West Seattle. Beaches here are exposed to the bigger waves of Puget Sound, and they make for moody, melancholy walks on wintry days, and the best bathing in the summer, if you can stand the cold water! See Swimming section of the Sports chapter for details.

The Ship Canal. One of the best places to walk along this canal is under the Montlake Bridge. You enter on the south side, by the Museum of History and Industry (2161 E Hamlin), walk under the old bridge right beside the yachts, and end up in a waterfront park neighboring the Seattle Yacht Club on Portage Bay. Bring a picnic.

The Ballard Locks. The premier place for boat-watching, with salmon windows to gaze into, a pretty park for picnics, and inspirational prose from the Army Corps of Engineers, who built these second-only-to-Panama-in-North-America locks. See the 12 Top Attractions in the Introduction.

Built Seattle

Seattle is not one of the important American cities, architecturally. Too few large corporations are headquartered here to commission the major architects, and the local cult of unostentation makes most of the major structures blend in and hold back. Even so, there are the elements of a distinctive style: the fondness for wood, the hovering, deep-eaved roofs that the rainy weather dictates, the feeling for detail, the hunger for light, the softened modernism, the way homes melt into a hilly landscape rather than rising above it. Most of the distinguished examples of this style are in private homes, hence difficult to see. But there is still enough good architecture to make up some interesting hours.

Pike Place Market. The Public Market, dating back to 1907, is a classic illustration of wonderful "architecture without architects"—accreted space that has been lovingly restored and organically modified. The Market is one of the finest urban-preservation schemes in the nation, keeping both the buildings and the social uses intact, and it has inspired some excellent buildings nearby. The Pike and Virginia Building, at the north end of the Market, is a concrete condominium-cum-shops project by Olson/Walker that successfully marries an industrial vocabulary with greenery, Market echoes, and intricate patterns of use. Another condominium project by the same firm is Hillclimb Court, just south of the Western Avenue skybridge: an ingenious solution to a difficult site that comes out strong, delicate, up-to-date, and original all at once. Seattle Garden Center building, at the end of Stewart and Pine streets, is a Market-like exercise in playfulness and bold Deco patterns by Arne Bystrom. Market Place North, north of Virginia, is an effort by The Bumgardner Architects to jumble together townhouses, arcades, shops, textures, and a slope-roofed condo tower and make it look like a longtime Market fixture: it demonstrates how hard that is to do.

Pioneer Square. Like the Market, the interest here is in the overall urban design, rather than the individual buildings. The design is so strong because most of the Square was rebuilt according to the dictates of one man, Elmer Fisher, an otherwise obscure architect who happened to be in town right after the great fire of 1889. Fisher put up dozens of buildings with the same overripe Romantic-Romanesque style, kept them relatively low (so the sun gets into the streets), and generally unified the streetscape. The area went into a long decline after 1920, so most of the buildings avoided the wrecking ball: there wasn't enough interest in the area to prompt demolition and new building. When Pioneer Square was rediscovered as a gallery district in the 1960s, Seattle suddenly had one of the nation's few extensive and stylistically consistent "old towns."

The Pioneer Building, facing on Pioneer Square (a triangle), is Fisher's gaudiest work: each floor has a different scheme for windows, while the rough-stone grand entrance arch is the unifying trademark of Fisher's work in the Square. Look inside at the grand skylighted atrium. The Maynard Building, on the northwest corner of First S and S Washington, is only three years younger (1892), but it shows how the more severe Chicago style was just coming to town, along with Sullivan-like tracery in the spandrels. The Smith Tower, Yesler Way and Second, was the highest building west of the Mississippi for years after it was built in 1914; it has a kind of goofy, off-kilter Siennese grandeur that endears it to the locals, and the shiny brass-and-marble interior is quite splendid.

Waterfront. The Aquarium, just north of Waterfront Park, provides an intricate weave of ramps and odd-angle views of the fish before you emerge (as if by fish ladder) to a splendid topside view of Elliott Bay; the architect is Fred Bassetti. Waterfront Center, inland from the Viaduct between Madison and Seneca, is a very ambitious project by a Weyerhaeuser development subsidiary, Cornerstone, that is reviving old buildings and erecting new ones to create a four-block neighborhood of apartments, shops, offices, restaurants, and a hotel. The major new buildings, particularly Watermark Tower at Spring and First, by The Bumgardner Architects, show a bold use of contextual principles (the tower echoes the Seattle Tower, uptown, and the terra cotta facing of many Seattle office buildings) and a post-modernist fondness for color and decoration. The entire project, the creation of Paul Schell, is one of the most visionary and sensitive efforts at reviving a large part of a city, at human scale, anywhere in the nation.

Downtown. As with other parts of the city, the downtown is more admirable for its generally unified massing and beige-to-white color harmony than for any outstanding buildings. The Seattle Tower, 1218 Third Avenue, is a 1928 masterpiece with great artistry in the massing of the piers and the brickwork. Rainier Tower, Fifth Avenue and University, by Minoru Yamasaki, draws gawks because of the pencil-point base; but the structure deserves praise for the way it opens up views of the surrounding older buildings (especially the handsome Skinner Building on Fifth), echoes another Yamasaki tower, the IBM Building, southeast across the intersection, and fits in with an elegant set of interlocking white boxes which form the shopping arcade on the rest of the block. Freeway Park, Sixth and Seneca, by Lawrence Halprin & Associates, is a wonderful idea (lidding a freeway) carried out with great skill: the concrete waterfall provides an imitation of the Cascades and serves also to drown out auto noise. The 1111 Third Avenue Building, by Gerald Gerron of The McKinley Architects, is one of the more interesting downtown office towers: the facade is given interest by seemingly peeling off, and the window patterns contradict the support columns seen behind them; the miniature courtyard, with glass pavilions, is especially successful. Seattle First National Bank Building, Fourth and Madison, is a nationally praised essay in modernism by Seattle's big architectural firm, NBBJ. It is sleek and well-detailed, but the windswept plaza is not even redeemed by a fine Henry Moore sculpture. Since downtown Seattle is built on sloping streets, one of its design problems is how to meet sharply inclined streets: the best solution is Fred Bassetti and John Graham's Federal Office Building, Second and Marion, with outside plazas decorated with local sculpture and steps cascading down the south side, reminiscent of Rome's Spanish Steps.

Seattle Center, Denny Regrade. The Regrade has little of architectural interest, though the eye is drawn to the chisel-topped Fourth and Blanchard Building, a truncated knock-off of Philip Johnson's Pennzoil Place in Houston. Elmer Fisher's small remaining imprint on the Regrade is the Bell Building, 2326 First Avenue, and his Barnes Building just south. Seattle Center has its famous Space Needle, designed by John Graham with the assistance of Seattle's leading architectural gadfly, Victor Steinbrueck; it is certainly one of the few graceful sky-restaurants yet constructed. The Pacific Science Center, by Yamasaki, is a gothic-overlay arrangement of white pavilions around a water courtyard—odd, but well-liked. Paul Thiry, a leading internationalist pioneer in Seattle, designed the overall plan for the Center, a recycled World's Fair site, and his powerful Coliseum, with a swooping, umbrella-like roof, is one of the best legacies of the build-it-quick Fair.

A few driving and walking tours:

First Hill, with old mansions from the first-families days nestling amid condo towers and expanding hospital empires, makes for a fine stroll with outstanding views over the city to the harbor. Start at Boren and University (at the Sunset Club, 1916) and head east on University; turn south at Minor and you come to the Stimson-Green mansion of 1899 at 1204 Minor, the work of society architect Kirtland K. Cutter of Spokane. Now turn west on Spring Street, passing by the Hafins House of 1902 at 1104 Spring, in Venetian Gothic style (it is now the Roman Catholic Archbishop's residence). Turn south on Terry Avenue and walk to the Hotel Sorrento, an Italianate structure of 1908 now handsomely restored as a hotel. Also of note on First Hill is the Yesler Terrace Housing Project, Yesler and Broadway, a marvelous complex of low-rent public housing built under the direction of Jesse Epstein in 1941: it is one of the rare housing projects that is simple, well-landscaped, respectful of privacy, and dignified. A comparable project is at 1800 36th Avenue S, tucked into a ravine near Lake Washington. Here Ellsworth Storey put up a set of small cottages in 1916 to prove imagination could go into low-cost housing. Both these projects exemplify Seattle's fine tradition of architecture with a social conscience.

Capitol Hill. Start at E Roy and Broadway E, where there is a lovely little stone shopping courtyard by Arthur Loveless. Now head west on Roy, past the Spanishy Cornish School (once home of Seattle's one true artistic circle) to Belmont Avenue E, turning north. At this corner you can see some of Fred Anhalt's revivalist apartments (710, 730, 750 Belmont E), among the most coveted in the city. Follow Belmont to its end, noting the handsome mansions on the western side. Bear around to the right and follow E Prospect to Harvard Avenue E; then turn south and follow Harvard back to E Roy. The Merrill House, at 919 Harvard, by Charles A. Platt, is a formalist masterwork from 1910 that is Platt's only building on the West Coast. All along this street you can see an intermix of styles, outstanding craftsmanship, and the jumble of social strata that typify Seattle residential neighborhoods at their best. A detour at E Prospect is to continue eastward until you come to Federal Avenue E, another glorious street for homes: swing north until E Highland Drive, and then cut up the hill into Volunteer Park. You'll come out at the top of the hill at the Seattle Art Museum, an elegant Moderne work of 1932 by Carl Gould, another leading architect in the city. Across the plaza from SAM is a fine piece of granite sculpture by Isamu Noguchi, *Black Sun*. The jewelbox museum, the lovely Victorian park designed by the Olmsted brothers, and the powerful sculpture focusing the eye on the distant harbor create a very moving composition of styles.

Denny Blaine. This lovely section is dotted with homes by Seattle's finest architect, Ellsworth Storey, an individualistic designer in the turn-of-the-century Craftsman mode. Start at Epiphany Church, E Denny Way and Madrona Place E, with a chapel by Storey; head north on Madrona Place E to see a Storey house at 123; turn west at E John, to see two Storey houses at 219 and 221 36th Avenue E, and a Paul Thiry contemporary work at 3410 E John; go north on 35th and east on E Thomas, joining Dorffel Drive E and turning south; Storey houses are at 232 Dorffel and the famous couplet of his houses at 260 and 270—Storey himself lived at 260; the road swings back, via Maiden Lane, to your starting place.

Queen Anne. Start at the Betty Bowen viewpoint, Highland Drive and Seventh Avenue W, and walk east along Highland to admire the mansions and the view of the city and Sound below. The Black House at 220 W Highland is by Andrew Willatsen, a disciple of Frank Lloyd Wright who brought a few specimens from the Prairie School style to Seattle.

University of Washington. Start at the Central Plaza, known as Red Square, a Sienna-inspired essay in Brutalism by Kirk/Wallace/McKinley; other notable buildings are the Faculty Center, by Paul Hayden Kirk and Victor Steinbrueck, in strict modernism, and Condon Hall (the law school) on NE Campus Parkway, a distinguished design by the famous Romaldo Giurgola; the library is particularly beautiful.

Mercer Island is the best place to see outstanding examples of the contemporary Northwest style, and the circuit along W Mercer Way to E Mercer Way is a lovely drive to soak up the Northwest residential mystique. You'll find homes by Wendell

191

Lovett, a marvelously inventive designer, at 7545 E Mercer Way and 5003 E Mercer Way; Paul Hayden Kirk, at 2711 60th Avenue SE, 7829 W Mercer Way, and 4458 Ferncroft Road (with a Lovett house just north of it); Hobbs/Fukui, at 5411 96th Avenue SE; and Ralph Anderson, at 6007 79th Avenue SE.

Hilltop on the east side of Lake Washington is the place to finish your pilgrimage, a complex of homes built mostly in the 1950s by many prominent architects: Perry Johanson, Jack Morse, Fred Bassetti, Paul Hayden Kirk, and Wendell Lovett. To get there, take 150th Avenue SE from I-90, following the road to the top of the hill. The homes display the feeling for landscape, indoor-outdoor continuity, humanized modernism, and the searching for light and views that came together in a once-distinctive "Northwest School."

Green Seattle — Parks

Seattle's 5,000 acres of parks, green throughout the year and abundant with flowers and trees, are one of the city's most distinctive attractions. They range from the classical mode with Capitol Hill's Volunteer Park and the University of Washington's Arboretum, to recreational Meccas at Green Lake and Alki Beach Park, to the mature forests of outlying parks at Fauntleroy, Carkeek, and Seward, to unusual and innovative newer parks such as those crafted over a freeway, an old railway track, a disused gasworks, or over the water itself.

The city's first park was established in 1884 with a five-acre donation by pioneer David Denny. In the early 1900s the nationally famous park planners, the Olmsted brothers, devised an ambitious parks plan for Seattle, comprised of major parks in all corners of the city to be linked by tree-lined boulevards, designed to sweep west to Golden Gardens, east to Green Lake, Ravenna, and the University, south along Lake Washington to Seward Park from where they were to branch north to Jefferson Park and to West Seattle and Alki Beach Park. Each park was given its own special feel: the central parks "neat and smooth" and the remote parks more "wild." Their plan also conceived of neighborhood mini-park playgrounds to be provided within one and a half miles of every house.

While their proposals to annex a great many new parks were not achieved immediately and the boulevards only partly completed, there has been a tremendous growth in parklands over the last 80 years, particularly during the 1960s with large bond investments. Today's parks system now greatly resembles the Olmsted vision and Seattle is justly proud of this legacy. In addition, the city's mild, moist climate has made gardening and horticultural design a local obsession.

L5 **Freeway Park** Sixth & Seneca

Freeway Park functions as a much-needed backyard for Seattle's downtown office-dwellers. Perched on a lid above the I-5 freeway, the seven-year-old park over a noisy freeway caused many skeptical comments in its early days but its popularity is now well established. One popular custom is to eat lunch by the rushing waterfall of the Canyon or by the Great Box Garden with its colorful seasonal flowers and lush green vines spilling casually over the garden beds. The upper level of the park is rather sparsely landscaped.

Q6 **Hing Hay Park** S King & Maynard S

A red-brick square with an ornate grand pavilion, Hing Hay Park is a meeting and gathering place for the International District's large Asian community. An enormous multicolored mural of a dragon (on the adjacent Bush Hotel) peers down on the park.

Kobe Terrace
Seventh S between S Main & S Washington

Named after Seattle's sister city in Japan, the delicately terraced hillside of Kobe Terrace, adorned with Mount Fuji cherry trees and ground vines, serves as a graphic example of the Japanese use of space. Even though it adjoins the noisy I-5 freeway, the park's winding pathways and superb viewpoints create a separate little world.

Waterfall Gardens   Second S & S Main

One of Seattle's smallest parks and one of its most unusual, Waterfall Gardens consists of a waterfall spilling over huge rocks in a cool grotto just off a street corner in Pioneer Square. While the concept may seem somewhat out of place among the period architecture of Seattle's old town, the park provides a secure and secluded rest spot, amid attractive design.

Myrtle Edwards Park   Alaskan Way, north of Pier 70

Merging almost unnoticeably into Elliott Bay Park just north along the waterfront, this pleasant green haven for city strollers and picnickers is also popular with joggers. A provocative concrete-and-granite sculpture, "Adjacent Against Upon," is an added feature. Parking is at a premium, but the Waterfront Streetcar stops inside the park.

Volunteer Park   15th E & E Prospect

Volunteer Park is like a stately dowager who holds court among the mansions on North Capitol Hill and commands a sweeping westward view across her moat, actually a reservoir, to Puget Sound and the Olympic Mountains. One of Seattle's oldest parks, Volunteer Park offers a feast of activities for the inner-city resident. The Seattle Art Museum's main collection (see Arts chapter for details) is housed in a striking Art Deco building on the park's central concourse; the conservatory with its three large greenhouses filled with exotic flora is free to the public and open every day from 9 to 5 (625-4043); and the old water tower offers an even grander panorama from its observation deck 75 feet above the park. A bandstand provides the location for many open-air concerts, and a children's play area in the northeast corner is another popular spot.

Washington Park/Arboretum
E Madison & Lake Washington Blvd E

Park open Every day from dawn to dusk
Visitor Center: 8-5 Mon-Fri; 10-5 Sun
April & May
543-8800

The gently sloping, wooded parkland of the Arboretum is a delight for serious park-goers as well as lovers who picnic under the many flowering trees. A degree in botany or Latin helps in identifying the 5,500 species of trees, shrubs, vines, and flowers from all over the world. The Arboretum jointly serves as a botanical research center for the University of Washington and as a public park filled with groves of rhododendron, azaleas, ornamental cherries, magnolias, maple, ashes, birches, and countless other temperate plants. The Arboretum Foundation and the Northwest Ornamental Horticultural Society, the two main support groups of the Arboretum, also sponsor tours, classes, and plant sales (call 325-4510 for information). There is a Japanese Tea Garden replete with a classical tea house, delicate ornamental plants, intricate rockeries, and tranquil pools. The marsh and island area, a haven for wildlife, canoeists, swimmers, fishermen, and peace lovers, is at the north end. This little sanctuary is actually a strange mixture of wilderness and "civilization" with the huge concrete pillars of freeway ramps mingling with the wildlife.

The Lake Washington Parks
Madrona, Leschi, Frink, Colman, Mount Baker, Lake Washington

A drive through Seattle's neighborhood parks dotted along the shores of Lake Washington is a very popular diversion. After leaving the Arboretum, Lake Washington Boulevard winds its way through the leafy suburb of Washington Park and on its curvilinear course past magnificent redwoods and cedar. Natural forest gives way to stately homes again, while little pockets of green dot street corners and splendid mansions sport exquisite gardens.

The first beachside park you will come to, Madrona Park, casually sprawls its grassy lawns beside the water. A hive of activity in the summer (as are all the beach parks), Madrona also has a thriving dance studio (625-4303). Continuing on the Boulevard, which runs alongside the water now, you will be treated by a burst of color at the Leschi Marina, home for the neighborhood's many sailing boats. Follow Lake Washington Boulevard as it veers right slightly and you'll drive under a delightful old stone bridge going nowhere in particular, and past a secluded tennis court. You then wind through the giant trees and voracious vines that are Frink Park, yet another wildlife haven only a couple of miles from downtown. Turn left on 35th and return to Lakeside Avenue, which soon passes under the Mercer Island Bridge and on to Colman and Mount Baker parks. Mount Baker Park snakes inland here with its undulating meadows and delicate fruit trees.

As you continue south you have an unrestricted view of the lake all the way to Seward Park and perhaps even a vista of Mount Rainier on a clear day. At one of the bends near another marina you may want to park and feed the ducks and geese—Canadian honkers love this part of the lake in summer. Continuing on, look across the reeds to the massive promontory of Seward Park, with majestic trees and grassy picnic grounds.

JJ5 ## Seward Park
Lake Washington Boulevard S & S Juneau

This glacier-carved, foot-shaped piece of land jutting out into Lake Washington has many personalities. On misty winter days, you can enjoy Seward with a solitary walk by the quietly lapping lake, and only a few bird cries breaking the silence. On hot summer days, Seward becomes a loud assemblage of music and barbecued hamburgers and ribs. There's a fine swimming beach and sunbathing lawn by the bathhouse near the entrance to the park. The bathhouse also houses Seward Park Art Studio (723-5780), part of the City Art Works program, which offers classes in pottery, painting, photography, and a host of other arts and crafts. A small loop road and southern access road, both with parking, open onto picnic meadows with lots of barbecue pits and picnic shelters (call 625-4671 for reservations). Even in the summer you can escape the crowds and cars by taking the two-and-a-half-mile lakeside trail encircling the park, or by exploring the forest preserve with its centuries-old Douglas fir, red cedar, and maples.

KK9 ## Lincoln Park   Fauntleroy SW & SW Webster

Lincoln Park is the quintessential multi-purpose park for thriving West Seattle and may be a well-kept secret from other Seattleites. Perched on a bluff overlooking Puget Sound just north of the Fauntleroy Terminal (where you catch a ferry to Vashon Island), Lincoln Park is amazingly diverse for its size. Its facilities include picnic shelters; numerous playfields; an outdoor, saltwater, heated swimming pool'; a children's play area; and lots of ocean beach to explore. It also offers the opportunity for quiet exploration and reflection: its benches face the Sound and the Olympic Mountains, and its network of bicycle and walking paths winds through groves of fir, madrona, cedar, and redwoods.

Touring Seattle

I9   Alki Beach   Alki Ave SW

This two-and-a-half-mile strip of beach running along Puget Sound at the edge of West Seattle has many moods, depending on the season: cool and peaceful in the fall, stormy in winter, and jammed with sunbathers and roller-skaters in the summer. The sandiest of all the saltwater beaches, it is also the most popular, especially with teenagers, who "cruise" the adjacent Alki Avenue strip regularly. Duwamish Head, at the north end of the strand, offers spectacular views.

F7   Gasworks Park   N Northlake Way & Meridian N

Looming, dark towers and a huge mound of grassy hillside combine to make a grimy old gas plant into a distinctive city park. There are spectacular views across Lake Union to the downtown Seattle skyline, a flotilla of colorful kites dancing above the mound, dozens of picnickers barbecuing under the enormous picnic shelter (call 625-4671 to reserve space), and kids playing among the gaily colored gasworks artifacts in the huge playbarn. Gasworks Park is an inspired example of urban reclamation conceived in the spirit of old amusement parks but with many new uses as well.

F7   Burke Gilman Trail
B5   From Gasworks Park to Kenmore Log Boom Park

A relatively recent addition to Seattle's parks network, the Burke Gilman Trail provides a lush corridor of green from Gasworks Park on Lake Union, through the leafy University of Washington, and all along Lake Washington to its northern tip at Kenmore's Log Boom Park. The 12.5-mile path is built over a disused railway and offers a delightfully scenic route past lakeside homes, groves of old trees and blackberry vines, and alongside neighborhood parks like the family-oriented Matthews Beach Park. An excursion on the trail reveals a community on the move —bicyclists of all shapes and persuasions, joggers, walkers, and strollers. Bicyclists often continue on to the Sammamish River Trail via a short stretch on Bothell Way.

EE7   Green Lake
Latona N & E Green Lake Dr N

When the sun shines and the jogging, tanning, and roller-skating crowd musters in mass, Green Lake seems like a slice of Southern California beamed to the button-down Northwest. Even on the dreariest winter days there's a steady stream of joggers and bicyclists on the three-mile lake circuit. What's now the center of Seattle exercise culture is the remnant of a large glacial lake, well on its way to vanishing into meadowland when the pioneers arrived (hence the name). The city eventually scrapped plans to turn it into a golf course or storm drain for I-5 and decided to bolster its declining waters with surplus from city reservoirs. Though the Adidas and Walkman perambulators now dominate, Green Lake offers a host of other pleasures: the Bathhouse Theater (good performances at family prices—see the Arts chapter), sailing, tennis, fishing, picnicking, swimming (the water is balmy compared to the shivery Sound and even to Lake Union), and of course duck- and people-watching. The commercial district around Ravenna and Green Lake Drive, next to the park and beach facilities, is also a sort of urban mini-beach resort with a host of sports stores offering equipment for rental or sale, and restaurants and snack bars catering to athletes' appetites.

EE7   Woodland Park   *Zoo hours: 8:30-sunset Every day; 625-2244*
N 55th & Phinney N   *$2.50 adults, $1 13-17 years,*
(west zoo entrance)   *$.50 6-12 years, under 6 free with adult*

FF7

The focus of Woodland Park is the **zoo**, one of the best in the country. Major emphasis is given to providing natural and healthy environments for the animals and

195

good viewing points and pleasant surroundings for visitors. Under its dynamic director, David Hancocks, the zoo is well on its way to fulfilling its master plan, which is the simulation of bioclimactic zones from around the world. The lush tropical forests for gorillas, apes, and lion-tailed macaques, and the large, wide-open rolling African savannah are major attractions. The savannah is particularly impressive: zebras and giraffes, patas monkeys, hippos, and lions all have their own areas but the barriers between them are carefully concealed, as are covered enclosures where the animals can be brought in from the cold, fed, and doctored. This is definitely state-of-the-art stuff where both the animals and people win. The children's zoo is another wonderful place where human youngsters can meet the offspring of other species during supervised sessions. Other fun summertime activities for kids include pony and hay rides and animal presentations in the open-air theater.

Woodland Park owes its character to an Englishman, Guy Phinney, who transformed the land into a private estate complete with formal rose garden, bandstand, a small zoo, and intricate pathways. Unfortunately, in a burst of urban expansion in the '30s, a six-lane highway, Aurora Avenue, was plowed through the middle of this tranquil setting. Today, the western half houses the zoo, the Poncho Children's Theater (see the Arts chapter), the still-magnificent rose garden, which is most colorful from late May through August, and picnic areas. The east side is mainly an informal picnic park that also has a variety of sporting facilities, including lawn bowling, a pitch-and-putt golf course, tennis courts, and athletic fields.

FF9	**Discovery Park**	*Visitor Center hours 8:30-5 Tues-Sun,*
	36th W & W Government Way	*closed Mon*
		625-4636

Seattle's largest park, Discovery Park is full of variety and even a little mystery—in 1982 a cougar was "discovered" and no one knows how it got there or how long it resided in the park's 520 acres. Once an Army base, the park is slowly growing over its military buildings and is now a haven for nature lovers. You'll find grassy meadows, dunes and steep sea cliffs, rocky and sandy beaches, and woods (some with self-guided nature trails). A fine way to explore the park is by taking the 2.8-mile loop. The Park's Ranger-Naturalists also offer an exciting range of nature walks and wildlife courses for adults, children, and whole families, and the Daybreak Star Arts Center (285-4425, hours 9-4:30 Mon-Fri, noon-4pm Sat & Sun) offers a chance to view some fine examples of Native American arts and crafts. The kids' playground boasts one of the most thrilling slide rides in town, not to mention great climbing and swinging equipment. There are also extensive picnicking areas, playfields, and a rigorous health path.

DD8	**Carkeek Park**	NW 110th off Greenwood N

Carkeek Park is 180 acres of wilderness perched at the northwest corner of the city. You can follow forest paths from the parking lots and picnic areas to the footbridge spanning the railroad tracks and then down a staircase to the broad beach. Extra caution is required around the railroad tracks since frequent trains run through the park and the acoustics on the curving beach can be misleading. The beach's views of the Sound and distant Olympic Mountains complement Carkeek's willow-shaded Piper Creek Trail and massed rhododendrons.

II4	**Luther Burbank Park**	2040 84th SE, Mercer Island

A delightful grassy park on the northern tip of Mercer Island, Luther Burbank's rolling green fields (great for sunning) tumble onto a sandy beach. Its extensive picnic facilities, first-rate playground, tennis courts, skateboard trails, fishing pier, and moorage make it a favorite family park.

J2 Kelsey Creek Park   455-6885
Entrance at SE Fourth Place & 130th SE, Bellevue

With its meandering creek running through wooded hillsides and open grassy fields, Kelsey Creek Park provides a variety of parkland spaces for the enjoyment of the Bellevue community. Children love to visit the farmyard and barn in the spring, where they can see newborn calves, ponies, piglets, lambs, and goats. Open grassy areas are just right for family picnics, while the creek's bolder path runs in a more wooded marshy area where, at dusk, it's fun to use flashlights to spy on raccoons and bullfrogs. A community pottery studio and a delicate Japanese garden with numerous wooden footbridges spanning the creek round out the park's offerings.

F2 Bridle Trails State Park
116th Ave NE & NE 60th St, Kirkland

Bridle Trails State Park is a heavily wooded outpost for horselovers in the Greater Seattle area. In fact, the whole community surrounding the park is infatuated with equestrian pursuits: there are numerous stables, which breed, board, and rent horses, dozens of homes with horses in their backyards, and the pleasant spectacle of people riding by on horseback. The park itself has an exercise ring and plenty of trails winding through its dense forest; one horse-and-hiking trail links up with Marymoor Park. Plenty of picnic sites, too.

F1 Marymoor County Park
6046 W Lake Sammamish Parkway NE, Redmond

A huge expanse of flat grasslands and playfields, Marymoor Park is located in rural Redmond, aptly named the bicycle capital of the Northwest. Marymoor has the area's only velodrome and serves as the start or finish point for the Sammamish River bike, jogging, and horse trail. The Park also hosts a wide variety of other activities: a historical museum and fine-arts center, picnic facilities, exercise course, a pea patch, model-airplane area, and a wealth of playing fields.

F1 Sammamish River Trail
From Marymoor Park to near Bothell Landing

A bicyclist's dream, the flat Sammamish River Trail hugs the quietly moving little river as it meanders through the wide, open Sammamish Valley. Occasional racers skillfully zip past family groups out for a sunny Sunday-afternoon ride. You'll also see diligent joggers, horse riders on their own track, lovers out for a quiet stroll, and occasionally even wheelchair riders. Other people fish or enjoy the river in a canoe or raft. The Chateau Ste. Michelle Winery (just off the trail at NE 145th St) is nestled in 87 acres of manicured lawns and colorful flower gardens, and makes the winery a delightful place to enjoy a picnic. Wines, cheeses, and other delicacies can be bought at the Chateau, and tours and complimentary tastings are also offered.

BB2 Bothell Landing   9929 NE 180th, Bothell

A quaint little community park on the Sammamish River near the northern edge of the Sammamish River Trail, Bothell Landing offers rolling green lawns for family picnics and Frisbee-throwing, an amphitheater, an historical museum housed in a turn-of-the-century frame building, and a nearby old-fashioned ice-cream parlor for treats. Canoes and small boats can tie up at the public pier where there are friendly ducks just waiting to be fed.

DD4 Juanita Beach   Juanita Dr NE & NE 97th

Juanita Beach is on Lake Washington on the northeast side (about five miles south of Bothell; five miles north of Bellevue). This large, shallow, sandy beach is extremely popular with families, particularly those with small children. Parking is plentiful and the beach is wheelchair-accessible.

HH3 **Chism Beach**	**1175 96th SE, Bellevue**
The largest of Bellevue's developed beach parks, sandy Chism Beach features docks and diving boards for swimmers, plenty of picnic areas, a playground, and a large parking area above the beach.	

Green Seattle — Gardens

The mild maritime climate and plentiful rainfall of the Greater Seattle area have created a lush environment where a wide variety of vegetation proliferates. "Proliferate" is the operative word. Diligent gardeners alternately rejoice and despair at the fecundity of flora here. The whole region benefits from a warm Japanese current so that it avoids the harsh winters typical of many areas at such a northern latitude. In fact, the climate closely resembles that of southern England, and local gardeners have profited well from England's successful development of better and more varied garden plants.

This is one of the world's most famous centers of rhododendron culture and rock gardening. Superb examples of azaleas, camellias, roses, magnolias, ornamental Japanese flowering cherries, and dogwoods are also found in great quantities. Not to be forgotten, of course, are the native conifers, notably the massive Douglas fir, hemlock, and majestic cedar. And the area abounds in a wide variety of bulbs in the spring; the Skagit Valley, just an hour's drive north of Seattle, is a center for commercial daffodil and tulip bulbs and a feast for the eye in March and April. Springtime is probably the best time to be in Seattle, when new plants or trees come into bloom every couple of weeks. There are several winter-blooming cherries which herald, with great delicacy, the coming of spring. February and March mark the real beginning of this colorful season with huge camellias blushing, flowering cherries of every hue, and pure white pear trees. April and May belong to the rhododendrons and azaleas. Roses take over as spring warms into summer, a season which reveals the rich variety of greens so prevalent in the Northwest's vegetation.

You can while away many a fine Sunday afternoon exploring the area's private gardens. Here are a few suggestions to get you going.

The Madison Park and Washington Park area with their neat little homes and grander mansions sport a spectacular cascade of soft blossoms in the springtime.

GG6 Take Madison from downtown and, after passing Broadmoor, turn right on McGilvra, perhaps the finest street in the city for spring regalia. Thirty-sixth Avenue E is also impressive for its elm trees. The Magnolia area overlooking

GG9 Puget Sound is another fine place to explore, both for its superb views of the city, Mount Rainier, and the Olympics, and for its neatly maintained gardens and rockeries. Topiary is also a popular art form here. Laurelhurst (to the northeast of

EE5 the University of Washington) is yet another bastion of the upper middle class where one can be sure of fine, upstanding gardens and well-manicured lawns. A drive along the bus route (start at NE 45th near the University Village) will reveal the subtle tones of the cream-and-magenta magnolias, and more cherries and

FF6 rhododendrons. Battelle Institute (4000 NE 41st St) also has a delightful little park complete with pond. Mercer Island offers a more Northwest woodsy feel with its

II4 large modern homes tucked amongst Douglas fir and cedar. A late-afternoon drive south along E Mercer Way will give you a good feel for the area. For other areas,

KK4 ask at one of the leading nurseries (see Shopping).

Indian Seattle

Before the arrival of white settlers in the 1850s, the Seattle area had been home to a considerable Indian population for thousands of years. During that long period the native people had developed a culture and a comfortable society wonderfully adapted to the natural environment. The land that the pioneers claimed may more accurately be described as a well-tended garden than a wilderness.

In the Greater Seattle area, Indians spent winter months with their stores of food in large cedarboard longhouses built near the waterfront. During the rest of the year, the people travelled from camp to camp, harvesting grains, berries, and fruit. When the clams fattened on the beaches, the salmon swarmed upstream, or the waterfowl crowded the lakes and bays, hundreds of Indians would gather to set up great nets and fish weirs. At such gatherings, noble families would recite myths which told how their heroes had subdued the monstrous forces of nature, so that the people could prosper in a dark and beautiful land. Many of the myths dwelt upon features of the land, such as hillocks and beach boulders, that are virtually ignored today, but were once extraordinary talismans where the powers that animated the world could be approached and even manipulated.

When the whites arrived, the peaceful native culture was destroyed by epidemics and the removal of the native people to reservations. But in fields such as art, in environmental consciousness, and in their celebration of a marvelous heritage, they still exert an influence on Northwest society and on the city named for Chief Seattle.

FF6 **Burke Museum** (543-5590). The institution that has done the most to preserve the native cultures of the Northwest Coast is the University of Washington, especially the Burke Museum. Its ethnographic collections from the British Columbian and Alaskan coasts are not as extensive as those at the Provincial Museum in Victoria or the University of British Columbia's anthropology museum, but they are outstanding and intelligently displayed. Most artworks made by the Puget Sound peoples, however, are in museums in the East. With the interests of the Museum's staff directed mostly outside Washington, the local field fell to the regional colleges, whose archaeologists and students have gained fame with their discovery of "Marmes Man" in the Columbia Basin, the Manis Mastodon Site near Port Angeles, and the finds at Ozette on the Pacific Coast, the "American Pompeii." Still, the great heraldic poles and canoes, the masks and rattles, and the beautiful baskets at the Burke are of great interest, and the Museum has added several cases of interesting pieces from the Columbia River area. Fine native baskets are on sale in the gift shop.

FF9 **Daybreak Star** (285-4425). The continuing Native American presence in the Seattle area is best seen at the Daybreak Star Arts and Culture Center in Discovery Park. The services provided are primarily educational, designed for native children on and off the reservations. The Center also seeks to educate the general public about the art and traditions of the Native American peoples. The Center holds a dinner-theater, generally on every other Friday evening, with native dances and fashion. An Indian Art Mart on the second Saturday of every month sells various native arts and crafts, and the public can also observe native artists at work.

C7 **Pacific Science Center** (625-9333). The longhouse there is a replica of a Haida longhouse; inside are exhibits detailing aspects of the Northwest Coast culture, and occasional demonstrations of native tool-making techniques and other skills.

Suquamish. In late Summer the Suquamish people hold their "**Chief Seattle Days**" celebration at Suquamish on the Port Madison Indian Reservation, continuing a tradition passed down to them by their ancestors: singing, dancing, canoe racing, and gambling, while salmon is cooked over pits of alder wood. Any time during the year, the public can visit the site of Old Man House at Suquamish, where a small replica of one section of the house has been rebuilt in the old manner.

The new **Suquamish Museum** within the Tribal Center is devoted to studying and displaying Puget Sound Salish Indian artifacts. Its opening exhibit deals with Chief Seattle and his times. (Open 10-5 Mon-Fri; 10-8 Sat & Sun, call 598-3311 for information.) The Tribal Center is located one-quarter mile north of the Agate Pass Bridge on Highway 305. **Chief Seattle's grave** can be found nearby, on the grounds of the Catholic Mission Church.

For galleries of Native American art see that section under gallery listings in the Arts chapter.

Notable Native American sites:

N8 **Jijila'lich, "little crossing-place."** A native village existed at the site of Pioneer Square, once the commercial hub of white Seattle.

Skwuduks, "below the point." At a native clamming beach and campsite just east of Duwamish Head, Seattle's pioneers first met Chief Seattle in 1851.

LL9 **Psaiya'hus, "where there is an aya'hos."** A supernatural site on the beach at Fauntleroy Cove, south of the Vashon ferry, where a reddish beach boulder was once thought to be an aya'hos, a horn-headed serpent believed to cause earthquakes and avalanches. (Between Fauntleroy-Vashon ferry dock and Brace Point.)

MM6 **Kula'had, "the barrier."** On the Duwamish River south of Boeing Field, near the community of Duwamish, was the home of the great seasonal myths of the Duwamish and their Puget Salish neighbors. This was the site of the climactic struggle between the icy wind of the north and the warm, wet wind from the south (which announced the return of the salmon) that established the cycle of the seasons and inaugurated the human era. The stone remains of the mythic ice fish-weir can still be seen on the east bank of the river. (Next to the old Duwamish Drive-in Theatre where the Pacific Highway S Bridge crosses the Duwamish River.)

MM6 **Sbabade'el "the little mountain."** The center of the world is a rocky hill on the west bank of the river just south of the Kula'had. (Southern abutment of the Pacific Highway S Bridge.)

Su-whee'-whee-wud, "whistling place." The present community of Eliot on the Cedar River, two miles east of Renton, was the site of an important trade mart where people from as far away as British Columbia and Alaska traded slaves and copper for foodstuffs from the Columbia Plateau east of the Cascades. It was later the site of a native settlement, a Catholic Chapel served by Father Chirouse, and a shamanic dance house.

BB5- **Ha'chu, "the lake."** In myth, Lake Washington appears as a great swallowing
MM4 monster that consumed Mercer Island, its heart, each night and yielded it up each morning to daylight.

FF6 **Stetee'chee, "little island."** Foster Island, at the north end of the Arboretum, was used as a burial ground for the people of Union Bay, the most powerful and numerous group on Lake Washington. The dead were hoisted in boxes into the trees.

J9 **Sh-chapau, "subterranean passage."** On the shore of Elliott Bay beneath the present Seattle Aquarium was a mythical entryway to an underground stream that allowed whales to enter Lake Union.

'*)D7* **Liu'ktid, "colored."** Reddish ooze still flows from Licton Springs in North Seattle, where shamans gathered mud for pigment to paint their paraphernalia. (N 97th & Ashworth Ave N.)

Sa'tsakal, "head of the slough." A village site near the modern community of Factoria, south of Bellevue. Hostile forces gathered from around the Sound and east of the mountains to attack the fledgling community of Seattle in January of 1856, as part of a larger, futile scheme to drive the invading whites out of the area. Along 18th Ave SE, just west of the Factoria Interchange.

Kidstuff

Many of Seattle's major attractions are particularly good places to explore with children, so as a first step, check the city's top 12 attractions, listed in the introduction. There are also a number of special children's attractions sprinkled around the city. Some of these are described below.

Children's Park
Seventh Ave S & S Lane

One of Seattle's newest parks, this one in the International District has been designed to reflect elements of Chinese, Japanese, and Filipino culture. There's a "yin and yang" landscape made of sand and grass, a wonderful dragon sculpture which is both an artwork and a fun playground piece (kids love to slide down its back), and a covered pavilion in the shape of a Japanese umbrella. Even the vegetation is Asian-influenced, and there are some traditional slides and a clatter bridge.

Island Crest Park
Island Crest Way & SE 56th St, Mercer Island

Designed by the Mercer Island Preschool Association, this delightful woodsy area is a hotbed for fantasy for little people. Slides, lean-to's, a huge crocodile that you can crawl in or walk on, trails, and sandboxes are sprinkled throughout trees. Picnic areas are also available.

Other parks which offer some special delights for children include: **Discovery Park**, where ranger naturalists organize special children's nature walks and wildlife classes, and the Daybreak Star Arts Center, which exhibits Native American arts and crafts; **Kelsey Creek Park**, with its farmyard of baby animals; and **Green Lake**, the **Arboretum**, several of the **Lake Washington beaches**, and **Bothell Landing**, for their gregarious ducks and geese who just love to be fed. Some especially nice playgrounds can be found at **Luther Burbank Park, Discovery Park, Volunteer Park,** and **Green Lake**, while **Gasworks Park** has a covered playbarn. See the Parks and Beaches section for more details.

Seattle Junior Theater
158 Thomas
Season: Oct-April
622-7246
Performances at Seattle Center Playhouse; ages: grades 1-6

Seattle Junior Theater has a three-play series—productions for fall, winter, and spring—and is immensely popular.

The Children's Museum
117 Occidental
Ages: 2-10
10-3 Wed-Sat; closed Sun-Tues
624-6192
Admission: $1.25

Hands-on involvement with the displays is happily encouraged. Exhibits change about four times a year and some popular exhibits, particularly the little village and the Victorian house, revolve regularly. Lots of bubble-making apparatus for good clean fun. Great for a rainy day.

Seattle Public Library	625-4992

The Seattle Public Library system has a full calendar of **storytimes** at various branches throughout the city. Call for place, times, and programs.

The **Poncho Theater** is one of the best children's theaters in the country. See the section on theater in the Arts chapter for more details. Other major arts organizations have some special programming for children, too. The **Discover Dance Series** (625-4303) introduces young people to different forms of dance with fully staged one-hour productions; while the **Seattle Symphony** (447-4747) presents the "Musical Galaxy Series" four times a year for younger audiences.

And, finally, there are several other general attractions which by their nature tend to have special interest for children. You should go to the **Seattle Center** via Monorail: even though the ride only lasts a few short minutes, kids are fascinated by it (in fact, you may have to ride back and forth several times from downtown!). Inside the Center there's plenty to entertain, including a ride up the Space Needle (447-3100), the Science Center (382-2887) with its hands-on exhibits, the seven acres of amusement rides at Seattle's resident carnival, the Fun Forest (624-1585). For more details, see Emmett Watson's section on the Seattle Center, and the 12 top attractions in the Introduction. When hunger strikes, the Center House has an ethnic kaleidoscope of foods.

Other in-town activities which fascinate kids are the **Underground Tours** (682-1164 or 682-1511), or a boat ride with **Seattle Harbor Tours** (623-1445; see Commercial Tour section). The waterfront streetcars (see Transportation section) are another popular attraction, while the Sports chapter has more fun activities for kids.

If you're into family fishing fun there are several convenient places you can go to get your feet wet. In all cases, tackle and bait are provided and no license is required. You pay by the inch or the number of fish you catch. And they clean them, too.

Ferncroft Springs Trout Farm and Hatchery	
9050 132nd Ave NE, Redmond	*822-1161*
Gold Creek Trout Farm	*483-1415*
15844 148th NE, Woodinville	
Lil Bit O' Heaven	*883-1654*
16636 NE 40th, Redmond	*$1 adults; $.50 children*
Springbrook Trout Farm	*852-0360*
19225 Talbot Rd S, Renton	

Other out-of-town family adventures could include: visiting **Northwest Trek** (832-6116), a native wildlife park on the way to Mount Rainier (see Mount Rainier tour for more details); a ride on the **Puget Sound Railway** for a run to the top of Snoqualmie Falls Gorge (888-3030; see Eastside tour for more details).

For more information on current kids' activities, get a copy of *Seattle's Child* (322-2594), a monthly newspaper devoted to the concerns of the city's younger population.

Commercial tours — Boat

| Anchor Excursions | 4250 21st W | 282-8368 |

Anchor Excursions provides a variety of excellent cruises around Puget Sound. They've a proven track record of marine education programs in the schools.

| Seahawk Sailing Tours | | 343-9480 |

Seahawk Sailing Tours sells luxury: a 40-foot Valiant sailboat, expensively appointed, for two-hour to all-day cruises of Puget Sound. The boat holds up to 26 people.

| Seattle Harbor Tours | | 623-1445 |

These boat tours, leaving from Pier 56, are excellent. The level of information imparted on the regular tour, which includes a lot of the working waterfront, is truly impressive—not the usual unbroken stream of groaning puns—and the harbor is not only busy, it is gorgeous on most days. The trips run daily May - Oct; call for times. Costs are $3.50 for adults, $1.50 for kids 5-11, children under 5 go free.

| Tillicum Village Tours | | 623-1445 |

Another popular tour is the boat excursion to Tillicum Village on Blake Island. An authentic (but somewhat touristy) Indian-style salmon bake in a traditional cedar longhouse is the highlight of the four-hour excursion. Other features include interpretive dances, artifacts and crafts displays, and nature trails. Blake Island, now a marine state park, was the birthplace of Chief Seattle. Tour times vary depending on the day and season. Call for information. Cost: $22 adults, $9 children.

| Virginia V Foundation | 911 Western | 624-9119 |

Virginia V offers cruises on the grand old steamer to Poulsbo–Suquamish Tribal Center ($15), north and south Puget Sound ($5–$7.50), and to Everett–Marysville–Port Townsend ($15).

Wind Works Sailing School and Charters
7001 Seaview NW   784-9386

Offers day-sail excursions, including waterfront tours under sail ($32.50 a person, four hours), sunset sails, and inter-island sails. Reservations required.

Also, if you are interested in chartering a yacht, look under Sailing and Cruising Charters in the Sport chapter.

Commercial tours — Bus

| Gray Line | | 343-2000 |

Gray Line has several standard guided tours, mostly by bus. The tours depart from the Four Seasons Olympic Hotel, with pickups at the Westin Hotel, the Space Needle, Westlake Mall, Pier 57, the Sea-Tac Red Lion/Thunderbird Inn, Sea-Tac Airport, and any downtown hotel with a call beforehand. Tours range from various bus tours around Seattle (including the popular two-hour orientation tour) to a two-hour boat tour between Fisherman's Terminal and Pier 57. Further afield, there are nine-hour bus trips to Mount Rainier and overnight bus trips (May-October) in the North Cascades.

Evergreen Trailways (American Sightseeing of Seattle)
666 S Stewart   624-5813

Evergreen Trailways, the tour arm of the commercial carrier, gives tours called American Sightseeing of Seattle. Trips include city land and lake excursions, a

Boeing plant tour, Tillicum Village, Mount Rainier, and a one-day jaunt to Victoria and the Butchart Gardens. Prices range from $10 to $50.

Commercial tours — Smaller, personalized

Antique Around	523-0917

Antique Around does just that in a choice of three all-day bus tours of notable Seattle and Eastside antique shops and historic mansions, with a one-hour lecture to start off and a stop for snacks and lunch along the way. Beginning mid-June 1983, for groups of 18 or less.

City & Country Tours	282-2301

City & Country Tours arranges unique walking and driving tours of such pleasant spots as Discovery Park/Magnolia, the Arboretum, Leavenworth's "Bavarian Village," and Coupeville/Deception Pass on Whidbey Island. All with meals. Seattle entertainment services also available. Tours cost $20–$100 per person ($8–$27 per person in a group).

DayTours	624-2377

DayTours provides groups and corporate visitors with an excellent alternative to standard tours. Custom trips throughout the Sound, airport greeting service and baggage transfers, a variety of transportation, catering, and introduction to cultural and sports events. Call for fee information.

EcoTrips	382-0900

Zig Zag has recently started offering a series of nature trips around Washington called "EcoTrips." They include jaunts to Mount St. Helens, the Yakima River Canyon, and the Hoh River Valley rainforest.

Emerald City Excursions	631-8232

Emerald City Excursions offers "personalized adventure tours" of Puget Sound: Seattle, Whidbey and Bainbridge islands, Mount Rainier, Mount St. Helens, the Olympic Peninsula, and Victoria. Vans transport groups of up to 10 passengers on these two- to eight-hour trips, $14–$35.

Hokubei Tour & Travel Service	
2033 Sixth Ave	623-9441

Offers Japanese tourists and business people bilingual escort-guide services (deluxe car or chartered bus) for sightseeing and shopping.

Seattle in Style	842-5082

Seattle in Style provides carefully tailored, European-style tours of Seattle, afternoon skiing excursions to Alpental, cozy island and beach picnics, tugboat cruises of Lake Union, and overnights at Sun Mountain Lodge in Winthrop for cross-country skiers. Prices range from $25 to $50 per person for most tours. Also a full-service travel agency.

Commercial tours — Walking

International District Tours	624-6342

Guided by Elizabeth Burke, these tours are an excellent way to learn about the

International District. They are run Monday through Saturday, by reservation only, and last about one and a half hours. They are primarily an exploration on foot of the International District, although they start with a 30-minute slide show about the area's history and end (by special arrangement) at a restaurant. Basic cost is only $2. Group and individual tours are available.

Pike Place Market Tours	625-4764

The Pike Place Preservation and Development Authority offers guided walking tours of the Market every Saturday morning at 9. Signs underneath the Market clock (intersection of Pike St and Pike Place) indicate the tour's starting point. Each tour begins with a 10-minute slide presentation highlighting the Market's history and development. Although reservations are not required, they can be made by calling the above number. There is no charge, although a 50-cent donation is requested.

Seattle Art & Architecture Tours
1500 Western   *682-4435*

Takes you on a fascinating series of mainly walking tours through Seattle: Art Deco (downtown), Seattle Neighborhoods, Houseboats, Shaping of Downtown, Anhalt Apartments, Ellsworth Storey Houses (Denny-Blaine area, "Northwest Style" architecture); as well as bus tours of the parks, Port Townsend Historic Homes in spring and fall, and LaConner/Skagit Valley.

The Underground Tours
610 First Ave   *682-4646*

These tours are mostly one story down, the level of the city before rebuilding from the Great Fire of June 6, 1889. (Poor drainage at the old, lower level made the higher streetline imperative.) The story told down there is corny and funny, and you'll get a salty taste of the pioneers' eccentricities, but you may fail to gain much appreciation for the buildings and the present vibrancy of the Square. The tours cost $3 adults, $2 senior citizens, and $1.50 for kids six to 12 years old; children under six go free. Group rates are available. The tour runs about one and a half hours. Tour times vary seasonally. Call ahead; reservations are strongly recommended.

Commercial tours — Other

Boeing	342-4801

Boeing offers tours of its 747 plant at the world's largest building, just outside Everett, 23 miles north of Seattle. The tour lasts an hour and a quarter, twice a day, Monday through Friday, 9am and 12:30pm. Groups up to 42; no children under 12. Doors open one half-hour before tour begins. No reservations. Call ahead for driving information.

Independent Ale Brewery
4620 Leary Way NW   *784-0800*

This is Seattle's first new brewery in half a century, and a Northwest leader in the revival of "boutique" breweries producing fresh, heady real ale strictly for local consumption. At press time the brewery and tasting room had not yet been opened for public tours. Something may be arranged by the time you call. And you should surely try Independent's rich, malty Redhook Ale (and the excellent, more bitter Grant's Scottish Ale from Yakima) at any number of Seattle taps.

Kingdome Tours	201 S King	628-3331

Unknown to many Seattleites, the Kingdome Stadium contains a sports museum and 45-minute guided tours are conducted May to October daily at 11, 1, and 3. Cost is $2 for adults, $1 for kids under 12 and senior citizens, and free for children five and under. Smaller groups meet at Gate B. Groups of over 25 people (requiring advance registration) meet at Gate D.

Rainier Brewery	3100 Airport Way S	622-2600

Rainier Brewery offers 40-minute tours without reservations between 1 and 5, Monday–Friday, every 30 minutes. Groups should call ahead. The tours are free; children should be accompanied by an adult and be able to walk; no bare feet. Complimentary tasting.

For information on tours through the local wineries, **Chateau Ste. Michelle**, **Associated Vintners**, and **Paul Thomas Wines**, see the Eastside tour in the Out of Town Tour chapter.

Neighborhoods — International District

Seattle's International District is a small one, and partly for this reason it is not a touristy sector, as in many cities. It is known for its family-style restaurants and groceries, and memories of the many distinguished artists and writers who have come out of this Asian-American center.

The history of the white treatment of Asians in Seattle is not a pleasant or inspiring one, however. By the 1880s, there were ugly episodes of anti-Chinese demonstrations and deportations; and during World War II the Japanese-Americans were given scant notice before being herded off to internment camps while most whites stood by silently. Still, Asian-American art has gotten into the bloodstream of Seattle more than almost any other city, and the International District (I.D.) is undergoing a major renovation as the third-generation offspring of the early immigrants rediscover (even improve on) their heritage.

The district is close to the Kingdome, so many Seattleites drop by for a delicious, inexpensive dinner here before a game. Perhaps the best time of all to visit the I.D. is Saturday or Sunday around lunchtime, when many of the area's 30,000 Asians come to the old district to shop, to have a dim sum lunch, and to renew old ties. The restaurants become jammed with loud family groups, and the atmosphere is irresistible.

The I.D. can be toured formally or on your own. The formal guided tour, conducted by Elizabeth Burke, is a good one, starting with a 30-minute slide show about the area's history, including a visit to an abandoned 1930s gambling den, and a walking tour that ends (by special arrangement) at a restaurant. Reservations must be made in advance (624-6342).

Once you've parked your car under the I-5 freeway bridge (it's covered and relatively cheap), or better yet taken one of the free buses from downtown (Numbers 1, 7, or 14; the last free stop is under the freeway), a good place to start your own walking tour is the **Wing Luke Museum** at 414 Eighth Avenue S between S King and S Jackson (call 623-5124 for hours). It's named for the first person of Asian ancestry elected to public office in Washington; city councilman Luke was killed in an airplane crash in 1965. The museum has historical photos of the district, unusual artifacts, and colorful costumes of the past. Across the street is the fancy new **House of Hong** with a Hong Kong–style barbecue out front.

Turn right up **King Street**, the main Chinese street in the International District. It is crowded on weekends with families shopping at the grocery and import stores, many of which look as if they are unchanged for the past 50 years: floors creak, bargains are found in utility baskets, and row upon row of cans and jars contain some of the secret ingredients of Asian cooking. Near the corner of Eighth and King is the **King Cafe**, a popular spot for dim sum lunches of Chinese rice pastries.

Continue on to **Barclay Seafoods**, where live crabs and geoducks wait like Shmoos to leap on your plate. On the corner of Seventh and King are two good Cantonese restaurants, the **Silver Dragon** and **Linyen**, the latter offering somewhat spicier dishes. Take a left on Seventh Avenue S, pausing to admire the **Bing Kong Building** on the right-hand side of the street. It's marked by a sign and an ornate third-floor balcony, an architectural enthusiasm imported by early Cantonese immigrants. The Bing Kong Association is the Chinese Freemasons, not to be confused with the tongs, or family associations. Both are fraternal organizations that played an important role in America, where many men were cut off from Asian families due to immigration policies.

Continue down Seventh, across S Weller and past a few odd-shaped turn-of-the-century houses, and you come to the new **Children's Park**, with the delightful brass dragon designed by Jerry Tsutakawa. (The Tsutakawa family is a living testimony to the diverse Asian impact on Seattle's culture: old man George is the granddaddy of Seattle sculpture, whose fountains adorn the Seattle Center and countless other city sites; daughter Mayumi was a *Seattle Times* art critic; her brother Deems is a prominent young jazzman.)

Now go back up Seventh and turn left on S Weller. Halfway up the block is **Maynard Alley**, one of only two alleys in the city with names and mail delivery. Halfway up the alley on your right is the Wah Mee Club, an old gambling club closed after a notorious evening in February 1983 when 13 people were shot there. It's not much to look at; but next door is Liem's Pet Shop which is: white mice, tarantulas, hundreds of fish, squid, snakes, and such scurry around under the care of Liem himself, a Malaysian who breeds his own finches and parakeets on the premises. When you emerge from Maynard Alley, you're looking straight at **Master Leung's Kung-Fu School** across the street; if you ask politely, they may let you watch them practice.

Continuing on down King Street (westward) you will be enticed by many more seductive cooking smells. **Kau Kau** on the right-hand side is a very popular hangout for Chinese families and it is easy to see why—the front window is filled with barbecued duck, pork, and ribs. Across the street is **Tai Tung**, one of the busiest restaurants in the International District, but not the best place to get authentic foods. Before turning right onto Maynard Street S you may want to make a detour left to the **Hong Kong** (507 Maynard S), widely considered to have the best dim sum in town.

Back on course, going north on Maynard, walk up to **Kue Hing**, where you can get a thousand kinds of Chinese herbs for a headache or whatever else ails you (you can also buy or rent Chinese videotapes). Walk across the street and into the spiffy **Bush Asia Center** where there is yet another fine eating establishment, called **Han Il**; spicy Korean food is the fare here. Wander around inside, past the Chinese newspaper, and downstairs, pausing perhaps at the Filipino pastry shop. Then go out into lovely **Hing Hay Park** with its grand pavilion from Taipei and a large mural depicting Asian Seattle history. Turn right onto S King and stroll down to **Uwajimaya** with its striking blue-tiled roof. The biggest Japanese supermarket on the West Coast, it has a wealth of multiethnic imported foods, an excellent selection of fresh fish, plus clothes, furniture, cooking implements, and untold other stuff.

Now go up Sixth Avenue S for a block and cross S Jackson. This area is the Japantown of the district. Check out **Higo** (604 S Jackson), a traditional pre-World War II Seattle department store. Nearby are two of the city's popular Japanese restaurants: **The Mikado** (514 S Jackson) is known far and wide for its sushi and robata bars, and omakase dinners. The more modest **Chiyoko** (610 S Jackson) offers fine sushi, tempura, and makunochi.

Back on the left-hand side of Sixth Avenue S, head north and you will come to the Main Street school, the second elementary school to be built in Seattle. Go up a long block to S Washington Street, walk to where the street meets the freeway, and there's the **Nippon Kan**, the Japanese Community Center. Deserted for years, the building has been refurbished for meetings and, in the upstairs theater, for performances. The stage has a fantastic curtain adorned with advertisements for products of long ago; it is only accessible to those taking the formal tour of the district. (Another tour you might try lining up if your visit coincides with Chinese New Year, the second moon of February, is a tour of the tong—family association —buildings. Call the Chinatown Chamber of Commerce for information—623-8171.)

Across the street is **Kobe Terrace Park**, with a tall stone lantern from Seattle's Japanese sister city Kobe, and a splendid view over the district and Pioneer Square, where Asian-American settlers first lived in Seattle.

Neighborhoods — University District

All roads—and a good many of the buses—in northeast Seattle are likely to run by the 680-acre **University of Washington campus**. Just three miles outside downtown Seattle, the 35,000-student university remains the senior partner in the state's college system, provides Seattle's secondary shopping and cultural center, and dominates surrounding residential neighborhoods.

The university grew from an unpromising start in downtown Seattle in 1861—since there weren't any qualified college students handy, the would-be University of a Thousand Years settled for tutoring elementary and secondary students. Major expansion began around 1895, the year the U moved north to its new wooded campus. Major academic importance came even later—during the last 25 years— when the ever-expanding institution became the nation's largest holder of federal research grants, a major center for medical studies, as well as the Northwest's top educational establishment. Today the building has slowed, the student population stabilized, and the U has fallen on hard financial times. But it doesn't show to a casual observer: the campus has meanwhile matured into a horticultural and architectural showpiece.

For day-long browsing, nothing in town matches University Way NE, universally dubbed **"The Ave."** The long north-south blocks reflect most student trends of the past two decades, from headshops and leatherworks to video games (even though some have grown up almost beyond recognition), while a large contingent of foreign students, particularly from the Mid and Far East, support a varied (and of varying quality) collection of inexpensive ethnic restaurants.

To begin a tour, start with coffee and calories at one of two longtime University District institutions: The Last Exit on Brooklyn (3930 Brooklyn NE), where the counterculture remnant brings its children for Saturday brunch (try the apple pie or sweet hot chocolate topped with mountains of whipped cream), or Woerne's European Cafe and Pastry Shop (4108 University Way NE—sample the strudels or other small pastries, skip the tortes).

Just up the street from the cafe, shopping begins in earnest at House of Rice (4112), one of the city's surest sources for exotic ingredients as well as utensils for Oriental cooking. In the same block, there's the Folk Art Gallery (4138), originally a Latin American import shop, now a fascinating collection of crafts ranging from exotic musical instruments to cotton clothing. The latter is especially popular with women looking for un-cutesy maternity wear.

Cross the street in the next block to reach the immensely popular China First Restaurant (4237) and Pastimes (4239), full of old-fashioned and inexpensive toys. (But watch out for the boggling price tags on Steiff teddy bears.)

On the corner is Ness Flowers, a reliable, traditional florist, sometimes pricey, but open at night and famous for a mirrored ceiling and seasonal window displays.

North of 43rd, it's tough to avoid criss-crossing the street. The west side of the block includes a Haagen-Dazs ice cream shop (4301), Place Two (4315), a student-fashion division of trendy Nordstrom, Benton's Jewelers (4333), with a historic street clock in front, and Pier 1 (4345), a chain import store in the rattan and shiny brass mode.

The east side of the same block is dominated by University Book Store, engaged in perpetual rivalry with Harvard Coop to see which ends up the largest and most varied bookshop in the US. The older, northern section of the store carries everything except books, including clothing, luggage, and row after row of greeting cards, but best stick to the books—some 60,000 titles in all. The main floor is good for browsing—the errant reader is politely ignored; upstairs, the mezzanine level features periodicals and the children's book department, with frequent Saturday-afternoon kids' programs.

Back out on the street, continue north. Those with a taste for lovely, expensive clothes may want to veer a half block west, to Nelly Stallion (1311 NE 45th). Back on course, the next block features more jewelry stores, more restaurants, and more import shops. On the right side, look for Miller-Pollard Interiors (4538)—great stuff from greeting cards to oak furniture (sales are a rarity, but worth watching for) or settle down and rest the feet with a (large) glass of wine at University Bar & Grill (4553) on the left. Farther north, rents go down and the scene becomes much more eclectic (not to mention erratic), with offerings ranging from fresh seafood to revolutionary books to Oriental rugs. Two stops worth the extra walk include the Grand Illusion (1403 NE 50th), a tiny 99-seat cinema adjoining a cozy espresso house and Avenue 52 (5247), a stunningly successful combination of Italian and Syrian food.

Better yet, save the last two for evening and take a picnic to the **University campus itself**, entering at NE 45th and 17th Avenue NE. Walk south, past the Burke Museum on the right, then veer left past Denny Hall, the oldest building on campus and (naturally) home of the Classics Department as well as the chiming clock heard all over campus. (Student pranksters have on occasion added a Mickey Mouse figure to the conspicuous clock face.) Then south again, to the Academic Quadrangle, better known as the Quad.

Here's the home of liberal arts at the U and a good stopping point—mellow academic Gothic brick buildings (the gargoyles are an especially nice touch) enclosing a grassy oblong, where gnarled flowering cherries provide a dazzling pink display to open spring quarter. History classes tend to sneak outside in May;

strange noises emanate from Music Building practice rooms.

Head right to leave the Quad, and step into the dramatic contrast of the New Quadrangle, dubbed Red Square—a striking, if slippery-when-wet, brick combination of Brutalism with Sienna's town square. To the right are the modern chunks—the massive, square Kane Hall, with accompanying sculpture, the Odegaard Undergraduate Library, and Meany Hall, a favorite location for major concerts. On the left is the main, Suzzallo Library—its soft stained-glass facade glows at night—while the university's central administration is housed on the south edge of the square.

Walk past the grey Administration Building, down a few steps to Drumheller Fountain, to reach one of the most spectacular views on campus, the aptly named Rainier Vista. Here's another good stopping place, with benches, densely planted rose bushes, and ducks paddling around the fountain. To the right and left are various science and engineering buildings. Head southeast, past Electrical Engineering, to reach a well-hidden surprise—the Sylvan Theater, a grassy glade complete with Greek columns. Despite the uncertainties of Northwest weather, plays are sometimes staged here in summer.

Back on the main track, veer southwest from the fountain, down Garfield Lane to reach the enchanting, and practical, Drug Plant Garden, then use the overpass to reach the Warren G. Magnuson Health Sciences Center, named after the state's long-time senior senator, and heart of the campus' medical research activities. University Hospital is on the left. Continue through a maze of signs and buildings to reach a newish student center, with a pleasant courtyard, for a good place to end the tour. Or, if feet hold out, stroll to the Montlake cut, and enjoy a walk along the canal path. With luck, members of the U's world-class crew will be out training on the blue water below.

Neighborhoods—Capitol Hill

Capitol Hill is the most cosmopolitan of Seattle's residential districts—a heady, sometimes bewildering hodgepodge of fine old homes and densely packed, modest apartments, of families, the elderly, artists, young professionals who moved back in-city in the gentrifying 1970s, and even younger single folks, including all manner of fringe fashions. At some times, on some blocks, it seems if you throw a stone you'll hit a new-wave rocker; one section is even semi-officially labeled the city's "gay district." Compared to San Francisco's Castro Street, however, Capital Hill is pretty tame; it might be fair to call it the Northwest's milder version of Greenwich Village.

Capitol Hill got its name from its first manifest destiny, when city fathers hoped to perch the state capitol atop it. But the legislators got packed off to the wilds of Olympia in true Jeffersonian fashion, and the Hill wound up a capitol of blue-blood social life and cultural diversity instead.

Though the Interstate 5 corridor has done horrors to chop them apart, Capitol Hill remains closely linked to downtown. It runs like a curtain east of the business district, Denny Regrade, and Lake Union, parallel to Elliott Bay, and offers many fine views of all of them.

Olive Way is a restaurant-goer's mecca with more than half a dozen eateries of all different persuasions and ethnic cuisines. Settebello (1525 E Olive Way) is a chic and very good Northern Italian restaurant and bar. Across the street is the Famous Pacific Dessert Company (4020 E Denny Way), an equally fashionable place catering to Seattle's elegant sweet teeth. Going east, Mamounia (1556 E Olive Way) offers pricelessly exotic, and apparently authentic, Moroccan fare, while a little further along, B&O Espresso (at the junction of Olive, Belmont, and Boylston) serves enormous cakes and pastries in an informal, bohemian atmosphere. Before you hit Broadway, you'll encounter Henry's Off Broadway (1705 E Olive Way), offering standard American elegance complete with valet service, sunny dining room, and plush piano bar.

Broadway. Olive soon hits Broadway and changes its name to John Street. At the corner sits **Lion O'Reilly's and B.J. Monkeyshines' Eating and Drinking Establishment.** A lively singles spot, with decor a combination of robust-pub and overstuffed-drawing-room; the grand old mirrored wood bar, transplanted from the Anaconda Hotel in Montana. **Funky Broadway East** (916 E John) is a classic barbecue joint featuring sweet-potato pie, homemade ice cream, and five grades of barbecue sauce; the hottest, labeled simply "fool," has been rumored to cleave palates.

Broadway, which just a decade ago was nearly written off to urban decay, has experienced a dramatic (some locals say excessive) revival. It's now a center of not just the Hill's but the city's trendy boutique culture, nightlife, and general street life; if you stop to eat there, get a window seat to watch the action. Broadway's free-stepping spirit is nicely expressed in some offbeat public artwork by Jack Mackie, running intermittently along its length. He has inlaid lifesize bronze "**dancing feet**" in the sidewalk in various patterns (is that a cha-cha or tango?) before La Cocina, Starbucks, and other establishments. Get in step and boogaloo down. . . .

Heading north on Broadway, you'll find a fair selection of unusual fashion and furnishing vendors, most located on the east side of the street: **Opus 204** (at 204, natch) for ethnic and original fashions; **All That Jazz** (across the street at 233), a fun, flashy boutiqueful of new-wave, post-pop, high-glitter, or whatever-you-want-to-call-it fashions, cards, accessories, etc.; **Keeg's Furniture** (310), one of the town's popular contemporary furnishings stores; **Seattle Design Store** (406), with sharp kitchenware, bright plastic furnishings, and everything else for the modern look (the plastic goose and fruit lamps in the window say it all); **A Different Drummer** (420), a new-and-used bookstore moving from countercultural to highcultural focus; and **Great Things**, an unpredictable selection of ceramics, gifts, and decorator items.

For all the panoply of trendy and designer merchandise on Broadway, you'll hardly find a bona fide art gallery here—or anywhere else on Capitol Hill, a fact that gives even some of the Hill's resident artists pause.

You'll do better if you're looking for food and drink. **La Cocina** (432), is a pleasant Mexican restaurant with a vaguely continental air. **The Dilettante** (416) is an excellent (and expensive) chocolate bar (its original confections can also be bought for home indulgence). It spearheaded Seattle's consuming passion for chocolate, which often seems to supplant lust, violence, and all other excesses in the supermoderate local sensibility.

The slick **Broadway Restaurant** (314), with valet parking, sits next to a Baskin-Robbins—an apt expression of Capitol Hill's patrician–populist blend. Nearby, on E Harrison, sits (or rather, lies) a cast-aluminum figure, an old fellow reclining on a bench under a newspaper, by popular and populist Seattle sculptor Rich Beyer. Nearby, Ernie Steele's Checkerboard Room, Andy's Cafe, and the 206 Tavern preserve some of the old Broadway's less assuming spirit.

Up Broadway sit two drab but clean Chinese restaurants, the Macfong-Ho (516, with no known relation to McDonald's or HoJo's) and the Jade Pagoda (606), which has good food with gracious service at reasonable prices. **Boondock's, Sundecker's & Greenthumb's** (611), the prototype of the fern bars that have spread so widely across the Hill and city (and they're a universal catchphrase joke), is still popular, especially among the late-night crowd. **Kernels Natural Foods Garden** (621) is a combination deli, bakery, and bulk-food outlet, with plenty of wholesome antidotes to all that chocolate you splurged on at the Dilettante. You may have to wait in line for an elbow-to-elbow niche at the **Deluxe Bar & Grill** (corner of Broadway and Roy Street), a long-popular tavern spiffed up and converted to full bar which, nevertheless, has maintained its hearty burgers, fries, and steak sandwiches.

If you turn the corner of an evening, you'll probably bump into a line for the **Harvard Exit**'s next show. This two-screen moviehouse usually hedges its bets with one esoteric import and one semi-mainstream feature. Once a women's club/concert hall, its Victorian parlor, with a piano and giant antique projector for centerpieces, chessboards for diversion, and coffee and spiced tea free for the sipping, makes waiting for the show a pleasure.

Across the street, in the quaint, stone Loveless Studio Building, **Le Petit Bateau** sells pricey kids' stuff and **Cinema Books** displays the town's best selection of film lore; if you can't get into the Harvard Exit, you can read about the film here. Also, take a peek inside the building's tiny, grassy courtyard—its tranquility is enough to make you want to pack up everything and move into one of its apartments tomorrow. In a cozy semi-basement, the new **Byzantine** (806 E Roy) Greek restaurant has fortunately preserved the fine floor-to-ceiling **murals** of the old (and sadly missed) Russian Samovar. These richly muted friezes are based on Ivan Bilibin's illustrations to Pushkin's fairy tale of Tsar Saltan.

Your Broadway tour ends at the **Cornish School for the Allied Arts**, at 710 E Roy across from to the tidy colonial DAR mansion. Cornish wants to be a West Coast Juilliard; it recently started awarding four-year degrees and bought a second building, the former St. Nicholas School next to St. Mark's Cathedral a half-mile north on 10th. As a college, Cornish is young; as an institution, it dates back to early in the century, when Miss Nellie Cornish drew a stellar faculty (Mark Tobey, John Cage, Merce Cunningham, et al.) to the remote Northwest by sheer force of personality. Over the years, students included Mary McCarthy, Robert Joffrey, and rock star Steve Miller. Today's students are uncommonly dedicated, and often give performances open to the public. Sunday nights are a good chance to catch them. (Call 323-1400 for information.)

North End. While you're in the neighborhood, **St. Mark's Cathedral** (1245 10th E) and the St. Nicholas School may be worth a side hike. St. Mark's is a tall, chunky, expressively unfinished neo-Romanesque vault, with a view of Lake Union and downtown from the grounds. If you're lucky, someone may be practicing on its marvelous organ; compline service at 9:30pm Sunday is a delight to hear. St. Mark's is the heart of blueblood, Episcopalian Seattle, and its neighborhood is equally patrician; head north on 10th, right on E Boston, then right again on Federal Avenue to see some of the city's most impressive, and diverse, homes and landscaping. Turn left at E Highland or Prospect to **Volunteer Park**, the stateliest of Seattle's parks (designed by the Olmsted brothers of New York Central Park fame) and site of the Seattle Art Museum's main building and a lush, lovely botanical conservatory.

On the park's north side spreads Lake View Cemetery, with the mausoleums of many of Seattle's founding families. Exiting at the cemetery's northeast corner, onto 15th Avenue E, brings you to another, smaller park, with a magnificent view north toward the University of Washington. Take Boston west to 11th Avenue E, turn right and right again on Delmar Drive. You'll immediately reach **Interlaken Drive**, a lovely, wildly overgrown, winding passage which was the Olmsteds' (never-finished) plan for a citywide network of wild parkways linking with all the major boulevards.

If you're in the mood for more parks (and perhaps a picnic), Interlaken will lead you to the spectacular spread of "wilderness," the University of Washington Arboretum (see Parks Section of Touring Seattle for details). If, however, you want to continue exploring inner-city neighborhoods, Capitol Hill has plenty more to offer.

Fifteenth Avenue E is a downhome, quietly bohemian retail-restaurant district that's only half as far as Broadway down the gentrification trail. (A two-block detour south on 13th Avenue to Harrison Street lets you see the **St. Spiridon Cathedral**, center for one of the United States' largest and most active Russian Orthodox communities.) At 15th E and Mercer, several blocks south on 15th E from the northeast exit of Volunteer Park, are two top choices for good, hearty food at skimpy prices: **Bloch's** (605), a beer, sandwiches, salads, and prime-rib cafeteria (with a Lower Queen Anne clone), and the **Canterbury** (534), a rambling neo-Tudor alehouse thickly decked with murals, stained glass, and animal skins, and well-provendered with burgers, homemade soups, salads, souffles, etc. Just to the south, the **Cause Celebre Cafe** (524) endures as a cozy home away from home for Hilltop radicals and literati, with poetry readings and music, homemade ice cream and espresso, vegetarian sandwiches, and an outdoor deck with a ringside view of the street life. Upstairs, **Red & Black Books** offers a literate selection with a political edge. Browse for who-knows-what in 15th's antique/junk stores, including Trinkets & Treasures (517) and Wicker Design (515).

Next stop heading south is **Matzoh Momma** (509), originally (and still, though the takeout selection is skimpy) an early outpost for New York–style deli, now more notable as a bar and relaxed showcase for local jazz musicians.

The Ritz Cafe (429), with low light, old prints, and continental menu, has supplanted an old hippie haven—more gentrification on the march. Next door, in a rambling old house, **Horizon Books** offers one of Seattle's largest selections of old volumes and discs, a book-search service, and the musty smell of true bibliophilia. Farther down, you'll pass the expansive Bagel Deli (340) and, by the mammoth **Group Health Cooperative's central hospital** at 15th and John, **Treats Restaurant & Confectionery** and the **Beach Seafood Bar**.

E Pike and E Pine streets. South of Olive, Pike and Pine streets also cross the freeway, but then cut due east instead of angling northeast as Olive does. Pike Street offers an interesting tour in itself, through aging apartments, warehouses, garages, and all manner of small specialty businesses.

As you pass the wide-windowed auto-restoration shop at 415 Pike, you may gawk at the antique beauties in the window. At 717, a chic balloon gallery, The Red Balloon, hunches against a classic stained-glass shop, La Fenetre. If all this evokes a less congested sort of SoHo, the resemblance is more than coincidental; the upper Pike area is a mecca for artists and a haven for offbeat creative enterprises.

One of the foremost is the **Empty Space Theater** (919 E Pike), the city's most consistently venturesome and, in some eyes, satisfying performing group. Its actors, local artists, and a few legends-in-their-own-time gather at the **Comet Tavern** across the street, a Seattle tradition which proves artsiness can be funky rather than affected. Around the corner, **and/or** (915 E Pine), Seattle's durable, highly experimental (and, some artists charge, cliquish) media arts center, no longer stages gallery shows, but offers good art and video libraries, video workshops and production facilities, and sundry special events

Up a block, between Pike and Pine on 11th, is a must-stop for visitors from towns where Sears is the closest thing to an outdoor outfitter: the **Recreational Equipment Inc.** (REI) co-op, purportedly the world's largest emporium for hiking, camping, and ski gear. In line with the times, REI offers many outdoorsy fashions for city wear, right down to briefcases of the same construction as its rucksacks. Purists complain that REI has moved too far into the conventional business world from its early co-op days, but its selection is better than ever and its prices still often good.

Head south on Pine; at Broadway you'll pass Seattle Central Community College on your right; the restored old masonry portion, which seems to fight to hold its own against a newer brick box, is the historic Broadway High School. Farther down, on the left, you'll spot the **Egyptian Theater** (801), which is well worth a peek inside even if you can't stop for a movie. The theater, a showcase for notable foreign films and for the dazzling Seattle International Film Festival each spring, seems a fortunate holdover from the era of grand movie palaces; its sculpted bric-a-brac, nicely highlighted with spots of color, suits the Egyptian theme nicely. In fact, the hall is an old Masonic Temple only recently converted to picture shows when the Egyptian's owners were forced to vacate their former digs at the Moore Theater downtown.

Finally, yet one more Capitol Hill religious haven is worth a detour on your way downtown: **St. James Cathedral**, Seattle's foremost Catholic center of worship, at Ninth Avenue and Marion Street (take Broadway south to Madison, then head west to Ninth). Its graceful vault is in sky blue and golden yellow—the two colors the Swiss metapsychoanalyst Carl Jung said represent infinity and illumination.

Sport

Spectator sport	216	Auto racing
	216	Baseball
	216	Basketball
	217	Bicycle racing
	217	Football
	217	Horse racing
	217	Hockey
	218	Soccer
	218	College sports
Participatory sport	219	Bicycling
	222	Boating
	222	Canoeing and kayaking
	224	Exercise clubs and facilities
	228	Fishing
	231	Golf
	232	Hiking, camping, climbing
	235	Jogging
	237	Rafting
	237	Sailboarding
	238	Sailing
	239	Skiing
	242	Swimming
	243	Tennis

Sports
Spectator sport

Auto racing

RR2 **Seattle International Raceway**, 31001 144th SE, Kent (take Exit 142A east off I-5; 631-1550), holds a busy schedule of races in the good-weather months. The dirt track for motorcycle races is not much, but the nine-turn, 2.25-mile road-racing track (originally built in 1959 for sports-car racing) is a very good facility. Closed in December.

Baseball

The **Mariners** have the best young manager in baseball, Rene Lachemann, a slew of good young pitchers, and ageless Gaylord Perry. Though some insist that baseball wasn't meant to be played indoors, the covered Kingdome is at least dry. Bring your own peanuts, because the Kingdome's are expensive and the rest of the food is poor. Parking and good seats are nearly always available. Better than driving, however, is to take a free bus from downtown and have dinner in Pioneer Square or the International District. For fun, try sitting in the left-field stands, where the crowd is the liveliest.

Season: Early April through September. Game time is 7:35pm except for rare weekday-afternoon games, which begin at 12:35pm. Sunday games start at 1:35pm.

Q9 **Where they play:** Kingdome.

Tickets: General admission is $3, except for those seats on the 200 level directly underneath the huge television screen, which run $1.50. All general-admission seats are in the outfield on all three levels and are available day-of-game only. Best are those on the 100 level in left field. Avoid the 300 level. Reserved seats start at $4.50 and run up to $7.50. The best and most expensive are closest to the field.

Information: 628-3555.

Basketball

The **Sonics** play smart, competitive basketball, lately vacillating between invincibility and indifference. In the cavernous Kingdome, tickets are always available for Sonic games, even if you have to, or, perversely, want to, sit in the third deck. Best seats are in the horseshoe-shaped "temporary stands." Parking in the Kingdome lot seldom is a problem.

Season: October through mid-April, when the play-offs begin. Games begin at 7:30pm on weekdays, 8pm on Fridays, and anywhere from 1:30pm to 7pm on Sundays.

Q9 **Where they play:** Kingdome.

Tickets: Most of the best seats are held by season-ticket holders. The only bargains are $3 seats in the 300 level; it's hard to see up there, but it's great fun when the crowd is large.

Information: 628-8430.

Sports

Bicycle racing

F1 Track racing at **Marymoor Park**, Redmond, runs from the first Friday in May through the first Friday in September at 7:30pm, every Friday unless it's raining. Track racing is a much more watchable sport than road racing, and many nights include national-caliber riding. The site, with good sunsets and Mount Rainier as a backdrop, is lovely; take a picnic. Also take a pad to protect yourself from the aluminum bleachers, or sit on the grass. $2 per person; $5 family. For information, call Cycling Activities at 329-7381.

Football

The **Seahawks'** new coach, Chuck Knox, seems a good bet finally to prod the team into becoming a contender. The Hawks' games in the Kingdome are always sellouts, no matter how well the team is playing, but scalpers are present at all games. Best to avoid the traffic/parking hassle by taking a free bus from downtown to the game. A walk through Pioneer Square is a good way to stretch beforehand; restaurants and takeout places abound, many offering pre-game brunches.

Season: August through December. Game time is 7:30pm in August, 1pm after that.

Q9 **Where they play:** Kingdome.

Tickets: The best 60,000 seats are grabbed by season-ticket holders, leaving about 5,000 available per game. Most of those are sold by mail beginning June 1. Some single seats in all three price levels—$15, $12, and $8—are usually available the week before a game.

Information: 827-9766.

Horse racing

The beautifully kept track at **Longacres** offers excellent minor-league racing April to October; dining facilities are open year-round. The fun is the variety of places to sit, walk, horse-watch, people-watch, eat, drink, and place bets. Don't challenge the kitchen and it will reward with decent sandwiches in the grandstand, often good and not overpriced meals in the clubhouse. Weeknight racing starts at 3:45, and there is no better place around to settle into a summer evening.

Season: Late April–late October; post time 3:45pm Wed-Fri; 1:15pm Sat-Sun & holidays; closed Mon & Tues.

004 **Where they run:** Longacres Racecourse, Renton (off Interstate 405; take exit from I-5 at Southcenter, heading east).

Tickets: $2.75 grandstand; $5 clubhouse.

Information: 226-3131.

Hockey

The **Breakers** have been providing Seattleites an uncompromising style of play from the Western Hockey League. It's not the NHL, true, but the action on the ice is all youthful dedication.

217

Sports

Season: September through March. Game time is 7:30 weekdays & Sat, 2:30 Sun.

B5 **Where they play:** Seattle Center Arena.

Tickets: $6 for lower sections near center ice; $5 for balcony seats; $4 general admission in the corners. There's not a bad seat in the cozy little Arena. Senior citizens, kids under 12, and military personnel get a 25-percent discount. Prices are subject to change before the 1983–84 season. Call 282-1880 for ticket information.

Information: 624-9121.

Soccer

Under new ownership, the normally excellent **Sounders** are trying to "Americanize" the game with faster action and young American players. The Kingdome is not ideal for soccer, but for the best view get seats about halfway up the Kingdome's first section. Parking and tickets are readily available for all games.

Season: Late April through August, when the playoffs begin. Games start at 7:30pm.

Q9 **Where they play:** Kingdome.

Tickets: Underneath the large television screen in the north end zone, seats cost just $5. For a view of the screen from the south end zone you'll pay $6.50. The best seats are in the temporary stands close to the action, and they all run $10. In the permanent stands, seats on the sides are $10 and those in the corners are $8.50.

Information: 628-3450.

College sports

For community-wide interest, University of Washington football dominates the local collegiate sports scene. That's not surprising, considering its record: since 1977, the Don James–coached Huskies have won two Rose Bowls, one Sun, and one Aloha Bowl, and have been ranked in the top 10 nationally several times.

As a result of this gridiron success, the 60,000-seat Husky Stadium is often sold out in advance for big games, so make ticket reservations as early as possible; scalpers prowl the north side of the stadium if you're desperate. Try to get seats in the covered sections of the stadium, since the weather can be miserable any time of the season. (Wear warm, rainproof clothing no matter how sunny game-day promises to be.)

On a clear day, Husky Stadium's setting on Lake Washington, with the Cascades looming behind the east end zone, is truly memorable. Parking-lot tailgate picnics and people arriving by boat create a festive atmosphere unmatched at any other sporting event in the city. You can buy picnic food nearby at University Village; some restaurants also sell a package including lunch and a boat trip to the game. Traffic and parking are a problem, so take a bus.

Season: Mid-September to mid-November. Games start at 1:30pm.

FF6 **Where they play:** Husky Stadium, University of Washington.

Tickets: All of the good seats are taken by some 45,000 season-ticket holders. Those that remain cost $14 for a powerful opponent such as USC and $12 for the

Sports

likes of, say, Oregon State.

Information: 543-2200.

The UW is also big-time in several other sports, including basketball, swimming, gymnastics, crew racing, track and field, and baseball. Tickets are much easier to come by for these sports, and you can watch the Huskies' world-class eight-oared crew for free in the Montlake Cut, a narrow canal at the southern edge of the University campus. Schedule and ticket information for all University of Washington sports is best obtained from the UW ticket office: 543-2200.

Other local collegiate sports of note are Seattle Pacific University soccer (played at Seattle Center's High School Memorial Stadium) and basketball (in the SPU Royal Brougham Pavilion, Third W and W Nickerson), both played well by this small college. For SPU ticket information, call 281-2854.

Participatory sport

Bicycling

With all the current emphasis on health and fitness, bicycling has been enjoying a renaissance in the Seattle area. Many people cycle to work and many more include cycling in their recreational pursuits. Listed below are some popular bicycle routes.

Bicycling — rides

Alki — *Alki Ave SW*

A flat West Seattle route along the beach at Alki and on to Lincoln Park; the road is wide enough for bikes and cars, and motorists are used to cyclists. The lighthouse at Alki is open for visits and tours. The round trip to Lincoln Park from the beginning of the Alki trail is about 12 miles. Avoid the beach area on sunny Sunday afternoons; it will be very crowded.

Bainbridge Island Loop

This is a signed bike route along fairly flat low-traffic roads, around the island. A pleasant 25-mile getaway for Seattle cyclists.

Burke Gilman Trail — *Gasworks Park at Lake Union to Kenmore Log Boom Park at north end of Lake Washington*

A wide, well-paved path cutting through the University of Washington and following Lake Washington. Plans are under foot to connect the Burke Gilman Trail with the Sammamish River Trail on the Eastside; meanwhile, many bicyclists make the short hop on Bothell Way to continue their off-road trail riding.

Sammamish River Trail — *near Bothell Landing to Marymoor Park, Redmond*

A very flat route following the quietly flowing Sammamish River—about 9½ miles one way. Great picnicking at the Ste. Michelle Winery just off the trail on NE 145th St. (Food and wine can be bought there.)

219

Sports

HH8- GG8	**Elliott Bay Bikeway**	*Pier 70 to Pier 9, Alaskan Way*

This trail is less than two miles but it runs right along Puget Sound and passes between the Grain Terminal and its loading dock. Start at the north end, off West Galer, buy the kids ice cream at Pier 70 and return.

EE7	**Green Lake**	*Latona NE & E Green Lake Way N*

The 2.8-mile paved path is half for cyclists, and half for pedestrians, runners, baby strollers, and dogs. On sunny weekends, it's great people-watching but poor riding; at other hours, the quiet trip around the lake may offer ducklings and geese to be fed, mountain views, some crewing to watch and lots of Frisbee players. The bikeway extends along Ravenna Blvd to the university; a green-painted line establishes the cycling lane.

NN5	**Interurban Trail**	*From Fort Dent Park in Tukwila to the King-Pierce County line*

This interesting multi-purpose trail for non-motorized use (jogging, cycling, riding, skating, etc.) is 16 miles long and runs along the old electric Seattle-Tacoma Interurban Railroad through the Green River Valley. Parts of it, like the Kent section from S 180th to 228th, are paved; other sections follow signed access roads.

GG6- KK5	**Lake Washington Blvd**

The asphalt path from Madrona Park to Seward Park is five miles long, and offers some great views of the lake. The road is narrow part of the way, but the southern half (from Mount Baker Beach south) has a separate asphalt path, which is safer if you're with children.

	Seward Park	*Juneau St. & Lake Washington Blvd.*

Two-and-a-half mile traffic-free paved road encircling the park which juts out into Lake Washington. Very peaceful; can be lonely.

GG9- EE9	**Magnolia–Discovery Park Bike Route**

Magnolia Blvd is wide and traffic isn't bad; you can also ride the roads of Discovery Park (formerly Fort Lawton). Ambitious riders can cross the Ship Canal at the Ballard Locks and continue toward Shilshole Bay and Golden Gardens Park. Smith Cove Bikeway offers access to Pier 91—just one mile away—and has great views.

II4- KK4	**Mercer Island Loop**

There are moderate rolling hills the whole distance, and, though roads are narrow, motorists are used to bikes; you might want to avoid rush hours. It's a good way to look at the varied architecture of the island. The loop trip is 14 miles.

Bicycling — rentals

Alki Bikes 'n Boats	*938-3322*
2722 Alki SW, near the bikeway	

From one- through 10-speeds, plus tandems; from $2.50 an hour. Closed Sunday in winter.

The Bicycle Centers	
4529 Sand Point Way NE,	*523-8300*
near Burke Gilman Trail	

Ten-speeds, $2.50 an hour; $9 a day; $30 a week.

Gregg's Greenlake Cycle　　　*523-1822*
7007 Woodlawn NE, at Green Lake

One- through 10-speeds, plus tandems and child carriers. $1.25 an hour to $35 a week.

Wheelsport Ltd　　　*454-2875*
12020 NE Bellevue-Redmond Rd, Bellevue

Bicycles start at $2.50 an hour; $7.50 a day.

Redmond Cycle　　　*885-6363*
16205 Redmond Way, Redmond

Bicycle rentals run $2.50 an hour; $10 a day.

Bicycling — information

Bicycle Hot Line　　　*522-BIKE*

A community service of the Cascade Bicycle Club, the Bicycle Hot Line has a recorded message of upcoming bicycle events in the area. Also, if you leave your name, phone number, and a biking question on the recording, someone will get back to you with the answer.

The Bicycle Paper　　　*329-7894*
Peggy Stewart

Published monthly, except in winter, and available in most bicycle shops for 75 cents, The Bicycle Paper carries a current schedule of group rides; names and addresses of local clubs; race results; and commentaries and general notices on bike-related issues.

Bicycle Sundays 1983　　*May 15, June 19, July 17, Aug 21, Sept 18*

Co-sponsored by the Seattle Department of Parks and Recreation and Coca Cola, Bicycle Sundays take place from 10-5 on the third Sunday of each month from May through September. Lake Washington Boulevard from Mt. Baker Beach to Seward Park is closed to motor traffic.

Cascade Bicycle Club　　　*325-2375*
Dave Shaw, President

With over 1,300 members, the Cascade Bicycle Club is one of the largest bicycle clubs in the nation. It is very active politically on bike-related issues and was instrumental in creating numerous local bike paths. The club also organizes group rides and special events, including the Seattle–Portland and Seattle–Vancouver, B.C. rides, and Seattle's Bicycle Week (normally the third week of May; in 1983 the activities are mainly being held during the League of American Wheelmen National Rally in Seattle in July.) Its bicycle education committee gives talks to clubs and school groups on cycling matters, including safety and maintenance. The club also operates the Bicycle Hot Line.

Northwest Bicycle Touring Society　　*Lloyd Jones, 232-2694*
**6166 92nd Ave SE,
Mercer Island 98040**

The Northwest Bicycle Touring Society schedules six or seven tours each summer, ranging from one to nine days; reservations are necessary because tours normally sell out in advance. For information, send a self-addressed stamped envelope to Lloyd Jones at the above address.

Bicycle racing

Informal training rides are held summer Wednesday evenings at Seattle International Raceway (631-1550), Kent; it's fairly easy for a novice to get involved. Or visit Marymoor Park Velodrome (329-7381), Redmond, on summer Friday evenings, where there is information available on track racing, and sometimes a novice race.

Boating

With its several lakes and proximity to Puget Sound, Seattle offers a plethora of boating opportunities within the city limits. There are also dozens of navigable rivers within a few hours' drive, beckoning with names Walt Whitman would love, like the Skagit, the Nisqually, the Stillaguamish, the Hoh, and the Humptulips. The state's 10,000 or so lakes and hundreds of miles of tidal shoreline along Puget Sound provide for even more nautical adventures.

Sailing, sailboarding, canoeing, kayaking, and rafting activities, rentals, lessons, clubs, and excursions are all listed under their own sections.

The individual municipal parks and recreation departments in the Greater Seattle area, as well as the King County Parks and Recreation Department, can provide information on boat ramps, docks, and moorage along Lake Washington, Lake Sammamish, and Puget Sound. Call the following numbers:

King County	344-3987	Kirkland	828-1271
Seattle	625-4671	Mercer Island	233-3545
Bellevue	455-6881	Redmond	882-6401
Issaquah	392-7131		

EE7 **Green Lake Small Craft Center** *General: 625-2975*
Southwest corner of Green Lake *Classes: 625-4673 or 625-4671*
Green Lake Boat Rental *Rental: 527-0171 or 362-3151*
Northeast corner of Green Lake

A wealth of rental and educational opportunities involving rowing, sailing, canoeing, and kayaking, and windsurfing (paddleboats are also for rent!) at these Seattle Department of Parks and Recreation facilities.

Canoeing and kayaking

These sports require a good deal of instruction and preparation before you ever reach a river, and it is best to go with experienced boaters. Information on group excursions, both river and sea, is listed below, along with canoe and kayak rental outlets, clubs, and lessons.

Sports

Canoeing and kayaking — excursions, lessons, and rentals

L8	**The Boathouse**	*763-0688*
	9812 17th Ave SW, White Center	

Canoes are definitely "to go" here, as there's no water nearby. You can rent completely outfitted canoes from $25 a day, $40 for a weekend, or $60 a week; rowboats, car-top racks, and eight-canoe car trailers also available.

Eddyline Kayaks *743-9252*
8423 Mukilteo Speedway, Mukilteo

Rents and sells ocean-going kayaks. Handy if you're at the Mukilteo or Edmonds ferry landings. $18-25/day for rentals.

E5 **Northern Lights** *524-1662*
8556 Sandpoint Way NE

Introductory sea-kayaking is the offering here, with weekends in the San Juans, May and June ($85); weeks in British Columbia, mid-June to September ($325-360); and Baja trips in the winter. Emphasis is on looking for whales and listening to sea life with underwater mikes.

F6 **Northwest Outdoor Center** *523-1982*
1009 Boat St

This organization provides an exciting array of lessons and excursions in sea kayaking, and whitewater kayaking and canoeing. Some lessons are held in Seattle while a number of others combine trips (to the San Juans, local rivers, or further afield to the Methow Valley), with practical training sessions. Other adventures include sea kayaking in Desolation Sound and Barkley Sound. A full range of sea kayaks can be rented by the hour, day, weekend, and week, while canoes and whitewater kayaks may be rented on a more limited basis. All instructors and guides have had extensive training in First Aid, CPR, and advanced rescue techniques, and are certified as instructors by the American Canoe Association.

O6 **Pacific Water Sports** *246-9385*
16205 Pacific Hwy S, east of Sea-Tac Airport

Canoes, whitewater rafts, and ocean or whitewater kayaks (for experienced kayakers only); instruction available, including ocean-touring kayaking and whitewater rafting. Rentals start at $12.

F6 **University of Washington Waterfront Activities Center**
Southeast of Husky Stadium *543-2217 or 543-9433*
University of Washington

One of the most beautiful places to enjoy canoeing is along the Arboretum near the University, on Lake Washington. You can rent canoes at the University of Washington Waterfront Activities Center every day, 9-5, for $2.50 an hour.

EE7 **White Water Sports** *523-5150*
307 NE 71st

In addition to their range of sea-touring and whitewater kayaks for sale, and their canoes which can be special-ordered, White Water Sports rents out sea-touring kayaks (starting at $25 a day and $40 a weekend).

See also: **The Good Sport** under Sailboarding section, and **Kelly's Landing** under Sailing section.

Sports

Canoeing and kayaking — clubs

Paddle Trails and Canoe Club	246-2871

As with most canoe organizations, kayakers are welcome.

University of Washington Canoe Club	543-2217

For UW students and alumni only.

Washington Kayak Club
PO Box 24264, Seattle, WA 98124

One of the oldest such clubs in the United States and the largest club outside Europe, this safety- and conservation-oriented club organizes several trips (with varying levels of difficulty) each weekend, and gives sea and whitewater kayaking lessons each spring—general public welcome but must have own equipment.

Exercise clubs and facilities

EE7	**Anderson Nautilus Fitness Center**	*6:30am-9pm Mon-Fri; 9am-6pm Sat;*
	7203 Woodlawn NE	*closed Sun; 524-7000*

Conveniently located for I-5 commuters and Green Lake joggers. Exercise room includes 36 Nautilus machines. Aerobic dance classes. Nine-member instructor staff includes seven kinesiology graduates who counsel members on a one-to-one basis. Three-month, one- and two-year memberships with payment plans. Facilities include sauna, Jacuzzi.

HH3	**Bellevue Athletic Club**	*5am-11pm every day*
	11200 SE Sixth, Bellevue	*455-1616*

Health and social club offering indoor and outdoor tennis courts, handball/racquetball courts, squash courts, Olympic indoor swimming pool, indoor running track, classes, steam and sauna, child care, restaurant and lounge, banquet and conference facilities.

HH7	**The Body Nautilus**	*6:45am-9pm Mon-Fri; 8:45am-6pm Sat;*
	1501 12th Ave	*11:45am-6pm Sun; 329-2639*

Men-only weight training and conditioning features special fitness assessments and periodic physiological profiles. Stationary bikes, 12 Nautilus machines, six instructors. Showers, sauna, whirlpool. Staff offers assistance in developing an individual exercise program and reaching goals. Monthly consultations.

GG7	**The Exercise Place**	*Hours vary*
	100 Mercer St, Hansen Baking Co.	*284-8940*

Aerobic conditioning and exercise studio for men and women. Dressing facilities, showers, no equipment. First class free.

J4	**Fitness, Inc.**	*6am-8pm Mon-Fri; 8am-6pm Sat; closed Sun*
	1529 Ninth Ave	*624-2153*

Men-only barbell gym. Works closely with members to achieve particular physical development objectives. Ten percent of clientele is involved in specific sports training and conditioning; 30 percent is on maintenance program; 60 percent is therapy-related. Facilities include steam room, sauna, ultraviolet tanning, showers, lockers. One instructor.

Sports

| **First Hill Nautilus**
Cabrini Medical Tower
901 Boren Ave | *6am-8pm Mon-Fri; 8am-3pm Sat;*
closed Sun; appointments required
625-9605 |

Offers extensive professional supervision for everyone from weekend joggers to professional athletes and post-surgical patients. Dietary and nutritional consultation. Twelve Nautilus machines, three stationary bikes. Showers and lockers. Three instructors.

| **Gallery Racquet Club**
11616 Aurora Ave N | *6am-midnight every day*
365-5710 |

Game courts include six indoor tennis courts and one racquetball court. Exercise weight room, classes. Aerobic exercise. Amenities include pro shop, social programs, some babysitting. Dance classes and suntanning facilities open to non-members. Lifetime and annual memberships available. Racquetball-only memberships offered.

| **Green Lake Health Club**
308 NE 72nd | *9am-8pm Mon-Sat; closed Sun*
523-1950 |

Men-only free-weight gym with emphasis on body building and conditioning. Individual instruction for all levels and all ages. Facilities available for runners. One instructor. Showers, steam bath.

| **Gymnastics and Dance Center**
7104 Woodlawn Ave NE | *9am-8pm Mon-Sat; closed Sun*
522-6282 |

Dance room and gymnastics equipment. Aerobic, dance, and gymnastics classes for children and adults; tap dance for adults. No showers. Classes by appointment. Prices vary with length of classes.

| **In Shape Fitness Center for Women**
6300 Roosevelt Way NE | *9:30am-9pm Mon-Fri; 9:30am-2pm Sat*
Appointments required; 524-6310 |

Gym reserved exclusively for women; men may use UVA tanning facilities. Variety of exercise equipment, free weights, and machines. Programs are individually designed, with continual monitoring and periodic reassessments. Special programs for pregnant women. Two instructors. Weight-control instruction. Sauna, steam room, lockers. Membership varies by program.

| **In-Trim Health Studio**
6423 Fauntleroy Way SW | *10am-9pm Mon, Wed, Fri (women)*
10am-9pm Tues, Thurs, Sat (men); 937-7026 |

Specializes in in-depth body-shaping instruction for people involved in professional activities in which appearance is important. Personal supervision includes attention to diet and eating habits. Offers weight-training machinery and free weights. Facilities include whirlpool, sauna, tanning lamps, showers, lockers. Exercise classes.

| **Ironworks Gym**
12708 Northrup Way, Bellevue | *6am-midnight Mon-Fri; 7am-6pm Sat;*
noon-6pm Sun; 883-6006 |

Body building for men and women. Barbells, some Universal gym equipment, tanning machines, showers, lockers, sauna. Award-winning powerlift instructors; nutritionist. Nutritional seminars are available. Prices vary.

| **Juanita Bay Athletic Club**
11450 98th Ave NE, Juanita | *6am-11pm Mon-Sat; 8am-8pm Sun*
821-0882 |

Offers water skiing and downhill skiing lessons. Has eight racquetball courts, swimming pool, basketball gym, running track. Weight-training facilities include 13

Sports

Nautilus machines, free weights, Universal gym. Fitness center equipped to measure body fat percentage, including hydrostatic weighing facilities. Sauna, steam room, whirlpool. Other facilities include pro shop, restaurant, hair salon, banquet facilities, daycare center, tanning facilities.

HH6	**Madrona Dance Center** **800 Lake Washington Blvd**	*7:30am-9:30pm Mon-Thur; 7:30am-7:30pm Fri; 7:30am-4pm Sat; closed Sun* 625-4303

Offers adult dance classes for men and women. Special programs available for pre- and post-pregnancy. Also has kids' and teenagers' programs, aerobics for seniors; conditioning classes to complement aerobics. Yoga, tumbling, floor exercise. No showers available, but lockers are provided; you supply your own lock. Tuition varies by class and quarter.

J7	**Metropolitan Health Club** **1519 Third Ave**	*5:30am-9pm Mon-Fri; 10am-6pm Sat; noon-5pm Sun;* 682-3966

Weight training and body building on a wide variety of equipment including Nautilus and other machinery, dumbbells, barbells, Universal machines. Nine Olympic sets. Separate room for power lifting. Emphasis on injury prevention. Nutritional consultation. Guidance from award-winning bodybuilder; co-ed. Facilities include steam room and sauna, snack bar.

F5	**Nautilus Northwest Athletic Club** **2306 Sixth Ave, 223-0480**	*6:30am-9pm Mon, Wed, Fri; 10am-9pm Tues & Thur; 9am-6pm Sat; noon-6pm Sun*

Weight training and exercise for men and women. First four workouts are supervised; programs are individually developed and reassessed every five weeks. Training available for particular athletic activities. Twenty-six Nautilus machines, free weights, aerobic dance, exercise room, Jacuzzis, saunas, showers, lockers, sun tanning, eight instructors. Affiliated with 1,800 clubs for worldwide reciprocal memberships.

FF8	**Olympic Racquet and Health Club** **5301 Leary Way NW**	*Open 24 hours every day* 789-5010

The only health club in the area which is open 'round the clock. Facilities include a women's Universal weight-training room, co-ed free weight room, and co-ed Nautilus floor. Also has swimming pool, game courts for racquet sports, indoor jogging track, classes in aerobics and aqua-aerobics. Massage, tanning lamps, child care, restaurant and lounge (open to public). Facilities for parties and tournaments.

	Pacific Nautilus	*5:45am-9pm Mon, Wed, Fri; 7am-9pm Tues*
PP4	**214 SW 43rd, Renton, 251-8848**	*& Thur; 9am-6pm Sat; noon-4pm Sun*
GG3	**12611 Northrup Way, Bellevue, 451-8848**	

Serious weight training and physical therapy; recreational workouts not allowed. Emphasis is on achievement of goals. Physical therapist available. Three lines of Nautilus equipment, indoor jogging, exercise machines, nutritional counseling, tanning rooms.

	Pacific West Sport and Racquet **Club** **1340 W Meeker, Kent**	*6am-10:30pm Mon-Fri; 7:30am-9pm Sat; 9am-9pm Sun;* 852-9500

Game courts, including tennis; exercise equipment and instruction; swimming pool. Special children's programs, nursery. Contracts with outside vendors for special recreational training in scuba diving, white-water rafting, windsurfing, and skydiving. Operates a private ski resort at Pacific Mountain, Snoqualmie, where special rates are available to members. Club costs vary according to membership

Sports

plan and activities.

Redwood Athletic Club
15327 140th Pl NE, Woodinville
6am-10pm Mon-Fri, 6:30am-10pm Sat & Sun
483-6111

Family club set around a small private lake, which offers picnic and fishing facilities, access to Burke-Gilman Trail. Indoor facilities include four racquetball courts, nine tennis courts, pool, running track, pickleball courts, weight-training room with barbells and Universal equipment. Outdoor facilities include horseshoe pits, shuffleboard, tennis court, Olympic pool, covered picnic area with barbecue pits, basketball hoops. Showers, lockers, saunas, whirlpool, steam room. Program offers socials, aerobic dance, swimnastics, junior participation in all sports, inter-club competition.

Samena Club
15231 Lake Hills Blvd, Bellevue
8am-10pm every day (exercise); 5am-10pm every day (pool only); 746-1160

Full facilities club emphasizing water activities. Swimming lessons available year-round (outdoor pool opens after May). Wading pool. Red Cross water-safety classes include advanced life saving, basic rescue. Other classes in aerobics, tennis, tumbling, calisthenics, flexibility, CPR, and first aid. All classes open to non-members. Facilities for softball, basketball. Also has game courts, Universal and free weights, sauna.

Seattle Athletic Club (Downtown)
2020 Western Ave
6am-11pm Mon-Fri; 8am-8pm Sat & Sun
625-1600

Has racquetball and squash courts, gym, all-purpose exercise room, complete Nautilus room including free weights and stationary bicycles, indoor pool, and running track. Also has massage therapist, tanning room, manicurist, squash and racquetball pros, exercise classes, locker rooms, showers, sauna, child care, social and recreational activities, restaurant, and conference room. Limited reciprocal agreements with the Northgate Seattle Athletic Club.

Seattle Athletic Club (Northgate)
333 NE 97th
6:30am-11pm Mon-Fri; 8am-8pm Sat & Sun
522-9400

Game courts (no court fees) and racquetball and squash pros, swimming pools, full Nautilus equipment and free weights, a combination gym and basketball/volleyball court. Also has aerobics classes, tournaments, leagues. Whirlpool, sauna, UVA tanning, restaurant, and babysitting services round out facilities. Limited reciprocal agreements with the Downtown Seattle Athletic Club.

Supersonics Racquet and Health Club
4455 148th Ave NE, Bellevue
6:15am-11pm Mon-Fri; 7:15am-10pm Sat & Sun
885-5566

Club specializing in racquet games—tennis, racquetball. Indoor track and soccer, basketball, Universal weight training equipment and 9 Nautilus machines. Co-ed aerobic conditioning classes offered. Parties and outdoor trips.

Washington Athletic Club
1326 Sixth Ave
6am-10pm Mon-Fri; 8am-5pm Sat & Sun
464-3073

Established downtown full service club. Separate conditioning departments for men and women feature free weights and Universal equipment, bicycles, saunas, Jacuzzis. Game courts include 6 handball/racquetball, 4 squash courts. Indoor track swimming pool. Wide variety of exercise and fitness classes. Massage and sun lamps. Restaurant, lounge, and banquet rooms. Open to members only; sponsors required. Variety of plans.

227

Sports

	Washington Conditioning Club	6am-9pm Mon-Fri; 10am-6pm Sat;
J6	1521-B Fourth Ave, 682-4036	noon-5pm Sun
GG1	2505 152nd Ave NE, Bellevue, 882-1660	

Conditioning for men and women. Specializes in designing individual exercise programs for the most effective 30-minute, three times weekly workouts. Comprehensive computer monitoring service includes hydrostatic weighing and EKG machine to perform aerobic fitness analysis. Flexibility testing, physical proportion monitoring of body size changes during program. Five lines of Nautilus equipment, aerobics, nutritional counseling, Jacuzzi, saunas, showers, lockers. Full-time staff includes three full-time physiologists, a kinesiologist, and a nutritionist.

	YMCA	Open Mon-Sat - hours vary; closed Sun
M6	Main branch, 909 Fourth Ave	382-5010
	13 other branches	

Memberships available for men and women. Facilities vary with branch but most include swimming pool, exercise rooms with Universal equipment and free weights, game courts, sauna, whirlpool. Variety of classes. Prices vary. The new Women's Fitness Center at the downtown YMCA has a complete set of Universal and free weights, stationary bicycles, rowing machine, treadmill and dance studio.

	YWCA	7am-8pm Mon-Fri; closed Sat & Sun
L6	Main branch: Fifth & Seneca	447-4869
	4 other branches	

Facilities for men and women include exercise equipment and classes at most locations; downtown location also has weight training, sauna, swimming. Programs for seniors, and parents and kids.

Fishing

The real fishing in Washington is for salmon and for its battling cousin, the steelhead, a seagoing trout that spawns in fresh waters and is often mistakenly referred to as a salmon.

If you are new to the area or to the sport, contact a local tackle shop for the latest information; listed are some with the most knowledgeable staffs. Also, before you do anything else, you should pick up a copy of *Fishing and Hunting News* (624-3845), a local, up-to-date journal on the sport. Both local daily newspapers also have weekly fishing columns. Washington State fishing licenses are required for all freshwater fish, salmon, and razor clams, and can be obtained at tackle shops, sporting-goods stores like Sportswest, and Ernst Home Centers, Fred Meyer, and most Pay 'n Save stores.

	Archer and Angler	
DD6	11714 15th NE	362-4030

A good source for fly-fishing information.

	Eddie Bauer, Inc.	
K5	1330 Fifth	622-2766

They have one of the few files in town with charter information, though it's not as comprehensive and up-to-date as it used to be.

	Linc's Tackle & Honda	
I16	501 Rainier S	324-7600

Sports

A well-established, no-nonsense tackle shop.

Warshal's
First & Madison   *624-7300*

Ditto.

Steelhead. The season is roughly from December through March, although there are some summer and fall steelhead runs. The best rivers for steelhead fishing are the Skykomish, Monroe to Index; the Skagit, a beautiful stretch of river between Sedro Woolley and Rockport (hurry, a dam may change all that in a few years); the Kalama, Green, and Cowlitz rivers to the south of Seattle; and the Hoh, Bogachiel, and Quillayute rivers in the rain forest of the Olympic Peninsula. There are weekly stream reports in both daily papers giving the flow heights and conditions of the rivers. For a pleasant introduction to steelhead fishing (from a boat), you can try going with a local guide, all of whom are registered with the state. For $35 to $50 a day, they supply all the tackle and gear, and will take you where the fish are biting. Check the Yellow Pages for guides in the localities where you are interested in fishing, or contact the Department of Game, 600 N Capitol Way, Olympia 98504 (753-5700) for a fishing-guide list.

Salmon. There are several charters for Puget Sound salmon fishing departing from Seattle and Edmonds, but the vast majority of charters operate out of coastal towns, salmon fishing being more properly an ocean sport. The coast season does, however, run only from May 28 through Labor Day or until the quotas are filled. The Seattle charters have a longer season, with south Puget Sound closed only in April–June, and the waters north of Edmonds open all year round.

The most popular coastal town is undoubtedly **Westport**, which draws 250,000 fishermen a year. For about $40 to $50 a person (add another $5 to rent gear), you can enjoy a day's pursuit on a charter boat. Boats range in size from a "six-man" to a "22-man"—the smaller the boat the slightly higher the cost, normally. Most companies serve coffee but no food, rent gear and tackle, and sell fishing licenses. All the charter companies are Coast Guard–approved. Some Westport companies are listed below with their year-round phone numbers; during the season many have toll-free numbers. Check with directory assistance before calling. Westport Charters, 268-9120; Gull Charters, 268-9186; Travis Charters, 268-9140; and Islander Charters, 268-9166. Be forewarned that you will need reservations, and well in advance for weekends.

Also good, and far more interesting in terms of Northwest culture, are **Neah Bay**, at the farthest tip of the United States on the Olympic Peninsula, an Indian village caught between the past and the present; and **Ilwaco**, a pretty little fishing village near the mouth of the Columbia River.

Several Seattle-based charters are listed below:

Bendixen's Puget Sound Charters
818 W Argand   *285-5999*

The fishing boat leaves from Shilshole every morning just before daylight, year round. A fully covered 40-footer, the boat accommodates groups of six people who can fish (troll, actually). The cost is $39 per person, which includes gear, hot sweet rolls and coffee in the morning, and a salmon bake aboard the boat on the way back in the afternoon. Bring your own salmon-fishing permit (or buy one from the charter operators for $3.25—yearly permit—or $1.25—one-day permit) and your own beer. The trip lasts about seven and a half hours, returning at 2pm.

Sports

EE9 Mager Fishing Charters
6049 Seaview Ave NW   763-1194

They guarantee fish or the next trip is free! The boat leaves from the Shilshole marina at 6:30am and returns at 1:30pm; the outing costs $17.86 per person, $3 for the day's bait, $3 for tackle, and $1.25 for a Washington State fishing license.

FF7 Viking Star Charters
3629 Bagley N   634-2939

The 58-foot boat *Viking Star* leaves every morning at 6am from Shilshole Bay Marina whenever 12 people are signed up. Cost is $42 per person in summer ($28 in winter), including bait and tackle. The catch, depending on the season, includes salmon, blackmouth cod, and bottomfish, which the crew will fillet for you. Coffee is available on board, along with a microwave oven to heat the sandwiches you should bring along. Return is at 4:30pm.

EE9 Ray's Boathouse   6am-2pm Wed-Sun; closed Mon & Tues
6049 Seaview NW   789-4130 or 783-9779

If you are not up to a full-scale charter, Ray's Boathouse at Shilshole Bay has 12- and 14-foot aluminum boats for rent for $14 per day (plus $6.50 per hour for motor). Tackle rentals and fishing licenses are also available.

Public fishing piers—Seattle

For more information, phone 625-4671.
Commodore Park, W Commodore Way & W Gilman
Golden Gardens Park, north end of Seaview N
Green Lake, E Greenlake Way & Latona NE (juvenile); W Greenlake Dr N & **Stone Way N;** W Greenlake Way N
North Leschi Moorage, Lakeside S & Alder E
Madison Park, Lake Washington Blvd & E Madison
Mount Baker Park, Lake Washington between Lake Park Dr S & S Horton
Seward Park, Lake Washington Blvd S & S Juneau
Waterfront Park, Pier 57, Alaskan Way, on Puget Sound

Public fishing piers—Kirkland

Houghton Beach, Lake Washington Blvd & NE 60th
Marsh Park, 6600 Lake Washington Blvd
Marina Park, foot of Kirkland
Waverly Park, Waverly Way & 6th W

Public fishing piers—Kenmore

Kenmore Logboom County Park, Hwy 522 & 60th Place NE

Public fishing piers—Mercer Island

Clarke Beach, 7700 E Mercer Way
Groveland Beach, 5800 W Mercer Way
Proctor Landing, foot of SE 32nd
Luther Burbank, 8400 SE 24th

Public fishing piers—Redmond

Johnson Park, 7901 196th NE
Fiorito Park, Avondale Road/Beer Creek Village

Sports

Golf — Public courses

FF2	**Bellevue Municipal Golf Course** **5450 140th NE, Bellevue**	*PNGA 66.1; 5,694 yards* *885-6009*

Sixteen years old, fairly level, easy.

HH1	**Crossroads Park Golf Course** **16000 NE 10th, due east of Crossroads Mall, Bellevue**	*453-4873*

A par-3, nine-hole course. 800 yards.

CC7	**Jackson Park Municipal** **Golf Course** **1000 NE 135th**	*PNGA 68.2; 5,997 yards* *363-4747*

A speedy, easy course over rolling hills.

JJ6	**Jefferson Park** **4101 Beacon St**	*PNGA 67; 6,282 yards* *762-4513*

Great views of the city from the hilltop fairways, which look easier than they really are.

Mount Si Golf Course **9010 Meadowbrook-North Bend Rd** **SE, northwest of North Bend**	*PNGA 65.4; 5,470 yards* *888-1541*

A beautiful, ego-boosting course with a marvelous, Bavarian setting; out of the way, but very pretty.

PP6	**Tyee Valley Golf Course** **2401 S 192nd**	*PNGA 66; 5,896 yards* *878-3540*

Right at the foot of the runway to Sea-Tac, this easy, short course is perfect for a fast game between planes.

JJ8	**West Seattle Golf Course** **4470 35th SW**	*PNGA 68; 6,054 yards* *932-9792*

A good, undulating course just over the Duwamish River, tucked into a hilly valley that makes for some surprising lies.

Lake Wilderness Golf Course **25400 Witte Rd SE, Maple Valley** **south on I-5 to I-405 and Maple Valley**	*PNGA 69; 6,220 yards* *432-9405*

A pretty, moderately challenging, rolling course.

Practice ranges

GG1	**Harris-Conley** **1440 156th NE, Bellevue**	*747-2585*

32 tees, automatic and grass.

GG8	**Interbay Golf Park** **2501 15th W**	*625-2820*

20 tees, none automatic.

231

JJ6	**Jefferson Park** 4101 Beacon S	763-8989
	24 tees, none automatic.	
DD7	**Puetz Evergreen** 11762 Aurora N	362-2272
	32 tees, automatic and grass.	
LL3	**Renton** 2000 Lake Washington Blvd N, Renton	255-1817
	20 tees, automatic.	

Hiking, Camping, and Climbing

There are three national parks, three forests, three wilderness areas, and numerous state parks, all within several hours' drive of Seattle. You can choose between rain forest and ocean beaches on the Olympic Peninsula, hike along the Pacific Crest Trail in the Cascades, or climb Mt. Rainier.

Access to campgrounds in National Parks and Forests is first come, first served. If your backcountry hiking includes overnight camping in any of the National Parks, you may be required to obtain a permit which you can get at the park when you start your hike. Limits on the size of your party (maximum 12, preferred six) are enforced even with the permit. Open fires may be prohibited in some areas.

Special wilderness permits are required for all Washington State wildernesses except the Alpine Lakes Wilderness Area. Permits and information may be obtained by mail, phone, or by visiting the Forest Service Ranger Station administering the particular wilderness you wish to visit. Like the backcountry use permits, they are free and are issued one per party for a single trip.

State parks tend to be at lower elevations, accessible year-round, and closer to populated areas. In lands administered by the State Department of Natural Resources, or the State Parks and Recreation Commmission, rules may vary. All veteran hikers recommend that you call or write the park ranger or administrator in the area you wish to travel for information about current rules, weather, and trail conditions.

US Forest Service/National Parks Service (joint) **Outdoor Recreation Information Office** 1018 First Ave, Seattle 98104	*7:45-4:30 Mon-Fri* *442-0170* *(Recording after hours)*
Has trail reports, maps, books, information on weather, camping areas, opening and closing dates of facilities, access roads, and backcountry skiing conditions. Can also give out information on wilderness and backcountry use permits.	
North Cascades National Park, **Ross Lake, and Lake Chelan** **National Recreation Areas** Marblemount, WA 98267	*8-4:30 Every day* *873-4590*
Mount Rainier National Park Tahoma Woods, Star Route Ashford, WA 98304	*8-4:30 Mon-Fri, 569-2211* *24-hour road and weather recorded message,* *569-2343*

Olympic National Park 600 E Park Ave Port Angeles, WA 98362	*8-4:30 Every day,* 452-4501 x230 *24-hour road and weather recorded message,* 452-9235
Washington State Parks and Recreation Department Public Information Office 7150 Clearwater Lane Olympia, WA 98503	*8-5 Mon-Sat,* 753-2027 *Toll-free number* *Early May to Labor Day:* 1-800-562-0990

There are a number of clubs and organizations of backpackers and climbers in the Greater Seattle area; several of them are listed below. Another good way to find out what is happening in the outdoors world, meet interested people, and choose a guide service or climbing school is to check in with some of the outdoors shops about town (see Outdoor Equipment in the Shopping Chapter for a listing of these).

The Mountaineers   623-2314
719 Pike

The Mountaineers is a very active outdoors club committed to enjoying and preserving mountain backcountry areas. The club is also an excellent source of information for newcomers to the area or to outdoors activities. The club maintains a fine library (open to non-members for browsing) on subjects such as backpacking trails, climbing techniques, nature study, and expedition history, and also publishes a series of reliable, inexpensive books that cover practically every major hike in the Northwest (the *101 Hikes* and *Footsore* series and more). They will send you a listing of their publications on request; the books are available in bookstores as well. The club also offers its members courses in such skills as alpine scrambling, basic climbing, and cross-country skiing as well as a plethora of organized bicycling, climbing, hiking, snowshoeing, canoeing, and other trips.

REI   323-8333
1525 11th

In addition to providing for all the equipment needs and fantasies of outdoor types, REI has an excellent outdoors book and map section and offers a free slide, lecture, and clinic series on Thursday evenings at 7 in the store's auditorium. Topics include slides and films on exotic adventures and nature photography. More in-depth workshops are also given on climbing, downhill and cross country skiing, sailboarding and bike maintenance, etc.

Sierra Club   621-1696
1516 Melrose

A national club dedicated to exploring, enjoying, and preserving wilderness areas, The Sierra Club also offers numerous day hikes and backpacking trips to members and non-members alike.

Camp Long   625-2570

The Seattle Department of Parks and Recreation operates a unique natural area within the City of Seattle, complete with all facilities for outdoor activities and camping. A range of workshops, training courses, and off-site field trips is offered year-round. These courses include: survival, winter camping, snowshoeing, backpacking, wild edible plant identification, and map and compass skills. Family-oriented nature walks and spring and summer youth camping programs are also offered.

Leavenworth Alpine Guide Service   *Carl Schneider*
837 Front St, Leavenworth   *939-4373 or (509) 548-5623*

This organization based on the eastern side of the mountains offers both instruction in all forms of alpine climbing and personally guided alpine climbing trips. Call or write for an informational brochure.

Backcountry Horsemen of Washington 20617 Poplar Way, Alderwood Manor	Ken Wilcox 775-2603

This club was formed to improve and increase trailriding opportunities in the state. It also organizes several outings a year.

Issaquah Alps Trails Club
PO Box 351, Issaquah, WA 98027

This club sponsors hiking trips in the Issaquah Alps. Write for more information.

Signpost Magazine 16812 36th Ave W, Lynnwood	743-3947

Published 12 times a year by the Northwest Trails Association, this is the best source of local information about the backpacking scene.

Signpost Books 8912 192nd SW, Edmonds	776-0370

The now-separate book-publishing arm of Signpost Magazine specializes in trail and river guides, biking and snow-touring books, and one on foraging for edible plants in the Northwest. Call for specific titles.

Climbing Mount Rainier

There are two ways to climb "The Mountain": with Rainier Mountaineering, the concessioned guide service, or in your own party. Unless you are qualified to do it on your own—and this is a big, difficult, and dangerous mountain on which several people a year are killed—you must climb with the guide service.

Rainier Mountaineering, Inc. Paradise, WA 98397 (summer) 210 St. Helens Ave, Tacoma, WA 98402 (winter)	569-2227; 9-5 Every day 627-6242; 9-noon Mon, Wed, Fri

Run by Lou Whittaker, Rainier Mountaineering is highly regarded nationally. In a one-day training session, they will teach you everything you need to know to make the climb—all you need is a good heart. The climb itself takes two days and can be done with them any time from late May till the middle of September. Call or write for their brochure.

If you plan to climb with your own party (solo climbing is prohibited), you must register at one of the ranger stations in Mt. Rainier National Park (at Paradise, Longmire, White River, or Carbon River). They will make sure you have adequate experience and the proper equipment, and will inform you of the route, avalanche conditions and weather forecast. Generally, the best time to climb is from late June through early September; a backcountry use permit is needed from June 15-Sept 30. Also, you must check in with the Ranger Station when you get back down. For more general information, call Mt. Rainier National Park at 569-2211.

Sports

Jogging

Seattle's natural beauty, its many parks, the mild climate, and the large number of soft grassy parking strips combine to make it an easy and attractive city in which to run. In fact, it's possible to step out of just about any front door in the area and make up an acceptable running course just by being adventurous. Most runners, though, like to know in advance where and how far they're going to run. The following list serves as a guide to the area's most popular running places, with distances and a short description of each area's surface and attractions. Addresses given are for the usual starting place.

Jogging — Parks and road courses

FF7- BB5	**Burke-Gilman Trail**	*See Bicycling section*
BB3	**Sammamish River Trail**	*See Bicycling section*
FF1	At its southern end, Marymoor Park offers a fitness course and many other recreational possibilities.	
EE5	**Warren Magnuson Park**	*Sand Point Way NE & NE 65th*
	A former Naval Air Station with many opportunities for running, including wide paved roads and varying grassy terrain, all nicely situated on Lake Washington.	
EE7	**Green Lake**	*See Bicycling section*
	The city's most popular running spot also features a three-mile dirt trail circling the lake.	
FF5	**Laurelhurst Park**	*NE 45th & 48th NE*
	An 880-yard dirt path winding around a small park in one of the city's nicest residential neighborhoods.	
EE7- EE6	**Ravenna Boulevard**	*Green Lake Way N & NE 71st*
	Wide grassy median strip, which begins at Green Lake and dips down into a woodsy ravine near its end at 25th NE.	
FF9	**Discovery Park**	*36th W & W Government Way*
	Many trails and settings await the runner here, including an 880-yard fitness course and a three-mile loop around the perimeter of the park.	
GG9	**Magnolia Bluff**	*W Galer & 31st W*
	A striking run when the weather is clear, offering vistas of the Olympic Mountains across Puget Sound. From the Magnolia Bluff parking lot it's 2.1 miles, with some hills, to the other end at Discovery Park.	
GG8	**Queen Anne Hill Scenic Loop**	*3rd W & W Smith*
	One of the city's most architecturally-pleasing runs, incorporating Highland Drive and other interesting parts of Queen Anne Hill in a three-mile loop on streets and parking strips.	
HH7	**Broadway Playfield**	*11th E & E Pine*
	Dirt running path around a reservoir.	

Sports

HH8- GG8	**Elliott Bay Waterfront**	
	A favorite with noon-time runners. Most start no farther south than Pioneer Square, and then run to and through Myrtle Edwards Park north of Pier 70. The Park's double paved loop course is two-and-one-half miles long, and incorporates a fitness course on its west path.	
HH6	**Lake Washington Boulevard**	*See Bicycling section*
	Interurban Trail	*See Bicycling section*
JJ5	**Seward Park**	*See Bicycling section*
II9	**Alki Point**	*Alki Ave SW*
	Crowded in summer, wind-swept in winter, but a nicely paved surface and great views of the Sound and the city.	
KK9- LL9	**Lincoln Park**	*Fauntleroy Way SW & SW Trenton*
	Varying paths and roads through a tree-filled park overlooking Vashon Island and the Sound.	
II4-	**Mercer Island**	*See Bicycling section*
KK4	**Pioneer Park**	*Island Crest Way & SE 68th, Mercer Island*
	Dirt paths and many horse trails of varying length (watch where you step).	
FF4- HH4	**Medina-Evergreen Point**	*Overlake Drive & Evergreen Point Rd, Bellevue*
	A scenic route on nicely maintained parking strips and offering views of Lake Washington and some of the area's most stunning homes. Two-and-a-half miles each way.	

Running Information

Seattle's large and well-organized running community offers many events year-round, from races to running clinics. For information on upcoming events, check out the sports sections of the *Seattle Times* (Thursdays) and *P-I* (Fridays), or get a copy of the *Norwester*, the local running magazine. Running shops are also good sources for running news and schedules of events. Best bets are Super Jock & Jill, 7210 E Green Lake Dr N (522-7711), The Runner's Place, 321 Broadway E (324-6537), and Fast Lady Sports, 14310 NE 20th, Bellevue (641-9696). (The Runner's Place store also has a recorded runners' hotline after hours.)

There are many good running races in the Seattle area, at least one every weekend once good weather begins. Some featured races include the Emerald City Marathon in late March, the 11-kilometer Mariner Freeway Run in late April, Seward-to-Madison seven-mile run in mid-July, the Seafair 10-kilometer through the city streets in early August, the Women's Sportswest 10-kilometer in mid-August, and the Seattle Marathon in late November.

Running clubs offer the chance to get together with other runners, wear a special T-shirt, and not too much else. The Seattle Track Club (447-2605) is the best bet for women and age-group runners (masters and juniors); it meets at least twice per week for group runs and some coaching is available. Serious male and female runners gravitate toward Club Northwest (522-7787) which has the most competitive orientation.

Sports

Rafting

There are half a dozen rafting companies in the area that would be more than willing to give you a taste of the region's rivers for $40–$60 a day. Each river is unique and each company has its own style of trip, though there are two basic types: peaceful float trips, often in protected wildlife areas; and those that run the rapids (varying degrees of difficulty). You should inquire beforehand about the type of trip, the cost, transportation included, rain gear and life jackets provided, meals, and so on. Regular trips are scheduled on the Sauk, Skagit, Methow, Wenatchee, Skykomish, and the Olympic Peninsula rivers.

Rafting — Excursions and lessons

DD6 **Orion Expeditions**　　　　　*364-9850*
10728 Lake City Way NE

Orion offers both lessons and expeditions for whitewater rafters. Their five-day school ($275) covers all phases of whitewater running on the Deschutes River in Oregon. One-, two-, or three-day trips, including an all-you-can-eat lunch, can be arranged on Washington and Oregon rivers. Orion's guides are all four- or five-year veterans who can recommend rivers based on the rafter's experience. Rates are lower on weekdays.

17 **Zig Zag River Runners**　　　　*8-6 Mon-Fri*
1932 First Ave　　　　　　　　　　*382-0900*

Runs exuberant guided scenic and whitewater rafting tours daily, March 1 through October 1, on 10 Washington rivers. Wenatchee is the big one, but the Skykomish, Methow, and Sauk are fun, too. Beginning to advanced, prices vary.

Pacific Northwest Float Trips　*Seattle: 855-0535*
PO Box 287, Burlington, WA 98233

Offers one- and two-day trips on most major Washington rivers including eagle-watching float trips on the Skagit, and whitewater trips on the Sauk, Suiattle, Wenatchee, and Methow.

Rivers Northwest　　　　　　　*842-2824*
Bainbridge Island

Offers rafting trips on the Olympic Peninsula rivers.

Sailboarding

DD7 **The Good Sport**　　　　　　*362-3151*
344 NE Northgate Way

This North End shop carries a good line of sailboards and accessories. Perhaps the best part of their operation, however, is their concession near Evans Pool at Green Lake. From there they rent sailboards, canoes, and paddleboats, and give sailboard lessons.

GG7 **Lake Union Sailboards**　　　*283-4799*
1844 Westlake Ave N

This is *the* sailboard specialist—selling boards, renting equipment, sponsoring lessons. By purchasing a membership you get access to the deli, changing and

237

Sports

sauna rooms, and board storage facilities. This is the only sailboard outlet that is located right on the water—their own pier connects the clubhouse to Lake Union.

Northwest Boardsailing Fleet   PO Box 396, Seattle, WA 98125

Established locally to help newcomers and challenge the advanced, this organization can answer just about any question regarding local windsurf activities. The group is a hub for those interested in the sporting and social events in sailboarding.

Northwest Sailboard Newsmagazine   *821-2940*
published by Windsurfing Northwest, PO Box 396, Seattle, WA 98125

This newsprint-format magazine, published four times yearly, is a good resource for local events. Subscriptions are available or single copies are distributed at all retail sailboard outlets.

EE7 **Whitewater Sports**   *523-5150*
307 NE 71st

Once known exclusively for their whitewater line of kayaks and canoes, Whitewater Sports is turning a lot of warm-weather attention to sailboarding. Their shop near Green Lake positions them well for lessons and rentals. Boards cost $7 per hour ($35 per day) and wetsuits can be rented at $1.50 per hour ($10 per day). Trips to Lake Chelan for windsurfing are often part of the summer plan, too.

Sailing — Rentals and instruction

FF6 **Kelly's Landing**   *Open weekends in May, 9-7:30 every day,*
1401 NE Boat St, Portage Bay   *June–mid-Sept; 634-3470*

Has a good selection of sailboats, 12-38 feet long. Rates are $3-$12 an hour and there are thrifty half- and full-day rates. Its larger sailboats have motors and can navigate the Montlake Cut into Lake Washington; there are no overnight rentals. Canoes are also for rent, for use on the lake or elsewhere (car racks are available).

GG7 **Sailboats Unlimited**   *Open every day: winter 9-4, summer 9-7*
2046 Westlake N (Lake Union)   *283-4664*

A variety of sailboats for rent at rates ranging from $7.50-$12 an hour ($50-$100 for a full day). They have one motor-equipped sailboat to get from Lake Union to Lake Washington.

EE9 **Seattle Sailing Club**   *782-5100*
7001 Seaview NW (Shilshole Bay)

This is a sailing club for those who don't own their own boats. Twenty-three and 27-foot boats are available at both Shilshole and Anacortes. Beyond the annual membership fee of $895, there is no charge for day-sailing; there is an overnight fee of $30 per night. Private lessons are $135/10 hours for non-members, $99/10 hours for members.

EE9 **Wind Works Sailing School**   *784-9386*
and Charters
7001 Seaview NW, Shilshole Bay Marina

Rentals by the day, charters by the week, sailboats 25 to 57 feet (from $55 a day), bareboat or skippered. Lessons, beginning through advanced, are given on Puget Sound, and there are also day-sail excursions.

Sailing and cruising charters

F8 **Ledger Marine Charters**   *283-6160*
101 Nickerson St, Suite 200

Big-time charters here, with sailboats from 27 to 47 feet (from $425/week), powerboats from 26 to 55 feet, and skippered boats up to 110 feet, all with one-week minimums. Special-occasion vessels (75 persons or less) available with three-hour minimum, from $450.

G7 **Northwest Marine Charters**   *283-3040*
2400 Westlake N

The big charter broker for yacht owners, Northwest Marine Charters leases yachts to qualified renters (u-drive or sail), and offers skippered and crewed sightseeing yacht trips. Costs range from $100 to $2,600 per day, depending on service.

F7 **Viking Star Charters**   *634-2939*
3629 Bagley N

E9 Offers skippered yacht tours from its Shilshole Marina to the San Juan Islands from June 1 through September. $250–$400 per person pays for three days and two nights of visual feasts, four meals, lodging at the Island Lopez resort, and a Dungeness crab picnic. Sport-fishing charters also available.

Downhill Skiing

They call it "Seattle Cement"—the rain-thickened, heavy snow on thousands of vertical feet of Cascade skiing. They say if you can ski it, you can ski anything. They also say you don't have to try it if you don't want to; the weekend parking lots are already crowded enough. Yet despite the constantly unpredictable weather, you can luck into an ideal day—and in Washington, when it's good it's very good. All the areas except Mt. Baker have night skiing, too. Remember to carry tire chains and a shovel whenever you are driving to a ski area and, before you leave, call 464-6010 to find out about highway conditions.

The closest ski areas to Seattle are on I-90's Snoqualmie Pass, just an hour's drive east of Seattle. **Alpental** (623-3415 or 434-6112) draws a more selective group, as a good portion of the layout is advanced-expert terrain; nevertheless the hill has a loyal following who learned to ski on the gentler, well-groomed novice runs.

A recent merging of two separate summit areas has opened a myriad of beginning and intermediate runs at the **Snoqualmie Summit-Ski Acres** operation (Summit at 434-6161, Ski Acres at 434-6371). One lift ticket will load skiers onto chairs at either of the neighboring areas although a narrow strip of privately owned land between the two keeps them from being adjacent. You can hop a shuttle bus for a quick half mile between the two for a change of scenery. The school buses park side by side here as the gradual ballroom slopes host numerous ski schools during high season.

Just a short mile to the east is **Pacific West** (633-2460), the new name for the old Mt. Hyak ski resort. New money and management seem to have stabilized conditions here. While the runs are more limited, Pac West has the cheapest lift tickets around. Night skiing is a popular draw with lifts running nightly until midnight, Friday and Saturday until 1.

The biggie for Seattleites is the two hour southbound ride to **Crystal Mountain** (634-3771—recorded message on snow conditions, 663-2265 to reach Crystal

239

Sports

Mountain directly), a World Cup ski race site in 1972 and the best ski resort in the state. The 7,000-foot vantage point at the top of Green Valley affords a tremendous view of Mt. Rainier, and even Mt. St. Helens on a clear day. The runs are extensive and varied, whether you're gobbling moguls in Green Valley's bowl or cruising down Queen's. You can rent condominiums with kitchens from Crystal Chalets (509-663-2311) or Silver Skis Chalet (663-2265).

Mount Baker, 56 miles east of Bellingham, (734-6771), is a terrific weekend destination even though most lodging is in or close to Bellingham. Its remote location limits day traffic and hours. Usually open only Friday, Saturday and Sunday during the day with the exception of select "Holiday Weeks" here and there, this mountain never lacks for snow. The runs are varied, predominantly intermediate with bowls, meadows, and trails. A favorite destination for the silly seriousness of Spring skiers—look for burgers on the grill at the chairlift bases.

Skiers not headed for Crystal often opt for **Stevens Pass** (973-2441). While its powder is overstated, the conditions are somewhat drier and the variety of time shifts for lift ticket purchases is a welcome customer courtesy. More advanced skiers will revel in burning down the face of Chief, skiing the back slopes of Tye Mill, or challenging the upper limits of Seventh Heaven. The newer day lodge and bar are quite attractive.

If you are looking for powder you have to journey east of the Cascade mountains.

Mission Ridge (509-663-7631 or 6543) is the closest area, though still a four-hour trip. The temperatures can get considerably chillier here than in Western Washington. There are more than 30 major runs, with different terrain from what Seattleites see close to home.

White Pass is a long 105 miles from Seattle but the Mahre twins have marked it forever on the Washington ski map. Other areas—**49 Degrees North, Mount Spokane,** and **Bluewood** are located at the Eastern extremities of the state. **Whistler** and **Blackcomb** Mountains in British Columbia are wooing more weekend dollars and week-long stays from Seattleites discovering with delight this enormous destination resort about five hours to the north.

Call the **Cascade Ski Report** (634-0200) for daily updates on skiing conditions in all the downhill areas.

Cross-Country Skiing

Cross-country ski buffs can have a dandy time in the nearby Cascades, or choose to take advantage of the drier snow and more stable conditions in Eastern Washington.

Cross-country skiing—Day trips

The Cascades offer many opportunities for enjoyable day trips on skinny skis; however, a word of warning should be issued: There is a constant threat of avalanche danger in this mountainous backcountry. Conditions change daily and sometimes hourly, so always check for current road and avalanche conditions before starting out.

Call 464-6010 (or 925-6151 if you are east of the mountains) for highway conditions. These are 24-hour recordings operating in winter only. You can also listen for up-to-date commercial radio reports from the Forest Service or National Weather Service. For avalanche conditions call 527-6677 for the Olympic and

Cascade Mountains, or call the local Forest Service Ranger Station. Local ski or Nordic patrols are also good sources of information. In an emergency contact the local ranger station or ski patrol office at a developed area. They will get in touch with the Cascade Nordic Ski Patrol which organizes search and rescue operations. The Snoqualmie Pass Snow Ranger (434-6111) has primary responsibility for search and rescue at Snoqualmie Pass.

In the Cascades, the National Park Service offers a wide variety of marked cross-country ski trails. The closest areas are the Mt. Baker-Snoqualmie National Forest, where there are numerous trailheads along both I-90 (Snoqualmie Pass) and Highway 2 (Stevens Pass). The Gold Creek and Bandera areas (near I-90), with their wide open spaces and gentle slopes, are good for beginners.

Further east, the Wenatchee National Forest offers more cross-country trails, especially around Lake Kachess (exit off I-90) and the alpine town of Leavenworth (Hwy 2) but these should be reserved for longer trips. For a longish day trip, you could also try one of the several trails in Mt. Rainier National Park. For more detailed information contact the US Forest Service/National Parks Service Outdoor Recreation Information Office at 1018 First Avenue in Downtown Seattle (442-0170). This office, which is open from 7:45-4:30 Mon-Fri, has listings of the cross-country ski trails in the National Parks and Forests, maps of the areas, and information on weather and backcountry ski conditions. Most of these areas (especially along I-90) require a Sno-park permit which costs $10 per vehicle per winter season. These can be purchased from the Office of Winter Recreation, Washington State Parks and Recreation Commission, 7150 Clearwater Lane KY-11, Olympia 98504. Phone 754-1253. (A number of retail outlets around the state also sell them.)

While some people prefer skiing the less crowded cross-country trails away from outposts of civilization, here are a couple of areas that offer the benefits of rentals, lessons, and nearby restaurants.

Pacific West Ski Area (434-6503). This Snoqualmie Pass destination is popular: The logging roads in the area make for a less strenuous trip, and can be easily followed. A single chairlift ride up the mountain is available for a few dollars if you don't wish to hike up the road to get to the higher trails. Pac West's shop has the only cross-country rental for the four downhill resorts on Snoqualmie Summit and boasts a good inventory, fitting small children and extra tall adults. Maps illustrating the various roads from the mountaintop into the back country can also be obtained at the rental shop. Cross-country ski lessons are available here as well.

Mountainholm, just north of Easton, (Exit 70 off I-90); contact Ski Rack Sports, 2118 Eighth Ave, Seattle (623-5595). For a fee you can take advantage of their double-tracked trails, some of which are along pretty Lake Kachess. Organized groups can arrange for moonlight tours. Instruction and rentals are available.

Crystal Mountain (663-2455, patrol). This area, though more famous for its downhill facilities, attracts cross-country skiers to the Silver Basin (just off chair 4). Ski Patrol here will monitor your whereabouts if you check in and out, and for 25 cents they supply topographical maps of the area. Single-ride tickets and equipment rental are available.

Mt. Rainier National Park (569-2211; 24-hour road and weather recorded message: 569-2343). There are several marked cross-country trails in the Paradise area—to Narada Falls, Nisqually Vista, and Reflection Lakes. These trails are famous for their breathtaking views of Mt. Rainier and the surrounding area but are also subject to avalanche dangers: Check with the ranger station office at Longmire for information on trail and avalanche conditions. Rentals and instruction are available from Rainier Ski Touring (569-2283). The Park rangers also

Sports

lead snowshoe walks along the Nisqually Vista Trail from Paradise on winter weekends.

Cross-Country Skiing—Longer Trips

Family Adventures, Inc., PO Box 312, Leavenworth 98828 (509-548-7330). Cross-country ski adventures out of two camps near Highway 2. Hearty meals and accommodations in heated tents and cabins make for a rustic weekend. If you want to try the Leavenworth area on your own, stay at the Pension Rohrbach (509-548-7024) or Der Ritterhof Motor Inn (509-548-5845), both just west of the town. Der Sportsmann sports shop in the town can arrange rentals and lessons.

Sun Mountain Lodge, PO Box 1000, Winthrop 98862 (509-996-2211). A cross-country skier's dream come true, Sun Mountain (nine miles southwest of Winthrop) offers spectacular views from its vantage point 1,500 feet above the gorgeous Methow Valley, as well as a 50-mile network of Nordic trails (30 miles groomed) over fine powder snow, a 50-unit lodge, pool, and fine restaurant. Book well in advance.

Mazama Country Inn, PO Box 223, Mazama 98833 (509-996-2681). A relatively recent addition to the "destination resort" offerings for cross-country skiers, Mazama Country Inn, 14 miles west of Winthrop in the Methow Valley, is a ranch house which has been converted to a family inn with five private rooms, a bunk room, and shared bathrooms. There are 12 miles of groomed trails right by the Inn, and, in 1983, Liberty Bell Alpine Tours, which is affiliated with the Inn, commenced helicopter ski trips both for downhill and cross-country skiers.

Swimming

There it is at long last—beautiful Puget Sound. You run right down to the lovely beach at Lincoln Park, past all the sunbathers, and dive into the blue water. You scream in pain and are soon back on the beach with the rest of the "bathers." Beautiful Puget Sound doesn't warm up much in the summer, rising only 10 degrees from its winter temperature, which makes it a nippy 56 degrees at best.

So the place to swim in Seattle, unless you are one of the hardy who prefer Sound water—and there are many—is one of the city's public swimming pools, or in Green Lake or Lake Washington. The Puget Sound beaches do not have lifeguards. (Seattle Parks and Recreation Department: 625-4671.) Eastside beaches are on Lake Washington and Lake Sammamish; several communities have public pools. Public beaches (except on Puget Sound) have lifeguards during summer months, weather permitting.

Public beaches — Seattle

Lake Washington:

GG5	**Madison Beach**	*1900 43rd E, at the foot of E Madison*
HH6	**Madrona Beach**	*800 Lake Washington Blvd*
EE5	**Magnuson Beach**	*NE 65th & Sand Point Way NE*
DD5	**Matthews Beach**	*9300 51st NE*
II6	**Mount Baker Beach**	*2301 Lake Washington Blvd S*
KK5	**Pritchard Beach**	*8400 55th S*
JJ5	**Seward Beach**	*5900 Lake Washington Blvd S*

EE7 **Green Lake:** The warmest water, excluding pools, in the city. *7201 E Green Lake Dr N*
  7312 W Green Lake Dr N

Puget Sound:
Alki Beach   *Alki Ave SW*
Carkeek Park   *NW 110th off Greenwood N*
Discovery Park   *36th W & W Government Way*
Golden Gardens   *North end Seaview NW*
Lincoln Park   *Fauntleroy SW & SW Webster*

Tennis — Public courts

In Seattle, the early tennis player usually gets the court. Tennis is immensely popular here and getting a public court without a reservation requires some advanced strategy. For further public court information call 625-2168.

A few tips: The best time to play is early in the day; from 6 pm onward, the courts are really crowded. The second thing to master is the rules of court occupancy, which must normally be cited, chapter and verse, in order to harass politely (persuade, if you wish) the player who got there before you did. Keep these rules in mind.
1. People using courts must relinquish at conclusion of one set or one hour for singles, two sets or 1½ hours for doubles. Warm-up time is included.
2. Priority of use is established by putting your racquet against the net of the court that you are waiting for.
3. Reservations for a public court may be made up to one week in advance. Purchase of a one-year $10 reservation card enables players to make phone reservations. Otherwise, reservations must be made in person at the Scheduling Office, 5201 Green Lake Way N, 625-4673, 8-5, Mon-Fri. Reservation times are from 10 to 10. Reservation fees are $2 for unlighted courts and $4 for lighted courts for 1½ hours of playing time.

Best Courts:
E9 Ballard Playfield, 28th NW and NW 60th
F9 Discovery Park, 36th W and W Government Way
K9 Lincoln, Fauntleroy SW and SW Webster
F7 Lower Woodland, Stone Way N and Green Lake Way N
D6 Meadowbrook, NE 107th and 30th NE
L5 Rainier Playfield, Rainier S and S Oregon
'6 Seattle Tennis Center, 2000 Empire Way S, 324-2980 (see next section for details)
G6 Volunteer Park, 15th E and E Prospect

Tennis — Public indoor courts

| Seattle Tennis Center | *7 am-10 pm, every day* |
| 2000 Empire Way S | *324-2980* |

Reservations for the 10 indoor and four outdoor public courts must be made no further in advance than eight days. There is a $10 yearly fee for phone reservations. Otherwise, reservations must be made in person. Rates are $7 for singles, $9 for doubles, for one hour and 15 minutes of play. The facility, incidentally, is an outstanding one, not heavily used except in evenings; one need not be a Seattle resident to get a reservation.

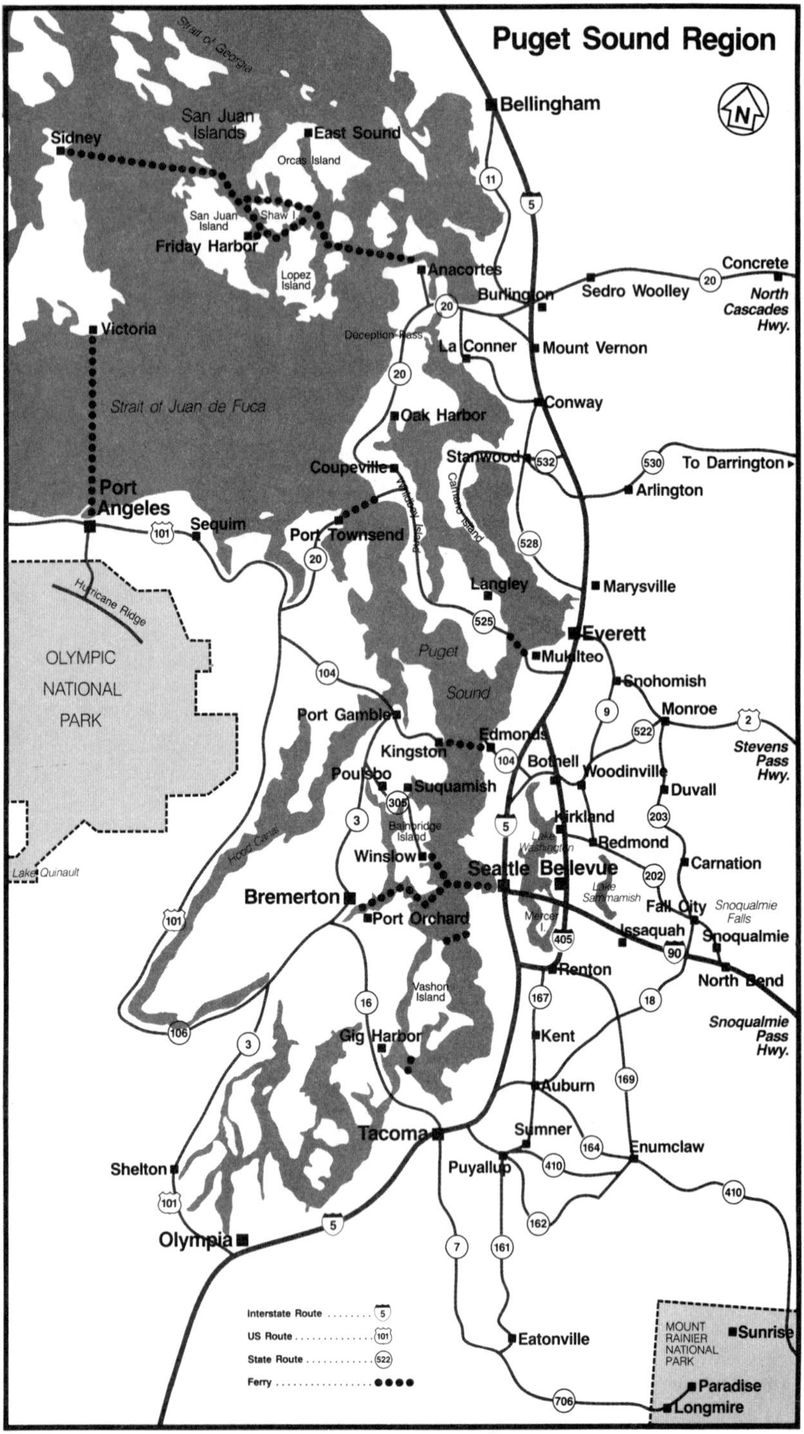

Puget Sound Region
N
Strait of Georgia
San Juan Islands
Sidney
East Sound
Orcas Island
San Juan Island
Shaw I.
Friday Harbor
Lopez Island
Anacortes
Bellingham
Burlington
Sedro Woolley
Concrete
North Cascades Hwy.
Victoria
Deception Pass
La Conner
Mount Vernon
Strait of Juan de Fuca
Conway
Oak Harbor
Stanwood
Camano Island
To Darrington
Arlington
Coupeville
Whidbey Island
Port Angeles
Sequim
Port Townsend
Marysville
Hurricane Ridge
Langley
OLYMPIC NATIONAL PARK
Everett
Mukilteo
Puget Sound
Snohomish
Monroe
Port Gamble
Edmonds
Kingston
Stevens Pass Hwy.
Bothell
Woodinville
Poulsbo
Suquamish
Duvall
Kirkland
Bainbridge Island
Hood Canal
Lake Washington
Redmond
Winslow
Carnation
Lake Quinault
Seattle
Bellevue
Lake Sammamish
Bremerton
Fall City
Snoqualmie Falls
Port Orchard
Mercer I.
Issaquah
Snoqualmie
Renton
North Bend
Vashon Island
Snoqualmie Pass Hwy.
Gig Harbor
Kent
Auburn
Tacoma
Sumner
Enumclaw
Shelton
Puyallup
Olympia
Eatonville
MOUNT RAINIER NATIONAL PARK
Sunrise
Paradise
Longmire
Interstate Route 5
US Route 101
State Route 522
Ferry ....

Out of Town Tours

Mount Rainier	245	
Mount St. Helens	247	
Mountain loops	247	Two-day northern loop
	248	One-day mid-Cascades loop
Heading east	249	Bellevue
	251	Issaquah
	251	Snoqualmie Falls
	252	Carnation and Duvall
	252	Woodinville
	253	Kirkland

Victoria 253

San Juan Islands 254

Skagit Valley & Bellingham 255

Bremerton, Poulsbo, Bainbridge triangle 256

Olympic Peninsula 257

Mount Rainier

Mount Rainier dominates the landscape of the Pacific Northwest. On clear, blue days, it seems like you could reach out and touch it; on other days, it could be a cloud on the horizon. For weeks on end, it may not be "out" at all, yet "The Mountain" has an undeniable effect on the moods of all who live in its shadow. If you are visiting Seattle and only have time for one out-of-town trip, this is probably the best choice.

Mount Rainier's volcanic cone rises 14,410 feet above sea level. The Visitor Center at Sunrise, at 6,400 feet, is the closest you'll get to the peak (road open only in summer) while the lodge and visitor center at Paradise, at 5,400 feet, offer more spectacular views. The mountain is famous for its many glaciers, and for a colorful display of wildflowers during its short summer. There are, in fact, two flower shows: the first growth comes in early July with lilies, mountain buttercups and marshmarigolds pushing up through the snow. The second and more extensive display occurs about a month later when entire meadows are covered in a

245

kaleidoscope of color. Snow may fall again by September, while in many years, Indian-summer weather continues into October, when fall colors are at their best. Chinook and Cayuse passes are closed in the winter; you can only take the loop trip or the road to Sunrise between late May and October. The road from Longmire to Paradise remains open during daylight winter hours. It is advisable to carry tire chains and a shovel during winter, and it is always wise to check current road and weather conditions by calling a 24-hour recorded message (569-2343). Park entrance fees are $2 per car and 50 cents per person in a bus.

Inns at Longmire (569-2565) and Paradise (569-2291) offer overnight accommodations and dining facilities. The massive old-fashioned lodge at Paradise, while not luxurious, is vastly preferable. With its exposed beams, log furniture, and lobby with two big stone fireplaces, it provides a suitably rustic atmosphere. It is, however, only open from late May through early October for overnight guests. The Paradise Visitors' Center, housed in a flying-saucer-like building, has a trail information office, cafeteria, extensive nature exhibits and films, and offers a superb view of the mountain from its observation deck. The old lodge at Sunrise has no overnight accommodations, but there is a snack bar. Longmire sells gas (if you're desperate; it's expensive). There are campgrounds (no reservations) and picnic sites scattered throughout the Park, and since the food concessions are merely passable, picnicking is the most enjoyable option anyway.

There are several ways of planning a trip to Mount Rainier from Seattle. Some one-day possibilities are listed below. (If you are interested in climbing the mountain, see the Sports chapter.)

Bus tours. Gray Line (343-2000) offers a nine-hour loop trip of the National park with a two-hour stop at Paradise, from mid-May through October. With advance notice, the tour bus will pick you up at your hotel soon after 9am and drop you back there between 6 and 7pm. Several smaller tour companies offer more personalized trips: try City & Country Tours (282-2301) and Emerald City Excursions (631-8232).

By car—Circumnavigation. You can drive around the mountain (in summer only) and get a sense of its massive size and variety of landscapes. Approach by Routes 7 and 706 from Tacoma and enter at Longmire: a hotel, small wildlife museum, and hiker information center are all found here as well as the starting points for several lowland nature trails and hikes. The road winds up through dense forest to magnificent vistas of the mountain and the Nisqually Glacier. Continue on to Paradise where you could have lunch and explore the flower fields. Then take Stevens Canyon Road past the glassy Reflection Lakes and up through Cayuse Pass. Then it's back to Seattle via Enumclaw and Renton on Routes 410 and 169. During the long summer days, if you leave early, this route gives you the whole picture of the mountain—and there may even be time for a side trip to Sunrise or the Crystal Mountain ski resort. But the round trip is more than 200 miles, and the miles on the mountain are apt to be under 40 mph; you'll spend a large amount of time in the car.

By car—Paradise and return. Rather than drive around Mount Rainier, return to Tacoma and the freeway from Paradise. You will have more time to explore and enjoy the area at Paradise; and, depending on the season, you could have a picnic among the wildflowers, slide on innertubes in the snowplay area, try a little cross-country skiing, or take a day hike along part of the Wonderland Trail which surrounds the mountain. You could stop at Alexander's Manor (569-2300) on Highway 706 at Ashford for a bite to eat on the way home, or, if it is still light, you could drop by Northwest Trek (832-6116, six miles north of Eatonville on Route 161), where the animals—native wildlife from caribou to mink—roam free and the people stay on the trails, in open-air buses (their summer and winter hours differ so call to make sure they are open). In the springtime you may want to make another detour on your way to or from the mountain to catch the daffodils in the Puyallup Valley. Take Route 167 out of Kent and in late March and early April you should be treated to some tremendous splashes of yellow between Sumner and Puyallup. After Puyallup, follow 16 until it connects with 7 and 706—the road to Longmire.

By car—Sunrise and return (road open in summer only). Drive through the pretty rural country of Maple Valley (Route 169) to Enumclaw and Greenwater (Route 410), climb almost to Cayuse Pass on the Mather Memorial Parkway, then take a side road to Sunrise passing through shaded evergreen forests and alpine meadows on the way. The old lodge has art displays and exhibits about the mountain, while the short nature trail nearby leads to a magnificent viewpoint of Emmons Glacier Canyon.

Mount St. Helens

Washington State's other famous mountain, Mount St. Helens, lies about two hours' drive south of Seattle via I-5. When the weather is clear it is well worth the trip to see what remains of this great mountain after the eruption of May 18, 1980. The volcano is best viewed from the north, the side on which the blast carved out a crater two miles across and half a mile deep. Turn east on Route 12 and follow the signs to Mossyrock; five miles farther east is Hopkins Hill viewpoint, overlooking Riffe Lake and aimed right into the gaping crater. If you want to glimpse the devastation close up, take Route 504 east from Castle Rock, heading up the valley of the Toutle River and its desolated mudflats. The best views of all are from the air; Columbia Air Services at Kelso Airport (577-8550) is a good place to line up a charter for a short flight; General Aviation at Chehalis (748-0035) is closer to Olympia. SpanaFlight (847-1919) offers flights over both Mount St. Helens and Mount Rainier, departing from Spanaway Airport, just south of Tacoma.

Mountain loops

One of the most inspiring one-day or two-day trips is a swing through the Cascades and over to the Columbia River, especially in the spring when the air is perfumed by fruit blossoms or in the fall when the trees are full of color. The roads are good, and you can view a variety of landscapes and Paul Bunyan-sized natural features. The following trips can, of course, be taken in either direction.

Two-day northern loop

(Possible only in summer as the North Cascades Highway is closed in winter.)

From Seattle, cross one of the floating bridges and head north on Interstate 405. Follow the signs to Route 9 and the town of Snohomish, passing through pretty dairy country en route. Snohomish, with a few nice antique stores, makes a good introduction to the countryside. Now go east on Route 2, which follows the Skykomish River up to Stevens Pass. The railroad towns along the highway offer little more than some tasty cheeseburgers (notable is Zeke's, two miles east of Gold Bar) and provisions for campers. There are many fine hiking trails leading off from Stevens Pass or just eastward at Lake Wenatchee.

From the pass to the town of Leavenworth, Route 2 is one of the most beautiful

247

roads in the state, carved alongside the dramatic rapids of the Wenatchee River; it is most spectacular in the fall. Some of the turnouts here make great picnic sites, or you can head into the Bavarianized town of Leavenworth for lunch (best is Cafe Christa, 801 Front St, 509-548-5074, with decent German food). Leavenworth is a good base for river rafting, golfing, climbing, hiking, riding, or some late-season cross-country skiing; it also has the best gift shops of any town on this route. If you want to stay overnight here, the Pension Rohrbach (12882 Ranger Rd, 509-548-7024), is an authentic Bavarian pension with very friendly proprietors.

So that the next day's drive is not too long, you might continue east on the first day, heading into the apple town of Wenatchee, set alongside the banks of the powerful Columbia River. The mighty basalt coulees of the river are set off with lacy orchards of fruit blossoms in the spring. (Apple Blossom Festival is the first weekend in May.) The best view of the river valley is from Ohme Gardens, four miles north of Wenatchee on Route 97, a rocky promontory festooned with small gardens from all climes. The place to dine here is a classic, tiny steakhouse called The Windmill (1509 N Wenatchee Ave, 509-663-3478). A twilight drive up Route 97, right along the Columbia, is a great way to finish the day, ending up at the town of Chelan, at the foot of the spectacular lake of the same name. Best lodging is at the fancy condo-resort, Inn at Wapato Point (at Manson, nine miles north of Chelan, 1-800-572-9531) or at the smallish motel, Cannon's Resort, near town (239 W Manson Rd, Chelan, 509-682-2932)—both expensive and tough to get into at peak summer season.

The second day's route takes you into remote, western country and back across the Cascades. You head north on Route 97, still along the rushing Columbia, turning west into the mountains on Route 153 at Pateros. Your route takes you into the Methow River valley, rolling rangeland, and fine trout country; join Route 20 at Twisp and continue north to the frontier town of Winthrop (good lunches can be had here at the spectacularly cantilevered Sun Mountain Lodge (Twin Lakes Rd, Winthrop, 509-996-2211), the finest mountain resort in the state. Before heading west to the North Cascades passes, you can shop in Winthrop, gussied up as a frontier town.

The North Cascades Highway (closed in winter) runs through the highest mountains of any state crossing, but the view of the mountains is normally obstructed by clouds or tall trees along the road. There are no facilities until you emerge in the spectacular gorge of the Skagit River, site of some engineering marvels by Seattle City Light. (Full-day tours must be arranged in advance at Seattle City Light, 625-3030, but there is plenty to see if you are a drop-in visitor.)

The road comes down through the lush farmland of the Skagit, as beautiful a river valley as the state offers, and you connect up with Interstate 5 at Burlington for a quick 80-minute run back to Seattle.

One day, mid-Cascades loop

You follow the same route as the first trip, heading across Route 2 to Stevens Pass and Leavenworth. If you are in a hurry, you can turn south six miles east of Leavenworth, heading across Blewett Pass on Route 97, cutting over to Cle Elum after the little town of Liberty; we'll rejoin that route after we take a wider loop to the east.

On this wider loop, continue east to Wenatchee, cross the Columbia River, and turn south on Route 28, right along the east bank of the river: you encounter the reclaimed sagebrush land of the Columbia plateau, turned into orchard country by the irrigation projects of the Columbia. A picnic overlooking the mighty river is a good idea, and the tiny town of Trinidad has a pretty site; or you can stop in at the Crescent Bar Resort (Route 28, eight miles west of Quincy, 509-787-1511), just about the only resort located right on the Columbia, though the food service is rather simple.

At Quincy, turn south on Route 281, joining Interstate 90 at the town of George, Washington (a tired joke), where you turn west for the return home. Just after crossing the Columbia at Vantage, you can visit a fascinating petrified forest at Gingko, where you can dig your own souvenir, if you wish. (Great view-picnic sites here as well.) The next town west, Ellensburg, is an attractive cowboy town, famous for its Labor Day rodeo, and sporting a fairly authentic downtown along Pearl Street; most of the buildings here date to 1889. McCullough's (402 N Pearl, 509-925-6545) is the restaurant for a good dinner before the drive home.

From Ellensburg, Interstate 90 rises through luscious grazing land and into the coal-mining towns of Cle Elum and Roslyn, worth a quick look-see. Snoqualmie Pass, the historic, low-lying trans-mountain route of the Indians, is a good jumping-off place for hikes and mountain sports. From here it is a quick hour's run back into Seattle, where the landscape will seem awfully tame.

Heading east

The Eastside—meaning a band of diverse communities east of Lake Washington—still inspires snobbish Seattleites to paraphrase Gertrude Stein on the lack of *"there there."* That's hardly fair. The Eastside is still Seattle's foremost suburb—just witness the commuter jams on the two floating bridges in early morning and late afternoon. But it's also increasingly where the business and good jobs, not just the bedrooms, are. Bellevue, the Eastside's largest city (and Washington's fourth-largest), is the nexus of the "Silicon Valley North" of computer and other high-tech companies, which have largely bypassed Seattle. You have only to watch the tall buildings mushrooming in Bellevue to realize this section is charting the path from suburban infancy to urban maturity at breakneck pace.

Still, there's a lot of country over past the big lake, and plenty of room to get away from it all on quiet drives and hikes. Begin by heading east on I-90, over Lake Washington on the floating bridge, and across Mercer Island.

Bellevue

Once you hit mainland again, take the first exit, **Bellevue Way**, north, and veer slightly right on 108th Avenue SE. Along this drive you'll see still-vacant meadows and woodsy Northwest-style homes cloistered in the trees, but don't be deceived by pastoral touches; with 85,000 people, Bellevue is fast losing its rural and suburban status. The gleaming square edges of its downtown highrises, outer-loop shopping centers, and "Hotel Row" along I-405 evoke Dallas or Phoenix more than any traditional Northwest cityscape, and leave many visiting Seattleites feeling lost in a glass-and-concrete sea.

But Bellevue has a past, and it's done a good job of preserving and polishing its remnants. Turn left on **Main Street** from 108th and you'll see a pleasant, old-fashioned—well, main street—renovated and revitalized with all manner of custom shops, galleries, and boutiques, many of them ensconced in the **Main Place** arcade. Back to 108th and two more blocks to NE Fourth Street brings you to the city's real retail hub, **Bellevue Square**—Kemper Freeman's influential, pioneering "regional" shopping center, whose 37 years correspond with Bellevue's mushroom growth. (If you suspect the Square might have had something to do with the city that resulted, you're right.) Bellevue Square has only lately begun to show a finished face, after its drastic reconstruction and conversion to a modern indoor mall. From the outside, the new mall is pretty much an austere box; inside, it's a lavish visual cacophony, obviously intended to achieve the lively bazaarness that Seattle's Pike Place Market expresses more humbly. Deep green coloring, down to the ubiquitous enameled metal rails, achieves a certain Northwesternness, the exposed glass elevator delights the kids, and you'll find the Square sights diverting, though they may distract you from actually shopping.

Bellevue Square's most notable attraction is an ingenious innovation in museum design, and proof that even shopping-center culture has its moments: the **Bellevue Art Museum**, located in a bright, clean third-story atrium by the elevator. This little eight-year-old museum (originally located in a former mortuary) is the apple of Bellevue's eye; in exhibitions, it shows the ambition and imagination of a much larger showplace. The museum, and the summer Pacific Northwest Arts and Crafts Fair (the region's largest), are supported by **PANACA** (the Pacific Northwest Arts and Crafts Association), which operates a major crafts gallery in the Square. The **Gail Chase Gallery** (22 103rd Avenue NE) is another leading showplace for Northwest crafts.

A quick detour to northeast Bellevue will give you an inside view (and heady taste) of another ancient art, just lately coming into its own in Washington: winemaking. Take the 120th Avenue NE exit off Highway 520 going east to reach **Associated Vintners** (1445 120th Ave NE, 453-1977). Washington's oldest premium and second-largest winery was founded in 1967 by academics from the University of Washington, largely to prove good wine could be made here. Associated Vintners proved it, and has since expanded to a 20,000-foot warehouse. You can take a tour (and sip samples) six days a week, 11-4 Tuesday through Saturday, noon-4 Sunday. The choicest times are during the crush, mid-September to early November, or bottling, late March through May; you can get up close to see how it's done. **Paul Thomas Wines** (1717 136th Pl NE, near Bellevue Crossroads), the state's third-largest winery, dares an offbeat specialty: fine wines from fruits and vegetables (rhubarb, Bing cherries, pears, as well as grapes) usually consigned to home hobbyists and sugary rotguts. They may surprise you. Thomas has no regularly scheduled tours, but gladly welcomes guests by special arrangement, preferably groups of six to 10 with two weeks' notice.

Bellevue has set aside some insurance against the crowding that comes with boom: an admirable (albeit inadequate, to some local critics) web of parks and greenbelts. Many lie in the lush **Mercer Slough**, which winds through the city's middle to enter Lake Washington where Bellevue Way meets I-5. One, **Kelsey Creek Park**, includes tranquil duck ponds, a Japanese tea garden (shades of Seattle's Arboretum), and a vintage-1888 log cabin which proves Eastside history did not begin in shopping centers. The in-city **Balatico Farm**, a living link with that history, still grows and sells pumpkins, corn, and blueberries farther down the slough, at 2810 Bellevue Way SE.

If you want more open space, head east on I-90, which takes you, in less than an hour, to the multitudinous ski slopes and trails of **Snoqualmie Pass**, and in another hour to the sunny steppes of Eastern Washington. First stop is **Lake Sammamish**, Lake Washington's little sister to the east. **Marymoor County Park** on the lake's north end offers vast stretches of play and picnic space; on the south shore, **Lake Sammamish State Park**, the Alki or Golden Gardens of the Eastside, has a fine, sandy, and busy beach, with boat ramps and picnic grills.

ssaquah

A few more minutes on I-90 brings you to Issaquah, which has grown quickly from village to town but still retains its rural character. Don't be startled if odd, brightly colored shapes seem to swoop toward you from the sky as you drive along: they're only parachutes, tow gliders, or ultralight airplanes coming in for a landing on the small recreational airstrip just north of the highway. You can take skydiving lessons from the **Issaquah Parachute Center** (392-2121) there, and learn gliding or just ride along at the **Issaquah Soaring Center** (392-8731).

One exit more to the west and south of the highway (on Gilman Blvd at Juniper St) is a private shopping development which recalls Henry Ford's Dearborn Village. A couple of dozen local wood farmhouses and bungalows, plus a garage, courthouse, granary, barn, and old-fashioned grocery, dating from 1910 to 1935, have been saved from getting chopped to kindling, hauled in close together, and named **Gilman Village** (Issaquah lost its original name, Gilman, to a rival in 1899). Brick walks, ornamental gardening, and cute wood signs complete the look; a variety of little boutiques, craft and clothing shops, and eateries fill the storefronts. If you get hungry browsing, **Original Ellen's** offers fine Sunday-brunch fare or a mean hamburger, depending on your mood and the time of day.

The state **salmon hatchery**, at 125 Sunset Way in downtown Issaquah (392-3180), is open every day from 8 till 4:30 and offers a vivid view of how that tasty pink fish flesh starts out.

If you hanker for a vigorous afternoon hike (great views for moderate exertion), you'll find plenty of apt ascents on Cougar and Tiger mountains and the other hills jokingly called the "**Issaquah Alps.**" Or head for the lovely Asahel Curtis Nature Trail and other pathways around Snoqualmie Pass. North Bend is the jumping-off point for this recreation area, though it's not much in itself: a few shops are redone in the Bavarian/Swiss chalet motif, in pale imitation of Leavenworth to the east.

Snoqualmie Falls

If you're not bound for the high mountains, take the Snoqualmie Falls exit north from I-90. You'll soon hit the little town of Snoqualmie, terminus for the volunteer-operated **Puget Sound Railway** (888-3030). From October through May the last electric trolley in Washington or Oregon departs each half hour from 11 to 4 Saturdays, for a run to the top of the Snoqualmie Falls gorge, and on Sundays from 11 to 5 a passenger train makes a longer run. From May to September a steam locomotive takes over the Sunday run; from June to September it also runs on Saturday. Fares: $3 adults, $2 children and seniors. You also get to see other engines, old cars, a rotary plow, a steam crane, and sundry artifacts at the nearby railroad museum.

Farther northwest on Highway 202 brings you to Western Washington's modest answer to Niagara, the popular (to locals as well as tourists) **Snoqualmie Falls**. You've a better chance of seeing the water roar over the cataracts, instead of disappearing into the electrogeneration turbines below, in a wet winter or spring. You can admire the falls from a covered overlook or take the path to the bottom of the gorge. The **Snoqualmie Falls Lodge** (888-2451) offers refreshments in a pleasant setting. The family-style breakfasts are long on quantity but variable in quality. Reservations are a must—well in advance for summer Sundays.

You can round out your fisheries study with a stop at the state's **Tokul Creek Fish Hatchery** (off Highway 202, 222-5464). Open to the public daylight hours seven days a week, it specializes in steelhead and rainbow trout, plus some cutthroat. At **Fall City**, you may choose to return to Seattle via Redmond and Kirkland on Highway 202, to stop at the **Stillwater Wildlife Recreation Area**, or to continue on 203 to Carnation and Duvall (and eventually Seattle).

Carnation & Duvall

If you choose the third option, after driving through a stretch of dairy country you'll reach **Carnation Research Farms** (788-1511), one of Seattle's original dairy bowls (since 1910). It's now devoted first to research, second to production; from 1 to 3 Monday through Saturday you can follow a self-guided tour through the calf barn, maternity ward, milking stations, museum (with a collection of antique buggies and carriages), and gardens, which reach peak bloom in July. While in Carnation, ask directions to **Remlinger Farms**, where you can shop in a refrigerated warehouse (bundle up) for terrific fruits and veggies, seven days a week from April's end to Christmas—from about 8 am till 8 pm once the season reaches its peak. If you'd rather save your pennies and get (briefly) back to the land, you can also pick your own here, as at many other Eastside and Kent Valley u-picks. Call Harvold Berry Farm, 333-4185, to see what's available.

Continue north of Carnation on 203 until you reach the little town of Duvall. The **Silver Spoon** restaurant on the main street (788-2734) serves delightfully eclectic and hearty fare—homemade soups, salads, hamburgers, prime rib, stir-fry—all very tasty. (It is also famous for its baked goods and breakfasts.)

Woodinville

West of Duvall (take the Woodinville-Duvall Road) is **Woodinville**, which offers two extravagant sightseeing treats, one horticultural and one vinicultural. With 28 greenhouses set on six acres, **Molbak's** (13625 NE 175th) makes most greenhouse operations look like window boxes. To say it has everything would be an understatement: the tropical conservatory is even stocked with chirping birds and a splashing waterfall. Nothing else brightens a winter day as well. **Chateau Ste. Michelle** (14111 NE 145th, 488-1133), one of Washington's leading wineries, turned only in the 1970s from cranking out sweet wines to bottling fine varietal vintages. It saluted (and doubtless stimulated) its resulting success in 1976 by opening an imposing yet bucolic new headquarters on the 87-acre Stimson estate in the Sammamish Valley, complete with a $6-million turreted French-style chateau, manicured lawns graced with trout ponds, experimental vineyards, and a winemaking complex. Chateau Ste. Michelle's displays and guided tours could make a vinophile of a hardened teetotaller. They're worth the stop any time of year—but September or October, when the grapes arrive from over the mountains for pressing, is best.

Out of Town Tours

Kirkland

Nearby **Kirkland** on Lake Washington, is named for British industrialist Peter Kirk, who once tried to build "the Pittsburgh of the West," with smokestack dreams fueled by local coal. But the Panic of 1893 shattered Kirk's schemes, and left Kirkland to develop peaceably as a suburb with a distinctly resort-like air.

Kirkland is home to the Seattle Seahawks pro-football team, while its other significant distinction is its extensive public lakefront parks and marinas—20-plus percent of its total waterfront. Especially popular—among waterfowl as well as human lake-lovers—is **Marina Park**, which offers shoppers coming to the nearby business center free boat moorage. Permanently moored by the park, as a floating museum, are the historic lightship *Relief* and ocean tug *Arthur Foss*, open (more hours in summer than winter) for tours. Local sports fishermen bring their salmon catches to the **Kirkland Custom Cannery** (640 Eighth Ave NE) for smoking and canning against a rainy or unlucky day; other delicacies are offered for sale.

Victoria

If you feel like a little bit of England here in the Northwest, you should go up to Victoria, B.C. for the day or, preferably, overnight.

You have a couple of fine choices as far as transportation goes: there's the **Princess Marguerite**, the grand old lady of Puget Sound cruise ships, which leaves Seattle (Pier 69) every summer morning at 8 and arrives back in Seattle at 9:45 pm, well-timed to take in the sunset. The ship is a relic, with proper English service, good breakfasts, and a few nice nooks to get away from the crowds. (See Transportation section of the Services chapter for details.) Or, if you have a little more money and a little less time, you could take a seaplane from Lake Union for the scenic one-hour flight over the islands. (Also look in the Transportation section for further information.)

As you enter Victoria's harbor, the stately **Empress Hotel** (604-384-8111) dominates the scene. The hotel is an interesting place to explore if you can handle the swarms of other tourists, avoid the high tea, and stick to a lunch in the Library Bar or breakfast in the Garden Cafe. Several places offer more pleasing accommodations: the Oak Bay Beach Hotel, if you want to be immersed in Old World English charm (604-598-4556), or, if modern is the style you're after, along with tennis courts, indoor swimming pool, and health spa, go to Delta's Laurel Point Inn (604-386-8721).

There are several fine little restaurants to try: Picchi's (604-383-4223), which can be loosely described as Roman Italian; Chez Daniel in Oak Bay (604-592-7424), ordinary of decor but distinctive in its nouvelle-oriented cuisine; and Chez Pierre (604-388-7711), another delightful little place offering classical French fare. Best of all is Deep Cove Chalet (604-656-3541), one of the finest French restaurants in the entire Northwest, a half-hour's drive north of Victoria and near the ferry to Vancouver.

For the anglophile, there are some fine shops stocking British goods; if it's antiques you are after, walk along Fort Street and you'll probably find what you're looking for. The Provincial Museum (Belleville and Government streets, 604-387-3701) is one of the finest museums in the country, with elaborately reconstructed street scenes from 1900, early logging operations, and a stunning Northwest Coast Indian exhibit. The Butchart Gardens is another fine attraction, 17 miles north of the city; its splendid array of gardens in various international styles is best appreciated late in the afternoon, after the tourist buses have left.

Out of Town Tours
San Juan Islands

There's something about islands—and whatever that is, the San Juan Islands seem to have their share. This mini-pelago lies just 80 miles, plus a 45-minute to two-hour ferry ride, north of Seattle. But the passage over water ensures a mood of exotic isolation that spells weekend heaven to city-frazzled Seattleites. That mood is bolstered by a slight change in climate: the islands lie at the north end of the famous Juan de Fuca "banana belt," under a rain shadow that allows more sunshine and less rain (as little as half Seattle's) though it can still fall as slowly and, it sometimes seems, as often).

In the San Juans, as elsewhere on Puget Sound, the state ferries tend to be undercleaned, badly overcrowded, tardy in summer, and underequipped with amenities beyond overpriced sandwiches and beer. Nevertheless, getting there is half the fun; the winding route between uncountable tree-blanketed isles and islets may be the loveliest ferry passage south of the Stockholm-to-Turku crossing. If you go by foot or bicycle (a favored and practical locomotion for island visitors), it's also wonderfully carefree. If you drive a car, queue up early in summer and on all sunny weekends and pray you squeeze onto the next boat.

Six ferries chug daily to the four largest San Juans; one more goes to the first three, and one pushes on to Sidney, near Victoria on the island of Vancouver in British Columbia. For information, call Washington State Ferries (464-6400). Last stop (short of Canada) is **San Juan Island**, whose ferry stop, **Friday Harbor**, is the nearest thing on the islands to a town. "Friday" is an amiable, Isle-of-Wightish stack of restaurants, craftsy galleries, and little hotels. It also boasts a Whale Museum (1-800-562-8832 or 378-4710), a little bed and breakfast, Collins House (378-5834), and a cutely misnamed hostel-style dormitory, Elite Hotel (378-5555) with spa and saunas in the basement. At the island's opposite end is the rambling old Roche Harbor Boatel Resort (378-2155); midway is its most noted restaurant, Duck Soup Inn (378-4878). On its shore sit the American and English camps, where those old adversaries squared off in the Pig War.

Watch for a big jazz festival on San Juan in the summer and a little one in spring. Half the folks on the islands seem to play music of one sort or other; that, and the prevalence of Greek fisherman's caps and down vests, should give some notion of the San Juans' informal ambience and surfeit of creative dropouts.

Just a tad larger than San Juan, **Orcas Island** is less urban, much hillier, and more resort-conscious. Rosario Resort (367-2222) is the island's most prominent all-purpose getaway. **Eastsound** offers a few shops and some good restaurants, chiefly the elegant Christina's (376-4904) and the New-Mexican-style Bilbo's Kitchen (367-4728). But Orcas' greatest prominence is geographic: the 2,409-foot Mount Constitution whose granite lookout tower offers a spectacular, 360-degree panorama of the islands, mainland, Vancouver Island and city, and of course all that bright water in between. Surrounding the mountain is 5,035-acre Moran State Park, with several lakes ready for camping, swimming, and fishing.

Shaw Island has no resorts or eateries, but a county park for camping and the jolly sight of Franciscan nuns who habitually dock the arriving ferries.

Lopez Island is flatter and quieter than its fellows; a mecca for bicyclists. Its rolling meadows are still largely devoted to sheep, cattle, geese, Shetlands, and chickens. This American pastoral can seem a welcome refuge when the other big islands get too lively in summer. The Islander Resort (468-2233) is less picturesquely sited than Orcas' Rosario, but offers rooms as good for less, plus pool and Jacuzzi, a bar with music, and a decent restaurant. Other Lopez havens: Betty's Place (468-2470), bed and breakfast; Chateau Rios (468-2368), cozy with classic French cuisine; and The Galley (468-2713), long on seafood and atmosphere.

Of course, the ferries are the biggest but not the only transport to and around the islands. San Juan Airlines (1-800-438-3880) flies several times daily from SeaTac Airport and Bellingham; check in off-times for half-price standby fares. From the San Juan airstrip you can buy passage to Stuart and other smaller islands on mail planes. You may get a custom sightseeing tour, if the pilot's not pressed, and an eye-to-eye with a soaring bald eagle. And of course charter boats, from various resorts, will take you to see the secret coves and, perhaps, the famous local orcas (killer whales).

Skagit Valley and Bellingham

For a day or weekend exploring rural Western Washington, the lush farmlands of the Skagit Valley are hard to beat. Spring is by far the best season to come here, as the valley is a center for commercial daffodil and tulip growing. Because the area is so flat, bicycling is a popular way to explore field after field of yellow, red, and pink. Drive a little farther north and you will be treated to one of the finest vistas of Puget Sound and the San Juan Islands along Chuckanut Drive to Bellingham.

The **Skagit Valley** is about a one-and-a-half hour drive north of Seattle by the I-5 freeway. Take the LaConner exit when you get up there. If you want to meander in the countryside a little earlier, leave the freeway at Marysville just north of Everett and follow Route 528 (turn left under the freeway) through classic Northwest woods of Douglas fir and cedar. Kayak Point Park on the Sound is a pleasant place to stretch your legs and have a picnic (plenty of covered picnic areas); there's good camping here too, in the summer. The forest soon gives way to the rich, flat farmland of the Pilchuck and Skagit valleys. You'll drive through the town of Stanwood, with its frontier storefronts, on past the turnoff to Conway, where you may want to make a brief detour into the town to check out its Saturday produce market, and then into the heart of Skagit Valley: tidy little farmhouses, red barns, and placid Holstein dairy cows, while in the distance the snow-capped peaks of the North Cascades overlook the calm, bucolic scene. Continue on till you reach the little town of LaConner.

A trading post and fishing town since 1867, **LaConner** has become a popular tourist stop with a mixed destiny. Its main street runs alongside the Swinomish Slough, so many of the stores and restaurants have wooden decks from which you can enjoy the sleepy river. A lot of care has been taken to provide little courtyards and benches all over the town. A spate of antique shops (Nasty Jack's is a fine one), two good bookstores, and "country" gift, clothes, and crafts stores make for enjoyable browsing. There are also several enticing eateries: Calico Cupboard (466-4451) offers hearty breakfasts, and homemade soup, salads, and sandwiches—their bakery produces many mouth-watering items as well. The tiny Black Swan Restaurant (466-3040) is a must if you can get in—tasty seafood dishes are their specialty. The LaConner Country Inn (466-3101) is the preferable place to stay: a new facility which looks like an old-fashioned country inn. On sunny weekends LaConner is mobbed with daytrippers on bicycles, motor bikes, and in cars, yet the atmosphere still manages to be relaxed and, so far, it has avoided becoming a spoiled Carmel. If you can, though, come on a weekday for a quieter visit.

The daffodils and tulips bloom at slightly different times each year, so call the Mount Vernon Chamber of Commerce (336-9555) during the week to find out when they will be at their finest and to get a map showing where the fields are. Over the years, Best and McClean streets (between LaConner and Mount Vernon) have proven to be very colorful. **Mount Vernon**, a rural trading center, is an interesting mix of traditional stores catering to the local farming and timber industries, along with a smattering of counterculture shops including a macrobiotic restaurant and a health food co-op. Monkey Business (309 Pine—a pedestrian mall) offers sprouty sandwiches on freshly baked bread. The older part of town, with its red-brick streets, is rather pleasant to wander through.

If you're going on to **Bellingham**, get back on the freeway going north for a short while, then take the exit for Chuckanut Drive (Route 11). Soon you will be marveling at the sweeping views of the Sound as the road hugs the coast all the way to Bellingham. If hunger strikes and you want to savor a sunset over the water, try The Oyster Bar (dinners only, 766-6185); but call ahead as reservations are hard to get.

Located on three rivers flowing into a broad bay, Bellingham is a delightful place to explore. The town is full of stately old houses and lovely parks, and the presence of Western Washington University gives it all the accoutrements of a full-fledged student town. The campus itself, on a hill overlooking the town, is a superb showcase of Northwest architecture, with its emphasis on warm materials and respect for the natural environment.

There are several walking or driving tours around the town's grand old homes, notably on the northern shoulder of Sehome Hill (near the university), around Eldridge Avenue, and in Fairhaven, which is just south of Bellingham on the Sound. If you're hungry, try the Fairhaven Restaurant (676-1520), the Italian Primo Provare (676-9136), or the new little uptown cafe, M'Sieur's (671-7855). Call BABS (Bread And Breakfast Service Registry) at 733-8642 if you're interested in a relatively inexpensive night's accommodation in a private home.

Bremerton, Poulsbo, Bainbridge triangle

Two state ferries leave from downtown Seattle, to two very different locations. If you bring your wheels, you can combine the Bremerton and Bainbridge Island runs into a day's circle, and get a good sample of the diversity and incongruities of Puget Sound.

Bremerton, as even many locals will admit, can seem a pretty dismal place. Its first reason for existing is its huge US Naval Shipyard (478-3466); the Trident nuclear submarine base, across the Kitsap Peninsula in Bangor, is now bringing a frenetic boom to the rest of the area. Bremerton sometimes seems built of tough sailors' taverns at the center, and endless roadside sprawl at the edges. You're advised to start your day here, so you'll wind up hungry at Poulsbo or Bainbridge Island. (If you're in Bremerton at dinnertime, the Neon Sky, 674-2664, at the airport, is the local posh spot, though the aviation decor is more interesting than the fare.)

But Bremerton is still a magnet for some 200,000 tourists a year, for one reason: the battleship *USS Missouri*, on which the Japanese surrendered in 1945. It's a special magnet for Pacific Theater vets (many of whom also remember Bremerton fondly as the site of their discharge). The surrender site is graced with historic displays, but most of the rest of the big boat is cordoned off; still, with smaller shipfellows floating nearby, the *Missouri* is an impressive sight. The Bremerton Naval Museum (479-7447), above the ferry terminal, tells of shipbuilding history back to bowsprit-and-sail days.

North on the overbuilt new Highway 3 brings you to **Poulsbo**. The "historic" downtown is a cheerfully corny collection of Scandinavian cuteness, with perhaps more murals per square foot of wall than any place outside the Vatican. The flashiest sits over Sluys Bakery (779-2798), along with the inscription "Giv Os Idag Vort Daglige Brod." Other shops offer gifts, crafts, and woodwork in a similar Nordic vein. The nearby wharf provides a pretty stroll, and the Olympic Inn (779-4655) serves fancy dinners in a historic setting. If you want to spend a night in rural elegance, stay at the Manor Farm Inn (779-4628), just outside Poulsbo. This country manor house with all the trappings is located on a working farm.

Follow Highway 305 southeast, then the signs past Agate Pass to **Suquamish** on the Port Madison Indian Reservation. A totem pole marks the sharp left turn to Chief Seattle's grave, behind St. Peter's Catholic Church. Twin dugout canoes rest on a log frame over the stone, which reads, "the firm friend of the whites, and for him the City of Seattle was named," lending a monumental melancholy. Nearby the Tide's Out and Tide's Inn taverns stand like sentinels on Main Street.

Back to Agate Pass and across the bridge lands you on **Bainbridge Island**. This is a commuter's dream: an island suburb. A 30-minute ferry ride about once an hour joins its only real town, Winslow, with Seattle. The island's population is still a mix of dropout, creative, and executive types, despite soaring land prices. But set against countercultural Vashon, Bainbridge enjoys a more or less blueblood (even snooty) reputation. That reputation is borne out on Country Club Road and other posh drives at the island's south end; there, a slice of Seattle's aristocracy can contemplate the city skyline from afar and cut their deals at the sequestered golf links.

But Bainbridge also offers simpler pleasures for the rest of us. You can camp at Fay Bainbridge State Park, at the island's northeast corner, and enjoy a beach and Seattle view as good as the country club's. At the south end, Fort Ward, one of many Puget Sound emplacements now left to leisure use, is a prime spot for hikes and picnics.

In **Winslow**, peruse the Bainbridge Arts and Crafts Gallery, stroll the marina, and stop for a hearty breakfast at the Streamliner Diner (842-8595), for seafood and varied beers and wines at the Saltwater Tavern (842-8339) by the Winslow wharf, or for pastry and cafe Romano at the Pegasus Espresso House (842-3113) next door.

Popular as it is with daytrippers, Bainbridge doesn't offer a single hotel (though one sign by a pen on Country Club Road near Toe Jam Hill announces, "No-Tell Goatel. No Vacancy"). But two bed-and-breakfast spots have opened lately: the Phoenix Inn (842-0341) at Lynwood Center, and Bombay House (842-3926) at Port Blakely. Bombay House is an especially impressive old wood rambler (with wide garden and cedar gazebo) packed with antiques and old curiosities, all for sale.

Olympic Peninsula

Even if you never get any closer to them than the view from Queen Anne Hill, you'll appreciate the Olympic Mountains: their jagged, ever-snowy peaks loom like a backdrop to some fantasy epic. The Olympic Peninsula can be an inhospitable place to live, thanks to isolation, winter gales, and rainfall averaging 140 inches a year on its west side and passing 200 inches in some parts. But it is a breathtakingly beautiful place to visit—certainly on a rare sunny day, and at other times the fog and drizzle enhance the mood.

You can make a quick dash along the Peninsula's north edge in one day, but you should allow at least one overnight to get your gasoline's worth. From either the Edmonds-to-Kingston, Seattle-to-Winslow, or Seattle-to-Bremerton ferries, follow the signs to the Hood Canal Bridge (reopened in 1982 after a spectacular sinking). As you pay your $2 toll, ask the collector for Olympic Peninsula maps and brochures.

After the bridge, follow the signs to **Port Townsend**. This historic port at the Peninsula's northeast corner is by far its most attractive town—a lovely collection of grand Victorian homes, some dilapidated but many beautifully restored. The Rothschild House is especially notable. Port Townsend hosts a string of festivals, offers galleries, antique shops, and bookstores, and boasts many charming bed and breakfast homes. Good ones to try are the James House (385-1238) and the Quimper Inn (385-1086). For dining, the Farmhouse (385-1411) offers a sublime setting and very interesting food; Lido by the Sea (385-1132) is more fun and has better seafood. Old Fort Worden, on the northern outskirts of town, hosts the summer arts festival and provides terrific picnic grounds on beach and bluff; you can stay in the old officers' quarters (385-4730).

Travel along a pretty inlet on Route 20 to US Highway 101, which loops around the Peninsula. The next main town is **Sequim** (rhymes with "whim"), a once-placid community in the sunny rain shadow, now falling to development sprawl. Its two main attractions are the Olympic Game Farm (Ward Avenue, 683-4295), home to some of Hollywood's top animal stars, and the Cedarbrook Herb Farm (986 Sequim Avenue S, 683-7733), a treasure trove of medicinal and culinary herbiculture. Both are closed in winter.

You're soon at **Port Angeles**, an unpretentious, rough-edged working port set against dramatic mountains. From their station west of town, the Puget Sound pilots go out to meet the big ocean ships and guide them into Seattle and other Sound ports. Two good restaurants here are the fancy C'est Si Bon (2300 Highway 101, 452-8888) and the crab-house called Dupuis (Highway 101, seven miles east of Port Angeles, 457-8033).

Port Angeles is the jump-off point to the north (and most popular) end of **Olympic National Park**. The park fills the interior of the Peninsula, and with inclement weather ensures a low human population and huge numbers of elk, deer, bear, and, on the highest crags, mountain goats. Follow the signs to the park headquarters, then up 17 miles of winding precipices to a subjective height that few mountains with twice the altitude can offer (the Olympics only make the 6,000-to-8,000-foot range). **Hurricane Ridge**, with restroom and snack facilities, sits amid spectacular vistas, with trails for hiking and, in winter, guided snowshoe tromps, and downhill and cross-country skiing. Snowshoes and downhill skis can be rented on weekends. The Hurricane Ridge road is open only weekend daylight hours in winter, and may even be closed then due to excessive snow. It is advisable to carry tire chains and a shovel during winter months, and it is always wise to check current road and weather conditions by calling a 24-hour recorded message (452-9235) before you set out.

A long side drive on Route 112 brings you to Neah Bay on the Makah Indian Reservation, site of an 18th-century Spanish settlement. At the museum (open 10-5 Tues-Sun; 645-2711) you can find out about guided tours of the reservation's attractions.

At the Peninsula's tip is **Cape Flattery**, supposedly the most perfect "land's end" in the United States, with the longest unbroken expanse of water before it.

If you push on around the Peninsula on 101, you'll see some of the eeriest scenery this planet allows: the perpetual, lushly desolate rain forest, most spectacular along the Bogachiel, Hoh, Queets, and Quinault river valleys; 300-foot fir and cedar trees, ribboned with near-perpetual fog and mist; and giant maples dripping moss. Ocean beaches offer more room for meditation and digging for tasty razor clams (state laws and red tides permitting; call the red tide hotline: 1-800-562-5632).

Park concessionaires maintain lodges at Sol Duc Hot Springs (end of Sol Duc River Road, off Highway 101, near Lake Crescent, 327-3583, open summer only), Lake Crescent (Highway 101, Lake Crescent, 928-3211; open summer only), and Kalaloch (Highway 101, Kalaloch, 962-2271).

If you want to venture inland, the private Lake Quinault Lodge (Quinault Rain Forest Road, off Highway 101, 288-2571), a massive cedar-shingled structure on rolling lawns overlooking the lake, also makes for a fine retreat.

Services

Auto emergencies	261	On the road
	261	24-hour towing
	261	All- and late-night service stations

Emergency numbers	262	
Business services	263	Computers
	264	Hotel meeting and conference facilities
	266	Non-hotel meeting and conference facilities
	269	Messenger services
	270	Private restaurant rooms
	272	Secretarial services
	274	Miscellaneous

Foreign visitors	274	Consuls
	274	Translators
	275	International services
	275	Banking

Lost and found	275	
Transportation	276	Air
	279	Land
	281	Water

Visitor information	283
Babysitting/childcare	283

Services

Automobile emergencies —
Vehicle breakdowns on the road

Seattle Police, traffic division: 911
Washington State Highway Patrol: 455-7700
AAA: 292-5409 in Seattle; 1-800-336-4357, other areas

Police recommend that drivers get their disabled vehicles off the road as far as possible without going into the ditch. Turning on flashers is advisable for short periods, but exercise common sense about length of usage. Don't sleep in the car while you're waiting for assistance—police are slower to attend to an apparently vacant vehicle. Put the hood up: this will be noticed. At night on the highway, women drivers should not leave their cars. Keep doors locked and roll down the window only slightly to communicate with anyone who stops to help. Be patient.

If you do not have AAA membership or other towing insurance, after-hours car problems usually mean turning to the nearest service station. Most of these all-night and late-night service stations in the greater Seattle area have access to towing and can do emergency minor repairs. Many have tow trucks on the premises. Hours and days for mechanics on duty vary widely, but help is generally available.

24-hour towing

A-1 Auto & Towing — 324-0330
Clyde's Chevron Service — 232-9772 (Mercer Island)
Crane Towing — 632-4233
Ibsen Towing — 454-7201 (Bellevue)
Jim's Northgate Towing — 364-1500
Lincoln Towing — 622-0415

All-night and late-night service stations

Central Seattle

M3	**Boren & Madison Chevron** 1101 Madison Hospital area	*Open 24 hours every day* 623-0833
GG7	**Broadway & Roy Union Service** 700 Broadway E	*7am-midnight every day* 329-4635
D7	**Dean's Texaco** 351 Broad St (Denny & Broad)	*Open 24 hours every day* 624-7070
C2	**Westlake Union 76** 600 Westlake	*Open 24 hours every day* 623-8272

North End

	Alderwood Shell 19930 44th W, Lynnwood	*Open 24 hours every day* 778-2243
BB7	**Bob's Aurora Union** 16510 Aurora N	*Open 24 hours every day* 542-8300

Services

BB5	**Bothell Way Chevron** 6504 NE Bothell Way, Kenmore	6am-midnight Mon-Fri; 7am-midnight Sat & Sun 485-5500
EE6	**Dan's View Ridge Shell** 7347 35th NE	7am-11pm Mon-Sat; 9am-9pm Sun 525-5925
BB5	**Forest Park Center Chevron Service** 17017 Bothell Way NE	6:30am-11pm Mon-Fri; 7:30am-8pm Sat; 9am-8pm Sun 365-7565
DD7	**Northgate Chevron** 2150 N Northgate Way	Open 24 hours every day 365-8980

Ballard

EE8	**Ballard Exxon Products** 6500 15th NW	Open 24 hours every day 783-7100
DD8	**Crown Hill Union 76** 8502 15th NW	Open 24 hours every day 782-4030

South End

I16	**Beacon Avenue Shell** 2424 Beacon S	Open 24 hours every day 322-7861
MM6	**John's Exxon Service** 12911 Empire Way S	Open 24 hours every day 772-6512
I16	**Rainier Chevron** 2800 Rainier S	Open 24 hours every day 723-3033
OO6	**Sea-Tac Union 76** 17606 Pacific Hwy S	Open 24 hours every day 242-6303
LL7	**Tom Mills Arco** 1505 SW Roxbury, White Center	7am-10pm Mon-Fri; 8am-10pm Sat & Sun 762-1662
MM5	**Tukwila Texaco** 13138 Interurban S	Open 24 hours every day 244-3520

Eastside

II4	**Bill's Chevron No. 2** 7725 Sunset Hwy SE, Mercer Island	Open 24 hours every day 232-2810
DD3	**Juanita Chevron Service** 11601 98th NE, Kirkland	Open 24 hours every day 823-6766
HH3	**Mobil Service Station** 804 NE Eighth, Bellevue	Open 24 hours every day 455-0850
CC3	**Totem Lake Chevron Service** 12500 Kingsgate Way NE, Kirkland	5:30am-midnight every day 821-1801

Emergency telephone numbers

POLICE, FIRE, MEDIC ONE: 911 (Seattle), 885-3131 (Bellevue)
Alcohol and Drug Help Line: 722-3700
Check Mart: 322-4811 (a check-cashing service at 1407 E Madison)
Child Protective Services (Family Crisis Intervention): 721-4115
Chiropractor (Washington Chiropractors' Association): 241-2668
Coast Guard: 442-7070

Services

Community Information Line: 447-3200
Community Service Officers (Seattle Police Department): **625-4661** (food, shelter, transportation, etc.)
Crisis Clinic: 447-3222
Dentist (24-hour answering service): **624-4912**
FBI: 622-0460
Language Bank: 622-4250
Locksmith: 325-1515 (AAA Locksmith), **634-2525** (A-A Acme Mobile Locksmith Service)
Missing Persons: 625-2882
National Runaway Switchboard: 1-800-621-4000
Physician (24-hour answering service): **622-6900**
Poison Center: 526-2121 (in Seattle); **1-800-732-6985** (toll-free in Washington State)
Quick Information (Seattle Public Library): **625-2665**
Rape Relief: 632-7273
Red Cross: 323-2345
Seattle Emergency Housing: 725-4066
Sexual Assault Center: 223-3047
Shelter for Battered Women (New Beginnings): **522-9472**
State Patrol (Seattle, Bellevue, Mercer Island): **455-7700**
Telephone Directory Information: 1-555-1212
Traveler's Aid Society: 447-3888
Veterinarian (Emergency veterinary care on nights and weekends): **284-9500** (downtown Seattle), **523-1900** (North End), **641-8414** (Bellevue)
Weather (KSEA Radio Weather Recording): **382-7246**

The Blue Pages of the Seattle telephone directory (pages B-2 through B-4) contain a list of community service numbers for such things as alcoholism, drug abuse, sexual abuse, information and referral services, emergency social services, community health care, legal, dental, and mental health clinics.

Business services

This section has been compiled with the needs of the out-of-town or new-to-town businessperson in mind. Listed below in alphabetical order is information on such things as secretarial and messenger services, meeting rooms, access to computers and audio/visual materials, and other resources of a similar nature.

Access to computers and word processors

FF6 **Academic Computer Center**
University of Washington
3737 Brooklyn Ave NE

Accounting & Production Control Office:
543-5925, Room 44B, 8:30-noon;
12:30-4:45 Mon-Fri; closed Sat & Sun
Operations: 543-5926;
24 hours a day Every day

While you will have to go through some red tape, the University of Washington Academic Computer Center also rents computer time to external, non-University users. Call the Accounting and Production Control Office for information. Basically you will need to write an explanatory letter and fill in an application form to get a user number, an ID, and a password. There are some restrictions on who can use

263

Services

the system, so check first. It will take three to four days to process the application but, once approved, you gain access to a new Cyber 750 main frame and a NOS operating system on a 24-hour basis for as little as a day or for as long as you like.

O9 **Anchor Computer Systems** *10-6 Mon-Sat; closed Sun*
323 First Ave S *621-9307*

Of particular interest to traveling businesspeople, Anchor Computer Systems specializes in computer rentals as well as sales. Customers can rent computers for as little as an hour at the store, or take units home or to their hotel rooms for a day, a week, or a month. Computer systems for rent or sale include KAYPRO II, OTRANA attache (both portable), Eagle II Business Computer, Epson QX 10/Valdocs Desktop System, and Epson HX-20 Notebook Computer. Printers and modems are also available.

FF7 **Computer Place** *9:30-9:30 Mon-Thur, 9:30-6 Fri,*
1314 NE 43rd Ave, Suite 209 *9:30-noon Sat, noon-6 Sun 632-8774*

Computer Place offers word processing and other computer programs (spelling, footnote, mail merge, data base, and super calc) at reasonable rates. An hour's training is $10, including a disc capable of holding 70 pages of material. Both letter- and draft-quality printing are available.

C7 **Pet Computer Lab (Building 5)** *1:30-4:30 Fri, 1:30-5:30 Sat & Sun*
Pacific Science Center, Seattle Center *625-9333, ext. 243*

If your needs and pocketbook are more limited, the Pacific Science Center's "open lab" hours may be more appropriate for you to practice your computing skills. For $1.50 a half-hour you can use one of their Pet Micro Computers, as long as you don't mind the chatter of kids playing computer games on the other machines. The School for Science also offers classes for a variety of age groups on both Apple II and Pet computers.

FF7 **Wordtronics** *8-11 Mon-Thur, 8-5 Fri, noon-5 Sat & Sun*
4556 University Way NE
(above North Face) *632-9798*

Wordtronics provides word processors for use by students, writers, businesspeople, and anyone else who finds this new technology useful. For $15 (with periodic discounts), the novice receives one hour's training and a diskette with 200-page storage capability. Rental rates are very reasonable and Wordtronics will also process your words for you.

Hotel meeting and conference facilities

L8 **Alexis Hotel** 1007 First Ave *624-4844*

Seattle's new small European-style luxury hotel provides two rooms, accommodating 13-22 people, with wood-burning fireplaces to warm up your meetings. Beautifully appointed suites are also available. Buffet lunches and complimentary coffee supplied. No special audio-visual equipment.

HH3 **Bellevue Hilton** *455-3330*
100 112th Ave NE, Bellevue

All the standard facilities here: Five meeting rooms of varying sizes, accommodating small and large groups. Audio-visual equipment.

HH3 **Bellevue Red Lion Inn** *455-1300*
300 112th Ave SE, Bellevue

A generous 11 meeting rooms are dotted throughout this glittering new addition to the Eastside hotel community. Audio-visual equipment is available, and there is no room charge when meals are ordered (20-person minimum for this).

HH3 Greenwood Inn   455-9444
625 116th NE, Bellevue

Six rooms are available at this comfortably charming Eastside hotel. The rooms hold up to 400 people; rental fee is waived if meals are ordered. There is a $100 deposit for large functions.

36 Mayflower Park   Fourth & Olive Way   623-8700

One of the last moderately priced, mid-scale small downtown hotels, the Mayflower Park has eight meeting rooms holding up to 200 people, for banquets and confabs. No room fee if a meal is ordered. Blackboards and audio-visual equipment supplied.

L6 Four Seasons Olympic Hotel
411 University   621-1700

Although not geared for the major conference hotel market, the elaborately refurbished Four Seasons Olympic has a number of exquisitely appointed small meeting/conference rooms. Popular for board meetings, they are equipped with pull-down screens, blackboards, and telephones. The ornate Spanish Ballroom accommodates up to 600 people and once again can house the grand receptions that made it famous many years ago.

L5 Park Hilton   Sixth & Seneca   464-1980

The elegant downtown hotel, next to Freeway Park, sports nine common rooms (holding four-550 people). Though built on a small scale, the hotel boasts excellent service for meetings, and full-range audio-visual facilities.

K5 Seattle Sheraton   Sixth & Pike   621-9000

With the newest conference facilities in town, the Sheraton is going after the convention business in a big way. Eight meeting rooms, all on the second floor, accommodate from 10 to 270 people, while the Grand Ballroom can house 1,400. Conference planning staff can assist or coordinate all events. State-of-the-art audio-visual equipment is available for rent. Room fees are negotiable depending on the utilization of catering services.

K5 Seattle Hilton   Sixth & University   624-0500

The drawing card for group meetings at this fairly typical Hilton is the variety of facilities and service. Besides five rooms holding 10 to 500 people, groups of 15 can rent suites. Audio-visual equipment available. All fees negotiable, depending on the size of the group and the catering services used.

M4 Sorrento Hotel   900 Madison   622-6400

This small luxury hotel does not aim to attract the convention crowds. Meeting facilities at the Sorrento are scaled to its wealthy clientele. Three rooms are available: The Top of the Town (40-100 people); the Sorrento Room (boardroom holding 20-45 people); and the Penthouse Executive Suite (receptions and buffets for up to 55 people, with a deck, piano, fireplace, blackboard, and blackout shading). Audio-visual equipment available. Prices are negotiable depending on the use of the hotel's catering services.

H5 Westin Hotel   1900 Fifth Ave   624-7400

Billing itself as a major convention hotel, the newly-refurbished Westin Hotel has

Services

the most extensive meeting facilities in Seattle: 24 meeting rooms of varying sizes and configurations, and a Grand Ballroom (the largest in the Northwest), which can accommodate 2,000 people for a stand-up reception and 1,800 for a sit-down dinner. Sophisticated audio-visual equipment is available for rent. Their convention-services staff assist with all convention coordination, and the catering department is especially skilled in providing food for large groups.

Non-hotel meeting and conference facilities

J9	**Aquarium**	Pier 59, Alaskan Way	625-4358

The Aquarium has three areas that it rents out to the general public: a conference room seating 12-20 people, an auditorium seating 242; and a large viewing area (accommodating over 500 people), which is separated into the underwater dome and the marine mammal area.

FF7	**Battelle Institute**	525-3130
	Seminars and Studies Program	
	4000 NE 41st St	

The internationally renowned Battelle Institute operates a fully equipped and staffed conference center in a retreat-like environment at its 18-acre wooded campus 10 minutes from downtown Seattle and not far from the University of Washington campus. Arguably the cream of Seattle's existing conference facilities, Battelle offers a broad spectrum of well-appointed meeting rooms in a variety of configurations to accommodate groups ranging from four to 100. The conference center has a full range of audio-visual and recording equipment as well as duplicating, Telex, word processing, and library services. Attractive and comfortable rooms and apartments can house up to 60 people and dining facilities (with a good selection of pre-arranged menus) can serve 100 people. Battelle staff can also offer a full range of professional conference management services. Rates are figured on a per-person daily basis.

II2	**Bellevue Community College**	*Theater, 641-2416;*
	3000 Landerholm Circle SE, Bellevue	*other facilities, 641-2376*

Bellevue Community College rents its Carlson Theater, with amphitheater seating for 350, and classrooms of varying sizes.

JJ8	**Camp Long**	5200 35th Ave SW	625-2570

A 68-acre camping site located in a wooded setting in West Seattle, Camp Long offers rustic residential conference facilities. A lecture room accommodates 60-80 people and a multi-purpose room holds 30-40. Ten overnight cabins sleep 120 and meals are cooked over wood fires. Blackboards, slide, and film projectors are also available.

DD7	**North Seattle Community College**	634-4646
HH7	**Seattle Central Community College**	587-6930
KK8	**South Seattle Community College**	764-5341

All the Seattle Community Colleges rent rooms for nominal fees to outside groups such as educational institutions, government agencies, and charitable and community organizations. Call the appropriate number to find out about room sizes and facilities.

L6	**Downtown YWCA**	Fifth Ave & Seneca	447-4865

Rents out several rooms seating 25-30 people, another for 100 people as well as its gymnasium accommodating 80-150 people. A slide projector and screen can be rented.

Eastside Unitarian Church   747-3780
12700 SE 32nd, Bellevue

Rents out its sanctuary (200-250 people), social hall and kitchen (80-100), and carpeted library (20) to non-profit groups.

Forest Ridge School   641-0700
4800 139th Ave SE, Bellevue

Forest Ridge School rents out its 305-seat theater, art gallery/reception area, and kitchen and dining room facilities at reasonable prices. A range of audio-visual equipment is available for an additional fee.

Gethsemane Lutheran Church
911 Stewart   682-3620

Religious organizations and other nonprofit groups may use the church's formal lounge (accommodating 50 people) and its auditorium with theater seating for 150. A donation is requested for use of the space. Screens and projection equipment for both movies and slides are available.

Lake Wilderness   *Conference arrangements 543-5380*
22500 SE 248th, Maple Valley   *Guest messages 432-4282*

The University of Washington Lake Wilderness Center is a residential conference site open to any educational organization. It is located about 15 miles (25-minute drive) east of Sea-Tac International Airport in a wooded retreat on the shores of Lake Wilderness. The Center houses four conference rooms with a capacity ranging from 10 to 100 persons, dining facilities for 100, and overnight facilities for 40. Conference and secretarial equipment is also available. The amenities are good but simple and the atmosphere is relaxed and casual.

Lutheran Bible Institute   392-0400
Providence Heights, Issaquah

Religious and nonprofit secular groups can rent this conference facility at Providence Heights, which has rooms seating from 12 to 400 people. Specializing in weekend conferences, the Center offers accommodations in both dormitory and motel rooms, has several dining rooms, and a gymnasium and indoor swimming pool.

The Meeting Place   Pike Place Market   447-9994

Located in the tastefully renovated Economy Market Building in the Pike Place Market, the Meeting Place has three rooms which can be rented for meetings, seminars, and parties. There's a 20-person boardroom, 50-person conference room overlooking Elliott Bay, and a 160-person meeting room. The doors between the latter two can also be opened to make one large room. The rooms are available at all hours, seven days a week, and may be reserved on an hourly, daily, or weekly basis. A full range of conference equipment is also available.

Museum of History and Industry   324-1125
2161 E Hamlin

Located near the Arboretum on the shores of Lake Washington, the Museum of History and Industry rents out its auditorium with theater-style seating for 475, sound and lighting equipment, a screen, projection booth and equipment. Also for rent is a general purpose room which accommodates 200 for sit-down functions and 300 for stand-up receptions. It has an adjoining food preparation area with dinnerware and coffee pots.

Pilchuck Retreat Conference Center
Winter office: 107 S Main, #324　　　　　　*621-8422*
Summer office: 1201 316th NW, Stanwood　　*445-3111*

Set in woodland and meadow in the foothills of the Cascade Mountains north of Seattle, and overlooking the lush Skagit Valley and Puget Sound, this residential summer glass-art school becomes a retreat and conference center during the other months of the year. The strikingly designed rustic lodge has a great hall with a cathedral ceiling and massive stove fireplace. It seats 100 for lectures and 80 for dining, and is equipped with projectors and screens. Also in the lodge are a kitchen, library, and classroom. Sleeping facilities (rooms with twin beds) accommodate 24 people.

Seattle Dept of Parks and Recreation
Community Centers　　　　　　　　　　　*625-4671*

The Seattle Department of Parks and Recreation has 24 community centers around the city which can rent rooms to both non-profit and profit-making groups. The former get priority and lower rental fees. For general information on the community centers and their facilities, call the Recreation Information Office at 625-4671. Bookings must be made through the relevant community center, however. The Parks Department also rents out pools.

Seattle Center　　　　　　　　　　*Facility Sales 625-4254*

The largest and most varied meeting and conference center in the city to date, the Seattle Center accommodates a vast range of meeting needs. It can provide for the likes of 1982's International Cancer Congress with its 8,000 delegates, who met in huge general meetings, symposia, round table discussions, lectures, and workshops, and viewed countless scientific and technical exhibits. The Center can also cater to the needs of local groups who need to meet in a small conference room on a monthly basis. Audio-visual facilities, catering services, conference planners, and other support staff are available.

Seattle First National Bank　　　　　　　*583-5100*

Seafirst Bank rents out its auditorium, which seats 212 people theater-style. Screen, podium, and PA system are supplied.

Seattle Pacific University　　　　　　　*281-2187*
Third W & W Nickerson

SPU has a range of classrooms and auditoriums for rent (35–2,000-person capacity). Reasonably priced food service, dormitory lodging, gymnasium.

Seattle Public Libraries　　　　　　　*Media Booking Desk*
Main Branch 1000 Fourth Ave　　　　　　*625-4986*

The Downtown Branch of the Seattle Public Library has a 225-seat auditorium, and some smaller meeting rooms which are available free of charge for groups holding public meetings. To reserve one, call the Media Booking Desk. A number of the branch libraries also have meeting rooms which they offer to community groups for meetings that are free and open to the public. Ask for details at your local library.

Seattle Trade Center　　2601 Elliott Ave　　*682-9222*

While it focuses on trade shows and exhibitions, the Seattle Trade Center also rents out its huge space on Elliott Bay for conferences, seminars, and banquets. On-site caterers provide a wide range of refreshments; there is no room rental fee if the caterers are used.

Seattle University	626-5371
Conference Office, 914 E Jefferson	

SU has a wide range of meeting and conference facilities, including small conference- and classrooms, auditoriums of varying sizes, and a ballroom which accommodates 600. Dormitory accommodations and catering services are also available, along with limited audio-visual equipment.

University of Washington	Allocation request office 543-7602
	Room assignment office 543-1080

Although you will have to go through some red tape, meeting rooms are available at the University of Washington's large campus. You have must be sponsored by an appropriate academic department, and fill out an application form (from the room assignment office). To find out what rooms and facilities are available, call the allocation request office.

Messenger services

Bucky's Messenger & Delivery Service	292-9280

Bucky's has developed a solid reputation for fast, efficient delivery service via its colorful, radio-dispatched bicycle riders, who seem to be able to outpace motorized transportation in the congested downtown area. One of their messengers can usually respond within 30 minutes in the downtown area; up to two hours in outlying areas. Bucky's service area extends as far south as Georgetown, north to 50th St, and east to 23rd Ave. They do not serve West Seattle, Beacon Hill, or west of 28th Ave W in Magnolia. In the Rainier Valley, they go as far south as the 2000 block of Rainier Ave S. Their riders will carry anything that fits on a bicycle, to a maximum of 20 pounds. A downtown-to-downtown delivery costs $2.50; the highest delivery fee is $6.80. A rush delivery costs $2 extra.

Business Services of Washington	624-1114

Business Services provides mail and courier services throughout greater Seattle and King County. Although they do primarily scheduled work charged on a monthly basis, they also pick up and deliver individual letters and packages. Rates are $3.50 per piece in the downtown area bordered by Denny Way, the King Street Station, I-5, and Elliott Bay. Weight and size are restricted to what will fit on a hand-truck. For areas outside those noted above, the charge is $20 per hour; adjustments to that rate are possible if other runs are scheduled in the same direction.

Crosstowne Courier Co.	621-1002

Crosstowne Courier's fleet of cars delivers smaller parcels (under 15 pounds) anywhere from Federal Way to Lynnwood and Bellevue. Downtown Seattle runs are made in 20 minutes at a cost of $4. Rates vary up to a $25 maximum. Because they deliver packages one-at-a-time, Crosstowne is one of the speedier messenger services available.

Dependable Messenger Service	624-3435

Dependable is a good choice for large packages (up to 85 pounds) and deliveries outside the close-in neighborhoods (they work anywhere within a 25-mile radius of downtown). Their radio-dispatched vehicles can usually make a pickup within one hour and delivery in one to two hours. Dependable's rate structure is based on four zones, which extend from downtown to SeaTac, Kent, Kirkland, Redmond, Renton, and Edmonds.

Fleetfoot Max	382-9442

Services

Fleetfoot Max, one step up from Bucky's on the vehicular evolutionary scale, makes its deliveries on mopeds. Package size is limited to what a moped can carry, generally small parcels. Fleetfeet travel as far north as Green Lake and as far south as Boeing Field, providing 60-minute downtown service. Rates range from $3 downtown to $9.50 for longer distances. Drivers are radio-dispatched and move quickly in heavy traffic.

Gelco Courier   *763-3660*

Gelco Courier's vans specialize in business delivery throughout the state of Washington. In King, Pierce, and Snohomish counties, the rates are $7 for deliveries scheduled 48 hours in advance and $9.30 for same-day calls. This is the place to call for large- and multiple-package delivery: they'll take boxes up to 70 pounds, with a limit of 250 pounds per day per customer.

Purolator Courier   *325-5400*

Purolator is a nationwide service with next-day delivery to many major cities. In this area, they provide same-day business delivery in Western Washington and next-day service to western Oregon. Delivery of 125-pound-or-less packages is made by truck. Prices vary, depending on frequency, distance, time, and number. It's best to call first for a quote on single-package service.

Restaurants with private rooms

DD7 **Andy & Jemmy's Wok**   **11030 Eighth Ave NE**   *364-6898*

The bar can be closed off for parties of up to 35 people. No gratuity or reservation fee. Chinese cuisine.

L5 **Asuka**   *682-8050*
1200 Sixth Ave (Park Place Bldg)

Eleven tatami rooms for lunch and dinner; fancier Japanese meals are usually served there and full-blown banquet menus can be arranged. For more than 10: 15-percent gratuity charge.

GG7 **The Austrian**   **2355 10th E**   *322-8028*

In the two downstairs rooms private parties of 15-50 people can be accommodated for lunch or dinner; 7-10 days' notice required; 15-percent gratuity charge. No reservation fee.

N8 **Brasserie Pittsbourg**   **602 First Ave**   *623-4167*

A beautiful back room here that's booked well in advance; reservations are recommended. 15-percent service charge for dinner. Menu negotiable. Classic French cuisine.

FF7 **Canlis**   **2576 Aurora N**   *283-3313*

Two private rooms: the "Executive," for 6-16, menu dining only, $25 fee; and the "Penthouse," for 16-100, buffets, receptions and cocktail parties, $30 fee.

Chez Claude   **417 Main, Edmonds**   *778-9888*

No deposit or room charge for the private room, seating 12-14 people. Groups are given three menu choices; can be ordered in advance.

DD7 **China North**   **12319 Roosevelt Way NE**   *362-3422*

The banquet menu costs about $15 per person and the banquet room holds up to

70-80 people. No room charge or deposit.

Crepe de Paris   Rainier Square   623-4111

One private room for 10-12 people. Reservations required. $12.50 fee for lunch. French-accented buffet and banquet menus can be arranged.

Fuller's   621-9000
Sixth & Pike (Sheraton Hotel)

The Wine Room takes up to 20 people in a private party. No room fee or deposit. There are various menu options.

Gerard's Relais de Lyon   485-7600
17121 Bothell Way NE, Bothell

Several private rooms are available here, accommodating 8-24 people. No weekend parties. The room fee is $10 and several days' notice is required. Classical French fare.

Gretchen's Of Course   1513 Sixth Ave   622-9487

The 1513 Sixth Avenue branch has a room that holds 25 to 30 people; no fee or service charge. All menus "custom-arranged." Any of Gretchen's outlets can be reserved (no charge) in the evenings (623-8194). Salads, quiches, and desserts.

The Georgian Room (Four Seasons Olympic)   621-1700
411 University

A private room, La Petite Georgette, accommodates 6-12 people in classic surrounding complete with the finest china, crystal, and hand-blown glassware. Special menus are also offered.

Henry's Off Broadway   1705 E Olive Way   329-8063

The Crystal Room takes 10-24 people. The chef likes to work closely with the client in selecting the menu. Room charge for lunch is $15, for dinner $30.

India House   4737 Roosevelt Way NE   Leslie Das: 632-5072

The room upstairs holds 40-60 people for meals. Menu available. No reservation fee.

Ivar's Indian Salmon House   632-0767
401 NE Northlake Way

Seattle's great seafood entrepreneur has one room at his Salmon House for 20-150, dinner or buffet. One week's notice; no fees; 15 percent gratuity.

Le Bonaparte   878-4412
S 216th & Marine View Dr, Des Moines

This house by the airport has three private rooms; the menu is French. Parties of 8-60 can be accommodated. No fees; deposit and menu negotiable.

F.X. McRory's   419 Occidental S   623-2424

The back dining room holds 20-55. The management requires large parties to choose from two entrees—prime rib or fish. One or more week's notice required; no fee; 15-percent gratuity.

Mikado   514 S Jackson   622-5206

Nine tatami rooms accommodate 6-35 persons. Minimum $8 charge per person; one week reservation recommended. Sushi, robatayaki (grilled appetizers) and seafood are the specialties here.

Services

M6 **Mirabeau**		624-4550
1001 Fourth Ave (Seafirst Bldg)		

Three private rooms are available for groups of 16-70 persons. No room fees; 15-percent service charge. Special menus to choose from, depending on the affair. French cuisine.

HH7 **Nikko**	1306 S King	322-4641

Nikko has a private room that accommodates 40 people. There is an $11.50 minimum meal charge per person; no room reservation fee. Banquet menus available. Japanese fare; sushi a specialty.

E7 **Rosellini's Four-10**	Fourth & Wall	624-5464

The "Library" and two other private rooms serve up everything from buffets to sit-down meals; 150-person maximum. Reservation fees: $15 lunch; $30 dinner.

B8 **Le Tastevin**	19 W Harrison	283-0991

Just short notice is required for one of two private rooms, seating 25 and 40 people respectively. Room fee for 10 or fewer people. The rooms can be rented together to accommodate a total of 75 people. Superb French cuisine.

GG7 **Sundays**	620 First Ave N	284-0456

Banquets for up to 450 people can be arranged in the upstairs lounge or the Terrace Bar (or even the main room). No room fee or reservation charge; 15-percent gratuity.

H5 **Trader Vic's**		624-8520
1900 Fifth Ave (Westin Hotel)		

With its legions of waiters, Trader Vic's provides excellent service for its private room that seats up to 65 people. Reservations are recommended one week in advance. Reservation fee negotiable. No fee if more than 25 people.

P9 **Umberto's**	100 S King	621-0575

The banquet room accommodates 80 people. Banquet menus available. No reservation fee. 15-percent gratuity charge. Italian fare.

N2 **The Wok**	1301 Columbia	324-9488

The private room accommodates up to 14 people. No reservation fee or service charge. Chinese cuisine.

Secretarial services

L7 **The Headquarters Companies** (offices and services)		
1111 Third Ave, Seventh Floor		621-1020

Promoting a new concept of office and secretarial support, the Headquarters Companies not only provide secretarial, word-processing, and sophisticated telephone-answering services, but will lease you executive office (and conference room) space in the heart of downtown for as little as two hours.

N8 **Help Mates**		
Suite 310, Market Place 2, 2100 Western Ave		624-4126
Suite 210, Pioneer Building, 600 First Ave		

With two offices, located in the Pike Place Market area and Pioneer Square, Help Mates supplies professional office services ranging from word processing and secretarial assistance to bookkeeping, inventory management, and clerical support. The

Pioneer Square office has a Vector Graphic microcomputer which is capable of fulfilling functions such as accounting, statistical analysis, list and data-base processing.

Professional Assistants
234 SW 43rd St, Suite B, Renton *251-0830*

Offers a broad spectrum of support services, including typing, word processing, photocopying, stenography, 24-hour dictaphone, notary public, mailing, bookkeeping, and errands and light deliveries. They also rent or lease individual offices.

Red Carpet Executive Service
155 NE 100th, Suite 403 *523-4575*

Offers a full range of secretarial services, including word processing, in addition to office rentals with accompanying answering and receptionist services, conference room, and general office support. All these needs can be met independently or as a package.

Seattle Medical Steno *325-2244, 323-5488*
900 Boylston Ave

Offers a telephone dictation/transcription service whereby the client never has to leave his or her office or hotel room: dictation is done over the phone, then the material is typed and delivered within 24 hours. Also provides word processing, specializing in text editing, mailing-list maintenance, and multiple letters. Trained personnel are thoroughly versed in medical terminology.

The Secretariat
65 Marion Street *623-0909*
310 First Ave S, Suite 200 *624-3822*

A newcomer to the field, The Secretariat has already developed a good reputation for providing services such as word processing (equipment staffed 24 hours a day), typing, dictation transcription, editing, photocopying, and telex. They also supply office support services such as telephone answering and mail drop. Their two offices are conveniently located in the Financial District and Pioneer Square.

SEL — A Secretarial Service
1402 140th Pl NE, #101, *643-3792*
Rockwood Office Park, Bellevue
10210 NE Eighth, #200, Downtown Bellevue *451-3399*

With its two offices in Bellevue, SEL provides computerized word processing (with WordStar software), typing, 24-hour call-in dictation, photocopying, and postage services. They also anticipate having telecommunications soon. Evening, weekend, and rush jobs are accepted, and pickup and delivery are provided.

The Word Processors *625-9692*
Suite 505, The Seattle Tower
Third & University

A very professional secretarial service located in the heart of the business district, the Word Processors offers a full range of word-processing services with equipment staffed 18 hours per day and on weekends; a 24-hour telephone dictation service; meeting attendance and note transcription; and list processing. They specialize in legal, medical, and engineering fields.

Services

Miscellaneous services

M6 **Seattle Public Library**
Main Branch *Quick Information 625-BOOK*
1000 Fourth Ave *Media Booking Desk 625-4986*

The first-floor Information Desk can help you with all general enquiries. The downtown branch has free typewriters for public use. Media and Program Services also lends out audiovisual materials, including 16mm projectors, 8mm and 16mm films, VHS video tapes, laser video discs, 35mm slides, and ¾-inch video cassette tapes. Available for in-house use are laser disc, ¾-inch video, VHS tape, and slide preview machines. This department can also help you locate speakers on any topic.

Foreign visitors

Consuls

The dean of Seattle's consular corps is the Consul-General of the Federal Republic of (West) Germany, 1200 Fifth, 1617 IBM Bldg., 682-4312.

Translators & interpreters

| **Language Bank** | *622-4250* |

A volunteer organization of professional women called the Altrusa Club organized the Language Bank some 11 years ago; they can put their finger on interpreters who speak 70 languages or dialects. In an emergency, the service is free; otherwise, the fee is negotiated with the individual interpreter. The 24-hour phone number is 622-4250.

Incidentally, the club is always looking for potential new translators; call their number is you think you're qualified (especially in Chinese, Filipino, Southeast Asian, or Middle Eastern languages).

| **Hokubei Tour & Travel Service** | *623-9441* |
| **2033 Sixth Ave, Suite 251** | |

This company provides Japanese/English business interpretation and bilingual tour guides.

| **Indochinese Language Bank** | *324-7835* |

This service provides translators for Cambodian, Laotian (Hmong and Mien), Vietnamese, and Chinese (Cantonese, Mandarin, Chou-jo) language needs.

| **Milmanco Corp** | *255-8656* |
| **620 S Seventh, Renton** | |

For those involved in international business and in need of technical written translation from foreign languages, Milmanco may be a good source. Rates vary.

| **Southeast Asian Refugee Federation** | *343-9773* |

This agency provides Laotian, Vietnamese, Cambodian, and Chinese language translators.

Most of the Seattle-area universities and colleges keep lists of people able and willing to translate and interpret for foreign visitors. Rates vary; many do not charge.

… # international services

The American Cultural Exchange 633-3239
1107 NE 45th, Suite 315-A
This organization provides English language classes for teachers, especially Japanese, from abroad. They also arrange for summertime exchanges and visits by foreigners to American homes. These should be set up ahead of time through schools and colleges.

Highline YMCA 244-5880
The YMCA offers a variety of international programs, from meeting students and government officials at the airport to arranging contacts between visiting foreigners and Seattle residents. Most airport meetings are set up beforehand. For information, call the Highline YMCA at the above number.

Banking

Money-changing facilities are available at almost every major bank. In addition, the largest Seattle banks also have foreign departments, which handle commercial banking requirements on an international basis.

Several foreign banks have also established branches in Seattle:

Bank of Tokyo 382-6000
1111 Third Ave

Canadian Imperial Bank of Commerce
801 Second Ave 223-7951

Hokkaido Takushoku Bank, Ltd 624-0920
3880 Fifth Avenue Plaza, 800 Fifth Ave

Hongkong & Shanghai Banking Corp., Ltd
705 Third Ave 622-8490

Sumitomo Bank Ltd 625-1010
1001 Fourth Ave, Suite 4600

Taiyo Kobe Bank, Ltd 682-2312
900 Fourth Ave

Lost and found

For stores, theaters, restaurants, etc., the best approach is to telephone the establishment directly. Some facilities do have special lost-and-found numbers, however:
AMTRAK: 382-4128
Metro: 447-4822
Seattle Center (except for Pacific Science Center, Space Needle, or Memorial Stadium): **625-4236**
Sea-Tac Airport: 433-5312 (or individual airlines)
Washington State Ferries: 464-6400
"Lost" Car: Call **625-2061** first to determine if your car has been towed and impounded; if the auto-records people can't trace it, call **911** to report it stolen.

Services

Transportation—Air

Seattle-Tacoma International Airport

Sea-Tac, 13 miles south of Seattle, is the nation's sixteenth largest airport. It's operated by the Port of Seattle and is used by nearly 10-million passengers a year. It is an uncommonly well-laid-out airport, close to downtown (25 minutes on the freeway), compact, easy to find your way around in, and recently modernized with successful architecture. In 1981, Sea-Tac was awarded the FAA's Aviation Environmental Award for planning and was ranked among the five best US airports by the Airline Passengers Association.

Most of the flights at Sea-Tac leave not from the main terminal (where you can buy tickets, claim baggage, buy gifts, and exchange money), but from two satellite terminals. A one-and-a-half-mile computer-controlled subway, reached by a series of escalators, connects the terminals and transports up to 4,500 passengers per hour. Most passengers, it is said, do not have to walk more than 600 feet once they are inside the terminal. But allow an extra 10 minutes for reaching gates at those satellite terminals; there are 56 loading gates and 20 baggage claim areas.

Airport Information. The Seattle–King County Convention and Visitors Bureau operates an information booth at the airport (433-5217) in the baggage claim area, near baggage carousel number 10 in the center of the terminal. It operates 9:30-7:30 seven days a week all year (except Christmas Day, Thanksgiving Day, and New Year's Day) and gives out tourist and regional travel information for Seattle, King County, and Washington State. Assistance is also given with airport directions and transit information.

Travelers' Aid also has a desk at Sea-Tac Airport (447-3888, on the ticketing level, just south of the center of the terminal). It operates 9:30am-10pm Mon-Fri, 11-7 Sat & Sun, and gives directions, general information, and assistance to travelers.

An **Observation Deck** is located in the main terminal building. Take the stairway to the right of the coffee shop to the second floor; either door to the balcony allows a good look at planes taking off and landing at the satellite terminals across the tarmac.

The best bar from which to watch planes is in **The Carvery** in the main terminal, the best restaurant (433-5622) in Sea-Tac. It is open every day for lunch and dinner, 11-2:30 and 4:30-10. The Deli snack bar (433-5643) is open 9-5:45 daily, and serves bagels, cheeses, and salads. The Cafe Northwest (433-5615), a larger cafeteria, is open 24 hours daily. Besides The Carvery's bar, visitors can try The Rim Bar (433-5217), open 6am-1am daily; the C Bar in Concourse C (433-5611), open 10:00am-10:30pm daily; and the new Gazebo Bar (433-5217) in Concourse A, open daily with varying hours. The Carvery Dining Room and all bars accept AE, MC, and V credit cards.

The Port of Seattle maintains a **Trade Center** for international businesspeople who want a place to meet or entertain potential clients of the Port (a Japanese manufacturer, for example, who might ship his product via Seattle rather than San Francisco). The facilities, on the mezzanine level of the main terminal, can accommodate several groups at a time; arrangements can be made to serve coffee or to have meals catered. Call 433-5386 for details.

The Port sponsors **"Operation Welcome"** to meet international flights. Interpreters greet passengers on flights from Europe and Asia and interpret for them during Immigration and Customs procedures. (There are 16 part-time interpreters with a combined command of 19 languages.)

The **Control Center** is located in the parking garage (fourth floor) between the fourth-floor skybridges. A bank of television monitors watches the subways come and go; corridors are scanned by TV cameras; lights indicate the path of subways and the temperature of the air. Kids (and their parents) can watch the glassed-in system (from the outside) as long as they like.

A **nursery** is located on the ticket level of the main terminal near the Northwest Gift Shop. It is available for feeding, changing, and caring for children; chairs, couches, and cribs are provided at no charge.

Seattle First National Bank operates an airport branch (behind Continental Airlines on the ticketing level of the main terminal, 583-6644). Hours are 9-5 Mon-Fri. A cash machine is also available.

AB Travel (several locations in the main terminal, 243-1231) offers money changing facilities from foreign currencies (cash only) as well as selling travel insurance. Hours are 6:30am-10:30pm every day of the week.

To and from the airport

The easiest way to get downtown from Sea-Tac (or vice versa) is to take the **Hustlebus** (343-2000). Departures from the airport are daily every 30 minutes, from 6:10am to 12:30am; the 20-minute trip is nonstop aboard a bus operated by Gray Line and costs $4.75; arrival is at the Four Season Olympic Hotel, the Park Hilton, Sheraton, and Westin hotels. It's easy to meet friends here, too; give them a call before leaving the airport and they'll be downtown when you get there without having to drive all the way out to the airport. Departures from the downtown hotels on the Hustlebus are daily every 30 minutes also, 5:05am-11:30pm. cc: from Sea-Tac, MC, V; from downtown, only from the Westin, AE, MC, V.

Metro Transit (447-4800) also provides bus service to and from the airport. Bus #174 leaves Second and Pike roughly every half hour (schedules vary) for a 40-minute trip to Sea-Tac; the fare is 50-75 cents, depending on the time of day. The same bus returns to town, leaving every half hour.

Howard Graves Limousine Service operates a Sea-Tac airport-shuttle service from the Park Hilton. Limousines leave the hotel every hour on the hour from 6am-2pm at a cost of $10 per person.

Suburban Airporter (455-2353) offers Eastsiders (and some Northenders) convenient airport transportation. Departures are daily every 45 minutes to one hour from 5:45am to 10:40pm. Return trips from Sea-Tac run daily from 6:25am to 11:45pm. The Suburban Airporter picks up passengers from the Red Lion, Thunderbird, Hilton, Greenwood, and Holiday Inn hotels in the Bellevue area; designated pick-up points in Edmonds, Lake Forest Park, Bothell, Kenmore, Woodinville, Kirkland, Redmond, Mercer Island, Issaquah, and Aurora Village; home pickups in Bellevue proper. Basic cost is $6.50, with additional charges for home pickups and designated points outside Bellevue. cc: none.

Tukwila guests at the Doubletree Inn (246-8220) receive free van service to and from Sea-Tac.

Services

Sea-Tac Airport parking — short-term

Sea-Tac's parking garage (433-5308) has four spiral ramps and six levels of covered parking. Signs direct you to parking areas closest to the airline you want to reach (via an elevator and a skybridge to the main terminal), but there are a couple of tricks. The lower levels of the garage are often full, and the first available level will be crowded; continue up one extra level, and you should be able to park near the elevators without much problem. Another idea is to follow the signs to "General Parking" on the ground level of the garage; it's usually less crowded than the others and, when you are ready to leave the garage, you avoid the slow, spiraling descent toward the toll booths. Rates start at $1 an hour, with a maximum of $6 per day.

There is also metered parking. Follow the signs to "Passenger Pickups"; the lot is just behind the Pan Am area. Meters function 24 hours a day.

Sea-Tac Airport parking — Long-term

It is considerably less expensive to park on lots outside the airport itself. Shuttle service is available from the lots to the terminal, and is either free or worked into the parking cost at reasonable rates. All the lots below are open 24 hours a day.

Budget Rent-A-Car (244-4008, 17808 Pacific Hwy. S) offers free parking to customers who rent a Budget car in Portland, Seattle, Pasco, or Spokane. Otherwise, it's $4.50 a day, and $30 per week. cc: AE, CB, DC, MC, V, Sears.

Huling Thrifty Airport Parking (246-7565, 18836 Pacific Hwy. S) charges $3.95 a day, $24 a week, but provides free parking to those who rent cars here. cc: AE, CB, DC, MC, V.

Mini-Rate Airport Parking (248-2442, 20620 Pacific Hwy. S) charges $2.75 a day, $17 a week. Free parking to car renters. cc: AE, DC, MC, V.

Dollar Park & Fly (433-6767, 17600 Pacific Hwy. S) gives AAA members the first day parking free. Charges are $4 a day, $24 a week. Free parking to car renters. cc: AE, CB, DC, MC, V.

Airplane charters

KK6   Most of the charters are based at **Boeing Field**; Everett (Paine Field) and Renton airports also serve as home base for charter operators. Many of the operators are dealers for aircraft manufacturers; many give lessons, and some offer helicopter rentals. Prior to departure, it's a good idea to call 767-4002 for the Transcribed Aviation Weather Broadcast.

Seaplanes

GG7   The largest seaplane charter service is **Kenmore Air Harbor**, which is located
BB5   both on Lake Union (1838 Westlake N) and the north end of Lake Washington, in Kenmore (6321 NE 175th, 486-1257 or 364-6990). The price for flying a couple to Friday Harbor, in the San Juan Islands, for example, runs about $117 with an hour of standby thrown in (additional standby is $30 an hour). That's for a single-engine Cessna 180; bigger planes would, of course, cost more. Kenmore also flies
B1   to British Columbia. **Lake Union Air Service** (1100 Westlake N, 284-0300) and
B1   **Kurtzer Flying Service** (950 Westlake N, 284-1234) also operate from Lake

Union, fly to Canada, and offer short scenic flights over Seattle. The biggest thrill is when the plane comes in for a landing, suddenly swooping down over the nearby office buildings and plopping itself onto the lake.

Transportation — Land

Bus charters

6 **Gray Line**, 1218 Third (343-2019 or 343-2003) is primarily a sightseeing service but will charter an entire bus or limousine for groups. cc: MC, V.

4 **Greyhound**, Eighth and Stewart (628-5510, 628-5537, or 1-800-528-0447) offers charters in addition to its intercity scheduled transportation. cc: none.

17 **Evergreen Trailways**, 720 S Forest (624-5077). cc: none.

Buses

Metro operates about 150 separate bus routes in the Seattle area. For the most part, they are new and comfortable coaches. Many are wheelchair-accessible, though not always at peak hours. Most lines go through downtown (with the exception of the Eastside suburban routes and the upcoming North End bus center). In the downtown core (between the waterfront and Sixth Avenue, between S Jackson and Battery) you ride free; just get on any bus. If you ride past the free zone (dubbed "Magic Carpet" by Metro), however, you pay when you get off.

Drivers don't carry change; the exact fare is 50 cents within the city limits (60 cents during peak hours in the morning and late afternoon), and 75 cents beyond the city limits, within King County (90 cents during peak hours). Don't forget to ask for a transfer when you purchase your ticket. It will enable you to travel on subsequent buses free of charge for an hour and a half. Senior citizens and disabled people with a $2 monthly pass ($24 yearly pass) pay only 15 cents.

Monthly passes are available ($23 for peak-hour travel within Seattle; $34.50 for peak-hour travel in King County) and allow unlimited travel; yearly passes ($253 for travel within Seattle; $379.50 for travel in King County) can also be purchased. The passes are for sale at many banks and at the Metro Customer Assistance Office, Exchange Building, 821 Second. Or try an All-Day pass, available for weekend and holiday travel only, for $1.25; or a Three-Day Pass, available anytime for $5. For information about route numbers and schedules, call Metro's 24-hour information number: 447-4800. Timetables are available at Bartell's, 7-11's and Wendy's.

14 **Greyhound**'s terminal is at Eighth and Stewart (624-3456). Greyhound no longer checks baggage in advance; it must be carried to the bus and picked up at busside upon arrival. Lockers are available.

H5 **Trailways** maintains its terminal at 1936 Westlake (624-5955).

Downtown parking

In addition to "expensive" street parking (limited, and with some of the highest parking ticket fines around), there are some good parking lots and garages in downtown Seattle. Rates vary.

P8 **Kingdome Parking**, north lot, (628-3663, 201 S King St). cc: none. Entrance at Second and King.

Services

I7 **The Bon Garage,** across from The Bon at Third and Stewart (344-7230). cc: AE, Bon, Chevron. Covered parking.

I5 **Systems Parking Garage,** across from Frederick & Nelson. (601 Olive Way, 623-0925). cc: none. Covered parking.

L6 **Four Seasons Olympic Garage** (Fifth & Seneca, 624-5767). Open 24 hours. cc: none. Covered parking.

Limousine services

AAA Limousine Service, 8016 Ashworth Ave N, 523-8000. cc: AE, MC, V.

Graves Limousine Service, 2341 Eastlake E, 329-6090. cc: none.

Monorail

C6- The Monorail (owned by the City of Seattle and operated by Metro) was built for
J6 the Seattle World's Fair in 1962 and has served Seattle ever since. It connects the Westlake Mall (downtown in the heart of the department store district) with Seattle Center, 1.2 miles to the north; the route along Fifth Avenue is mostly straight with two banked turns thrown in. Designed to travel along elevated concrete guideways at 60 mph, the Monorail has slowed down to 45 mph in recent years because of wear and tear on the system (the company that manufactured it, Alweg of Sweden, has gone out of business), so the trip now takes all of 90 seconds. The fare has gone up, too: one-way tickets cost 50 cents. The ride is a delight for children, since it has a touch of space age to it; it also affords surprisingly good views even though you are only a few stories above the street. Seattleites use the Monorail often as a way out to Seattle Center for lunch or to beat the evening parking crush for events at the Center: drive downtown, park, have a drink at a hotel bar, then hop onto the Monorail for an easy ride and walk to the Opera House. Hours: Sun-Thur: 10am-9pm. Fri-Sat: 10am-12:30am. Departs every 15 minutes. Wheelchair-accessible. Hours are extended during summer months.

Mountain driving

If you are driving the mountain passes, be sure to have chains in the car; some passes will allow you to pass with studded tires, but authorities can also require chains, and you'll be turned back if you don't have them. Some passes, including Chinook, Cayuse, and the North Cascades Highway, are closed entirely in the winter. For information on pass conditions: call 464-6010 or listen for up-to-date commercial radio reports from the Forest Service or National Weather Service. Incomplete combustion is a characteristic of driving in higher altitudes, so keep a window open slightly or carbon monoxide may build up in the car.

Railroads

P8 Seattle used to have two train stations; now there is but one. The King Street Station at Third and Jackson is the terminus for AMTRAK trains going south (to Portland, Salt Lake City, San Francisco, and Los Angeles), as well as eastbound trains to Spokane and Chicago. For schedule information and reservations, call 464-1930. AMTRAK's local ticket offices can be reached by calling 382-4127; the package express and baggage offices are at 382-4128.

Taxis

The June 1979 deregulation of the city's taxi system fulfilled one of the ordinance's goals: the number of cabs in Seattle and King County has risen to 525, thus accommodating more tourists, the elderly, and people with medical problems. A concomitant benefit from the larger taxi fleet—lower fares—is, at this point, a debatable prospect. The mushrooming of unregulated taxis has led to the expected horror stories of indifferent service and uncontrolled prices. Standard, long-time cab companies, however, continue to carry passengers at consistent prices and with courteous service.

Farwest (622-1717) maintains Seattle's largest fleet of cabs, and drivers take MC and V. A one-way ride to Sea-Tac costs $18.

Yellow Cab (622-6500) also takes MC and V credit cards. A one-way ride from Sea-Tac costs about $15.

Graytop (622-4949) charges $15 for the airport run, no credit cards accepted.

Checker Cab (937-1515) charges just $16 for a ride into town from Sea-Tac in one of their three taxis.

Hansom Cab (323-0365), with its formally dressed drivers and personalized service, adds a special touch. cc: MC, V. The fare to Sea-Tac is $23.

The flag drop charge in King County tends to range between one and two dollars, plus about $1.20 to $1.50 per each additional mile. Cab stands are located at or near the major hotels, as well as at Fourth and Pine, Frederick & Nelson's, the Medical-Dental Building downtown, on Seneca between Fifth and Sixth, at Eighth and Madison, at Fifth and Stewart, at the bus depots, the waterfront Ferry Terminal, at University Plaza at NE 45th and Brooklyn, and at The Bon at Northgate. If no cabs are in sight, it's best to telephone one of the companies listed above; they can usually dispatch a cab by radio within a matter of minutes (although the wait may be up to an hour at 4pm on a rainy Friday afternoon). Legally, cabs cannot stop if you flag them down from the curb, but some will.

Waterfront streetcar

HH7- Seattle's long-awaited waterfront streetcar, the brainchild of City Councilman
HH8 George Benson, has been phenomenally popular since it first started rolling in June 1982. Operated by Metro (cost 60 cents; conductors do not carry change), the mahogany, 1927-vintage Australian cars run on rails next to Alaskan Way, from Myrtle Edwards Park south to Pioneer Square. Every 15-30 minutes, the three handsome wooden cars carry passengers daily until 6pm (11pm in summer) along the waterfront; with a transfer, stops and starts can be made at no additional cost. Round trip takes about 30 minutes. Morning start-up times vary.

Transportation — Water

Ferries

Washington's fleet of ferries is the largest in the country; the system carried some 18.5 million passengers in 1982, nearly half of whom drove aboard. Eight routes serve 20 terminal locations. Often there are more cars than can be accommodated (especially in summer and on weekends) so it makes sense to park the car and walk if possible. Food service is available on almost all routes; beer is now sold on

281

Services

some routes, too. The Saga food service concession is a convenience to travelers with hungry children after a long car ride, but don't get your hopes up about the food.

For information on ferry schedules, call 464-6400; outside of Seattle there are toll-free numbers from 8am to 6pm: 1-800-542-0810 or 1-800-542-7052. In the Victoria area the number is (604) 381-1551 or (604) 656-1531. Ferry schedules vary in summer and winter. Destinations from Seattle and surrounding areas, with prices for a car and driver:

Winslow, for Bainbridge Island and beyond. Many islanders commute to Seattle; the trip lasts 30 minutes and the ferries run frequently. This is also an excellent round trip for a summer lunch hour or sunset cruise. The two new "super-ferries" are usually assigned to this run, which leaves from Seattle Ferry Terminal, Pier 52, at the foot of Marion Street and Alaskan Way. $4.80 one way.

Bremerton, for the Navy Ship Yard, the battleship *Missouri*, Hood Canal, and the Olympic Peninsula. Crossing takes one hour. Also leaves from the Seattle Ferry Terminal, Pier 52, $4.80 one way.

Vashon Island, an idyllic retreat just west of Seattle, is the first stop on a trip leaving from Fauntleroy, in West Seattle. The boat continues to Southworth, on the Kitsap Peninsula, before returning to Seattle. Fifteen minutes for the trip to Vashon; $6.50 for the round trip.

Kingston, close to the northern tip of the Kitsap Peninsula, is reached from Edmonds (about 15 miles north of Seattle; take the Edmonds-Kingston Ferry exit from I-5 and head northwest on Highway 104). The crossing takes 30 minutes and costs $4.80 one way. Highway 104 continues westward (toward the Olympic Peninsula) across the Hood Canal Bridge, a floating bridge also operated by the ferry system, and finally repaired in October 1982. The bridge toll is $2.50 per car, including all occupants.

Clinton, on Whidbey Island, is reached from Mukilteo, 27 miles north of Seattle. Boeing's giant Everett plant is along the approaches to the ferry dock; the crossing takes 20 minutes and costs $3.25. From **Keystone,** on Whidbey Island, another ferry goes to **Port Townsend,** one of the most enchanting towns in the state. The trip takes 30 minutes and costs $4.80.

The San Juan Islands are reached by ferry from Anacortes, 88 miles north of Seattle. The boat makes stops at Lopez, Shaw, Orcas, and Friday Harbor on San Juan Island, for costs ranging from $5.25 to $6.80. Once a day (twice in summer) at noon the ferry continues to Sidney on Canada's Vancouver Island, just 15 minutes from **Victoria.** It returns at 12:30pm. $22.60 for the trip to Sidney from Anacortes, car plus driver. Evergreen Trailways (624-5813) offers an $18 one-way package that includes the bus ride from downtown Seattle to Anacortes, ferry to Sidney, and bus to Victoria. The bus departs from the Trailways Terminal at 6:15am and returns from the Olympic Best Western Hotel in Victoria at 11:20am.

Direct service to **Victoria,** the capital city of British Columbia, is available on the *Princess Marguerite* (623-5560), a beloved old passenger and car steamer built in Scotland in 1948 and belonging now to the British Columbia Steamship Company. The Princess leaves Pier 69 on the Seattle waterfront at 8am every day from April 23rd to October 6th, and arrives in Victoria at 12:15pm. It leaves Victoria at 5:30pm the same day for the return trip to Seattle, arriving at 9:45pm. One-way fares per person are $18; round trip is $29. Cars cost an additional $27 each way; reservations for cars are required. Food service, particularly a proper British breakfast, is rather good. If you are going at a crowded time the throngs of teenagers and children might spoil your mood, so you might consider renting a stateroom (get one with a view for $20 including private bath); the budget staterooms aren't worth the extra money.

Victoria can also be reached from Port Angeles by the *Coho* ferry owned by the Black Ball Transport company, leaving Port Angeles at 9am in winter and up to four times a day in summer months. Call 622-2222 for schedules. Fare is $20 each way for car and driver. Additional adult passengers are $5.25. Greyhound (628-3456) makes daily runs to Port Angeles.

Visitor information

The Seattle-King County Convention and Visitors' Bureau and the King County East Convention and Visitors' Bureau provide tourist and regional travel information pertaining to Seattle, King County, and Washington State for both the tourist and business traveler. They are also responsible for booking and coordinating many of the conferences that come to the area. Their information outlets are listed below.

15	**(S-KC) Downtown Seattle office** 1815 Seventh Ave	*8:30-5 Mon-Fri, closed Sat & Sun* *447-7273*
006	**(S-KC) Sea-Tac Airport office**	*9:30-7:30 every day except Thanksgiving,* *Christmas, and New Year's days; 433-5217*
C6	**(S-KC) Seattle Center office** At base of the Space Needle, near Monorail terminal	*10-6 every day (summer only: Memorial Day* *to Labor day); 447-7280*
	(S-KC) North Bend office Exit 31 From I-90	*9:30-6 every day (Memorial Day weekend to* *Labor Day weekend); 888-1678*
CC7	**(KC East) office** Ashwood Center, NE 12th & 108th NE	*455-1926 9-5; brochures & maps 9-9*

Babysitting/childcare

There are a handful of bonded babysitting services listed in the *Yellow Pages* under 'Babysitting.' The rates are $4-$5/hour with a four-hour minimum. If you are staying at one of the hotels, make arrangements for child care through the concierge. Often rates will be a little bit lower.

Babysitting & drop-in childcare

These child-care centers accept drop-ins on a first-come, first-served basis. Each facility listed is state-licensed and therefore has a legal capacity which it cannot exceed: call ahead whenever possible.

Day Care Referral Service	*9-5 Mon & Fri; 11-5 Tues & Thur; 5-9* *Wed; closed Sat & Sun; 447-3207*

This complimentary service tries to line up your child-care needs, drop-in or otherwise, with computerized files of 1,500 state-licensed day care homes, centers, or mini-centers.

Services

Fifth Avenue Kiddy Korner
2133 Fifth Avenue
Ages: 1-8 years

6:30-6:30 Mon-Sat, closed Sun
624-5437
Rates: 1-2½ years, $2.25/hour; 2½-8 years, $1.50/hour; $6 minimum

Only four blocks from the Seattle Center, Kiddy Korner provides a loosely structured environment with some light academics in the late morning. There is an outside play area with gym equipment and a small library off the large playroom inside. Tumbling classes and swimming classes are offered in the summer; frequent field trips. Lunch is not provided, but morning and afternoon snacks are complimentary.

Frederick & Nelson's Downtown
Fourth floor, Fifth & Pine
Ages: 3-8 years

9:30-5:30 Mon-Sat; closed Sun
682-5500, ext. 2191
Rates: 1 child, $1.50/hour; 2 children, $2.75/hour

A well-supervised playroom with lots of table activities and play equipment. There are no napping facilities and lunch is not provided.

His Divine Love Day Care Center
Woodlawn Ave. & N 43rd
Ages: 1 month–5 years

6:30-6 Mon-Fri; closed Sat & Sun
634-3491
Rates: 1-18 months, $2.50/hour; 18 months-3 years, $2.25/hour; 3-5 years, $2/hour

Separate cribroom for infants and different classrooms for each age group. Access to real kitchen allows for some kiddie culinary creations. Snacks and lunch are included and are homemade from natural ingredients. There is a nearby park for outdoor exercise and a large gym with mats for rainy day activities.

The Little Red Schoolhouse
The Bon, Third & Pine, third floor
Ages: 2½-9 years

10-6 Mon-Sat; closed Sun
344-8799
Rates: 2½-3 years, $1.50/hour; 3-9 years, $1.25/hour; second child $1.15/hour

Art, music, storytimes, and a large play area with lots of table activities and play equipment. Napping facilities are provided. Snacks are complimentary and lunch is available for $1.25, or you can bring your own.

Pike Place Market Childcare Center
1500 Western Ave., second floor
Ages: 2½-6 years

9-5 Sat
625-5045
Rates: $2.50/hour

The indoor area has several rooms to provide spaces for different activities such as art, dramatic play, and reading; there is also a partially covered outdoor playyard. They provide snacks but you must provide lunch.

Seattle Early Education Center
1624 Eighth Ave.
Ages: 2½-8 years

6:30-6 Mon-Fri; closed Sat & Sun
682-9120
Rates: $12/day; $6/half day

A structured day with emphasis in the morning on a light curriculum—social studies, drama, art, literature, small and large motor development. There are five classrooms with a small library and a large upstairs play area for preschoolers with blocks, a slide, a fort, and lots of table activities. They have an enclosed play roof and their own bus provides a lot of field trips. Breakfast and two snacks are provided; parents must provide lunch for their child.

Index

ACT (theater) see A Contemporary Theater
A Contemporary Theater, 66
A la Francaise, 11
Abruzzi 55
Acapulco y los Arcos, 82
Accessories and luggage, 101
Ad Lib Tavern, 92
Adriatica, 11
Airplanes
   Charter flights, 278
   Out of town, 247
Al-Waaha, 12
The Alaska Junction, 12, 53
Alex's Cafe, 59
Alexis Hotel, 1
   Bar, 78
   Dining room, 12
   Lodging, 1
   Mark Tobey, 85, 36
   Meeting & conf. facilities, 264
Alexis Restaurant, see Alexis Hotel
Alki Beach Park, 195
Alternative art spaces, 77
America's Cup, 95, 12, 53
American Pie, 62
The Americana Cafe, 12
Andy and Jemmy's Wok, 13
   Private rooms, 270
Anthony's Home Port, 13, 53
Antiques, 138
Apres Vous Cafe, 13
The Aquarium, *vii*
Arboretum, 193 *vi*
Art Galleries, 72, 250; see also
   Alternative art spaces
   Crafts galleries
   Glass galleries
   Native American art galleries
Arts, 65; see also individual entries
Associated Vintners, 250
Astor Park, 88
Azuka, 13
   private rooms, 270
Athenian Inn, 13, 82
The Attic, 56
Auctions, 141
Aurora Village shopping, 98
Aurora's of Mexico, 14
The Austrian, 14
   Private rooms, 270
Auto emergencies, 261
Auto racing, 216
The AxelRock Saloon, 84
Avenue 52, 14
Azteca, 61

B&O Espresso, 62
Babysitting/childcare, 283
Back Court Tavern, 90
Backstage, 90
Bainbridge Island, 257
Bakeman's Restaurant, 54
The Baker Apartment Hotel, 1
Bakeries, 120
The Bakery, 52, 54
Ballard, 185
Bangkok Hut, 14
Barbecue restaurants, 58
Bars, 78
   Downtown, 78
   Gay, 84
   Other areas, 80
   Piano, 93
      Downtown, 93
      North End, 95
      Other areas, 95
   View, 82
   Wine, 84
Baseball, 216
Basketball, 216
Bathhouse Theater, 66
Bed & Breakfast, 7
Bellevue, 249
Bellevue Art Museum, 71, 250
Bellevue Hilton
   Lodging, 6
   Meeting & conf. facilities, 264
Bellevue Red Lion Inn
   Lodging, 6
   Meeting & conf. facilities, 264
Bellevue Square shopping, 99, 250
Bellevue Thunderbird, 6
Bellingham, 256
Belltown Cafe, 15
Benihana of Tokyo, 15
Benjamin's, 15, 82
Beth's Cafe, 52
Bicycle racing, 217
Bicycling, 219
Blarney Stone, 88
Blue Moon Tavern, 85
Boating, 222
The Boiserie, 62
The Bon, 99
Books, 149
Boondock's, Sundecker's, and Greenthumb's, 80
Bothell Landing, 197
Brasserie Pittsbourg, 15
   Private rooms, 270
Brazilian restaurants, 58
Breakers, 217
Breakfast, 52
Bremerton, 256
Bridle Trails State Park, 197
British Pantry, 58
The Broadway, 15, 80
Browny's Seafood Broiler, 16

Brunch, 53
brusseau's, 16
The Buckaroo, 85
Buffalo Tavern, 90
Bugsy's, 55
Burke Gilman Trail, 195
Burke Museum, 71, 199
Burk's Cafe, 16
Burnie's Cafe, 52
Bus tours, 203
   Mount Rainier, 246
Buses, 279
Business services, 263
Butchers, 122
Byblos, 60

Cafe Allegro, 63
Cafe Botanica, 16, 53
Cafe Casino, 16
Cafe Juanita, 17
Cafe Loc, 17
Cafe Optimum, 17
Cafe Sabika, 17
Cafe Society, 17
Cajun/Creole restaurants, 58
Camera, 152
Camera repair, see camera
Camlin Hotel
   The Cloud Room, 93
   Lodging, 1
Camping, 232
Candies and Chocolate, 123
Canlis, 17, 82
   Private rooms, 270
Canoeing and kayaking, 223
Clubs, 224
Canterbury Ale & Eats, 56, 84
Cape Flattery, 258
Capitol Hill, 191, 210
   Shopping, 98
Captain's Table, 18
Carkeek Park, 196
Carnation, 252
Carpets, see Rugs
Casa Lupita, 61
Catering, see Gourmet take-out, 124
Cause Celebre, 18
Caveman Kitchen, 18
Central Tavern, 85, 95
Century House, 4
Charters
   Airplane, 278
   Bus, 279
Chateau Ste. Michelle, 252

285

Index

Cheese, 127
Chez Claude, 18
  Private rooms, 270
Children's activities, 201
Children's clothing, 103
Children's Museum, 201
China First, 18
China Gate, 19
China North, 19
  Private rooms, 270
Chinese restaurants, 58
Chism Beach, 198
Chiyoko, 19, 95
Chocolate, see Candies and Chocolate
Cirrus, see Sheraton Hotel
City Picnics, 54
City Stage, 67
Claremont Prime Rib & Salmon House, 19
Clifford's, 19
Climbing, 232
Cloth, see Fabric
Clothing, 101
  Children's, 103
  Large, tall, maternity, petite sizes, 109
  Lingerie, 110
  Men's and women's wear, 110
  Rainwear, 117
  Vintage clothing, 118
Cloud Room, see Camlin Hotel
Clubs
  Other areas, 92
  Pioneer Square and Downtown, 88
  University District and North End, 90
Coffee houses, see Dessert and Coffee Houses
Coffees and Teas, 127
The College Inn, 6
College Inn Pub, 85, 90
College sports, 218
Colman Park, 194
Comedy Underground, 89
Comet Tavern, 85
Computers
  Sales, 154
  Rentals, 263
Concord Garden, 20
Condominiums, 9
Consuls, 274
Consumer food cooperatives, 128
Continental Restaurant and Pastry Shop, 59, 63
Cooking equipment, see Kitchenware, Gifts, and Imports
Cooperative, see Consumer food cooperatives

Copacabana, 20
Costas, 20
Costas Opa, 20
Craft galleries, 74, 250
Crepe de Paris, 20, 79
  Private rooms, 271
Crossroads Mall shopping, 99
Czechoslovakia restaurants, 58

The Daily Grind, 63
Daly's, 57
Dance, 69
D'Andrea, 21
Dandy's, 21
Daniel's Broiler, 21
Dante's, 85
Daybreak Star Center, 199
De Laurenti's, 56
Delis, 129
Deluxe One Bar & Grill, 21, 81
Denny Blaine neighborhood, 191
Denny Regrade, 190
Department stores, 98
Dessert and coffee houses, 62
Dez's 400, 90
Dick's, 57
The Dilettante, 62
Discos, 93
  Downtown, 93
  North End, 95
  Other areas, 95
Discover Dance, 70
Discovery Park, 196
Doc Maynard's, 89
Dog House, 93
Domani, 21
Dominic's, 63
Doubletree Inn, 5
  Infinity Lounge, 92
  Lodging, 5
Doubletree Plaza, 5
  Boojum Tree Lounge, 96
  Lodging, 5

East Pike & East Pine streets, 213
East-West Garden, 60
Edgewater Inn,
  Bar, 93
  Lodging, 4
El Cafe, 61
El Gaucho, 22
El Puerco Lloron, 22
Elliott Bay Cafe, 22
Emergency telephone numbers, 262
Emmett Watson's Oyster Bar, 23
Empty Space, 66

English restaurants, 58
Enoteca, 23, 84
Entertainment, 87; see also individual entries
Ernestine's, 89
Ethiopian restaurants, 59
Ethnic restaurants, 58; see also Delis
Executive Inn, 4
Exercise, 224

F.X. McRory's Steak, Chop & Oyster House, 79,37
  Private rooms, 271
Fabric, Sewing and knitting stores, 105; see also Imports, Dept. stores
Factoria Square, 99
The Famous Pacific Dessert Company, 63
Fat Albert's, 85
Ferries, vii, 255, 281
Fifteenth Avenue E, 213
5th Avenue Theater, 65
50th Street Deli and Cafe, 54
Filiberto's, 23
Filipino restaurants, 59
Films, see Movies
The Fireside Room, see Sorrento Hotel
First Hill, 190
The Fisherman's, 82
Fishermen's Terminal, vii
Fishing, 228
Fitzgerald's, see Westin Hotel
Flame, 91
Flor de Mexico, 61
Food cooperatives, see Consumer Food Cooperatives
Food stores, 120
Football, 217
Foreign banking, 275
Foreign visitors, 274
Fortnum's, 63
Four Seasons Olympic Hotel, 2
  Garden Court, 79, 93
  Georgian Room, 24, 53
    Private rooms, 271
  Lodging, 2
  Meeting & conf. facilities, 265
  Shuckers, 46, 80
Franco's Hidden Harbor, 23, 82
Franglor's Creole, 58
Frederick & Nelson, 99
Freeway Park, 192
The Fremont Cafe, 54
French restaurants, 59
French Invention, 23
Frink Park, 194
Frye Museum, 71
Fuller's, 23
Funky Broadway East, 58
Furniture, see Home Furnishings

286

Index

G-Note Tavern, 91
Galleries, see Art galleries
Garden Court, see Four Seasons Olympic Hotel
Gardens, 198
Gasworks Park, 195
Gatsby's, 92
Gelateria Di Freddie, 63
Gene's Place, 15, 93
Gepetto's Gelateria, 63
The Georgian Room, see Four Seasons Olympic Hotel
German/Austrian restaurants, 59; see also Delis
Gerard's Relais de Lyon, 24
　Private rooms, 271
Gift stores, 158
Gilbert and Sullivan Society, 67
Gilman Village, 99, 251
Girvan's, 24, 83
Glass galleries, 76
Godfather's, 56
Golden Crown, 89
Golden Palace, 24
Golf, 231
The Goose, 25, 79, 84
Gourmet take-out, 124
Grand Illusion, 64
Greek restaurants, 59; see also Delis
Green Lake, 183, 195
Greenlake Grill, 25
Greenlake Jake's, 52, 57
Greenwood, 184
Greenwood Inn,
　Lodging, 6
　Meeting & conf. facilities, 265
Gretchen's Of Course, 25
　Private rooms, 271
The Group, 66

Haagen Dazs, 64
Hall of Fame, 91
Hamburgers, 56
Han Il, 26
Handbags, see Accessories and Luggage
Hardware stores, 141
Harry's, 57
Health food stores, 132
Hector's, 26
Henry Gallery, 71
Henry's Off Broadway, 25, 81, 96
　Private rooms, 271
The Hi-Spot Cafe, 26
Hibble & Hyde's, 89
Hill Brothers Barbecue, 58
Hiking, 232

Hing Hay Park, 192
Hiram M. Chittenden Locks, vii
Hiram's at-the-Locks, 26, 53, 83
Hisago, 26
Hobbies, see Toys
Hockey, 217
Home furnishings, 143; see also Antiques
Hon's, 27
Hong Kong, 27
Horatio's, 27, 83
Horse racing, 217
Hostels, 10
Hotel Seattle, 2
Hotels and motels, 1
　Downtown, 1
　Denny Regrade/Seattle Center, 4
　airport area, 5
　Eastside, 6
　University District and North End, 6
House of Hong, 27
Hungry U, 56
The Hunt Club, see Sorrento Hotel
Hurricane Ridge, 258
Huskies, 218
Hyatt Seattle, 5

I. Magnin, 100
Il Bistro, 28, 78
Import shops, 161
India House, 28
　Private rooms, 271
Indian restaurants, 59
Indian Seattle, 199
Indonesian restaurants, 59
Inn Bin, 28
International District, vii, 206
　Tours, 204
International services, 275
Interpreters, 274
Intiman Theater Company, 66
Issaquah, 251
Italian restaurants, 59; see also Delis
Italo's Casa Romana, 28
Ivar's Indian Salmon House, 29
　Private rooms, 271

J & M Cafe, 29, 86
Jake O'Shaughnessey's, 29, 81
Jalisco, 30
Japanese restaurants, 60
Java restaurant, 29
Jazz Alley, 91
Jewelry, 107
Jogging, 235
Jolly Roger Roadhouse, 91
Jonah and the Whale, 29, 96
Juanita Beach, 197
Julia's 14-Carrot Cafe, 30

Kaleenka Russian Cafe, 30
Karawan, 30
Kau Kau, 30
Kayaking, 223
Kelsey Creek Park, 197
Kennedy Hotel, 2
Kidd Valley Hamburger Company, 57
Kidstuff, 201
Kikuya, 30
Kimberley's, 64
King Cafe, 31
Kirkland, 253
Kirkland Custom Cannery, 253
Kitchen appliances (small); see Dept. Stores, Kitchenware
Kitchenware, 146
Kites, see Toys
Klahowyan, 31
Klondike Gold Rush National Historical Park, 72
Knight's Diner, 57
Knitting stores, see Fabric, Sewing, and Knitting
Kobe Terrace, 193
Kokeb, 31
Korea House, 31
Korean restaurants, 60
Kosher restaurants, 60

La Concha, 62
Labuznik, 31, 79
LaConner, 255
Lake Sammamish, 250
Lake Union Cafe, 23
Lake Washington, 194
The Lakeside, 32, 83
Large venues, 87
The Last Exit on Brooklyn, 32
Latitude 47, 95
Le Bonaparte, 32, 53
　Private rooms 271
Le Petit Cafe, 41
Le Pigalle, 32
Le Provencal, 33
Le Tastevin, 33, 84
　Private rooms, 272
Les Copains, 33
Lebanon, 60
Leschi Lakecafe, 34, 83
Leschi Park, 194
Library, Seattle Public, 274
Limousine services, 280
Lincoln Park, 194
Lingerie, 110
Linyen, 34

287

Index

Lion O'Reilly's & B.J.
Monkeyshine's, 34, 53, 81
Liquor stores, see State Liquor Stores
Lodging, 1
Lofurno's, 34, 91
Lone Star Cafe, 58
Longacres, 217
Longhorn Bar & Grill, 91
Lopez Island, 254
Lost and found, 275
Louie's Cuisine of China, 35
Lounges, 93
  Downtown, 93
  North End, 95
  other areas, 95
Lowell's, 52
Loyal Inn, 14
Luggage, see Accessories and luggage
Luther Burbank Park, 196

Mad Anthony's, 35
Madison Hotel, 2
Madison Park, 183
Madison Park Cafe, 35
Madrona Park, 194
Magazines and newspapers, 163
Maharaja, 59
Malaysian restaurants, 60
Malia's Northwest, 35, 79
Mama Lontoni's, 35
Mama's Mexican Kitchen, 62
Mamounia, 35
The Mark Tobey, see Alexis Hotel
Marymoor County Park, 197, 250
Maternity clothing; see Large, tall, maternity and petite clothing
Matzoh Momma's, 36, 93
Maximilien-in-the-Market, 36
Mayflower Park Hotel, 2
  Lodging, 2
  Meeting & conf. facilities, 272
  Oliver's, 2
McCormick's Fish House & Bar, 36, 79
Medieval Cellar, 92
Mediterranean Kitchen, 37
Mediterranean restaurants, 60; see also Delis
Meeting & conference facilities, 264
  Hotels, 264
  Other, 266
  Restaurants, 270
Men's wear, 110; see also Dept. stores, Vintage clothing

Mercer Island, 191, 198
Merchants Cafe, 37, 89
Messenger services, 269
Mexican restaurants, 61
Michael J's, 89
Middle Eastern restaurants, 60
Mikado, 37
  Private rooms, 271
Mikado Fish & Tempura Company, 52
Mint, 89
Mirabeau, 38, 83
  Private rooms, 272
Miya's, 38
Monorail, 280
Morgan's Lakeplace, 38, 81
Morilles; see Park Hilton Hotel
Morningtown Pizza, 56
Moroccan restaurants, 60
Motels; see Hotels and motels
Mount Baker Park, 194
Mount Rainier, vii, 245
  Tours, 245
Mount St. Helens, 247
Mount Vernon, 255
Mountain driving, 280
Mountain loops, 247
  Northern loop tour, 247
  Mid-Cascades loop tour, 248
Movie theaters, 67
Movies, 67
Mukilteo Cafe, 38
Murphy's, A Pub, 85, 92
Museum of History and Industry, 72
Museums, 70, 250
Music, classical, 73
MusiComedy Northwest, 67
Myrtle Edwards Park, 193

Native American art galleries, 76
Neighborhoods, 206
  Capitol Hill, 191, 210
  Intl. district, 204, 206
  University district, 208
New City Theater, 67
New Conservatory Theater, 67
Newspapers, see Magazines & Newspapers
Nightlife, 78
Nikko, 39
  Private rooms, 272
1904 Restaurant/Bar, 37, 84
The Nooner, 54
Nordstrom, 100
Northgate shopping, 98
Northlake Tavern & Pizza House, 56, 86
Northwest Chamber Orchestra, 68
Northwest Wine Sampler, 137

O'Banions, 92
O'Leary's, 39
Olde Bellevue shopping, 99, 249
Olive's East, 55
Oliver's, see Mayflower Park Hotel
Olympia Pizza & Spaghetti House, 56
Olympic Hotel, see Four Seasons Olympic
Olympic National Park, 258
Olympic Peninsula, 257
On the Boards, 70
One Stop Restaurant, 57
Opera, 69
Orcas Island, 254
Oriental food, see Delis, Ethnic restaurants
Original Ellen's, 39, 250
The Other Place, 39
Outdoor Equipment, 164
Owl Cafe, 92
Oyster Grotto, 40

Pacific Northwest Ballet, 69
Pacific Plaza Hotel, 2
Pacific Science Center, vi, 199
The Palm Court, see Westin Hotel
Panales, 40
Panchito's, 41
Park Hilton Hotel, 3
  Lodging, 3
  Meeting & conf. facilities, 265
  Morilles, 94
Parker's, 92
Parking, 279
  Downtown, 279
  Airport, 278
Parks, 192
Participatory sports, 264
Pasta, 133
Paul Thomas Winery, 250
Paul's Place, 41
Pavilion Outlet Center, 99
Performing arts, 65; see also individual entries
Petit Cafe, 41
Petite women's clothing, see Large, tall, maternity and petite clothing
Philadelphia String Quartet, 68
Phinney Ridge Cafe, 52
Phoenicia, 41
Photo equipment, see Camera
Photo labs, see Camera
Piccolo's, 56
Piecora's, 56
Pier 70, 89
Pike and Pine neighborhood, 213

288

Index

Pike Place Market, vi, 175, 189
  Shopping, 98
  Tours, 205
The Pink Door, 41
Pioneer Square, vi, 178, 189
  Shopping, 98
  Tours, 205
Pioneer Square Tavern, 90
Pioneer Square Theater, 66
Pizza, 55
Place Pigalle, 42
Polynesian restaurants, 60
Ponce's Pastelleria, 59
Poncho Theater, 66, 202
Poquito de Mexico, 62
Port Angeles, 258
Port Townsend, 258
Poulsbo, 256
The Price Is Right, 79
Primo Gelato, 64
Princess marguerite, 253, 282
Private rooms, restaurants, 270
Procopio Gelateria, 64
Produce markets, 133
Pubs, 84
Puget Sound Railway, 251
Purses, see Accessories and luggage

Queen Anne, 184, 191
Quick Info, Public Library, 263, 274
Quinn's Fishmarket, 42, 53, 95
Quintana Roo, 42

Rafting, 237
Railroads, 280; see also Puget Sound Railway
Rainbow Tavern, 92
Rainier Pub, 42
Rainier Square shopping, 98
Rainwear, 117
Rainy Town Folk Music Club, 92
raison d'etre, 42
Rama House, 42
Ramada Inn, 7
Rasa Malaysia, 43
Ray's Boathouse, 43, 83
Records, 168
The Red Cabbage Restaurant, 43, 80, 94
Red Robin, 57, 83
Regency Motor Inn, 5
The Restaurant Alki, 43
The Restaurant Queen Anne, 43

Restaurants, 11
  Top 200, 11
  Breakfast, 52
  Brunch, 53
  Soup, salad, sandwich, 54
  Pizza, 55
  Hamburgers, 56
  Ethnic, 58
  Dessert and coffee houses, 62
Rio Cafe, 90
Ristorante Pony, 43
Roanoke Exit, 44
Roanoke Inn, 86
Roanoke Park Place, 86
Roosevelt Bakery, 64
Rosellini's Four-10, 44, 80, 94
  Private rooms, 272
Rosita's, 62
Rugs, 148
Russet's, 44, 53
Russian restaurants, 60

Sabra, 60
Saigon over the Counter, 44
Sailboarding, 237
Sailing, 238
  Charters, 239
Ste. Michelle Winery; see Chateau Ste. Michelle
Salads, see Soup, salad, sandwich
Saleh al Lago, 44
Sammamish River Trail, 197
San Juan Islands, 254
Sandwich, see Soup, salad, sandwich
Santa Fe Cafe, 45, 54
Santa Fe Chamber Music Festival, 69
Scandia Cafe, 45
Scandinavian food, see Delis, Ethnic restaurants
Scandinavian restaurants, 61
Seafood Shanty of Singapore, 45
Seafood stores, 134
Seahawks, 217
Seaplanes, 278
Sea-Tac Airport, 255
Sea-Tac Holiday Inn, 5
Sea-Tac Red Lion Inn, 5
Seattle Airport Hilton Hotel, 5
Seattle Art Museum, vi, 70
Seattle Center, 181, 190
Seattle Chamber Music Festival, 69
Seattle Hilton Hotel, 3
  Lodging, 3
  Meeting & conf. facilities, 265
  Top of the Hilton, 94

Seattle International Film Festival, 67
Seattle Marriott at Sea-Tac, 5
Seattle Opera Association, 69
Seattle Repertory Theater, 65
Seattle Symphony Orchestra, 68
Seattle-Tacoma Airport, 276
  To and from, 277
  Airport parking, 276
Seattle Youth Symphony, 68
2nd Avenue Extension, 57
Second-hand clothes, see Vintage clothes
Secretarial services, 272
Sequim, 258
Service stations, late-night, 261
Services, 260
Settebello, 45, 81
Seward Park, 194
Sewing shops, see Fabric, sewing, and knitting
Shamper's, see Westin Hotel
Shanghai, 46
Shaw Island, 254
Sheraton Hotel, 3
  The Cafe, 3
  Fuller's 23
  Private rooms, 270
  Green's, 94
  Lodging, 3
  Cirrus, 3
  Meeting & conf. facilities, 265
Sheraton Renton Inn, 6
  Brandy's piano lounge, 96
  Lodging, 6
  The Penthouse, 96
Sherwood Town and Country Inn, 7
Ship canal, vii
Shopping, 97
Shopping areas, 97
Short-size clothing, see Large, tall, maternity, petite clothing.
Shortztop Cafe, 46
Shuckers, see Four Seasons Olympic Hotel
Silver Dragon, 46
Silver Spoon, 93, 252
Simon's, 46
Simonetti's, 95
Simply Desserts, 64
Skagit River tours, 248
Skagit Valley, 255
Skid Road Theater, see City Stage

289

Index

Skiing, 239
   Downhill, 239
   Cross-country, 240
Smuggler, 94
Snoqualmie Falls, 251
The Snug, 55
Soccer, 218
Sorrento Hotel, 3
   Fireside Room, 81
   Hunt Club, 27
   Lodging, 3
   Meeting & conf. facilities 265
Soul food, 61
Sounders, 218
Soup, salad, sandwich, 54
The Soup and Salad, 55
Soupourri, 55
South China, 47
Southcenter shopping, 98
Space Needle, 47
Specialty stores, see shopping
Spectator sports, 216
Sport, 215
State liquor stores, 135
Steam railway, see Puget Sound Railway
Stereo equipment, 148
Stereo records, see records
Stereos, see Stereo equipment
Streamliner Diner, 47
Stuart's at Shilshole, 47, 84, 95
Sundays, 47, 54, 84, 96
   Private rooms, 272
Sunlight Cafe, 55
Suquamish, 199, 257
   Museum, 200
The Surrogate Hostess, 48
Swannie's, 48; see also Comedy Underground
Sweets, see Candies and chocolate, Bakeries
Swimming, 242

Tacoma Actors Guild, 66
Tai Tung, 48
Take-out food, 124
Tally Ho, 94
Targy's Tavern, 86
Taverns, 85
Taxis, 281
Teas, see Coffees and teas
Tennis, 243
Teriyaki Sagano, 48
The Thai Kitchen, 61
Thai restaurants, 61
Thai Taste, 61
Thanh Lan, 48
Theater, 65
Thirteen Coins, 48
318 Tavern, 57
Three Girls Bakery, 55
Ticket outlets, 70

Tien Tsin, 49
Tijuana Tilly's, 90
To-go food, 124
Tony's, 56
Top of the Hilton, see Hilton Hotel
Top of the Needle, 47, 83
Toshi's Teriyaki, 49
Tours, bus, see Bus tours
Tours, commercial, 203
   Boat, 203
   Bus, 203
   Smaller, personalized, 204
   Walking, 204
   Other, 205
Tours—out of town, 245
   Mt. Rainier, 245
   Mt. St. Helens, 247
   Mountain loops, 247
   Heading east, 249
   Victoria, 253
   San Juan Islands, 254
   Skagit Valley & Bellingham, 255
   Bremerton, Poulsbo, Bainbridge Triangle, 256
   Olympic Peninsula, 257
Towing, 24-hour, 261
Toys, 168
Trader Vic's, see Westin Hotel
Translators & interpreters, 274
Transportation, 276
   Air, 276
   Land, 279
   Water, 281
Trattoria Mitchelli, 49
Trattoria Pagliacci, 49
TraveLodge, 5
Treats, 64
Tropics Bar, 95
Truffles, 55
Tugs Belltown Tavern, 84

Umberto's, 50, 80
   Private rooms, 272
The Unicorn, 50
Union Bay Cafe, 50
University Bar & Grill, 82
University District, 184, 208
   Shopping, 98
University of Washington, vi, 191
   Film Series, 68
   School of Music, 69
University Village shopping, 98
Uruapan, 50
Used clothes, see Vintage clothing
University Tower Hotel,
   Bar, 82, 95
   Lodging, 7

Vaersgo, 50
Val's Cafe, 53
Vance Hotel, 3
Vehicle breakdowns, 261
Victoria, 253
Vietnam, 50
Vietnamese restaurants, 61
Villa Real, 62
Vintage clothes, 119
Virginia Inn, 80
Visitor Information, 283
Visual arts, 70; see also individual entries
Vito's, 51
Vogue, 94
Volunteer Park, 193

Wallingford, 183
Warwick Hotel, 4
Washington Hall Performance Gallery, 67
Washington Park/Arboretum, vi, 193
Washington Post Cafe, 51, 54
Washington State Ferries, vii, 255, 256, 281
Waterfall Gardens, 193
Waterfront, 177, 189
Waterfront Streetcar, 281
Watertown Tavern, 86
Weaving stores, see Fabric, sewing and knitting
Westin Hotel, 4
   Fitzgerald's, 79
   Lodging, 4
   Market Cafe, 4
   Meeting & conf. facilities, 265
   Palm Court, 40, 53
   Shamper's, 84
   Trader Vic's, 49, 80
   Private rooms, 272
Wheedle's, 47
William's, 57
Wine shops, 135; see also Eastside tours, 250, 252
Wineries, 250, 252; see also Northwest Wine Sampler.
Wing Luke Memorial Museum, 71, 206
Winslow, 257
Woerne's European Cafe, 51
The Wok, 51
   Private rooms, 272
Women's wear, 110; see also Dept. stores, large, tall, maternity, petite; Lingerie; Vintage
Woodinville, 252
Woodland Park, 195
Woodland Park Zoo, vii, 195

Yangtze Szechwan, 51
Yung Ya, 51

**Seattle Best Places
Report Form**

Send to:
    David Brewster, editor
    Seattle Best Places
    1932 First Avenue, Suite 605
    Seattle, Washington 98101

Based on my personal experience, I wish to nominate/confirm for listing/disapprove for listing the following place(s):

_____
_____
_____

(Please include address and telephone number, if convenient.)

Report:

I am not connected, directly or indirectly, with the management or ownership of these establishments.

Signed _____

Address _____

(Note: It is easiest to Xerox this form from the book, thus keeping the form handy for subsequent reports.)

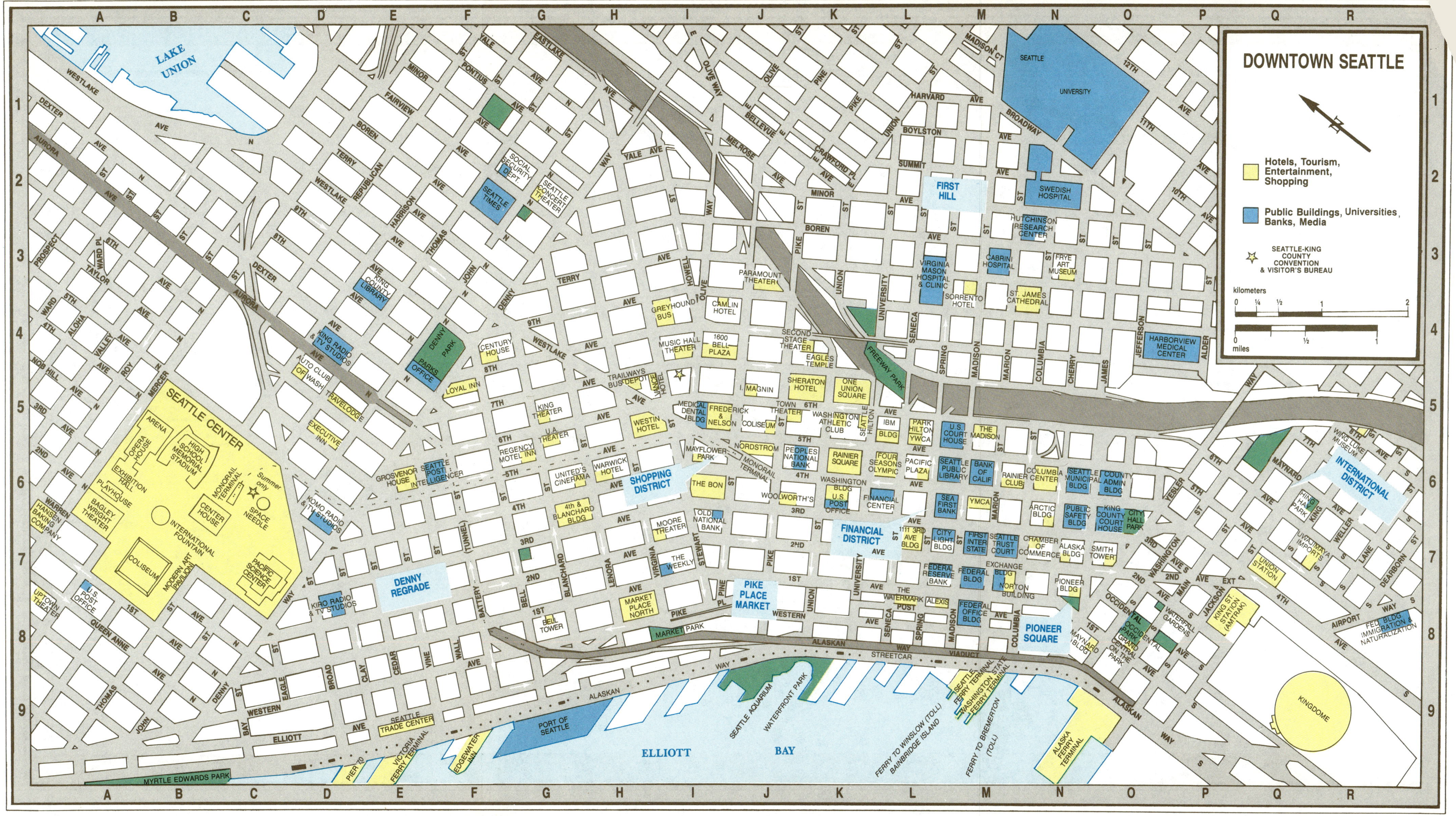
DOWNTOWN SEATTLE
Hotels, Tourism, Entertainment, Shopping
Public Buildings, Universities, Banks, Media
SEATTLE-KING COUNTY CONVENTION & VISITOR'S BUREAU
kilometers
0
¼
½
1
2
miles
0
½
1
LAKE UNION
ELLIOTT
BAY
SEATTLE CENTER
OPERA HOUSE
ARENA
HIGH SCHOOL MEMORIAL STADIUM
EXHIBITION HALL
PLAYHOUSE
BAGLEY WRIGHT THEATER
CENTER HOUSE
MONORAIL TERMINAL
SPACE NEEDLE
INTERNATIONAL FOUNTAIN
COLISEUM
MODERN ART PAVILION
PACIFIC SCIENCE CENTER
HANSEN BAKING COMPANY
UPTOWN THEATER
U.S. POST OFFICE
KING COUNTY LIBRARY
KING RADIO & TV STUDIOS
KOMO RADIO & TV STUDIOS
KIRO RADIO & TV STUDIOS
AUTO CLUB OF WASH
TRAVELODGE
EXECUTIVE INN
DENNY PARK
PARKS OFFICE
LOYAL INN
CENTURY HOUSE
SEATTLE TIMES
SOCIAL SECURITY DEPT.
SEATTLE CONCERT THEATER
KING THEATER
U.A. THEATER
REGENCY MOTEL INN
GROSVENOR HOUSE
SEATTLE POST INTELLIGENCER
UNITED'S CINERAMA
WARWICK HOTEL
4th & BLANCHARD BLDG
WESTIN HOTEL
TRAILWAYS BUS DEPOT
VANCE HOTEL
GREYHOUND BUS
CAMLIN HOTEL
MUSIC HALL THEATER
1600 BELL PLAZA
PARAMOUNT THEATER
SECOND STAGE THEATER
EAGLES TEMPLE
I. MAGNIN
SHERATON HOTEL
ONE UNION SQUARE
MEDICAL DENTAL BLDG
FREDERICK & NELSON
COLISEUM
TOWN THEATER
WASHINGTON ATHLETIC CLUB
SEATTLE HILTON
IBM BLDG
PARK HILTON YWCA
U.S. COURT HOUSE
THE MADISON
MAYFLOWER PARK
NORDSTROM
MONORAIL TERMINAL
PEOPLES NATIONAL BANK
RAINIER SQUARE
FOUR SEASONS OLYMPIC
PACIFIC PLAZA
SEATTLE PUBLIC LIBRARY
BANK OF CALIF
RAINIER CLUB
COLUMBIA CENTER
SEATTLE MUNICIPAL BLDG
COUNTY ADMIN BLDG
SHOPPING DISTRICT
THE BON
WOOLWORTH'S
WASHINGTON BLDG
U.S. POST OFFICE
FINANCIAL CENTER
SEA FIRST BANK
YMCA
ARCTIC BLDG
PUBLIC SAFETY BLDG
KING COUNTY COURT HOUSE
CITY HALL PARK
MOORE THEATER
OLD NATIONAL BANK
THE WEEKLY
FINANCIAL DISTRICT
1111 3RD AVE BLDG
CITY LIGHT BLDG
FIRST INTERSTATE
SEATTLE TRUST COURT
CHAMBER OF COMMERCE
ALASKA BLDG
SMITH TOWER
FEDERAL RESERVE BANK
FEDERAL BLDG
EXCHANGE BLDG
NORTON BUILDING
PIONEER BLDG
THE WATERMARK
ALEXIS
FEDERAL OFFICE BLDG
DENNY REGRADE
PIKE PLACE MARKET
MARKET PLACE NORTH
BELL TOWER
MARKET PARK
PIONEER SQUARE
MAYNARD BLDG
OCCIDENTAL PARK
GRAND CENTRAL ON THE PARK
WATERFALL GARDENS
KING ST. STATION (AMTRAK)
UNION STATION
FED. BLDG IMMIGRATION & NATURALIZATION
KINGDOME
INTERNATIONAL DISTRICT
WING LUKE MUSEUM
HING HAY PARK
UWAJIMAYA IMPORTS
FIRST HILL
SEATTLE UNIVERSITY
SWEDISH HOSPITAL
HUTCHINSON RESEARCH CENTER
VIRGINIA MASON HOSPITAL & CLINIC
CABRINI HOSPITAL
FRYE ART MUSEUM
SORRENTO HOTEL
ST. JAMES CATHEDRAL
HARBORVIEW MEDICAL CENTER
FREEWAY PARK
MYRTLE EDWARDS PARK
SEATTLE TRADE CENTER
PIER 70
VICTORIA FERRY TERMINAL
EDGEWATER INN
PORT OF SEATTLE
SEATTLE AQUARIUM
WATERFRONT PARK
FERRY TO WINSLOW (TOLL) BAINBRIDGE ISLAND
FERRY TO BREMERTON (TOLL)
SEATTLE FERRY TERMINAL
WASHINGTON STATE FERRY TERMINAL
ALASKA FERRY TERMINAL
ALASKAN WAY
STREETCAR
VIADUCT
A B C D E F G H I J K L M N O P Q R
1 2 3 4 5 6 7 8 9

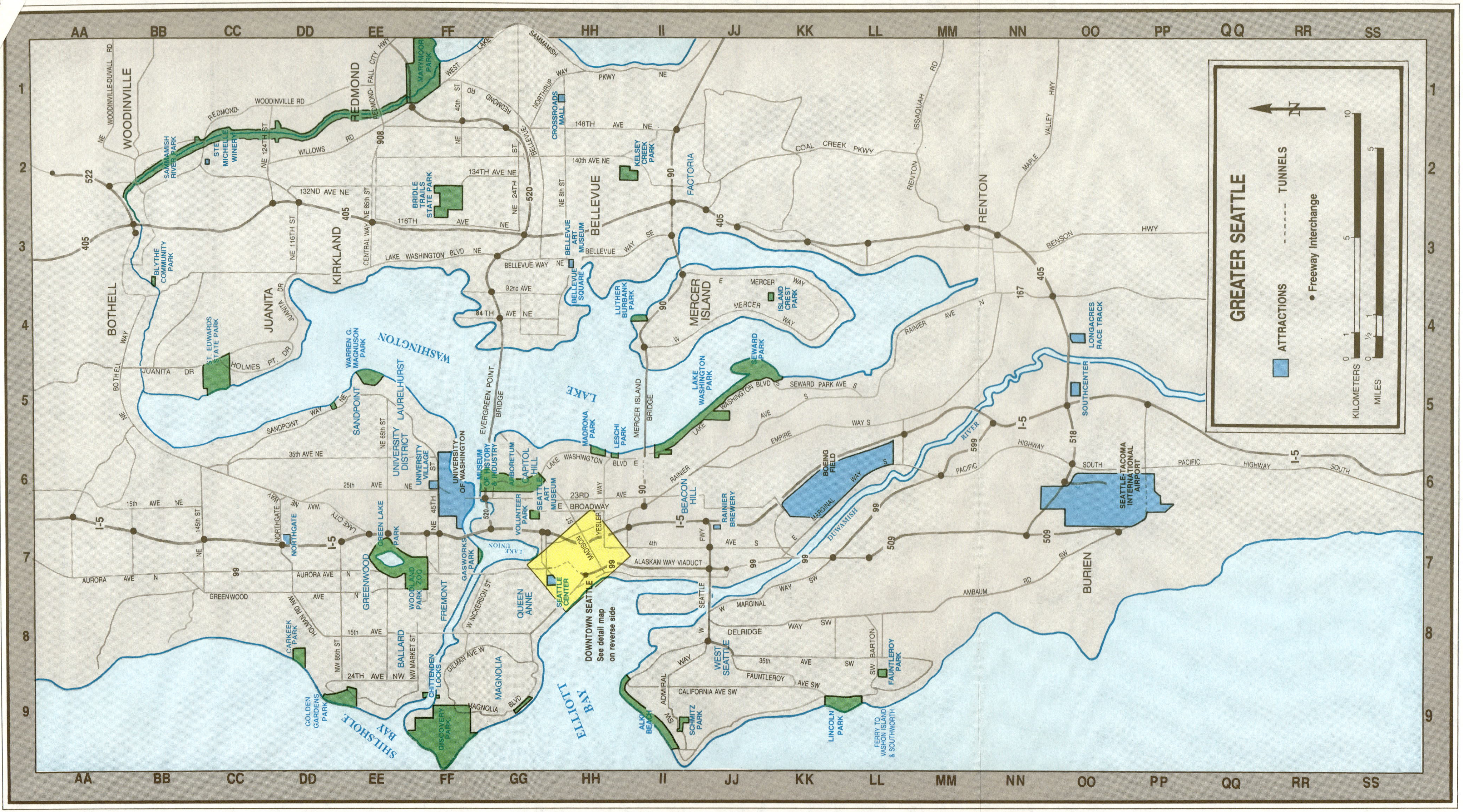
GREATER SEATTLE
ATTRACTIONS
TUNNELS
Freeway Interchange
KILOMETERS
MILES
N
DOWNTOWN SEATTLE
See detail map
on reverse side
WOODINVILLE
REDMOND
BOTHELL
KIRKLAND
JUANITA
BELLEVUE
FACTORIA
MERCER ISLAND
RENTON
BURIEN
LAKE WASHINGTON
LAKE UNION
ELLIOTT BAY
SHILSHOLE BAY
SAMMAMISH RIVER PARK
STE. MICHELLE WINERY
MARYMOOR PARK
BRIDLE TRAILS STATE PARK
CROSSROADS MALL
KELSEY CREEK PARK
BLYTHE COMMUNITY PARK
BELLEVUE ART MUSEUM
BELLEVUE SQUARE
LUTHER BURBANK PARK
ISLAND CREST PARK
ST. EDWARDS STATE PARK
WARREN G. MAGNUSON PARK
SANDPOINT
LAURELHURST
UNIVERSITY DISTRICT
UNIVERSITY VILLAGE
UNIVERSITY OF WASHINGTON
MUSEUM OF HISTORY & INDUSTRY
ARBORETUM
CAPITOL HILL
MADRONA PARK
LESCHI PARK
LAKE WASHINGTON PARK
SEWARD PARK
LONGACRES RACE TRACK
SOUTHCENTER
BOEING FIELD
SEATTLE-TACOMA INTERNATIONAL AIRPORT
NORTHGATE
GREEN LAKE PARK
GREENWOOD
WOODLAND PARK ZOO
FREMONT
GASWORKS PARK
VOLUNTEER PARK
SEATTLE ART MUSEUM
SEATTLE CENTER
QUEEN ANNE
BEACON HILL
RAINIER BREWERY
CARKEEK PARK
BALLARD
CHITTENDEN LOCKS
MAGNOLIA
GOLDEN GARDENS PARK
DISCOVERY PARK
WEST SEATTLE
ALKI BEACH
SCHMITZ PARK
LINCOLN PARK
FAUNTLEROY PARK
FERRY TO VASHON ISLAND & SOUTHWORTH
DUWAMISH RIVER
I-5
405
520
90
99
509
518
599
167
522
908
ALASKAN WAY VIADUCT
BROADWAY
YESLER
MADISON
AURORA AVE N
COAL CREEK PKWY
BENSON HWY
PACIFIC HIGHWAY SOUTH
EVERGREEN POINT BRIDGE
MERCER ISLAND BRIDGE